Pittsburgh Series in Bibliography

NATHANIEL HAWTHORNE

A Letter from the Portrait Artist

The studio which I occupied when I painted the portrait of Hawthorne was on the corner of West & Washington Sts. Boston. I remarked to my wife after the 1st. sitting, I never had a young lady sit to me who was half so timid as the great author whose work we so much admired, she wondered how he had mustered courage enough to propose. I said, depend upon it Darling, he had encouragement! . . .

He impressed me as a poetical Webster, complexion olive, the eyes rest in my mind as dark grey full of expression and intelligence. Mrs. Hawthorne approved of her husband's portrait and regretted that it was not for her instead of General Pierce.

G. P. A. Healy to George A. Holden, Paris,
1 September 1885 (Collection of CEFC)

overleaf

Nathaniel Hawthorne, by G. P. A. Healy, 1852. 24¹/₂″ × 29¹/₄″

Nathaniel Hawthorne

A DESCRIPTIVE BIBLIOGRAPHY

C. E. Frazer Clark, Jr.

UNIVERSITY OF
PITTSBURGH PRESS
1978

Published by the University of Pittsburgh Press, Pittsburgh, Pa. 15260

Copyright © 1978, C. E. Frazer Clark, Jr.

Feffer and Simons, Inc., London

Manufactured in the United States of America

Library of Congress Cataloging in Publication Data

Clark, C. E. Frazer.
  Nathaniel Hawthorne: a descriptive bibliography.

  (Pittsburgh series in bibliography)
  Includes index.
  1. Hawthorne, Nathaniel, 1804–1864—Bibliography.   I.   Series.
Z8393.C56 [PS1881]   016.818′3′03   76-50885
ISBN 0-8229-3343-8

for MATT

who made it happen

Contents

These scholars have my special gratitude:

MATTHEW J. BRUCCOLI

WAYNE ALLEN JONES

DAVID KESTERSON

JOHN D. MCDONALD

NORMAN HOLMES PEARSON

DENHAM SUTCLIFFE

ARLIN TURNER

Acknowledgments

I BELIEVE that collecting is an essential act of scholarship and that serious collectors have a special obligation to share their libraries and their knowledge. Collectors assemble the material and know it intimately; no one else sees more multiple copies of a title, no one has as much contact with knowledgeable dealers, no one spends as much time with other collectors and their books. The scholar who teaches or studies an author needs to know everything the specialist collector knows about that author and his writings—for scholarship is no better than the resources it is based on, just as collecting is no better than the help and guidance the collector receives. Since a great many people have helped me build my Hawthorne collection, the basis of this bibliography, I feel this volume is truly a collaborative effort.

Dealers are the real strength behind any substantial collection, and I owe a special debt to many. Charles S. Boesen was the first dealer I knew. He sold me my first rare book (a presentation copy of the first printing of *The Scarlet Letter*) and taught me the fundamentals of collecting. Seven Gables Bookshop has done the most for me and I owe much to Michael Papantonio and John S. van E. Kohn. John was special. Others who helped are Bart Auerbach, James M. Babcock, Gordon T. Banks, Richard S. Barnes, Jack Bartfield, Roderick Benton, Robert K. Black, Blackwells, Joseph F. Bowes, Van Allen Bradley, John R. B. Brett-Smith, C. K. Broadhurst, Harold M. Burstein, Roger Butterfield (a great friend), James Carters, Mrs. B. C. Claes, Ethel Claes, Lloyd Currey, Grace David, Walter S. Dougherty, I. D. Edrich, Lew David Feldman, John F. Fleming, H. M. Fletcher, Alla T. Ford, Frognal Bookshop, George T. Goodspeed (who supplied many treasures), Harold Graves, Hamill & Barker, Frank Hammond, Frank Hollings, Ken Hottle, Peter B. Howard, Warren R. Howell, Irene M. Jackson, Everett D. Jewett (who made an uncommon contribution), Norman Kane, Ruth Kennedy, S. Clyde King, David Kirschenbaum, Lawrence Kunetka, Harold A. Landry, Ken Leach, Larry McMurtry, G. A. Maddock, Robert Rulon Miller, Sam Morrill (who found incredible treasures), Harold Mortlake and Alixe Bartley (who parted with English titles I could find nowhere else), Howard S. Mott (who always found rare necessities), Winifred A. Myers, Kenneth Nebenzahl, Julia Sweet Newman, Tom Nicely, Roger O'Connor, David L. O'Neal, Kenneth W. Rendell, Anthony Rota, Bertram Rota, Joseph Rubenfine, Don and Ruth St. John, G. Reed Salisbury (a great scout), G. F. Sims, Fuller d'Arch Smith, Eric and Joan Stevens, Ronald Taylor, and many more.

I thank the following librarians and libraries: Marcus A. McCorison and the staff of The American Antiquarian Society; William Runge, Joan St. Crane, and John Via of The Barrett Collection, Alderman Library, University of Virginia; Lola Szladits (who deserves a special thanks) of the Berg Collection, The New York Public Library; the Bodleian Library; T. A. J. Burnett and the superb staff of The British Library; Columbia University Library; Concord Free Public Library, Concord, Mass.; Gloria Francis and the staff of The Detroit Public Library; Dorothy Potter of the Essex Institute, Salem, Mass.; O. B. Hardison of The Folger Shakespeare Library; William H. Bond, Roger Stoddard, and the gracious staff of the Houghton Library, Harvard University; James Thorpe of The Huntington Library; Susan Manakul and the staff of The Library of Congress; William R. Cagle of The Lilly Library, Indiana University; George Chandler of the Liverpool City Libraries, Liverpool, England; Herbert T. Cahoon of The Morgan Library; Arthur Monke, Richard B. Reed, and Mary Hughes of The Nathaniel Hawthorne—Henry Wadsworth Longfellow Library, Bowdoin College; The New York Public Library; Ohio State University Libraries; Charles W. Mann, Jr., of the Pennsylvania State University Library; The University of California General Library, Berkeley; Harriet Jamieson of The University of Michigan Library; Robert L. Volz of the University of Rochester Library; and Donald Gallup of the Yale University Library.

My work has benefited from the help of the following collectors and scholars: Nelson F. Adkins, C. Waller Barrett, Fredson Bowers, Kenneth W. Cameron, B. Bernard Cohen, J. M. Edelstein, Charles E. Feinberg (who first encouraged me and to whom I owe much), Otto O. Fisher, Lillian B. Gilkes, Richard B. Harwell, Parkman D. Howe (the other Hawthorne collector and a generous friend), Wayne Allen Jones, Ernest Kroll (who understands the rarity of reprints), Richard Layman, George Monteiro (who helped much), Andrew Myers, Arlin Turner, and Don Weeks; and I acknowledge a great debt to my friend Norman Holmes Pearson.

Hawthorne scholars everywhere, myself among them, owe a great debt to the editors of *The Centenary Edition of the Works of Nathaniel Hawthorne,* who have virtually completed the monumental task of establishing the definitive text of Hawthorne's writings. I am particularly indebted to Fredson Bowers, Matthew J. Bruccoli, the late William Charvat, and the late Claude Simpson. My special gratitude goes to L. Neal Smith, who generously shared information with me. I thank Weldon A. Kefauver, Director of Ohio State University Press, for information he supplied.

Providing the numerous illustrations was a huge task. Grateful acknowledgment is given to the Henry W. and Albert A. Berg Collection, The New York Public Library, Astor, Lenox and Tilden Foundations for permission to reproduce illustrations used for A 4.1.a₁, A 5.1, and A 13.1.b. The Bodleian Library furnished the illustrations for A 12.2.a₂. The British Library supplied the illustrations for A 21.2. Robert L. Volz provided the illustration of one of the two variants wrappers of A 13.6. The remaining illustrations were furnished from my collection. Earle A. Williamson sacrificed long evenings to the painstaking photography required to supply illustrations. Margaret Ann Clark, my wife, gave unstintingly of her time and special artistic talents in preparing all the illustrations and tabular artwork for production.

A number of people have made a special contribution to this bibliography. William R. Cagle and Charles W. Mann read the manuscript and provided valuable comment. I thank Frederick A. Hetzel, Director of the University of Pittsburgh Press, for his support. I am deeply indebted to Louise Craft, Editor of the University of Pittsburgh Press, for her final editing of the manuscript, which has contributed enormously to the quality of this work. Without the support and help of my family, from whom I took the time this work required, I could not have completed this undertaking. I thank C. E. Frazer Clark, III; Douglas Alexander Clark, for his alphabetizing; and my wife, Margaret Ann Clark, for her willing spirit and love. Without the encouragement and challenge provided by Matthew J. Bruccoli, the best scholar I know, this book would never have been started or finished.

Introduction

THIS descriptive bibliography of the writings of Nathaniel Hawthorne is limited to writings by Hawthorne. Writings about Hawthorne are not listed, except in cases where they include something by Hawthorne published for the first time or are special cases which merit inclusion.

FORMAT

Section A lists chronologically all books, pamphlets, and broadsides wholly or substantially by Hawthorne, including all printings of all editions in English through 1883 and selected reprintings to 1975.

The numbering system for Section A indicates the edition and printing for each entry. Thus for *Mosses from an Old Manse, A 15.1.a₁* indicates that it is the fifteenth separate Hawthorne work published *(15)* and that the entry is for the first edition *(1)*, first printing *(a)*. States and issues are designated by inferior numbers *(a₁, a₂)* and are specifically identified at the beginning of each entry, for example:

A 15.1.a₁
First edition, first printing, American issue [1846]

2 vols.

First printing has Craighead and Smith imprints below copyright notice in both volumes and text can be distinguished from later printings on the basis of type batter (see table).

and

A 15.1.a₂
First edition, first printing, English issue [1846]

2 vols. Sheets of the first printing with a cancel English title in each volume.

In each case, the means of distinguishing the state or issue is given at the beginning of the entry.

Section B lists all collected works of Hawthorne's writings through 1900 that were published, advertised, or sold as "Hawthorne's Works" by Ticknor and Fields and the successor copyright holders (Fields, Osgood; James R. Osgood; Houghton, Osgood; and Houghton, Mifflin). Selected collected works and certain one-volume collections by other publishers through 1975 have been included. All works printed from the same plates are grouped together and listed in chronological order; a table, "Pedigree of Primary Collected Works," is provided at the beginning of the section.

Section C lists chronologically all titles in which material by Hawthorne appears for the first time in a book or pamphlet. The first American and English printings of these titles are described, and selected reprintings up through 1850 are noted to show the exposure and spread of Hawthorne's name and work prior to the publication of *The Scarlet Letter*. When a contribution is signed by Hawthorne or attributed to him, the wording is given exactly as it originally appeared. Unsigned contributions are noted. Certain reprintings are given in this section in cases where the fact of republication have special importance to collectors. I have also listed selected offprints of articles that include Hawthorne material. These all have special importance to collectors; in a number of instances the offprints represent the first separate publication of Hawthorne material.

Section D lists chronologically the first American and English publication in magazines and newspapers of material by Hawthorne. Selected reprintings up through 1850 are noted to show the exposure and spread of Hawthorne's name and work prior to the publication of *The Scarlet Letter*. When a contribution is signed by Hawthorne or attributed to him, the wording is given exactly as it originally appeared. Unsigned contributions are noted. Although Hawthorne's verse is included in Section H, two appearances of Hawthorne's poem "The Ocean" are included in this section (D 1 and D 2) because they represent, respectively, the earliest located newspaper and magazine appearance of the author's work.

Section E lists special material and selected ephemera arranged chronologically.

Section F lists chronologically selected bibliographical material.

Section G lists chronologically prose material attributed to Hawthorne. If known, the source of the attribution is given, and any contending views are identified.

Section H lists chronologically verse by Hawthorne and verse attributed to him. The source and authority for each inclusion are given.

TERMS AND METHODS

Edition. All copies of a book printed from a single setting of type—including all reprintings from the standing type or plates made from that typesetting.

Printing. All copies of a book printed at one time (without removing the type or plates from the press).

State. States are created when some copies of a particular printing are altered *before* publication—that is, by stop-press correction or cancellation of leaves. There must be two or more states.

Issue. Issues are created by the alteration of some copies of a single printing *after* publication in a way that affects the circumstances of publication, sale, or distribution—frequently by the alteration of the title page or other preliminary matter. There cannot be a first issue without a second. Issues occur in various Hawthorne titles, such as *Mosses from an Old Manse* (A 15.1.a₁ and A 15.1.a₂) where some of the American sheets of the first printing were bound with a cancel English title.

While the terms *edition, printing,* and *state* have been applied only to descriptions of the printed sheets of the book, the term *issue* has been used to describe alterations of sheets and/or bindings created deliberately for the purpose of influencing the conditions of sale. For example, English publishers like Henry G. Bohn and George Routledge who were exploiting the expanding Railway Library market regularly bound the same sheets in various binding formats for the express purpose of retailing the same product at different price levels.[1] These English buccaneers would offer pirated Hawthorne titles in a cheap paper binding at a shilling, package the same sheets in cloth for sale at a shilling sixpence, bind the same sheets in any one of a number of leather bindings at a fancy price, or combine the same sheets of a given title with sheets of a second Hawthorne title (for example, *The Scarlet Letter* and *The House of the Seven Gables*) at a price of two shillings sixpence. I have described these different binding formats as binding issues because they represent deliberate alteration of some copies of a single printing *after* publication for the express purpose of changing the circumstances of publication, distribution, and sale.

Ticknor, Reed, and Fields actively promoted its books. For example, it was a common practice to insert advertisements for current and forthcoming T,R&F titles in new books being bound for sale. Usually—but not always—these ads are found between the pastedown front endpaper and the free front endpaper. Sometimes the ads are found between the rear endpapers or elsewhere. Common practice was to print these ads separately; that is, they were printed independently of the sheets of the book with which the ads were bound. The ads were constantly revised and/or reprinted as needed, and it was customary for Ticknor, Reed, and Fields (later Ticknor and Fields) to date them.

Over the years dealers and collectors have used these dated ads to distinguish printing priorities. A "first edition" of *The Scarlet Letter* is regularly described in catalogues as the "earliest state with March ads." However, first printings of *The Scarlet Letter* have been found with ads dated April and May 1850, and some copies are without ads. In addition, March 1850 ads have been found in much later printings. No point has raised as much discussion in Hawthorne collecting as the question of using the date of the ads to distinguish first editions. It should be stated unequivocally that the date on the inserted ads in a Ticknor, Reed, and Fields volume of Hawthorne has no bearing on the priority of the printing. When ads can be demonstrated to be an integral part of the text, the information they contain does bear on printing priority since they were printed right along with the text. Publishers often set up ads to fill the blank space that otherwise would have been wasted when the last few pages of the final signature were blank. For example, the first printing of *Our Old Home* (A 24.1.a) is distinguished by the presence of advertisements on p. 399; in the second printing the ads are omitted and p. 399 is blank. The important fact is that *only when the ads are*

---

1. For a discussion of the pirating of Hawthorne's works by English publishers and the Railway Library market, see my article "Hawthorne and the Pirates," *Proof,* ed. Joseph Katz (Columbia: University of South Carolina Press, 1971), pp. 90–121.

an integral part of the text (that is, printed along with the rest of the book) can they have any bearing on determining the priority of the text. The more common inserted ads, as in the case of *The Scarlet Letter,* have no bearing on determining the printing priority.

For binding-cloth designations I have used the method proposed by Tanselle.[2] Most of these cloth grains are illustrated in Jacob Blanck, ed., *The Bibliography of American Literature* (New Haven: Yale University Press, 1955–).

Color specifications are taken from the *ISCC-NBS Color Name Charts Illustrated with Centroid Colors* (National Bureau of Standards). However, fading and other color deterioration of nineteenth-century bindings make precise color description difficult, and no specification is given in those cases when I could not give the reader an accurate guide. As a further aid in binding identification, the publisher's standard binding formats are illustrated for most Section A titles. If there are significant variations in binding formats, they are shown. The basic Ticknor and Fields trade and "gift" bindings are pictured. In Section A the binding illustrations usually precede each entry. However, in some instances in Section A, especially toward the end, and in later sections, the bindings from a number of entries are grouped together, so that an illustration of a binding may not be with its entry.

Illustrations of the title pages and sample text pages of both the American and English first printings of each Section A entry are provided. The captions give outside dimensions of the title leaf, with the height preceding the width. The captions for the text-page illustrations give first the height of the text block on the page from the top of the highest ascender in the first line of text (excluding the running head) to the lowest descender in the bottom line of type on the page. The following measurement (in parentheses) gives the height including the running head. The last measurement given is the line length. Page numbers have not been included in text-page measurements.

All information on the verso of the title page is illustrated in the copyright cuts. When the first printing is a two- or three-volume set, all copyright pages are illustrated. A jagged line has been drawn through the cut to indicate the omission of blank space.

In the descriptions or quasi-facsimile transcriptions of title pages, the color of the lettering is always black unless otherwise stipulated. Dates provided within brackets do not appear on the title page; these dates come from the copyright page, Library of Congress records, British Library records, or reviews and notices.

The listings of the contents in the entries in Sections A and B follow the spelling and capitalization found in the tables of contents of the titles being described. When significant variations or changes in the title of a work exist, they are noted. A dagger (†) following a title indicates its first collected appearance. The use of a number sign (#) following a title indicates the first appearance of that title in print. A section sign (§) following a title indicates that it is attributed to Hawthorne.

---

2. G. Thomas Tanselle, "The Specifications of Binding Cloth," *The Library,* 21 (September 1966), 246–247.

Quotation marks are used around edition titles when that title does not appear on the half-title page, the title page, or anywhere in the published works but is used elsewhere to identify or promote the edition. For example, the first collected works of Hawthorne's writings are referred to in the publisher's records *(Cost Books)* as the *"Tinted Edition"* and the publisher's advertisements identify it as the *"Tinted Edition,"* but it is not so identified in the books. If the title does appear in the published works, no quotation marks are used. Also, when volume numbers appear in the published works, they are used without brackets. When volume numbers do not appear in the published works, they are put inside brackets. When the sequence of the volumes has not been identified in the published works, either I have established the order based on the publisher's records (if possible), the dates of publication (if available), or the advertised order, or I have established an arbitrary order based on my best estimate of the circumstances.

Locations are given in the National Union Catalogue list of symbols—with the following exceptions:

BM: The British Museum (now The British Library)
CEFC: Collection of C. E. Frazer Clark, Jr.
Lilly: Lilly Library, Indiana University
MJB: Collection of Matthew J. Bruccoli
PDH: Collection of Parkman D. Howe

A bibliography is outdated the day it goes to the printer. Addenda and corrigenda are earnestly solicited.

Bloomfield Hills, Mich.
1977

Source Identifications

Athenaeum: *Athenaeum; a Journal of Literature, Science, the Fine Arts, Music and the Drama* (London).

Browne: Nina E. Browne, *A Bibliography of Nathaniel Hawthorne* (Boston and New York: Houghton, Mifflin, MDCCCCV).

Cathcart: Wallace Hugh Cathcart, *Bibliography of the Works of Nathaniel Hawthorne* (Cleveland: The Rowfant Club, MCMV).

Centenary: *The Centenary Edition of the Works of Nathaniel Hawthorne,* 11 vols. (Columbus: Ohio State University Press, 1963–1974).

Cost Books: *The Cost Books of Ticknor and Fields and Their Predecessors. 1832–1858,* ed. with an introduction and notes by Warren S. Tryon and William Charvat (New York: The Bibliographical Society of America, 1949). Information in this bibliography is taken from the original T&F *Cost Books* on deposit at the Houghton Library, Harvard University.

Critic: *Critic; a Record of Literature, Art, Music, Science and the Drama* (London).

Letter Books: *The Letter Books of Ticknor & Fields,* now on deposit at the Houghton Library, Harvard University.

Literary Gazette: *Literary Gazette. A Weekly Journal of Literature, Science, and the Fine Arts* (London).

Literary Gazette (New York): *Literary Gazette and American Athenaeum* (New York).

Publishers' Circular: *Publishers' Circular and Booksellers' Record* (London).

Publishers' Weekly: *Publishers' Weekly* (New York).

A. Separate Publications

All books, pamphlets, and broadsides wholly or substantially by Hawthorne, including all printings of all editions in English through 1883 and selected printings to 1975, arranged chronologically.

Bindings for A 1.1 and A 1.2.a

FANSHAWE,

A TALE.

"Wilt thou go on with me?"—SOUTHEY.

◆

BOSTON:
MARSH & CAPEN, 362 WASHINGTON STREET.

PRESS OF PUTNAM AND HUNT.

1828.

Doctor Melmoth had followed his own fancies in the mode of laying out his garden; and, in consequence, the plan that had undoubtedly existed in his mind, was utterly incomprehensible to every one but himself. It was an intermixture of kitchen and flower garden,—a labyrinth of winding paths, bordered by hedges and impeded by shrubbery. Many of the original trees of the forest were still flourishing among the exotics, which the Doctor had transplanted thither. It was not without a sensation of fear, stronger than she had ever before experienced, that Ellen Langton found herself in this artificial wilderness, and in the presence of the mysterious stranger. The dusky light deepened the lines of his dark, strong features, and Ellen fancied that his countenance wore a wilder and a fiercer look, than when she had met him by the stream. He perceived her agitation, and addressed her in the softest tones of which his voice was capable.

'Compose yourself,' he said, 'you have nothing to fear from me. But we are in open view from the house, where we now stand; and discovery would not be without danger, to both of us.'

'No eye can see us here,' said Ellen, trembling at the truth of her own observation, when they stood beneath a gnarled, low-branched pine, which Doctor Melmoth's ideas of beauty had caused him to retain in his garden. 'Speak quickly; for I dare follow you no farther.'

The spot was indeed sufficiently solitary, and the stranger delayed no longer to explain his errand.

'Your father,' he began,—'Do you not love him? Would you do aught for his welfare?'

'Every thing that a father could ask, I would do,' exclaimed Ellen, eagerly. 'Where is my father; and when shall I meet him?'

A 1.1: Title page, 7⁷/₁₆″ × 4⁵/₈″. Page format, 5³/₈″ (5⁵/₈″) × 3¹/₈″

A 1 FANSHAWE

A 1.1
First edition, only printing [1828]

District of Massachusetts....to wit.

DISTRICT CLERK'S OFFICE.

Be it Remembered, that on the twenty second day of July, A. D.
1828, in the Fifty Third Year of the Independence of the United States
of America, Marsh & Capen, of the said District, have deposited in
this Office the Title of a Book, the Right whereof they claim as Proprietors in the words following, to wit:

"FANSHAWE.

A TALE.

'Wilt thou go on with me?'—Southey."

In conformity to the Act of the Congress of the United States, entitled "An Act for the Encouragement of Learning, by securing the Copies of Maps, Charts and Books, to the Authors and Proprietors of such
Copies, during the times therein mentioned:" and also to an Act entitled
"An Act supplementary to an Act, entitled, An Act for the Encouragement of Learning, by securing the Copies of Maps, Charts and Books
to the Authors and Proprietors of such Copies during the times therein
mentioned; and extending the Benefits thereof to the Arts of Designing.
Engraving and Etching Historical and other Prints."

JOHN W. DAVIS,

Clerk of the District of Massachusetts.

Note one: Dropped type at 33.19 [from   [rom] and 52.34 [has   [ha] is responsible for four possible states of the book: 'from'/'has', 'from'/'ha', 'rom'/'has', 'rom'/'ha'.
(See Matthew J. Bruccoli, "States of *Fanshawe*," *Papers of the Bibliographical Society
of America,* LVIII [First Quarter, 1964], 32.)

[1–3] 4–141 [142–144]

[1]⁶ 2–12⁶

Contents: p. 1: title; p. 2: copyright; pp. 3–141: text, headed 'FANSHAWE. | [rule] |
CHAPTER I. | Our court shall be a little academy. | Shakspeare.'; pp. 142–144: blank.
Errata list appended at conclusion of text on p. 141; corrections noted for five items.

Typography and paper: See illustration, A 1.1 page format. Running heads: rectos
and versos, 'FANSHAWE.' White wove paper.

Binding: Tan (79. 1. gy. y Br) paper-covered boards with violet (215. gy. V) smooth
V-like muslin shelfback. Printed paper label pasted on spine (see illustration, A 1
bindings). White wove endpapers. Single white wove flyleaf inserted at front and rear.
All edges untrimmed.

Publication: 1,000 copies published last week of October 1828. Announced as "Published this day" in the *Boston Daily Advertiser,* 27 October 1828; "just been published," *New England Galaxy,* 31 October; listed for 25 October, *Boston Statesman,* 4
November.

Printing: Printed from type metal by Putnam and Hunt, Boston.

Locations: 'from'/'ha': ViU; 'rom'/'has': OU; 'rom'/'ha': CEFC. Robert Manning copy:

Lilly; Susan D. Manning copy: CEFC; publisher's copy: MB; other copies: Berg, CSmH, CtY, ICN, ICU, LC, MeB, PDH, PU.

Note two: According to Hawthorne's sister Elizabeth (*Nathaniel Hawthorne and His Wife*, I, 123–125), he advanced $100 toward the publication of *Fanshawe*, which, while widely advertised and reviewed, did not sell. The money probably came from the estate of Richard Manning (see Wayne Allen Jones, "Hawthorne's Slender Means," in *The Nathaniel Hawthorne Journal 1977*, [Detroit: Gale Research, 1977], forthcoming). Although Hawthorne later suppressed knowledge of the existence of *Fanshawe*, the scarcity of this work results primarily from destruction in a warehouse fire of the publisher's inventory (see publisher's notes kept with the Marsh & Capen copy of *Fanshawe* at MB; see also *Centenary*, I, 310).

A 1.2.a
Second edition, first printing [1876]

FANSHAWE | AND | OTHER PIECES. | BY | NATHANIEL HAWTHORNE. | [Osgood logo] | BOSTON: | JAMES R. OSGOOD AND COMPANY. | 1876

Contents: Fanshawe, combined with the following other pieces: "Biographical Sketches:—Mrs. Hutchinson,"† "Sir William Phips,"† "Sir William Pepperell,"† "Thomas Green Fessenden,"† "Jonathan Cilley."† Daggers (†) indicate first collected appearance.

Printed from stereotype plates made from a new setting of type based on the 1828 edition (A 1.1). Published in a format uniform with the *"Tinted Edition,"* with the James R. Osgood logo goldstamped at foot of spine (see illustration, A 1.2 bindings). Bound in the style of Ticknor format D (see illustration, B 1 bindings), with a classical male figure blindstamped on covers. Green (146. d. G) pebble-grain P cloth with blindstamped-rules panel on covers. Undetermined number of the first printing of the second edition with 'VOL. 22' goldstamped on spine immediately under 'WORKS' (see B 1[22]). Covers noted beveled or plain. White wove endpapers brown coated one side. 1,000 copies printed 27 May 1876. Price $1.50, royalty 15¢ per copy.

Locations: Berg, CEFC, Lilly, MeB, MH, ViU.

LATER PRINTINGS WITHIN THE SECOND EDITION

A 1.2.b
Boston: James R. Osgood, 1876.

Combined with *The Dolliver Romance* in two-volumes-in-one format and published as the twelfth volume of the *Illustrated Library Edition*. 1,000 copies printed 12 September 1876. Price $2.00, royalty 20¢. See B 2 for reprintings of the *ILE*.

A 1.2.c
Boston: Houghton, Mifflin, 1880.

Combined with *Our Old Home, Septimius Felton*, and *The Dolliver Romance* in four-volumes-in-one format and published as the third volume of the *Globe Edition*. 1,500 copies printed August 1880. See B 3 for reprintings of the *Globe Edition*.

A 1.2.d
Boston: Houghton, Mifflin, [1886].

Combined with *Our Old Home, Septimius Felton*, and *The Dolliver Romance* in four-volumes-in-one format and published as the third volume of the *"New" Fireside Edition.* 1,000 copies printed May 1886. See B 4.

PRINTINGS FROM THE "LITTLE CLASSIC EDITION" PLATES

A 1.3.a

[All following within red and black double-rules frame] [red] Fanshawe, | [black] AND OTHER PIECES. | BY | NATHANIEL HAWTHORNE. | [vignette of Bowdoin College] | [red] BOSTON: | [black] JAMES R. OSGOOD AND COMPANY, | Late Ticknor & Fields, and Fields, Osgood, & Co. | [red] 1876.

Vol. [XXII], *"Little Classic Edition."* Contents same as in the second edition (A 1.2.a). Printed from plates made from a new setting of type. Sheets bound with James R. Osgood and, later, Houghton, Osgood spine imprints. 1,280 copies printed 1 September 1876. Price $1.25, royalty 12.5¢ per volume. See B 5 [XXII] for reprintings of the *"Little Classic Edition."*

A 1.3.b
Boston: Houghton, Osgood, 1879.

Combined with *The Dolliver Romance* in two-volumes-in-one format and published as vol. XII of the *"Fireside Edition."* 500 copies printed 20 September 1879. See B 6 for reprintings of the *"Fireside Edition."*

A 1.3.c
Boston: Houghton, Mifflin, [1891].

Combined with *The Snow-Image, Septimius Felton,* and *The Dolliver Romance* in four-volumes-in-one format and published as vol. IV of the *Popular Edition.* 1,000 copies printed June–August 1891. See B 7 for reprintings of the *Popular Edition.*

A 1.3.d
Boston: Houghton, Mifflin, [1899].

Vol. [XXII], *Concord Edition.* See B 8.

PRINTINGS FROM THE RIVERSIDE EDITION PLATES

A 1.4.a₁
Riverside Edition (trade), first printing, American issue [1883]

THE DOLLIVER ROMANCE | FANSHAWE, AND SEPTIMIUS FELTON | WITH AN APPENDIX CONTAINING | THE ANCESTRAL FOOTSTEP | BY | NATHANIEL HAWTHORNE | [vignette of seated girl] | BOSTON | HOUGHTON, MIFFLIN AND COMPANY | New York: 11 East Seventeenth Street | The Riverside Press, Cambridge | 1883

Four volumes in one published as vol. XI of the Riverside trade printing. Contents includes *Fanshawe,* with "Introductory Note" by George Parsons Lathrop added, but "Other Pieces" is omitted. 3,000 copies printed June 1883. Price $2.00. See B 9 for reprintings of the Riverside trade printing.

A 1.4.a₂
Riverside Edition (trade), first printing, English issue [1883]

London: Kegan Paul, Trench, 1883.

Sheets of vol. XI, first printing (A 1.4.a₁), with cancel title, in a Kegan Paul binding. 250 Kegan Paul title pages printed by Houghton, Mifflin, June–July 1883. Later issues noted with dated and undated Kegan Paul, Trench, Trübner title pages. See B 11.

A 1.4.b
Riverside Edition (large paper), second printing [1883]

[red] THE DOLLIVER ROMANCE | [black] FANSHAWE, AND SEPTIMIUS FELTON | WITH AN APPENDIX CONTAINING | THE ANCESTRAL FOOTSTEP | BY | NATHANIEL HAWTHORNE | [vignette of seated girl] | [red] CAMBRIDGE | [black] Printed at the Riverside Press | 1883

Four volumes in one published as vol. XI of the Riverside large-paper printing. 250 copies printed July 1883. See B 10.

A 1.4.c
Boston and New York: Houghton, Mifflin, 1884.

Combined with *The Dolliver Romance* in two-volumes-in-one format and published as vol. XXI of the *Wayside Edition*. 500 copies printed September–October 1884. See B 12.

A 1.4.d
Boston and New York: Houghton, Mifflin, [1891].

Combined with *The Dolliver Romance, Septimius Felton,* and *The Ancestral Footstep* in four-volumes-in-one format and published as vol. XI of the *Standard Library Edition.* 500 copies printed October 1891. See B 13.

A 1.4.e
Boston and New York: Houghton, Mifflin, [1902].

Combined with *The Dolliver Romance, Septimius Felton,* and *The Ancestral Footstep* in four-volumes-in-one format and published as vol. XI of the *"New" Wayside Edition.* 500 copies printed September–October 1902. See B 14.

A 1.4.f
Boston and New York: [Houghton, Mifflin], MDCCCCIX.

Combined with *The Dolliver Romance, Septimius Felton,* and *The Ancestral Footstep* in four-volumes-in-one format and published as vol. XI of the *Fireside Edition.* See B 15.

A 1.4.g
Boston, New York: Jefferson Press, [1913].

Combined with the *American Note-Books, The Dolliver Romance,* and *Septimius Felton* in four-volumes-in-one format and published as vol. [IX] of the *"Jefferson Press Edition."* See B 16.

A 1.5.a
Boston and New York: Houghton, Mifflin, MDCCCC.

Combined with *Tales and Sketches* in omnibus volume and published as vol. XVI of the *Autograph Edition*. Contents includes *Fanshawe*, but "Other Pieces" is omitted. 500 copies. Deposited 5 March 1901. See B 20.

A 1.5.b
Boston and New York: Houghton, Mifflin, MDCCCC.

Combined with *Tales and Sketches* in omnibus volume and published as vol. XVI of the *Large-Paper (Autograph) Edition*. 500 copies. See B 21.

A 1.5.c
Boston and New York: Houghton, Mifflin, 1903.

Combined with *Tales and Sketches* in omnibus volume and published as vol. XVI of the *Old Manse Edition*. See B 22.

OTHER EDITIONS

A 1.6
Fanshawe. A Tale. New York: Thomas Y. Crowell, [1902].

Introduction by Katherine Lee Bates. Prints *Fanshawe* without "Other Pieces." Printed on heavy laid stock. Same plates used to manufacture vol. [13] of the *Crowell "Lenox Edition."* See B 23.

A 1.7
Fanshawe, Grandfather's Chair, Biographical Stories. New York: Thomas Y. Crowell, [1902].

Introduction by Katharine Lee Bates. Omnibus volume published as vol. [1] of the *Crowell "Popular Edition."* See B 24.

A 1.8
The Complete Novels and Selected Tales of Nathaniel Hawthorne. New York: Modern Library, [1937].

Combined with *The Scarlet Letter, The House of the Seven Gables, The Blithedale Romance, The Marble Faun,* and 36 tales and sketches in an omnibus Modern Library "Giant." See B 27.

A 1.9
The Blithedale Romance and Fanshawe. [Columbus]: Ohio State University Press, [1965].

Fanshawe and *The Blithedale Romance* combined in a two-volumes-in-one format and published as vol. III of the *Centenary Edition*. 1,000 copies published 27 December 1965. See B 32 for reprintings of the *Centenary Edition*.

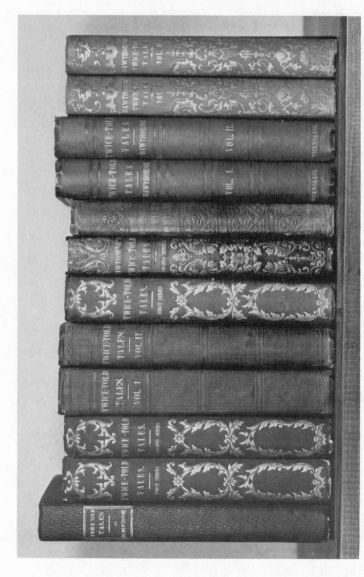

Bindings for (1) A2.1; (2–5) A2.3₁; (6 & 7) A2.3₂, mixed bindings; (8) A2.4₁; (9 & 10) A2.6, trade; (11 & 12) A2.6, "gift" (see also illustrations at A2.6 and A2.9.a)

and drinking in the words of their champion, who spoke in accents long disused, like one unaccustomed to converse, except with the dead of many years ago. But his voice stirred their souls. They confronted the soldiers, not wholly without arms, and ready to convert the very stones of the street into deadly weapons. Sir Edmund Andros looked at the old man; then he cast his hard and cruel eye over the multitude, and beheld them burning with that lurid wrath, so difficult to kindle or to quench; and again he fixed his gaze on the aged form, which stood obscurely in an open space, where neither friend nor foe had thrust himself. What were his thoughts, he uttered no word which might discover. But whether the oppressor were overawed by the Gray Champion's look, or perceived his peril in the threatening attitude of the people, it is certain that he gave back, and ordered his soldiers to commence a slow and guarded retreat. Before another sunset, the Governor, and all that rode so proudly with him, were prisoners, and long ere it was known that James had abdicated, King William was proclaimed throughout New England.

But where was the Gray Champion? Some reported, that when the troops had gone from King-street, and the people were thronging tumultuously in their rear, Bradstreet, the aged Governor, was seen to embrace a form more aged than his own. Others soberly affirmed, that while they marveled at the venerable grandeur of his aspect, the old man had faded from

B

TWICE-TOLD TALES.

BY

NATHANIEL HAWTHORNE.

BOSTON:
AMERICAN STATIONERS CO.
JOHN B. RUSSELL.
1887.

A2.1: Title page, 7¹³/₁₆″ × 4⁵/₈″. Page format, 4¹⁵/₁₆″ (5¹/₄″) × 2¹⁵/₁₆″

A 2 TWICE-TOLD TALES

A 2.1
First edition, only printing [1837]

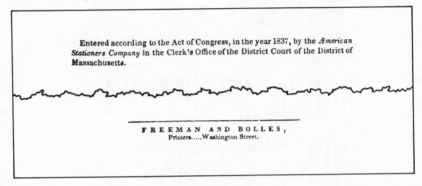

Entered according to the Act of Congress, in the year 1837, by the *American Stationers Company* in the Clerk's Office of the District Court of the District of Massachusetts.

F R E E M A N   A N D   B O L L E S ,
Printers.....Washington Street.

Note: Contents page in all copies incorrectly lists p. 78 for p. 77. Also, contemporary reviews suggest that some copies may exist with a double title-page imprint, although none has been located. (See Matthew J. Bruccoli, "Nathaniel Hawthorne Stalks Columbus: An Ohio Ghost?" *Serif,* 1 [1964].)

[1–11] 12–334 [335–336], with all blanks, section titles, and initial pages of tales unnumbered.

a⁴ [A]⁶ B–I⁶ K–U⁶ W–Z⁶ 2A–2C⁶ 2D²

Contents: pp. 1–4: ads; p. 5: title; p. 6: copyright; p. 7: contents; p. 8: blank; p. 9: section title 'THE GRAY CHAMPION.'; p. 10: blank; pp. 11–334: text, headed 'THE GRAY CHAMPION. | [rule]'; pp. 335–336: blank. Each tale preceded by leaf with tale section title on recto and verso blank.

Tales: All previously printed (see Sections C and D) and assembled and edited by Hawthorne for this collection. They include: "The Gray Champion,"† "Sunday at Home,"† "The Wedding Knell,"† "The Minister's Black Veil,"† "The May-Pole of Merry Mount,"† "The Gentle Boy,"† "Mr. Higginbotham's Catastrophe,"† "Little Anne's Ramble"† (corrected to "Little Annie's Ramble" in the text title), "Wakefield,"† "A Rill from the Town Pump,"† "The Great Carbuncle,"† "The Prophetic Pictures,"† "David Swan,"† "Sights from a Steeple,"† "The Hollow of the Three Hills,"† "The Vision of the Fountain,"† "Fancy's Show Box,"† "Dr. Heidegger's Experiment"† (first appeared as "The Fountain of Youth," see D 28). Daggers (†) indicate first collected appearance.

Typography and paper: See illustration, A 2.1 page format. Running heads: rectos and versos, tale titles. White wove paper.

Binding: Brown (58. m. Br), black (267. Black), purple blind-embossed patterned sand-grain CM-like cloth. Also blue (186. gy. Blue), black (267. Black), brown (62. d. gy. Br), green, and rose coarse-ribbed morocco AR-like cloth. Spine goldstamped (see illustration, A 2 bindings). Single white wove endpaper front and rear. Found with 8, 12, 14, and 16 pp. American Stationers Company catalogues bound in at rear. Edges untrimmed.

Publication: 1,000 copies published 6 or 7 March 1837. Price $1.00, with Hawthorne receiving $100 from profits.

Printing: Printed from type metal by Freeman and Bolles, Washington Street, Boston.

Locations: CEFC, Lilly, MH, NN, OU, PSt, ViU.

Manuscript: Manuscript of "The Wedding Knell" in the Berg Collection, New York Public Library.

THE GENTLE BOY:

A

THRICE TOLD TALE;

BY

NATHANIEL HAWTHORNE:

WITH AN ORIGINAL ILLUSTRATION.

Boston:

WEEKS, JORDAN & CO. 121 WASHINGTON STREET,

NEW YORK & LONDON:

WILEY & PUTNAM.

1839.

---

[18]

persecutors the unmitigated agony of my soul, when I believed that all I had done and suffered for Thee was at the instigation of a mocking fiend! But I yielded not; I knelt down and wrestled with the tempter, while the scourge bit more fiercely into the flesh. My prayer was heard, and I went on in peace and joy towards the wilderness.'

The old man, though his fanaticism had generally all the calmness of reason, was deeply moved while reciting this tale; and his unwonted emotion seemed to rebuke and keep down that of his companion. They sat in silence, with their faces to the fire, imagining, perhaps, in its red embers, new scenes of persecution yet to be encountered. The snow still drifted hard against the windows, and sometimes, as the blaze of the logs had gradually sunk, came down the spacious chimney and hissed upon the hearth. A cautious footstep might now and then be heard in a neighboring apartment, and the sound invariably drew the eyes of both Quakers to the door which led thither. When a fierce and riotous gust of wind had led his thoughts, by a natural association, to homeless travellers on such a night, Pearson resumed the conversation.

'I have well nigh sunk under my own share of this trial,' observed he, sighing heavily; yet I would that it might be doubled to me, if so the child's mother could be spared. Her wounds have been deep and many, but this will be the sorest of all.'

'Fear not for Catharine,' replied the old Quaker; 'for I know that valiant woman, and have seen how she can bear the cross. A mother's heart, indeed, is strong in her, and may seem to contend mightily with her faith; but soon she will stand up and give thanks that her son has been thus early an accepted sacrifice. The boy hath done his work, and she will feel that he is taken hence in kindness both to him and her. Blessed, blessed are they, that with so little suffering can enter into peace!'

The fitful rush of the wind was now disturbed by a portentous sound; it was a quick and heavy knocking at the outer door. Pearson's wan countenance grew paler, for many a visit of persecution had taught him what to dread; the old man, on the other hand, stood up erect, and his glance was firm as that of the tried soldier, who awaits his enemy.

'The men of blood have come to seek me,' he observed, with

calmness. 'They have heard how I was moved to return from banishment; and now am I to be led to prison, and thence to death. It is an end I have long looked for. I will open unto them, lest they say, "Lo, he feareth!"'

'Nay, I will present myself before them,' said Pearson, with recovered fortitude. 'It may be that they seek me alone, and know not that thou abidest with me.'

'Let us go boldly, both one and the other,' rejoined his companion. 'It is not fitting that thou or I should shrink.'

They therefore proceeded through the entry to the door, which they opened, bidding the applicant 'Come in, in God's name!' A furious blast of wind drove the storm into their faces, and extinguished the lamp; they had barely time to discern a figure, so white from head to foot with the drifted snow, that it seemed like Winter's self, come in human shape to seek refuge from its own desolation.

'Enter, friend, and do thy errand, be it what it may,' said Pearson. 'It must needs be pressing, since thou comest on such a bitter night.'

'Peace be with this household,' said the stranger, when they stood on the floor of the inner apartment.

Pearson started, the elder Quaker stirred the slumbering embers of the fire, till they sent up a clear and lofty blaze: it was a female voice that had spoken; it was a female form that shone out, cold and wintry, in that comfortable light.

'Catharine, blessed woman,' exclaimed the old man, 'art thou come to this darkened land again! Art thou come to bear a valiant testimony as in former years? The scourge hath not prevailed against thee, and from the dungeon hast thou come forth triumphant; but strengthen, strengthen now thy heart, Catharine, for Heaven will prove thee yet this once, ere thou go to thy reward.'

'Rejoice, friends!' she replied. 'Thou who hast long been of our people, and thou whom a little child hath led to us, rejoice! Lo! I come, the messenger of glad tidings, for the day of persecution is overpast. The heart of the king, even Charles, hath been moved in gentleness towards us, and he hath sent forth his letters to stay the hands of the men of blood. A ship's company of our friends hath arrived at yonder town, and I also sailed joyfully among them.'

A2.2.a₁: Title page, 9¹/₂″ × 12¹/₂″. Page format, 7¹/₁₆″ (7¹/₂″) × 9¹⁵/₁₆″ (full two-column width), first state with 'faccs' at 18-1.9

A 2.2.a₁

First separate edition of The Gentle Boy, *only printing, first state* [*1839*]

Note one: Probable first state has 'faccs' at 18-1.9 (see illustration, A 2.2 page format); corrected to 'faces' in second state. First state uncommon. After some review copies had been distributed, the work was withheld while the frontispiece engraving was altered and new frontispiece inserts printed. Either a stop-press correction of the error at 18-1.9 was made, or, more likely, the mistake was noted and corrected and the sheet involved reprinted while the frontispiece was being revised.

Note two: Frontispiece exists in three states, the illustration having been corrected by the engraver at the insistence of the artist, Sophia A. Peabody: (1) printed on plate paper with artist's initials and date ¹/₈+″ high; (2) printed on proof tissue and mounted on plate paper with artist's initials and date reset ¹/₁₆″ high; and (3) printed on plate paper with artist's initials and date ¹/₁₆″ high (see illustration).

Note three: Text from the 1837 *TTT,* edited and with portions omitted by the author. First appearance of Hawthorne's "Preface."

[i–ii] [1–5] 6–20

Plate leaf + [1]⁴ 2⁴ 3²

Contents: In most copies inserted frontispiece leaf has illustration on verso with recto blank; some copies noted with illustration on recto, verso blank. Protective tissue tipped in to title page. P. i: blank; p. ii: frontispiece illustration; p. 1: title; p. 2: copyright; p. 3: dedication; p. 4: preface; pp. 5–20: text, headed 'THE GENTLE BOY. | [double rules].'

Typography and paper: See illustration, A 2.2 page format. White wove paper.

Binding: Printed gray paper wrappers. All edges trimmed.

Publication: Advertised in the *Evening Transcript* (Boston), 22 December 1838, and noticed 2 January 1939. Apparently review copies were distributed in January 1839. Reviewed in the *Christian Register and Boston Observer,* 19 January 1839, by Washington Allston who complained about the engraver's handling of the face of the boy in the original drawing. Allston also noted that "this portion is to be retouched, and that the printing of the edition is delayed for a few days." *Transcript* for 23 February 1839 advertised that "a new edition is this day issued." Allston reviewed the "new edition" in the *Observer,* 23 February 1839. Presumably the "new edition" was made up from the balance of the undistributed sheets bound with the corrected frontispiece.

Locations: 'faccs': CEFC; 'faces': CEFC; plate state 1: CEFC, Lilly; state 2: CEFC; state 3: CEFC, Lilly, LC, MH, NN, PSt.

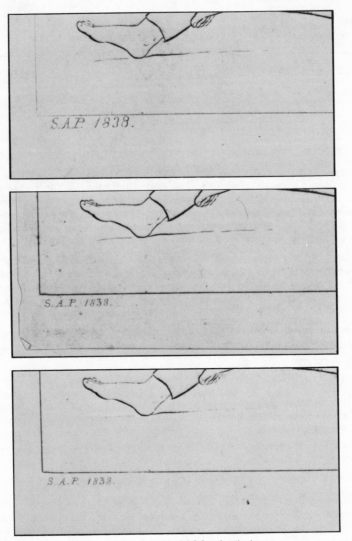

States 1, 2, and 3 (from top to bottom) of A 2.2.a₁ frontispiece

A 2.2.a₂

First separate edition of The Gentle Boy, *only printing, second state* [*1839*]

Note: Probable second state has 'faces' at 18-1.9. Otherwise, same as probable first state. First and second states of text found with various states of the frontispiece.

belong to some old champion of the righteous cause, whom the oppressor's drum had summoned from his grave. They raised a shout of awe and exultation, and looked for the deliverance of New England.

The Governor, and the gentlemen of his party, perceiving themselves brought to an unexpected stand, rode hastily forward, as if they would have pressed their snorting and affrighted horses right against the hoary apparition. He, however, blenched not a step, but glancing his severe eye round the group, which half encompassed him, at last bent it sternly on Sir Edmund Andros. One would have thought that the dark old man was chief ruler there, and that the Governor and Council, with soldiers at their back, representing the whole power and authority of the Crown, had no alternative but obedience.

'What does this old fellow here?' cried Edward Randolph, fiercely. 'On, Sir Edmund! Bid the soldiers forward, and give the dotard the same choice that you give all his countrymen — to stand aside or be trampled on!'

'Nay, nay, let us show respect to the good grandsire,' said Bullivant, laughing. 'See you not, he is some old round-headed dignitary, who hath lain asleep these thirty years, and knows nothing of the change of times? Doubtless, he thinks to put us down with a proclamation in Old Noll's name!'

'Are you mad, old man?' demanded Sir Edmund Andros, in loud and harsh tones. 'How dare you stay the march of King James's Governor?'

'I have staid the march of a King himself, ere now,' replied the gray figure, with stern composure.

vol. i. 2

TWICE-TOLD TALES.

BY

NATHANIEL HAWTHORNE.

VOLUME I.

BOSTON:
JAMES MUNROE AND COMPANY.
MDCCCXLIII.

A2.3: Title page, 6¹³/₁₆″ × 4⁵/₁₆″. Page format, 4¾″ (5¹/₁₆″) × 2⁷/₈″

A 2.3₁
Second edition, only printing, first issue [1842]

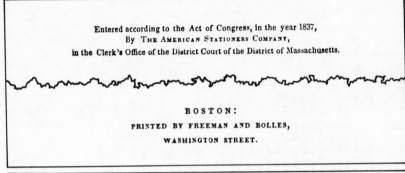

Entered according to the Act of Congress, in the year 1837,
By THE AMERICAN STATIONERS COMPANY,
in the Clerk's Office of the District Court of the District of Massachusetts.

BOSTON:
PRINTED BY FREEMAN AND BOLLES,
WASHINGTON STREET.

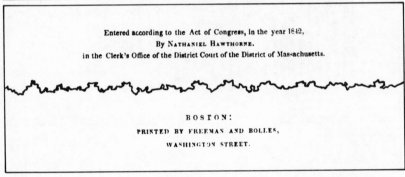

Entered according to the Act of Congress, in the year 1842,
By NATHANIEL HAWTHORNE.
in the Clerk's Office of the District Court of the District of Massachusetts.

BOSTON:
PRINTED BY FREEMAN AND BOLLES,
WASHINGTON STREET.

I: [i–iv] [1]–331 [332], with all section titles, blanks, and initial pages of tales unnumbered.

II: [i–iii] iv [1]–356, with all section titles, blanks, and initial pages of tales unnumbered.

I: π^2 1–20⁸ 21⁶; signature 21 also signed "21*" at 21₃r

II: π^2 1–22⁸ 23²

Note one: Contents for this two-volume 1842 edition were assembled and, in some cases, revised by Hawthorne.

Note two: The type metal in some of the forms loosened during the printing process requiring stop-press rearrangement. For example, the "r" in "throughout" at II, 98.10 and the "at" in "breathing" at II, 98.15 dropped out or moved and had to be pulled up or replaced (see illustration). Spacing rearrangements were made between words at II, 97.17, 18, 23–25, and 31; 112.3, 13, and 23; 209.14; 217.7, 11, and 18; 218.27.

Throughout   Th.oughout
as before, but   as before, but
   As your hea   As your hea
  — in a whisper   — in a whispeɪ
night solitudes   night solitudes
ter breathing   ter breɪ hing

State x   State y

Contents: *I:* p. i: title; p. ii: copyright; p. iii: contents; p. iv: blank; p. 1: section title 'THE GRAY CHAMPION.'; p. 2: blank; pp. 3-331: text, headed 'THE GRAY CHAMPION. | [rule]'; p. 332: blank. Each tale preceded by leaf with tale section title on recto and verso blank.

II: p. i: title; p. ii: copyright; pp. iii–iv: contents; p. 1: section title 'LEGENDS OF THE PROVINCE HOUSE. | NUMBER I.'; p. 2: blank; pp. 3–356: text, headed 'HOWE'S MASQUERADE. | [rule]'. Each tale preceded by leaf with tale section title on recto and verso blank.

Tales: *I:* Same as 1837 *TTT* (A 2.1) with the addition of "The Toll-Gatherer's Day."†
II: "Legends of the Province House: No. I.—Howe's Masquerade,"† "No. II.—Edward Randolph's Portrait,"† "No. III.—Lady Eleanore's Mantle,"† "No. IV.--Old Esther Dudley,"† "The Haunted Mind,"† "The Village Uncle,"† "The Ambitious Guest,"† "The Sister Years,"† "Snow Flakes,"† "The Seven Vagabonds,"† "The White Old Maid,"† "Peter Goldthwaite's Treasure,"† "Chippings with a Chisel,"† "The Shaker Bridal,"† "Night Sketches,"† "Endicott and the Red Cross,"† "The Lily's Quest,"† "Foot-Prints on the Sea-Shore,"† "Edward Fane's Rosebud,"† "The Threefold Destiny."† Daggers (†) indicate first collected appearance.

Typography and paper: See illustration, A 2.3₁ page format. Running heads: rectos and versos, chapter heads. White wove paper.

Binding: Brown (62. d. gy. Br), black (267. Black) bold and fine-ribbed T cloth in at least five varieties of blind-embossed cover designs one of which has 'HAWTHORNE' blind embossed in the center of a decorative frame. Spines goldstamped (see illustration, A 2 bindings). Cream and yellow endpapers, some coated one side. Also white wove endpapers faded to tan. Single flyleaf inserted at front and rear in some copies. Top edges untrimmed.

Publication: Contract with publisher specified "one edition not exceeding fifteen hundred copies," published December 1841 (*NHJ 1972*, 138). Price for two-volume set $2.25, with a 10% royalty.

Printing: Printed from type metal by Freeman and Bolles, Washington Street, Boston.

Locations: CEFC, Lilly, MH, NN, PSt.

Manuscript: Manuscript of "The Lily's Quest" in the William A. Strutz collection.

TWICE-TOLD TALES.

BY

NATHANIEL HAWTHORNE.

FIRST SERIES.

BOSTON:
JAMES MUNROE AND COMPANY.
MDCCCXLV.

Sabbath came twice as often, for the sake of that sorrowful old soul! There is an elderly man, also, who arrives in good season, and leans against the corner of the tower, just within the line of its shadow, looking downward with a darksome brow. I sometimes fancy that the old woman is the happier of the two. After these, others drop in singly, and by twos and threes, either disappearing through the door-way, or taking their stand in its vicinity. At last, and always with an unexpected sensation, the bell turns in the steeple overhead, and throws out an irregular clangor, jarring the tower to its foundation. As if there were magic in the sound, the sidewalks of the street, both up and down along, are immediately thronged with two long lines of people, all converging hitherward, and streaming into the church. Perhaps the far-off roar of a coach draws nearer — a deeper thunder by its contrast with the surrounding stillness — until it sets down the wealthy worshipers at the portal, among their humblest brethren. Beyond that entrance, in theory at least, there are no distinctions of earthly rank; nor, indeed, by the goodly apparel which is flaunting in the sun, would there seem to be such, on the hither side. Those pretty girls! Why will they disturb my pious meditations! Of all days in the week, they should strive to look least fascinating on the Sabbath, instead of heightening their mortal loveliness, as if to rival the blessed angels, and keep our thoughts from heaven. Were I the minister himself, I must needs look. One girl is white muslin from the waist upwards, and black silk downwards to her

A 2.3₂
Second edition, only printing, second issue [1845]

Entered according to Act of Congress, in the year 1837, by
THE AMERICAN STATIONERS COMPANY,
in the Clerk's office of the District Court of the District of Massachusetts.

Entered according to Act of Congress, in the year 1842, by
NATHANIEL HAWTHORNE,
in the Clerk's Office of the District Court of the District of Massachusetts.

I: [i–iv] [1]–331 [332], with all section titles, blanks, and initial pages of tales unnumbered.

II: [i–iii] iv [1]–356, with all section titles, blanks, and initial pages of tales unnumbered.

I: $\pi^2(\pm\pi_1)$ 1–20^8 21^6

II: $\pi^2(\pm\pi_1)$ 1–22^8 23^2

2 vols. 1842 sheets with cancel titles. Contents and collation same as 1842 issue except for title and copyright-page imprints.

Various bindings and spine imprints as with the 1842 set (see illustration, A 2 bindings). Probably less than 600 sets of the original 1842 printing refurbished for advertisement and sale in 1845. Price remained $2.25 for the set.

Location: CEFC.

aim, and merely smashed a looking-glass; and the next morning, when the incident was imperfectly remembered, they had shaken hands with a hearty laugh. Yet, again, while Memory was reading, Conscience unveiled her face, struck a dagger to the heart of Mr. Smith, and quelled his remonstrance with her iron frown. The pain was quite excruciating.

Some of the pictures had been painted with so doubtful a touch, and in colors so faint and pale that the subjects could barely be conjectured. A dull, semi-transparent mist had been thrown over the surface of the canvas, into which the figures seemed to vanish, while the eye sought most earnestly to fix them. But, in every scene, however dubiously portrayed, Mr. Smith was invariably haunted by his own lineaments, at various ages, as in a dusty mirror. After poring several minutes over one of these blurred and almost indistinguishable pictures, he began to see, that the painter had intended to represent him, now in the decline of life, as stripping the clothes from the backs of three half-starved children. "Really, this puzzles me!" quoth Mr. Smith, with the irony of conscious rectitude. "Asking pardon of the painter, pronounce him a fool, as well as a scandalous knave. A man of my standing in the world, to be robbing little children of their clothes! Ridiculous!"—But while he spoke, Memory had searched her fatal volume, and found a page, which, with her sad, calm voice, she poured into his ear. It was not altogether inapplicable to the misty scene. It told how Mr. Smith had been grievously tempted, by many devilish sophi-

TWICE TOLD TALES.

BY

NATHANIEL HAWTHORNE.

LONDON:

KENT AND RICHARDS,
PATERNOSTER-ROW.

A2.4: Title page. 6³/₄″ × 4¹/₈″. Page format, 4¹⁵/₁₆″ (5³/₁₆″) × 3″

A 2.4₁
First English edition, only printing, first issue, a piracy [1849]

[i–viii] [1]–312, with initial pages of tales unnumbered.

[A]⁴ B–I⁸ K–U⁸ X⁴; also signed at $2r.

Contents: p. i: half title; pp. ii–iii: blank; p. iv: frontispiece; p. v: title; p. vi: blank; pp. vii–viii: contents; pp. 1–312: text, headed 'FOOT-PRINTS ON THE SEA-SHORE. | [rule]'.

Tales: "Footprints on the Sea Shore," "Fancy's Show Box. A Morality," "The White Old Maid," "A Rill from the Town Pump," "The Hollow of the Three Hills," "Mr. Higginbotham's Catastrophe," "The Haunted Mind," "The Prophetic Pictures," "The Ambitious Guest," "Chippings with a Chisel," "Wakefield," "Sunday at Home," "The Threefold Destiny," "David Swan. A Fantasy," "The Vision of the Fountain," "Little Annie's Ramble," "The Lily's Quest. An Apologue," "Snow Flakes," "Edward Fane's Rosebud," "Sights from a Steeple," "Lady Eleanore's Mantle. A Legend of the Province House," "Dr. Heidegger's Experiment," "Night Sketches, Beneath an Umbrella," "The Toll Gatherer's Day. A Sketch of Transitory Life," "The Great Carbuncle. A Mystery of the White Mountains."

Typography and paper: See illustration, A 2.4, page format. Running heads: rectos and versos, chapter titles. White wove paper.

Binding: Rose (43. m. r Br) fine-ribbed T cloth blind embossed with decorative frame and central element on covers. Spine goldstamped (see illustration, A 2 bindings). White wove endpapers. Edges untrimmed.

Publication: Unknown number of copies published prior to 13 February 1849. No royalty paid.

Printing: Printed by Ward & Griffith, Bear Alley, Farringdon Street, London.

Locations: BM, 12704.c.15 (deposit-stamp 2 $\frac{49}{29}$ 13 [ie., 13 February 1849, ledger entry 29]); CEFC.

A 2.4₂
First English edition, only printing, second issue, a piracy

London: William Tegg and Co., 1850.

[i–viii] [1]–312, with initial pages of tales unnumbered.

[A]⁴ (±A₃) B–I,⁸ K–U⁸ X⁴; also signed at $2r.

1849 Kent and Richards sheets with a cancel title. (See *Centenary*, IX, 557.)

A 2.5
First Irish edition, only printing, a piracy

Dublin: James M'Glashan, MDCCCL.

Reprints the contents of vol. II of the 1842 Munroe edition plus three tales nowhere else attributed to Hawthorne: "Ethan Allen and the Lost Children," "An Indian's Revenge," and "The Fairy Fountain."

Location: CEFC.

TWICE-TOLD TALES.

NATHANIEL HAWTHORNE.

IN TWO VOLUMES

VOL. I.

A NEW EDITION.

BOSTON:

TICKNOR, REED, AND FIELDS.

M DCCC LI.

---

belong to some old champion of the righteous cause, whom the oppressor's drum had summoned from his grave. They raised a shout of awe and exultation, and looked for the deliverance of New England.

The Governor, and the gentlemen of his party, perceiving themselves brought to an unexpected stand, rode hastily forward, as if they would have pressed their snorting and affrighted horses right against the hoary apparition. He, however, blenched not a step, but glancing his severe eye round the group, which half encompassed him, at last bent it sternly on Sir Edmund Andros. One would have thought that the dark old man was chief ruler there, and that the Governor and Council, with soldiers at their back, representing the whole power and authority of the Crown, had no alternative but obedience.

'What does this old fellow here?' cried Edward Randolph, fiercely. 'On, Sir Edmund! Bid the soldiers forward, and give the dotard the same choice that you give all his countrymen — to stand aside or be trampled on!'

'Nay, nay, let us show respect to the good grandsire,' said Bullivant, laughing. 'See you not, he is some old round-headed dignitary, who hath lain asleep these thirty years, and knows nothing of the change of times? Doubtless, he thinks to put us down with a proclamation in Old Noll's name!'

'Are you mad, old man?' demanded Sir Edmund Andros, in loud and harsh tones. 'How dare you stay the march of King James's Governor?'

'I have staid the march of a King himself, ere now,' replied the gray figure, with stern composure.

A.2.6: Title page, 7" × 4¹/₂". Page format, 5³/₁₆" (5¹/₂") × 3"

A 2.6
Third American edition, only printing [1851]

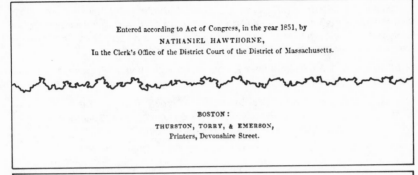

Note one: Hawthorne's "Preface" first appears in this edition.

Note two: Frontispiece engraved portrait of Hawthorne in vol. 1 exists in two states: (A) portrait only and (B) portrait with Hawthorne's signature and engraver's notice added.

I: [1–5] 6–287 [288], with initial pages of tales unnumbered. Frontispiece portrait on verso (recto blank) of leaf tipped in before title page.

II: [1–5] 6–288

I: π^2 1–17^8 18^4 19^2

II: π^2 1–17^8 18^4 19^2

Contents: *I:* p. 1: title; p. 2: copyright; p. 3: contents; p. 4: blank; pp. 5–12: preface; pp. 13–287: text, headed 'TWICE-TOLD TALES. | [rule] | THE GRAY CHAMPION.'; p. 288: blank.
    II: p. 1: title; p. 2: copyright; p. 3: contents; p. 4: blank; pp. 5-288: text, headed 'TWICE-TOLD TALES. | [rule] | LEGENDS OF THE PROVINCE HOUSE | I. | HOWE'S MASQUERADE.'

Tales: *I:* Same as vol. I, 1842 edition of *TTT* (A2.3₁) with added "Preface."
    II: Same as vol. II, 1842 edition (A 2.3₁).

Typography and paper: See illustration, A 2.6 page format. Running heads: rectos, chapter titles; versos, 'TWICE-TOLD TALES.' White wove paper.

Binding: See illustration, A2.6 binding, Ticknor format A. Brown (81. d. gy. y Br) bold-ribbed T cloth. Blind-embossed covers. Also Ticknor "gift" binding (see illustration, A2.6 binding, Ticknor format B ["gift" version]), with oval designs on covers goldstamped and edges gilded; red (13. deep Red) and green bold-ribbed T cloth, and faded rose (43. m. r Br) weave-grain EC-like cloth. Spines goldstamped. Yellow endpapers. Single white wove flyleaf inserted at front and rear. Ticknor ads inserted between front endpapers in some copies. All edges trimmed.

Publication: 2,000 copies of the two-volume set published 8 March 1851. Price for set $1.50, with a 10% royalty.

Printing: Printed from type metal by Thurston, Torry, & Emerson, Devonshire Street Boston. Probably bound by Benjamin Bradley & Co., Boston. Frontispiece engraved by T. Phillibrown from the C. G. Thompson portrait.

Locations: Trade: CEFC, LC, MH, NN, OU, PSt; "gift": CEFC, OU, PSt.

Manuscript: Manuscript of Hawthorne's "Preface" at the Houghton Library, Harvard University.

A2.7

THE GENTLE BOY. | BY | NATHANIEL HAWTHORNE. | AUTHOR OF "THE SCARLET LETTER," ETC. | [bird's nest vignette] | LONDON: | PUBLISHED BY KNIGHT AND SON, | 11, CLERKENWELL CLOSE.

[1852]. [1–5] 6–64. Prints "The Gentle Boy" only. A piracy.

Location: BM, 12651.a.25 (deposit-stamp 5 AP 1852).

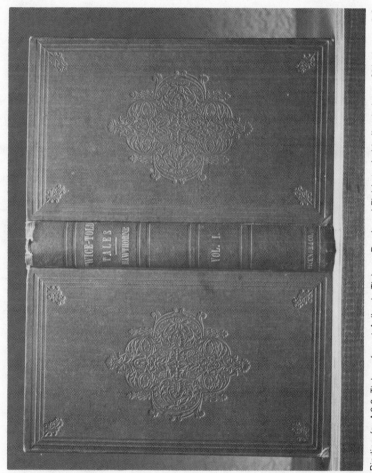

Binding for A2.6. Ticknor format A (basic Ticknor, Reed, and Fields trade binding in brown [81. d. gy. y Br]
bold-ribbed cloth with all binding rules and elements blindstamped)

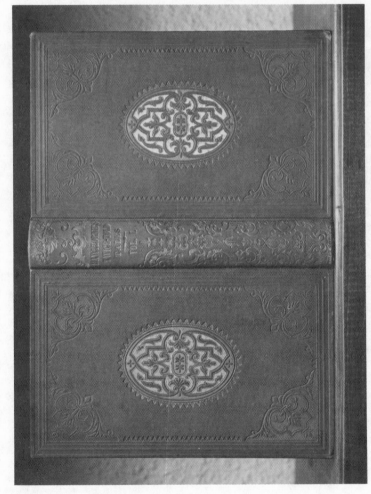

Binding for A2.6. Ticknor format B (basic Ticknor, Reed, and Fields "gift" binding in bold-ribbed T cloth in various colors with oval elements on covers and spine decoration goldstamped, all edges gilded)

A 2.8.a

Fourth American edition, first printing, first stereotyped edition

Boston: Ticknor, Reed, and Fields, M DCCC LIII.

I: [1–5] 6–287 [288], with initial pages of tales unnumbered. Portrait of Hawthorne (state B, see A 2.6) on verso (recto blank) of leaf tipped in before title page.

II: [1–5] 6–288, with initial pages of tales unnumbered.

I: π^2 1–17^8 18^4 19^2

II: π^2d 1–17^8 18^4 19^2

Note: First and second printings both bear 1853 date on title page. First and second printings of vol. I indistinguishable. Variant collations of vol. II exist. See A 2.8.b.

2 vols. Printed from stereotype plates made from a resetting of the 1851 edition (A 2.6). 500 copies printed 20 December 1852. Price for set $1.50, with a 10% royalty.

REPRINTINGS FROM THE T&F STEREOTYPE PLATES (IN 2 VOLS.)

A 2.8.b
Second printing

Boston: Ticknor, Reed, and Fields, M DCCC LIII.

Note: First and second printings of vol. I indistinguishable. Second printing of vol. II collates: π^2 1–17^8 18^6.

500 copies printed September 1853. Price $1.50, royalty 10%.

A 2.8.c
Boston: Ticknor and Fields, M DCCC LIV.

500 copies printed September 1854. Price $1.50, royalty 10%.

A 2.8.d
Boston: Ticknor and Fields, M DCCC LVII.

500 copies printed March 1857. Price $1.50, royalty 10%.

A 2.8.e
Boston: Ticknor and Fields, M DCCC LX.

280 copies printed February 1860. Price $1.50, royalty 10%.

A 2.8.f
Boston: Ticknor and Fields, M DCCC LXI.

280 copies printed March 1861. Price $1.50, royalty 10%.

A 2.8.g
Boston: Ticknor and Fields, 1863.

280 copies printed February 1863. Price $2.00, royalty 15¢.

A 2.8.h
Boston: Ticknor and Fields, 1864.

280 copies printed May 1864. Price $2.50, royalty 15¢.

A 2.8.i
Boston: Ticknor and Fields, 1865.

Vols. 1 and 2 of untitled *"Tinted Edition"* on laid paper. 500 copies printed October 1864. Price $1.50 per volume, royalty 12¢ per volume. See B 1[1,2] for reprintings of the *"Tinted Edition."*

A 2.8.j
Boston: Ticknor and Fields, 1865.

375 copies printed December 1864. Price $3.00, royalty 24¢.

A 2.8.k
Boston: Ticknor and Fields, 1866.

Note: Three printings with 1866 title-page date (see A 2.8.l, A 2.8.m), priority undetermined.

280 copies printed December 1865. Price $3.00, royalty 24¢. Printed on laid paper. Probably precedes 1866 printing on wove paper (A 2.8.l).

A 2.8.l
Boston: Ticknor and Fields, 1866.

500 copies printed July 1866. Price $3.00, royalty 24¢. Printed on wove stock of heavier weight than A 2.8.k and A 2.8.m.

A 2.8.m
Boston: Ticknor and Fields, 1866.

300 copies printed August 1866. Price $3.00, royalty 24¢.

A 2.8.n
Boston: Fields, Osgood, 1871.

280 copies printed September 1870. Price $4.00, royalty 40¢.

A 2.8.o
Boston: James R. Osgood, 1871.

Printed on laid paper.

A 2.8.p
Boston: James R. Osgood, 1871.

Combined in two-volumes-in-one format and published as the first volume of the *Illustrated Library Edition*. 500 copies printed 16 June 1871. Price $2.00, royalty 20¢. See B 2 for reprintings of the *ILE*.

A 2.8.q
Boston: James R. Osgood, 1872.

280 copies printed January–March 1872. Price $4.00, royalty 20¢.

A 2.8.r
Boston: Houghton, Mifflin, 1880.

Combined with *The House of the Seven Gables* and *The Snow Image* in four-volumes-in-one format and published as the first volume of the *Globe Edition*. 1,500 copies printed August 1880. See B 3 for reprintings of the *Globe Edition*.

A 2.8.s
Boston: Houghton, Mifflin, [1886].

Combined with *The House of the Seven Gables* and *The Snow Image* in four-volumes-in-one format as the first volume of the *"New" Fireside Edition*. 1,000 copies printed May 1886. See B 4.

PRINTINGS FROM THE BOHN EDITION PLATES

A 2.9.a

[I:] TWICE-TOLD TALES | BY | NATHANIEL HAWTHORNE. | A NEW EDITION. | LONDON: | HENRY G. BOHN, YORK STREET, CONVENT GARDEN. | 1851.

[II:] TWICE-TOLD TALES. | BY | NATHANIEL HAWTHORNE. | SECOND SERIES. | LONDON: | HENRY G. BOHN, YORK STREET, COVENT GARDEN. | 1851.

2 vols., continuously paged. Contents same as in 1851 T&F edition (A 2.6). A piracy.

Note: Various binding issues produced by Bohn from the same sheets for marketing to various classes of trade, priority uncertain:
    A. *Bohn's Cheap Series*. Nos. 35 (First Series) and 36 (Second Series) in *BCS*. Green (135. 1. y G) paper-covered boards, imprinted in blue ink (see illustration, A 2.9.a bindings). Price 1s. per volume. Location: CEFC.
    B. *Uniform with Bohn's Standard Library*. Both First and Second Series combined with *The Snow-Image* (A 19.2.a) in three-volumes-in-one format and published as vol. I of *Nathaniel Hawthorne's Tales*. Price 3s. 6d. Location: CEFC.

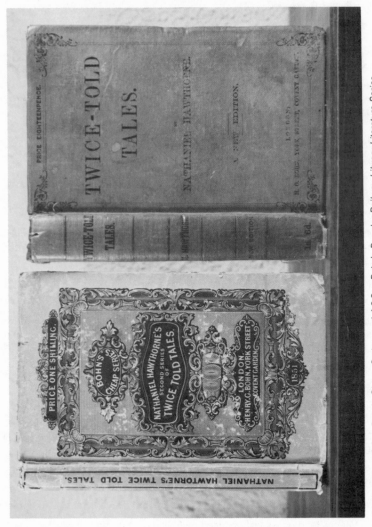

Bindings for A.2.9.a, *Bohn's Cheap Series*, and A.2.9.a, *Bohn's Popular Railway Library Literature Series*

C. *Bohn's Popular Railway Library Literature Series*. First and Second Series combined in two-volumes-in-one format and published in orange brown (54. br O) linen-covered boards (see illustration, A 2.9.a bindings). Price 1s. 6d. Location: CEFC.

D. First and Second Series also found in separate cloth and custom leather-bound volumes in various formats.

A 2.9.b
London: Bell & Daldy, 1866.

First and Second Series of *Twice-Told Tales* combined with *The Snow-Image* in three-volumes-in-one format and published as vol. I, *Nathaniel Hawthorne's Tales*, with omnibus volume title added. First and Second Series of *TTT* paged consecutively, *SI* paged independently. B&D volume title followed by a secondary title page for the two series of *TTT*. *TTT* title noted with London: Bell & Daldy, 1869 title-page imprint. Other title imprint dates are probable. Also Second Series *TTT* title noted with London: Henry G. Bohn, 1851 title-page imprint. Also *SI* section title noted (see A 19.2.b).

A 2.9.c
London: George Bell, 1875.

Same three-in-one format as A 2.9.b. *TTT* secondary title with London: Bell & Daldy, 1871 title-page imprint, no Second Series *TTT* listed. Also *SI* secondary title noted (see A 19.2.c). Other title imprints and combinations probable.

OTHER EDITIONS

A 2.10

TWICE-TOLD TALES. | BY | NATHANIEL HAWTHORNE. | A New Edition. | LONDON: | GEORGE ROUTLEDGE & CO., FARRINGDON ST. | 1852.

Paged continuously. Contents same as in 1851 T&F edition (A 2.6). A piracy.

Note: Various binding issues produced by Routledge from the same sheets for marketing to different classes of trade in competition with Bohn, priority undetermined:
A. *The Railway Library*. Advertised as two separate volumes in Routledge's *RL*. Probably bound in green (135. l. y G) paper-covered boards, imprinted in blue ink (uniform with other volumes in the *RL* series [see illustration, A 16.5 binding]). Price 1s. per volume. Also probably in cloth at 1s. 6d.
B. *Routledge's Standard Novels*. The two volumes of *Twice-Told Tales* combined in two-volumes-in-one format and published in the *RSN* series. Price 2s. 6d. With frontispiece portrait of Hawthorne. Title goldstamped on front cover. Location: Berg (copy presented to Hawthorne by publisher).

A 2.11
Halifax, [England]: Milner and Sowerby, 1853.

One-volume selection including 32 tales of 39 appearing in the 1851 T&F edition (A 2.6); omits "Howe's Masquerade," "Edward Randolph's Portrait," "Lady Eleanore's Mantle," "Old Esther Dudley," "The Sister Years," "The Lily's Quest," "Footprints on the Sea-shore."

Location: BM, 12707.6.66.

A 2.12

LITTLE ANNIE'S RAMBLE, | AND OTHER TALES. | BY | NATHANIEL HAWTHORNE. | HALIFAX: MILNER AND SOWERBY, | [rule] | 1853.

One-volume selection including "Little Annie's Ramble," "The Hollow of the Three Hills," "The Vision of the Fountain," "Dr. Heidegger's Experiment," "The Gentle Boy," "The Toll-Gatherer's Day," "The Haunted Mind," "The Village Uncle," "The Ambitious Guest," "The Seven Vagabonds," "The White Old Maid," "The Shaker Bridal," "Endi-cott and the Red Cross," "Chippings with a Chisel." Omits Hawthorne's "Preface." Made from the standing type of the Milner and Sowerby edition of *Twice-Told Tales* (see A 2.11). A piracy.

Location: CEFC.

A 2.13

A | RILL FROM THE TOWN PUMP, | BY HAWTHORNE. | WITH REMARKS | BY TELBA. | [rule] | PUBLISHED FOR THE ALBION SOCIETY, | BY W. AND F. G. CASH, 5, BISHOPSGATE WITHOUT. | [rule] | 1857. [all preceding within double-rules frame ornamented at corners] | PRICE TWOPENCE.

Cover title. A piracy.

Location: BM, 8435.a.106.(12) (deposit-stamp 6 JA 1857).

PRINTINGS FROM THE T&F "BLUE & GOLD EDITION" PLATES

A 2.14.a
First printing

Boston: Ticknor and Fields, 1865.

Note: First and second *B&G* printings have title pages dated 1865 and are indistin-guishable. *Cost Books* give separate entries.

2 vols. Contents of vol. I (excluding preface) and the first nine stories of vol. II of the 1851 T&F *Twice-Told Tales* (A 2.6) are combined and published as vol. I of the *"Blue & Gold Edition."* The conclusion of vol. II of *TTT* is combined with *The Snow-Image* and published as vol. II of the *B&G* edition (see A 19.5). New authorial note appended to "Dr. Heidegger's Experiment," *B&G,* vol. 1, p. 264. Goldstamped spine title imprint with and without Hawthorne's name. 1,500 two-volume sets published 28 October 1864. Price $3.00 per set, royalty 20¢ per set.

A 2.14.b
Second printing

Boston: Ticknor and Fields, 1865.

1,236 copies of vol. I and 1,225 copies of vol. II printed 26 January 1865. Price $2.75 per set, royalty 24¢ per set.

A 2.14.c
Third printing

Boston: Ticknor and Fields, 1866.

500 copies printed 16 July 1866. Price $3.00 per set, royalty 24¢ per set. Plates used for an unknown number of reprintings, including Boston: Houghton, Mifflin, 1879.

PRINTINGS FROM THE WARNE EDITION PLATES

A2.15.a

London: Frederick Warne, 1873.

Chandos Classics, no. 17.

A2.15.b

London: Frederick Warne, [1883].

Colophon has date of 4/6/83. 'New Edition,' noted on title page.

A2.15.c

London: Frederick Warne, [n.d.].

Warne shield on title page. Bungay, Clay and Taylor, Printers, imprint on verso of title page.

A2.15.d

London: Frederick Warne, [n.d.].

Warne shield on title page replaced with wings and horseshoe device. Morrison and Gibb, Printers, Edinburgh, on verso of half title. Reprinted an unknown number of times in various bindings.

A2.15.e

London: Frederick Warne, 1893.

PRINTINGS FROM THE "LITTLE CLASSIC EDITION" PLATES

A2.16.a

[All following within red and black double-rules frame] [red] Twice-Told Tales. | [black] BY | NATHANIEL HAWTHORNE. | VOL. I. [VOL. II.] | [seashore vignette] | [red] BOSTON: | [black] JAMES R. OSGOOD AND COMPANY, | Late Ticknor & Fields, and Fields, Osgood, & Co. | [red] 1876.

Vols. [I] and [II], *"Little Classic Edition."* Contents same as in 1851 T&F edition (A2.6). Sheets bound with James R. Osgood and, later, Houghton, Osgood spine stampings. 3,000 copies of each of the two volumes printed 26 November 1875. Price $1.25 per volume, royalty 12.5¢ per volume. See B 5[I,II] for reprintings of the *"Little Classic Edition."*

A2.16.b

Boston: Houghton, Osgood, 1879.

Two volumes in one combined as vol. I of the *"Fireside Edition."* 500 copies printed 20 September 1879. See B 6[I] for reprintings of the "Fireside Edition."

A2.16.c

Boston: Houghton, Mifflin, [1891].

Combined with *The House of the Seven Gables* in three-volumes-in-one format and published as vol. I of the *Popular Edition.* 1,000 copies printed June–August 1891. See B 7 for reprintings of the *Popular Edition.*

A 2.16.d
Boston and New York: Houghton, Mifflin, 1893.

Combined in two-volumes-in-one format with *'SALEM EDITION'* slug on title page. Reprinted with 1894 title-page date.

A 2.16.e
Boston: Houghton, Mifflin, [1899].

Vols. [I] and [II], *Concord Edition.* See B 8.

OTHER EDITIONS

A 2.17

Legends | *of* | *The Province House.* | BY | NATHANIEL HAWTHORNE. | [vignette] | BOSTON: JAMES R. OSGOOD AND COMPANY, | *Late Ticknor and Fields, and Fields, Oogood* [*sic*]*, & Co.* | 1877.

Contains "Howe's Masquerade," "Edward Randolph's Portrait," "Lady Eleanore's Mantle," "Old Esther Dudley." 1,000 copies printed 31 May 1877; 500 copies, 6 July 1877.

A 2.18

Tales | *of* | *The White Hills.* | BY | NATHANIEL HAWTHORNE. | [vignette] | BOSTON: | JAMES R. OSGOOD AND COMPANY, | *Late Ticknor and Fields, and Fields, Osgood, & Co.* | 1877.

Contains "The Great Stone Face," "The Great Carbuncle," "The Ambitious Guest." 1,500 copies printed 5 June 1877.

A 2.19

Legends | *of* | *New England,* | BY | NATHANIEL HAWTHORNE. | [vignette] | BOSTON: | JAMES R. OSGOOD AND COMPANY, | *Late Ticknor and Fields, and Fields, Osgood, & Co.* | 1877.

Contains "The Gray Champion," "The May Pole of Merry Mount," "Endicott and the Red Cross," "Roger Malvin's Burial." 1,500 copies printed 5 June 1877.

PRINTINGS FROM THE RIVERSIDE EDITION PLATES

A 2.20.a₁
Riverside Edition (trade), first printing, American issue [1883]

TWICE-TOLD TALES | BY | NATHANIEL HAWTHORNE | [vignette of Maypole scene] | BOSTON | HOUGHTON, MIFFLIN AND COMPANY | New York: 11 East Seventeenth Street | The Riverside Press, Cambridge | 1883.

Two volumes in one published as vol. I of the Riverside trade printing. Contents same as in 1851 T&F edition (A 2.6), with "Introductory Note" by George Parsons Lathrop added. 1,500 copies printed December 1882. Price $2.00. See B 9 for reprintings of the Riverside trade printing.

A 2.20.a₂
Riverside Edition (trade), first printing, English issue [*1883*]

London: Kegan Paul, Trench, 1883.

Sheets of vol. I, first printing (A 2.20.a₁), with cancel title, in a Kegan Paul binding. 250 Kegan Paul title pages printed by Houghton, Mifflin, June–July 1883. Later issues noted with dated and undated Kegan Paul, Trench, Trübner title pages. See B 11.

A 2.20.b
Riverside Edition (large paper), second printing [*1883*]

[red] TWICE-TOLD TALES | [black] BY | NATHANIEL HAWTHORNE | [sepia vignette of Maypole scene] | [red] CAMBRIDGE | [black] Printed at the Riverside Press | 1883.

Combined in two-volumes-in-one format and published as vol. I of the Riverside large-paper printing. 250 copies printed January 1883. See B 10.

A 2.20.c
Boston and New York: Houghton, Mifflin, 1884.

Vols. I and II of the *Wayside Edition*. 500 copies printed September–October 1884. See B 12.

A 2.20.d
Boston and New York: Houghton, Mifflin, [1891].

Combined in two-volumes-in-one format and published as vol. I of the *Standard Library Edition*. 500 copies printed October 1891. See B 13.

A 2.20.e
Boston and New York: Houghton, Mifflin, [1902].

Combined in two-volumes-in-one format and published as vol. I of the "New" Wayside Edition. 500 copies printed September–October 1902. See B 14.

A 2.20.f
Boston and New York: [Houghton, Mifflin], MDCCCCIX.

Combined in two-volumes-in-one format and published as vol. I of the *Fireside Edition*. See B 15.

A 2.20.g
Boston, New York: Jefferson Press, [1913].

Combined in two-volumes-in-one format and published as vol. [I] of the *"Jefferson Press Edition."* See B 16.

OTHER EDITIONS

A 2.21
Printings from the Paterson-Scott plates

2 vols.

[I:] TWICE-TOLD TALES. | BY | NATHANIEL HAWTHORNE. | [portrait of Hawthorne] | EDINBURGH: | WILLIAM PATERSON. | 1883.

[II:] Paterson's Shilling Library—New England Novels. | [rule] | LEGENDS | OF THE | PROVINCE HOUSE, | ETC. | BEING SECOND SERIES OF | TWICE-TOLD TALES. | BY | NATHANIEL HAWTHORNE. | [portrait of Hawthorne] | EDINBURGH: | WILLIAM PATERSON. | 1883.

Nos. 11 and 12, *Paterson's New England Novels.* Contents same as in 1851 T&F edition (A 2.6). Published in cloth, top edges gilded, at 2s. per set; in ornamental paper covers at 1s. Also combined in two-volumes-in-one format and published as vol. [III] of the *"Paterson Edition."* See B 17. Also reprinted spearately without date on title page. Also Paterson sheets noted with cancel Walter Scott title. Also remanufactured from Paterson plates with Walter Scott title-page imprints. Published in 1894 as vols. [IX] and [XI] of the *"Walter Scott Edition"* (gravure). See B 18.

A 2.22
Some Twice-Told Tales. New York: John B. Alden. 1884.

Vol. I, no. 30, *The Irving Library,* 9 January 1884. Contains "Night Sketches," "A Rill from the Town Pump," "The Toll-Gatherer's Day." Printed wrappers.

A 2.23

Modern Classics. | [rule] | HAWTHORNE. | By JAMES T. FIELDS. | TALES OF THE WHITE HILLS, | LEGENDS OF NEW ENGLAND, | By NATHANIEL HAWTHORNE. | *ILLUSTRATED.* | [floral device] | BOSTON: | HOUGHTON, MIFFLIN AND COMPANY. | The Riverside Press, Cambridge.

[1884]. Manufactured from the plates of the separate titles (see A 2.18, A 2.19). 500 copies printed January 1884.

A 2.24
Boston: Houghton, Mifflin, 1884.

Two volumes in one, *School Edition.* 500 copies printed May 1884. Price $1.00.

A 2.25
Printings from the Alden plates

2 vols.

[I:] TWICE-TOLD TALES | FIRST SERIES | BY | NATHANIEL HAWTHORNE | [rule] | New York | JOHN B. ALDEN, PUBLISHER | 1886

[II:] TWICE-TOLD TALES | SECOND SERIES | BY | NATHANIEL HAWTHORNE | [rule] | NEW YORK | JOHN B. ALDEN, PUBLISHER | 1886

Contents same as in the *Riverside Edition,* omitting "Preface" in vol. I. Alden plates used to manufacture Hurst and Lupton printings in various formats.

A 2.26
Tales of the White Hills and Sketches. Boston, New York, Chicago: Houghton, Mifflin, [1889].

No. 40, *Riverside Literature Series,* printed February 1889. Contains "The Great Stone Face," "The Ambitious Guest," "The Great Carbuncle," "Sketches from Memory," "My Visit to Niagara," "Old Ticonderoga," "The Sister Years." Printed wrappers.

A 2.27

TWICE-TOLD TALES. | BY | NATHANIEL HAWTHORNE. | [rule] | PHILADELPHIA: | DAVID McKAY, PUBLISHER, | 23 SOUTH NINTH STREET. | 1889.

Two volumes in one, *American Classic Series*. Contents same as in the 1851 T&F edition (A 2.6), omitting the "Preface."

A 2.28

The Riverside Aldine Series | [rule] | THE GRAY CHAMPION | AND OTHER STORIES AND SKETCHES | BY | NATHANIEL HAWTHORNE | [dolphin and anchor device] | BOSTON AND NEW YORK | HOUGHTON, MIFFLIN AND COMPANY | The Riverside Press, Cambridge | 1889.

Contains "The Gray Champion," "The Canterbury Pilgrims," "My Kinsman, Major Molineux," "The Snow Image: A Childish Miracle," "The Old Manse," "Feathertop: A Moralized Legend," "Drowne's Wooden Image," "The Wives of the Dead," "Wakefield," "Mr. Higginbotham's Catastrophe."

A 2.29

FOOTPRINTS ON THE SEASHORE | BY NATHANIEL HAWTHORNE | WITH ETCHED ILLUSTRATIONS BY | LOUIS K. HARLOW. | [sepia vignette] | BOSTON • SAMUEL E • CASSINO • | MDCCCXCII

Prints title story only. Imitation vellum covers.

A 2.30

SNOW FLAKES. | BY | NATHANIEL HAWTHORNE. | [vignette of winter scene] | ILLUSTRATED BY | LOUIS K. HARLOW. | BOSTON: | SAMUEL E. CASSINO. | Copyright 1892.

Prints title story only. Printed wrappers.

A 2.31
Philadelphia: Henry Altemus, 1893.

Two volumes in one. Contents same as in the *Riverside Edition* (A 2.20), omitting "Preface." Reprinted with 1894 and 1895 title-page dates. Also reprinted without date on title page. Altemus plates for vol. I only used to manufacture *Twice-Told Tales* in the *Altemus Illustrated Vademecum Series*.

A 2.32
London: Richard Edward King, n.d.

[1893?]. Printings on different grades of paper, apparently for different classes of trade, in various bindings. Frontispiece inserted in some. Customized booksellers' titles found in some copies as cancels.

A 2.33
Colonial Stories. Boston: Joseph Knight, 1897.

Contains "Howe's Masquerade," "Edward Randolph's Portrait," "Lady Eleanore's Mantle," "Old Esther Dudley." Also issued with Boston: L. C. Page, 1897 cancel title. Also issued with London: Bliss, Sands, 1898 cancel title.

A 2.34
New York: Maynard, Merrill, n.d.

[c. 1897]. Nos. 188–189, *Maynard's English Classic Series*. Contains "The Gray

Champion," "The Minister's Black Veil," "The Maypole of Merry Mount," "Howe's Masquerade," "Edward Randolph's Portrait," "Lady Eleanore's Mantle," "Old Esther Dudley," with biographical sketch and notes. Price 24¢.

PRINTINGS FROM THE AUTOGRAPH EDITION PLATES

A 2.35.a
Boston and New York: Houghton, Mifflin, MDCCCC.

Vols. I and II of the *Autograph Edition*. Contents same as in the *Riverside Edition* (A 2.20.a), with addition of "General Introduction" and "Introductory Note." 500 copies. See B 20.

A 2.35.b
Boston and New York: Houghton, Mifflin, MDCCCC.

Vols. I and II of the *Large-Paper (Autograph) Edition*. 500 copies. See B 21.

A 2.35.c
Boston and New York: Houghton, Mifflin, 1903.

Vols. I and II of the *Old Manse Edition*. See B 22.

OTHER EDITIONS

A 2.36
Howe's Masquerade. Boston: Educational Publishing Co., 1900.

No. 210, *Young Folk's Library of Choice Literature*, printed 1 September 1900. Prints title story only. Printed wrappers.

A 2.37
New York: Thomas Y. Crowell, n.d.

[c. 1900]. 2 vols. *Crowell Handy Volume Classics Series*. Introduction by Katharine Lee Bates. Also same plates used to manufacture vols. [1] and [2] of the *Crowell "Lenox Edition."* See B 23.

A 2.38
The Gentle Boy and Other Tales. Boston, New York, Chicago: Houghton, Mifflin, 1900.

No. 145, *Riverside Literature Series*. Contains "The Gentle Boy," "Roger Malvin's Burial," "The Wedding Knell," "The Gray Champion."

A 2.39
Selected Twice-Told Tales. Boston, New York, Chicago: Houghton, Mifflin, 1901.

No. 147, Extra (R), *Riverside Literature Series*, printed April 1901. Contains "Introductory Note," "Preface," "The Minister's Black Veil," "Howe's Masquerade," "Lady Eleanore's Mantle," "Old Esther Dudley," "Mr. Higginbotham's Catastrophe," "The Prophetic Pictures," "David Swan," "Sights from a Steeple."

A 2.40
Selections from Twice-Told Tales. New York: Macmillan, 1901.

Macmillan Pocket Classics. Contains "Prefatory Note," "Introduction" by Charles Robert Gaston, "David Swan," "Sights from a Steeple," "The Prophetic Pictures," "Mr. Higginbotham's Catastrophe," "The Minister's Black Veil," "Howe's Masquerade," "Lady Eleanore's Mantle," "Old Esther Dudley," "Notes," "Index."

A 2.41
New York: Thomas Y. Crowell, [1902].

Combined in a two-volumes-in-one format and published as vol. [6] of the *Crowell "Popular Edition."* See B 24.

A 2.42
New York: P. F. Collier, MCMIII.

Two volumes in one, *American Authors in Prose and Poetry* series. Contents same as in the *Riverside Edition* (A 2.20), omitting "Preface."

A 2.43
Chicago, New York: Scott, Foresman, n.d.

[c. 1903]. Two volumes in one, *The Lake English Classics*. Contents same as in the *Riverside Edition* (A 2.20), omitting "Preface," with new preface and introduction added.

A 2.44
Boston, New York, Chicago: Houghton Mifflin, n.d.

[c. 1907]. Two volumes in one, the *Riverside Literature Series*. Contents same as in the *Riverside Edition* (A 2.20), with synopsis, introductory note, and critical notes added.

A 2.45
London and Toronto: Dent; New York: E. P. Dutton, n.d.

[c. 1911]. Two volumes in one, no. 531, *Everyman's Library*. Contents same as in the *Riverside Edition* (A 2.20), with introductory note added. Reprinted 1913 and regularly thereafter.

A 2.46
Little Annie's Ramble. Cedar Rapids, Iowa: privately printed for Jean and Josephine Fisher, Nineteen Thirteen.

Prints title story only. Limited to 20 copies. Boards, printed paper label on front cover.

A 2.47
The Seven Vagabonds. Boston and New York: Houghton, Mifflin, Mdccccxvi.

Prints title story only. Boards, with printed paper label. Dust jacket.

A 2.48
Tales by Nathaniel Hawthorne. Selected, edited, with an introduction by Carl Van Doren. London, Edinburgh . . . Peking: Oxford University Press, 1921.

Contains "Introduction," "The Wives of the Dead," "My Kinsman, Major Molineux," "Roger Malvin's Burial," "The Canterbury Pilgrims," "The Seven Vagabonds," "Mr. Higginbotham's Catastrophe," "The Grey Champion," "Young Goodman Brown," "Wakefield," "The Ambitious Guest," "The Maypole of Merry Mount," "The Minister's Black Veil," "The Great Carbuncle," "Dr. Heidegger's Experiment," "Endicott and the

42 A 2.49 *Twice-Told Tales*

Red Cross," "Legends of the Province House: Howe's Masquerade," "Edward Randolph's Portrait," "Lady Eleanore's Mantle," "Old Esther Dudley," "The Birthmark," "The Celestial Railroad," "The Christmas Banquet," "Earth's Holocaust," "The Artist of the Beautiful," "Drowne's Wooden Image," "Rappaccini's Daughter," "The Great Stone Face," "The Snow Image," "Ethan Brand," "Feathertop." Trade and limp-leather formats, boxed.

A 2.49
Mr. Higginbotham's Catastrophe. Boston: The Berkeley Printers, n.d.

[c. 1931]. Prints title story only. Boards.

A 2.50
Legends of the Province House. New York: William R. Scott, [1936].

Contains "Howe's Masquerade," "Edward Randolph's Portrait," "Lady Eleanore's Mantle," "Old Esther Dudley." Boards, paper label on spine.

A 2.51
The Gray Champion and Other Tales. New York: Editions for the Armed Services, Inc., n.d.

[1945?]. No. 863. Contains "The Gray Champion," "Mr. Higginbotham's Catastrophe," "David Swan," "Dr. Heidegger's Experiment," "The Birthmark," "Rappaccini's Daughter," "Drowne's Wooden Image," "The Snow-Image," "The Great Stone Face," "Ethan Brand," "My Kinsman, Major Molineux," "The Shaker Bridal." Printed wrappers.

A 2.52
The Maypole of Merrymount. [Boston]: Merrymount Press, MDCCCCXLVII.

Prints title story only. Stiff paper covers.

PRINTINGS FROM THE LIMITED EDITIONS CLUB PLATES

A 2.53.a
First printing

New York: The Limited Editions Club, 1966.

Selected and introduced by Wallace Stegner. Illustrated by Valenti Angelo. Contains "Introduction," "The Snow-Image: A Childish Miracle," "The Great Stone Face," "Ethan Brand," "My Kinsman, Major Molineux," "Alice Doane's Appeal," "Young Goodman Brown," "Rappaccini's Daughter," "The Celestial Railroad," "The Birthmark," "Egotism, or, The Bosom Serpent," "Earth's Holocaust," "The Artist of the Beautiful," "The Wedding Knell," "The Minister's Black Veil," "The Maypole of Merry Mount," "Mr. Higginbotham's Catastrophe," "The Hollow of the Three Hills," "Dr. Heidegger's Experiment," "Lady Eleanore's Mantle," "Old Esther Dudley," "The Ambitious Guest," "Feathertop: A Moralized Legend," "The Prophetic Pictures," "Peter Goldthwaite's Treasure." Boxed. Limited to 1,500 copies, signed by the illustrator.

A 2.53.b
Second printing

New York: The Heritage Press, n.d.

[c. 1966]. Manufactured from *The Limited Editions Club* plates. Same contents. One of the colors used in the *LEC* printing eliminated. Printed on lighter-weight stock, and trimmed and bound in a smaller format.

OTHER EDITION

A 2.54
[Columbus]: Ohio State University Press, [1974].

Vol. IX of the *Centenary Edition*. 2,547 copies published 1 October 1974. See B 32.

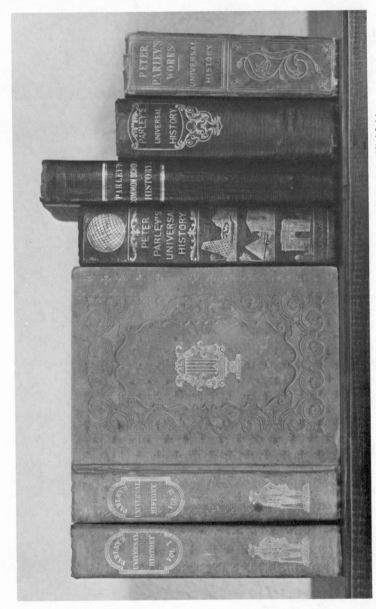

Bindings for (1 & 2) A3.1.a, with B. Bradley lyre goldstamped on covers; (3) A3.2; (4) A3.3; (5) A3.4.a; (6) A3.4.b

PETER PARLEY'S

UNIVERSAL HISTORY,

ON THE BASIS OF

GEOGRAPHY.

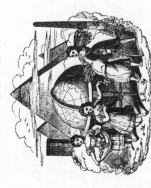

FOR THE USE OF FAMILIES.

ILLUSTRATED BY MAPS AND ENGRAVINGS

VOL. I.

BOSTON:

AMERICAN STATIONERS' COMPANY.
JOHN B. RUSSELL.
1837.

PETER PARLEY'S

UNIVERSAL HISTORY,

ON THE BASIS OF

GEOGRAPHY.

FOR THE USE OF FAMILIES.

ILLUSTRATED BY MAPS AND ENGRAVINGS.

VOL. II.

BOSTON:

AMERICAN STATIONERS COMPANY.
JOHN B. RUSSELL.
1837.

A.3.1.a: Title pages, 6⁹/₁₆″ × 5¹/₁₆″

ried away the treasures of the temple and of the palace.

2. The other ten tribes of Israel, which had revolted from Rehoboam, were thenceforward governed by kings of their own, the country being called the kingdom of Israel. Most of these kings were wicked men, and idolaters. Their palace and seat of government was in the city of Samaria.

3. When the kingdom of Israel had been separated from that of Judah about two hundred and fifty years, it was conquered by Salmaneser, king of Assyria. He made slaves of the Israelites, and carried them to his own country, and most of them never returned to the land of Canaan.

4. The people of the two tribes of Judah and Benjamin continued to reside in Canaan. They were now called Jews. The royal palace and seat of government was at Jerusalem. Some of the Jewish kings were pious men, but most of them offended God by their sinfulness and idolatry.

5. The whole nation of the Jews were perverse, and underwent many severe inflictions from the wrath of God. In the year 606 B. C., Nebuchadnezzar, king of Babylon, took Jerusalem. He destroyed the

F

THE HEBREWS.   81

ried away the treasures of the temple and of the palace.

2. The other ten tribes of Israel, which had revolted from Rehoboam, were thenceforward governed by kings of their own, the country being called the kingdom of Israel. Most of these kings were wicked men, and idolaters. Their palace and seat of government was in the city of Samaria.

3. When the kingdom of Israel had been separated from that of Judah about two hundred and fifty years, it was conquered by Salmaneser, king of Assyria. He made slaves of the Israelites, and carried them to his own country, and most of them never returned to the land of Canaan.

4. The people of the two tribes of Judah and Benjamin continued to reside in Canaan. They were now called Jews. The royal palace and seat of government was at Jerusalem. Some of the Jewish kings were pious men, but most of them offended God by their sinfulness and idolatry.

5. The whole nation of the Jews were perverse, and underwent many severe inflictions from the wrath of God. In the year 606 B. C., Nebuchadnezzar, king of Babylon, took Jerusalem. He destroyed the

VOL. I.   F

A 3.1.a: First-printing page format, 4⁹/₁₆″ (4¹³/₁₆″) × 3¹¹/₁₆″. A 3.1.b: Second-printing page format

A 3 PETER PARLEY'S UNIVERSAL HISTORY

A 3.1.a
First American edition, first printing [1837]

Entered according to Act of Congress, in the year 1837, by
S. G. GOODRICH,
In the Clerk's Office of the District Court of Massachusetts.

CAMBRIDGE:
FOLSOM, WELLS, AND THURSTON,
PRINTERS TO THE UNIVERSITY.

Entered according to Act of Congress, in the year 1837, by
S. G. GOODRICH,
In the Clerk's Office of the District Court of Massachusetts.

CAMBRIDGE:
FOLSOM, WELLS, AND THURSTON,
PRINTERS TO THE UNIVERSITY.

Note: Edited by Hawthorne and his sister Elizabeth.

2 vols. At least two printings bear 1837 title-page dates. First printing can be distinguished by absence of volume designation at foot of first page of each signature. Volume designation added to first page of signatures of second 1837 and later reprints. See illustration.

3. In this way, after many years, they grew rich, and built large cities, with fine houses, temples and
A

3. In this way, after many years, they grew rich, and built large cities, with fine houses, temples and
VOL. II.   A

Vol. II, p. 17: (top) first printing; (bottom) reprintings

I: [i–vii] viii [i] ii–vii [viii] [9] 10–380 [381–384], with full-page illustrations and first pages of some chapters unnumbered.

II: [i–vii] viii–xii [13] 14–374 [375–376], with full-page illustrations and first pages of some chapters unnumbered.

I: π^8 A^4 B–X^8; also signed π^4 [1]^6 2–32^6

II: π^8 A^4 B–I^8 K–X^8; also signed π^4 1–30^6 31^4

Contents: I: p. i: half title; p. ii: frontispiece; p. iii: engraved title; p. iv: blank; p. v: title; p. vi: copyright; pp. vii–viii: preface; pp. i–vii: contents; p. viii: map; pp. 9–380: text, headed 'UNIVERSAL HISTORY. | [rule] | CHAPTER I.—INTRODUCTION.'; pp. 381–384: blank.

   II: p. i: half title; p. ii: frontispiece; p. iii: engraved title; p. iv: blank; p. v: title; p. vi: copyright; pp. vii–xii: contents; pp. 13–374: text, headed 'UNIVERSAL HISTORY. | [rule] | CHAPTER I.—EUROPE CONTINUED.'; pp. 375–376: blank.

Typography and paper: See illustration, A 3.1.a page format. Running heads: rectos, chapter titles; versos, 'UNIVERSAL HISTORY.' White wove paper.

Binding: Found in a wide variety of cloths and embossed patterns, including rose (19. gy. Red), brown (58 m. Br), and black fine diaper H cloth; brown pebble-grain P cloth; rose bold-ribbed T cloth; blue and green (127. gy. Ol G) wavy-grain TR cloth; blue coarse-ribbed morocco AR cloth; salmon diagonal fine-ribbed S cloth, variously embossed with oak leaf pattern, assorted floral patterns, and blindstamped frames on the covers. Some covers goldstamped with lyre or great elm cuts. Name of binder, B. Bradley, incorporated in goldstamping or embossing on some covers. Spine gold-stamped with and without Parley figure at base (see illustration, A 3 bindings). Found with yellow, cream, gold endpapers. Flyleaf inserted at front and rear. Blank leaves at end of final signature removed during binding in some copies. All edges trimmed. Bound by Benjamin Bradley & Co., Boston.

Publication: The work in two volumes was deposited for copyright 29 July 1837. Hawthorne wrote his sister Elizabeth (12 May 1836), "Our pay as Historians of the Universe, will be 100 dollars, the whole of which you may have."

Locations: First printing: Berg, CEFC, ViU; second printing: CEFC, Lilly.

A 3.1.b
First American edition, second printing (1837)

2 vols.

Second printing has volume designations added to first page of signatures—see illustration under A 3.1.a. Otherwise the same as first printing.

OTHER PRINTINGS

A 3.1.c
Boston: American Stationers Company, John B. Russell, 1838.

2 vols.

A 3.1.d
New York: S. Colman, 1839.

2 vols. Later reprinted in two-volume format with various title-page imprints, including: New York: Nafis & Cornish; Philadelphia: J. B. Perry, 1845. Also produced in two-volumes-in-one format from the original plates and reprinted with various title-page imprints, including:

New York: J. A. Hoisington [1840].
New York: William Robinson, [n.d.]. *Sixth, Seventh, Eighth Edition.*
New York: Van Amringe & Bixby, 1844. *Eighth Edition.*
New York: Mark H. Newman, 1847. *Twelfth Edition.*
New York: Mark H. Newman, 1850.
New York: Ivison & Phinney, MDCCCLVI.

'A NEW EDITION, BROUGHT DOWN TO THE PRESENT DAY,' was produced in 1860 in 700 pp., revised in 1874 (718 pp.), further revised in 1886 (718 pp.).

5. He publicly proclaimed that God had sent him to convert the world to a new religion. The people of Mecca would not at first believe Mohammed. He was born among them, and they knew that he had been a camel-driver, and was no holier than themselves. Beside, he pretended that he had ridden up to heaven on an ass, in company with the angel Gabriel; and many of his stories were as ridiculous as this.

6. So the men of Mecca threatened to slay Mohammed, and he was therefore forced to fly to Medina, another city of Arabia, on July 16, 622. This flight is called *Hegira* by the Mohammedans, and from it they date events, as Christians do from the birth of Christ. There, in the course of two or three years, he made a great number of converts, He told his disciples that they must compel others to adopt his religion by force, if they refused to do so from conviction.

7. This conduct brought on a war between the disciples of Mohammed and all the other Arabians. Mohammed won many victories, and soon made himself master of the whole country.

8. Mohammed was now not only a pretended prophet, but a real king. He was a very terrible man, even to his own followers; for, whenever he was angry, a vein between his eyebrows used to swell, and turn black. This gave him a grim and frightful aspect.

9. His power continued to increase; but he died suddenly, at the age of sixty-three. He was buried at Medina, where his tomb may still be seen. Many pilgrims go every year to visit the place.

10. The religion of Mohammed was speedily diffused over nearly all Asia and Africa, and is still believed by many millions of people. Its precepts are contained in a book called the Koran. Mohammed affirmed that the angel Gabriel brought him the doctrines contained in this book from heaven.

PETER PARLEY'S

UNIVERSAL HISTORY,

ON THE BASIS OF

GEOGRAPHY.

LONDON:

JOHN W. PARKER, WEST STRAND.

M.DCCC.XXXVII.

A.3.2: Title page, 6⁷/₁₆″ × 4¹/₁₆″. Page format, 5³/₈″ (5⁵/₈″) × 3¹/₈″

A 3.2
First English edition, a piracy [1837]

[i–v] vi–viii [ix] x–xv [xvi–xx] [1] 2–512

π² a⁶ χ² B–I⁸ K–U⁸ X–Z⁸ 2A–2I⁸ 2K⁸

Contents: p. i: blank; p. ii: frontispiece; p. iii: title; p. iv: blank; pp. v–viii: preface; pp. ix–xv: contents; pp. xvi–xvii: blank; pp. xviii–xix: maps; p. xx: blank; pp. 1–512: text, headed 'UNIVERSAL HISTORY. | [rule] | CHAPTER I. INTRODUCTION.——*About travelling in a | Balloon, and what curious things one may meet with.*

Typography and paper: See illustration, A3.2 page format. Running heads; rectos, chapter titles; versos, 'UNIVERSAL HISTORY.' White wove paper.

Binding: Blue (187. d. gy. B) diagonal fine-ribbed S cloth blind embossed with geometric patterns. Spine goldstamped (see illustration, A3 bindings). Wove endpapers pale yellow coated one side. Single flyleaf inserted at front and rear. Four pages of ads for John W. Parker 'SELECT BOOKS' inserted at rear. All edges trimmed.

Publication: Advertised in the London *Literary Gazette* and *Athenaeum,* 21 October 1837.

Locations: BM, 1210.d.17; CEFC.

PETER PARLEY'S

COMMON SCHOOL

HISTORY.

ILLUSTRATED BY ENGRAVINGS.

BOSTON:
AMERICAN STATIONERS' COMPANY.
J. B. RUSSELL.

1838.

A.3.3: Title page, 7⁷⁄₁₆″ × 4½″. Copyright page

A 3.3
Second American edition

Boston: American Stationers' Company, J. B. Russell, 1838.

A new edition in one volume of *Peter Parley's Universal History*, completely reset from A 3.2. The text is slightly abridged and modified, and some illustrations are omitted. S. G. Goodrich later merchandised the *Universal History*, in two volumes in a deluxe format, to the general trade and produced this compact *Common School History* for the school trade (see statement on A 3.3 copyright page). Bound in blue (182. m. Blue) pebble-grained P cloth, navy-leather backstrip. Spine goldstamped (see illustration, A 3 bindings). Deposited for copyright 14 December 1837.

Locations: CEFC, ViU.

Note: Reprinted. Revised and new editions manufactured with various title-page imprints, including: Philadelphia: E. H. Butler, 1843 ('14TH EDITION, REVISED AND CORRECTED'); copyrighted by Butler and reprinted 1849. Reprinted 1851. Butler imprint recopyrinted by Goodrich and reprinted 1854. Reprinted 1856, 1857.

UNIVERSAL HISTORY,

ON THE

BASIS OF GEOGRAPHY.

BY

PETER PARLEY,

AUTHOR OF TALES ABOUT NATURAL HISTORY; THE SUN, MOON, AND STARS:
A GRAMMAR OF GEOGRAPHY, ETC.

FOR THE USE OF FAMILIES.

ILLUSTRATED BY MAPS.

Second Edition.

LONDON:
PRINTED FOR THOMAS TEGG, No. 73, CHEAPSIDE:

TEGG AND CO. DUBLIN; GRIFFIN AND CO. GLASGOW; AND
J. AND S. A. TEGG, SYDNEY, AND HOBART TOWN.

1839.

UNIVERSAL HISTORY,

ON THE

BASIS OF GEOGRAPHY.

BY

PETER PARLEY,

AUTHOR OF TALES ABOUT NATURAL HISTORY; THE SUN, MOON, AND STARS:
A GRAMMAR OF GEOGRAPHY, ETC.

FOR THE USE OF FAMILIES.

ILLUSTRATED BY MAPS.

LONDON:
PRINTED FOR THOMAS TEGG AND SON, 73, CHEAPSIDE:

TEGG AND CO. DUBLIN; GRIFFIN AND CO. GLASGOW; AND
J. AND S. A. TEGG, SYDNEY, AND HOBART TOWN.

1838.

A3.4.a: Title page. A3.4.b: Title page

A 3.4.a
Second English edition, first printing

London: Thomas Tegg, 1838.

Listed by *Athenaeum,* 13 January 1838, and reviewed 17 February 1838.

Location: CEFC.

A 3.4.b
Second English edition, second printing

London: Thomas Tegg, 1839.

Title page bears 'Second Edition' slug.

Location: CEFC.

A 3.4.c
Second English edition, third printing

London: Thomas Tegg, MDCCCXLI.

Title page bears 'Third Edition' slug.

Location: CEFC.

A 3.4.d
Fourth printing

London: Thomas Tegg, [n.d.].

[1849?] Title page bears 'The Fourth Edition' slug.

Location: CEFC.

OTHER TEGG PRINTINGS

The British Museum has copies of the following Tegg printings: MDCCCLIV ('Sixth Edition'), 1860 ('Seventh Edition'), 1862 ('Eighth Edition'), 1867 ('Twelfth Edition'), 1869 ('Thirteenth Edition'). Also a new edition prepared 'Corrected to Date,' 1871 ('Fourteenth Edition'), revised and expanded. Also 'Corrected to Date', 1876 ('Fifteenth Edition'). Also 'Corrected to Date' ('Twenty-second Edition').

A 3.5
Third English edition

London: John W. Parker, M dccc.XXXIX.

A new edition, slightly expanded, of the 1837 Parker edition (A 3.2). Page size: 6³/₄" × 4¹/₈".

Location: CEFC.

A4.1.a1: Broadside. Sheet size: 21″ × 16³/₈″; outside dimension of ornamental border: 19³/₈″ × 14¹/₄″; column width: 3″

A 4 TIME'S PORTRAITURE

A 4.1.a₁
First edition, first printing, first issue [*1838*]

Broadside.

Anonymous. Printed from type metal and published as a New Year's keepsake for distribution by the carrier boys who delivered the *Salem Gazette*. Unknown number of copies probably printed December 1837. First issue on white wove paper. Presumed second issue on silk.

Locations: On paper: Berg, MSaE.

Manuscript: Fragment 1: Berg; fragment 2: ViU.

A 4.1.a₂
First edition, first printing, second issue [*1838*]

At least one copy, probably produced as a press souvenir, printed on a pink silk handkerchief from the standing form used to print A 4.1.a₁.

Location: MSaE.

A 4.1.b
First edition, second printing [*1838*]

Salem Gazette, LII, New Series XVI, 1(2 January 1838), 1.

Same type metal used to print the broadside (A 4.1.a) rearranged and included in the makeup of the front page of the 2 January 1838 *Gazette* under the title "The Carrier's Address."

Locations: CEFC, MSaE.

TIME'S PORTRAITURE.

BEING

THE CARRIER'S ADDRESS TO THE PATRONS

OF THE

SALEM GAZETTE,

AND

ESSEX COUNTY MERCURY,

————o————

FOR THE FIRST OF JANUARY, 1853.

TIME'S PORTRAITURE.

BEING

THE CARRIER'S ADDRESS TO THE PATRONS

OF THE

SALEM GAZETTE,

AND

ESSEX COUNTY MERCURY.

————o————

FOR THE FIRST OF JANUARY,
1853.

A.4.2.a: Printing A cover title. A.4.2.b: Printing B cover title

A 4.2.a
Second edition, printing A [*1853*]

[Salem, Mass.]   Salem Gazette and Essex County Mercury, 1853.

Note: Two printings of the second edition distinguished by the type makeup of the cover title, priority undetermined.

[1] 2–8. 1838 text (A 4.1) slightly revised, including contemporizing of political, place, and time references. Wove paper. Cover title (see illustration, A 4.2 cover titles).

Locations: Berg, MSaE.

A 4.2.b
Second edition, printing B

Same as printing A except for cover-title imprint.

Location: MSaE.

THE

SISTER YEARS:

BEING THE

CARRIER'S ADDRESS,

TO THE PATRONS

OF THE

SALEM GAZETTE,

FOR THE

FIRST OF JANUARY,

1839.

[signature]

SALEM.
1839.

'Why my course here in the United States', said the Old Year—'though (perhaps) I ought to blush at the confession—my political course, I must acknowledge, has been rather vacillatory, sometimes inclining towards the Whigs—then causing the Administration party to shout for triumph—and now again uplifting what seemed the almost prostrate banner of the Opposition; so that historians will hardly know what to make of me, in this respect. But the Loco Focos—

'I do not like these party nicknames,' interrupted her sister, who seemed remarkably touchy about some points 'Perhaps we shall part in better humor, if we avoid any political discussion.'

'With all my heart,' replied the Old Year, who had already been tormented half to death with squabbles of this kind. 'I care not if the names of Whig, or tory, with their interminable brawls about Banks and the Sub Treasury, Abolition, Texas, the Florida War, and a million of other topics—which you will learn soon enough for your own comfort—I care not, I say, if no whisper of these matters ever reaches my ears again. Yet they have occupied so large a share of my attention, that I scarcely know what else to tell you. There has indeed been a curious sort of war on the Canada border, where blood has streamed in the names of Liberty and Patriotism; but it must remain for some future, perhaps far distant, Year, to tell whether or no those holy names have been rightfully invoked.—Nothing so much depresses me, in my view of mortal affairs, as to see high energies wasted, and human life and happiness thrown away, for ends that appear oftentimes unwise; and still oftener remain unaccomplished. But the wisest people and the best keep a steadfast faith that the progress of Mankind is onward and upward, and that the toil and anguish of the path serve to wear away the superfluities of the Immortal Pilgrim, and will be felt no more, when they have done their office.'

'Perhaps,' cried the hopeful New Year—'perhaps I shall see that happy day!'

'I doubt whether it be so close at hand,' answered the Old Year, gravely smiling. 'You will soon grow weary of looking for that blessed consummation, and will turn for amusement (as has frequently been my own practice) to the affairs of some sober little city, like this of Salem. Here we sit, on the steps of the new City Hall, which has been completed under my administration and it would make you laugh to see how the game of politics, of which the Capitol at Washington is the great chess-board, is here played in miniature. Burning Ambition finds its fuel here; here Patriotism speaks boldly in the people's behalf, and virtuous Economy demands retrenchment in the emoluments of a lamplighter; here the Aldermen range their senatorial dignity around the Mayor's chair of state, and the Common Council feel that they have liberty in charge. In short, human weakness and

A 5.1: Cover title, 9⅝″ × 5½″. Page format, 6⅞″ (7³/₁₆) × 3½″

A 5 THE SISTER YEARS

A 5.1
First edition, only printing [*1839*]

[1–3] 5–8

π^4

Contents: p. 1: cover title; p. 2: ' "HAPPY NEW YEAR." '; pp. 3–8: text, headed 'THE SISTER YEARS. | [rule]'.

Pamphlet. Page size varies slightly from copy to copy; noted $9^9/_{16}'' \times 5^1/_2''$ to $9^3/_4 \times 5^{13}/_{16}''$. Wove paper. See illustration, A 5.1 page format.

Locations: CtY, MH, MHi, MSaE, NN, PDH, ViU.

A 5.2
Second edition [*1892*]

[Salem, Mass.]: Salem Gazette and Essex County Mercury, 1892.

[1–2] 3–8. Cover title. Page size: $9^1/_2'' \times 5^{15}/_{16}''$. Wove paper. 1839 text, slightly revised, with an unsigned introduction by latter-day carrier boy added.

Locations: CEFC, LC, MSaE, NN.

Bindings for (1) A 6.1; (2) A 6.2.a₁; (3) A 7.1; (4) A 7.2.a₁

old, took the privilege of the youngest, and climbed his knee. It was a pleasant thing to behold that fair and golden-haired child in the lap of the old man, and to think that, different as they were, the hearts of both could be gladdened with the same joys.

"Grandfather," said little Alice, laying her head back upon his arm, "I am very tired now. You must tell me a story to make me go to sleep."

"That is not what story-tellers like," answered Grandfather, smiling. "They are better satisfied when they can keep their auditors awake."

"But here are Laurence, and Charley, and I," cried cousin Clara, who was twice as old as little Alice. "We will all three keep wide awake. And pray, Grandfather, tell us a story about this strange looking old chair."

GRANDFATHER'S CHAIR:

A

HISTORY

FOR

YOUTH.

BY NATHANIEL HAWTHORNE.
Author of Twice-Told Tales.

BOSTON:
E. P. PEABODY.
NEW YORK:—WILEY & PUTNAM.
1841.

A 6.1: Title page, 5¹³/₁₆″ × 3³/₁₆″. Page format, 3⅜″ (3⁵/₈″) × 2¼″

A 6 GRANDFATHER'S CHAIR

A 6.1
First edition, only printing [1841]

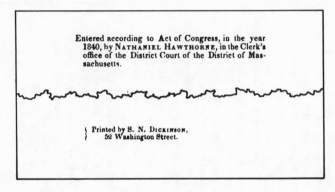

[i–iii] iv–vii [viii] [9] 10–140

π^4 1–8⁸ 9²

Contents: p. i: title; p. ii: copyright; pp. iii–vii: preface; p. viii: blank; pp. 9–140: text, headed 'GRANDFATHER'S CHAIR. | [rule] | CHAPTER I.'

Includes "Preface," "Grandfather's Chair," and the following subtitled stories within the chapters of *GC:* "The Lady Arbella," "The Red Cross," "The Pine-Tree Shillings," "The Indian Bible," "The Sunken Treasure."

Typography and paper: See illustration, A 6.1 page format. Running heads; rectos and versos, 'GRANDFATHER'S CHAIR.' White wove paper.

Binding: Brown (47. d. gy. r Br), plum bold-ribbed T cloth. Also basket-weave-grained bluish plum and slate T cloth. Gilt imprinted paper label on front cover (see illustration, A 6 bindings). White wove endpapers. Single white wove flyleaf inserted front and rear. All edges trimmed.

Publication: Published 3 December 1840.

Printing: Printed from type metal by S. N. Dickinson, 52 Washington Street, Boston.

Locations: CEFC, LC (deposited 28 December 1840), Lilly, MH, NN, PSt.

GRANDFATHER'S CHAIR:

A

HISTORY

FOR

YOUTH.

BY

NATHANIEL HAWTHORNE,
AUTHOR OF "TWICE-TOLD TALES."

SECOND EDITION,
REVISED AND ENLARGED.

BOSTON:
TAPPAN AND DENNET,
114 WASHINGTON STREET.
1842.

thing to behold that fair and golden-haired child in the lap of the old man, and to think that, different as they were, the hearts of both could be gladdened with the same joys.

"Grandfather," said little Alice, laying her head back upon his arm, "I am very tired now. You must tell me a story to make me go to sleep."

"That is not what story-tellers like," answered Grandfather, smiling. "They are better satisfied when they can keep their auditors awake."

"But here are Laurence, and Charley, and I," cried cousin Clara, who was twice as old as little Alice. "We will all three keep wide awake. And pray, Grandfather, tell us a story about this strange looking old chair."

Now the chair, in which Grandfather sat, was made of oak, which had grown dark with age, but had been rubbed and

A.6.2.a: Title page, 6¹/₁₆″ × 3¹¹/₁₆″. Page format, 4⁵/₁₆″ (4⁹/₁₆″) × 2¹¹/₁₆″

A 6.2.a₁
Second edition, first printing, first issue [1842]

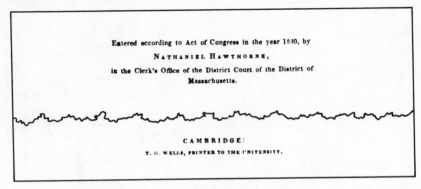

Hawthorne very slightly revised the first edition text and added five passages of new material.

[i–v] vi–vii [viii] [9] 10–26 [27] 28–139, ²[1] 2–5

1–12⁶

Contents: p. i: blank; p. ii: frontispiece cut of grandfather's chair; p. iii: title; p. iv: copyright; pp. v–vii: preface; p. viii: blank; pp. 9–139: text, headed 'GRANDFATHER'S CHAIR. | [rule] | CHAPTER I.'; pp. ²1–5: ads. Room scene with Lady Arbella seated in grandfather's chair on p. 27.

Typography and paper: See illustration, A 6.2.a, page format. Running heads: rectos and versos, 'GRANDFATHER'S CHAIR.' White wove paper.

Binding: Brown (58. m. Br), dark brown (81. d. gy. y Br), olive (113. Ol Gy), black bold-ribbed T cloth. Covers blindstamped with floral design or blindstamped with floral frame, gilt chair inside frame on front cover. Title goldstamped on spine (see illustration, A 6 bindings). Cream endpapers coated one side, light yellow endpapers, or white wove endpapers. Single white wove flyleaf inserted at front and rear in some copies. All edges trimmed. Bound by Benjamin Bradley & Co., Boston.

Publication: Printed from type metal by T. G. Wells, Cambridge, Mass. Published December 1841.

Locations: CEFC, CtY, LC, NN.

A 6.2.a₂
Second edition, first printing, second issue [1842]

For second issue, sheets of A 6.2.a₁ were incorporated in vol. I of two-volume *Historical Tales for Youth* (see A 10).

Note: Grandfather's Chair was incorporated in collection entitled *True Stories* (see A 12). *Grandfather's Chair* was also used as a title for different collections incorporating various combinations of *Grandfather's Chair, Famous Old People, Liberty Tree,* and *Biographical Stories.* These collections are listed under A 12.

A 6.3
True Stories From New England History 1620–1692 . . . Grandfather's Chair Part I . . . .
Boston, New York: Houghton, Mifflin, 1883.

No. 7, *Riverside Literature Series*. Contents same as in second edition (A 6.2.a₁).
1,500 copies printed May 1883. Printed wrappers. Reprinted by H,M an unknown
number of times.

FAMOUS OLD PEOPLE:

BEING

OF

THE SECOND EPOCH

GRANDFATHER'S CHAIR.

BY NATHANIEL HAWTHORNE
Author of Twice-Told Tales.

BOSTON:
E. P. PEABODY
13 West Street
1841.

thus, perhaps, there was something in Grandfather's heart, that cheered him most with its warmth and comfort in the gathering twilight of old age. He had been gazing at the red embers, as intently as if his past life were all pictured there, or as if it were a prospect of the future world, when little Alice's voice aroused him.

"Dear Grandfather," repeated the little girl, more earnestly, "do talk to us again about your chair."

Laurence, and Clara, and Charley, and little Alice, had been attracted to other objects, for two or three months past. They had sported in the gladsome sunshine of the present, and so had forgotten the shadowy region of the past, in the midst of which stood Grandfather's chair. But now, in the autumnal twilight, illuminated by the flickering blaze

A7.1: Title page, 7³/₄″ × 3³/₁₆″. Page format, 3³/₈″ (3⁵/₈″) × 2⁵/₁₆″

A 7 FAMOUS OLD PEOPLE

A 7.1
First edition, only printing [1841]

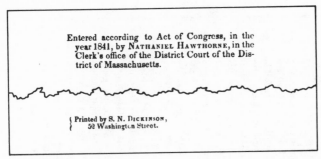

Entered according to Act of Congress, in the year 1841, by NATHANIEL HAWTHORNE, in the Clerk's office of the District Court of the District of Massachusetts.

{ Printed by S. N. DICKINSON,
52 Washington Street.

[i–iii] iv–vii [viii] [9] 10–158 [159–160]

π^4 1–9^8 10^4

Contents: p. i: title; p. ii: copyright; pp. iii–vii: preface; p. viii: blank; pp. 9–158: text, headed 'FAMOUS OLD PEOPLE. | [rule] | CHAPTER I.'; pp. 159–160: blank.

Includes "Preface," "Famous Old People," and the following subtitled stories within the chapters of *FOP:* "The Old-Fashioned School," "The Rejected Blessing," "The Provincial Muster," "The Acadian Exiles."

Typography and paper: See illustration, A 7.1 page format. Running heads: rectos and versos, 'FAMOUS OLD PEOPLE.' White wove paper.

Binding: Purple (234. d. p Gray) C, P, and fine-ribbed S-like cloth with and without a net-like pattern; slate cloth embossed with a basket-weave pattern. Gilt-imprinted black paper label on front cover (see illustration, A 7 bindings [at A 6]). White wove endpapers. Single white wove flyleaf inserted at front and rear. All edges trimmed.

Publication: Probably published 18 January 1841.

Printing: Printed from type metal by S. N. Dickinson, 52 Washington Street, Boston.

Locations: CEFC, CtY, LC, Lilly, MH, NN.

FAMOUS OLD PEOPLE:

BEING

THE SECOND EPOCH

OF

GRANDFATHER'S CHAIR.

BY

NATHANIEL HAWTHORNE,

AUTHOR OF "TWICE-TOLD TALES."

SECOND EDITION.

———

BOSTON:
TAPPAN & DENNET,
114 WASHINGTON STREET.
1842.

And thus, perhaps, there was something in Grandfather's heart, that cheered him most with its warmth and comfort in the gathering twilight of old age. He had been gazing at the red embers, as intently as if his past life were all pictured there, or as if it were a prospect of the future world, when little Alice's voice aroused him.

"Dear Grandfather," repeated the little girl, more earnestly, "do talk to us again about your chair."

Laurence, and Clara, and Charley, and little Alice, had been attracted to other objects, for two or three months past. They had sported in the gladsome sunshine of the present, and so had forgotten the shadowy region of the past, in the midst of which stood Grandfather's chair. But now, in the autumnal twilight, illuminated by the flickering blaze of the wood-fire, they

A 7.2.a₁
Second edition, first printing, first issue [*1842*]

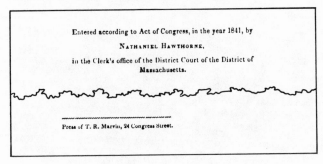

Entered according to Act of Congress, in the year 1841, by

NATHANIEL HAWTHORNE,

in the Clerk's office of the District Court of the District of
Massachusetts.

Press of T. R. Marvin, 24 Congress Street.

[i–v] vi–viii [9] 10–30 [31] 32–158, ²[1] 2

1–13⁶ 14²

Contents: p. i: blank; p. ii: frontispiece cut of grandfather's chair; p. iii: title; p. iv: copyright; pp. v–viii: preface; pp. 9–158: text, headed: 'FAMOUS OLD PEOPLE. | [rule] | CHAPTER I.'; pp. ²1–2: ads. Cut of 'MASTER CHEEVER'S SCHOOL' on p. 31. Contents same as first edition (A 7.1).

Typography and paper: See illustration, A 7.2.a₁ page format. Running heads: rectos and versos, 'FAMOUS OLD PEOPLE.' White wove paper.

Binding: Brown (62. d. gy. Br) bold-ribbed T cloth. Front blindstamped with floral frame, gilt chair inside frame. Title goldstamped on spine (see illustration, A 7 bindings). Yellow endpapers coated one side. All edges trimmed. Bound by Benjamin Bradley & Co., Boston.

Publication: Printed from type metal by T. R. Marvin, 24 Congress Street, Boston. Probably published January 1842.

Locations: CEFC, LC (deposited 23 December 1841).

A 7.2.a₂
Second edition, first printing, second issue [*1842*]

For second issue, sheets of A 7.2.a₁ were incorporated in vol. I of two-volume *Historical Tales for Youth* (see A 10).

Note: Famous Old People was incorporated in collections entitled *True Stories* and *Grandfather's Chair* (see A 12).

A 7.3
True Stories from New England History 1692–1763 . . . Grandfather's Chair Part II . . . .
Boston, New York: Houghton, Mifflin, 1883.

No. 8, *Riverside Literature Series.* Contents same as in second edition (A 7.2.a₁). 1,500 copies printed May 1883. Printed wrappers. Reprinted by H,M an unknown number of times.

Bindings for (1) A8.1; (2) A8.3.a₁, format A; (3) A8.3.a₁, format B; (4) A9.1.a₁; (5 & 6) A10.1

LIBERTY TREE:

WITH THE

LAST WORDS

OF

GRANDFATHER'S CHAIR.

BY NATHANIEL HAWTHORNE,
Author of Twice-Told Tales.

BOSTON.

E. P. PEABODY, 13 WEST STREET.
1841.

of Massachusetts proposed that delegates from every colony should meet in a Congress. Accordingly nine colonies, both northern and southern, sent delegates to the city of New York."

"And did they consult about going to war with England?" asked Charley.

"No, Charley," answered Grandfather; "a great deal of talking was yet to be done, before England and America could come to blows. The Congress stated the rights and the grievances of the colonists. They sent an humble petition to the king, and a memorial to the Parliament, beseeching that the Stamp Act might be repealed. This was all that the delegates had it in their power to do."

"They might as well have staid at home, then," said Charley.

"By no means," replied Grandfather.

A 8.1: Title page, 4¹³/₁₆″ × 3¹/₈″. Page format, 3³/₈″ (3¹¹/₁₆″) × 2¹/₄″

A 8 LIBERTY TREE

A 8.1
First edition, only printing [1841]

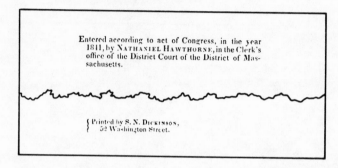

Note: The first and second editions can be distinguished by variants between type-settings. The following examples are sufficient to make the distinction:

	FIRST EDITION (1841)		SECOND EDITION (1841)
24.2	meet in a Con-	[	meet in Con-
30.13	half burned out,	[	half burnt out,
41.19	be a governor	[	be governor
82.8,9	after- | wards	[	after- | ward

[i–iii] iv–vii [viii] [9] 10–160

π^4 1–9^8 10^4

Contents: p. i: title; p. ii: copyright; pp. iii–vii: preface; p. viii: blank; pp. 9–160: text, headed 'LIBERTY TREE. | [rule] | CHAPTER I.'

Typography and paper: See illustration, A 8.1 page format. Running heads: rectos and versos, 'LIBERTY TREE.' White wove paper.

Binding: Green (127. gy. Ol G), blue (183. d. Blue) pebble-grain P cloth embossed with coral branches and flowers; mauve fine-ribbed S-like cloth embossed with flowers; blue (183. d. Blue) bold-ribbed T cloth; black bold-ribbed T cloth embossed with elaborate pattern. Gilt-imprinted black paper label on front cover (see illustration, A 8 bindings). Yellow and tan endpapers. All edges trimmed.

Publication: Printed from type metal by S. N. Dickinson, 52 Washington Street, Boston. Published March 1841.

Locations: CEFC, Lilly, MH, NN.

A 8.2.a₁
Second edition, first printing, first issue

Boston: E. P. Peabody, 1841.

A partial resetting. With the exception of pp. 1–104, 118, which were reset, the book was either printed from standing type used in the first edition (A 8.1) or made up from overrun sheets from the first edition.

Locations: CEFC, NN.

A 8.2.a2
Second edition, first printing, second issue

Boston: Geo. W. Briggs, Libertry Tree Bookstore, 1851.

Presumably remaindered sheets, with a cancel title.

Location: CEFC.

LIBERTY TREE:

WITH THE

LAST WORDS

OF

GRANDFATHER'S CHAIR.

BY NATHANIEL HAWTHORNE,

Author of "Twice-Told Tales."

BOSTON:

TAPPAN AND DENNET,

114 Washington Street.

1842.

---

imaginative boy was gazing at the historic chair. He endeavored to summon up the portraits which he had seen in his volume, and to place them, like living figures, in the empty seat.

"The old chair has begun another year of its existence, to-day," said Laurence. "We must make haste, or it will have a new history to be told before we finish the old one."

"Yes, my children," replied Grandfather, with a smile and a sigh, "another year has been added to the two hundred and ten which have passed since the Lady Arbella brought this chair over from England. It is three times as old as your Grandfather; but a year makes no impression on its oaken frame, while it bends the old man nearer and nearer to the earth; so let me go on with my stories while I may."

2

A 8.3.a₁
Third edition, first printing, first issue [1842]

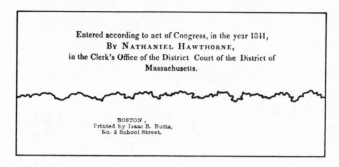

Entered according to act of Congress, in the year 1841,
By NATHANIEL HAWTHORNE,
in the Clerk's Office of the District Court of the District of
Massachusetts.

BOSTON,
Printed by Isaac R. Butts,
No. 2 School Street.

[i–v] vi–viii [9] 10–13 [14] 15–156

1–13⁶

Contents: p. i: blank; p. ii: frontispiece cut of grandfather's chair; p. iii: title; p. iv: copyright; pp. v–viii: preface; pp. 9–156: text, headed 'LIBERTY TREE. | [rule] | CHAPTER I.' Room scene with children before grandfather seated in his chair on p. 14.

Typography and paper: See illustration, A 8.3.a page format. Running heads: rectos and versos, 'LIBERTY TREE.' White wove paper.

Binding: Medium brown (61. gy. Br), dark brown (62. d. gy. Br) bold-ribbed T cloth with covers noted in two formats: (A) blindstamped oval floral frame on front and back covers with goldstamped grandfather's chair on front, and (B) blindstamped cover panels consisting of central element and four corner elements inside plain-rules frame. Title goldstamped on spine (see illustration, A 8 bindings). Also black (267. Black) ribbed morocco A-like cloth in cover format A. Cream endpapers coated one side; light yellow endpapers. Single white wove flyleaf inserted at front and rear in some copies. All edges trimmed. Probably bound by Benjamin Bradley & Co., Boston.

Publication: Printed from type metal by Isaac R. Butts, No. 2 School Street, Boston. Published February 1842.

Locations: CEFC, PSt.

A 8.3.a₂
Third edition, first printing, second issue [1842]

For second issue, sheets of A 8.3.a₁ were incorporated in vol. II of two-volume *Historical Tales for Youth* (see A 10).

Note: Liberty Tree was incorporated in collections entitled *True Stories* and *Grandfather's Chair* (see A 12).

A 8.4
True Stories from New England History 1763–1803 . . . Grandfather's Chair Part III . . . .
Boston, New York: Houghton, Mifflin, 1883.

No. 9, *Riverside Literature Series*. Contents same as in third edition (A 8.3.a₁). 1,500 copies printed May 1883. Printed wrappers. Reprinted by H,M an unknown number of times.

BIOGRAPHICAL STORIES

FOR CHILDREN.

| Benjamin West, Sir Isaac Newton, Samuel Johnson, | Oliver Cromwell, Benjamin Franklin, Queen Christina. |

BY

NATHANIEL HAWTHORNE,

Author of "Historical Tales for Youth," "Twice-Told Tales," &c.

BOSTON:

TAPPAN AND DENNET,

111 Washington Street.

1842.

"I will sit by you all day long," said Emily, in her low, sweet voice, putting her hand into that of Edward.

"And so will I, Ned," said George, his elder brother,—"school time and all, if my father will permit me."

Edward's brother George was three or four years older than himself, a fine, hardy lad, of a bold and ardent temper. He was the leader of his comrades in all their enterprises and amusements. As to his proficiency at study, there was not much to be said. He had sense and ability enough to have made himself a scholar, but found so many pleasanter things to do, that he seldom took hold of a book with his whole heart. So fond was George of boisterous sports and exercises, that it was really a great token of affection and sympathy, when he offered to sit all day long in a dark chamber, with his poor brother Edward.

A 9.1.a: Title page, 6¹/₁₆″ × 3³/₄″. Page format, 4⁵/₁₆″ (5⁹/₁₆″) × 2¹¹/₁₆″

A 9 BIOGRAPHICAL STORIES FOR CHILDREN

A 9.1.a1
First edition, first printing, first issue [1842]

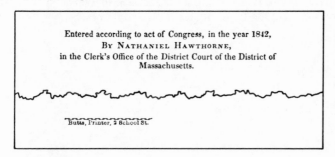

[i–iii] iv–v [vi] [7] 8–161 [162]

1–12⁶ 13⁸ [14]¹

Contents: p. i: title; p. ii: copyright; pp. iii–v: preface; p. vi: blank; pp. 7–161: text, headed 'BIOGRAPHICAL STORIES. | [rule] | CHAPTER I'; p. 162: blank.

Includes "Preface," "Biographical Stories," and the following subtitled sketches included within the chapters of *BS:* "Benjamin West," "Sir Isaac Newton," "Samuel Johnson," "Samuel Johnson. Continued," "Oliver Cromwell," "Benjamin Franklin," "Benjamin Franklin. Continued," "Queen Christina."

Typography and paper: See illustration, A 9.1.a1 page format. Running heads: rectos and versos, 'BIOGRAPHICAL STORIES.' White wove paper.

Binding: Medium brown (61. gy. Br), dark brown (62. d. gy. Br), black (267. Black) bold-ribbed T cloth. Covers blindstamped with a central element and corner elements featuring an arrow inside a plain-rules frame; title goldstamped on spine (see illustration, A 9 bindings [at A 8]). Yellow endpapers. Single white wove flyleaf inserted at front and rear. All edges trimmed.

Publication: Printed from type metal by Isaac R. Butts, No. 2 School Street, Boston. Deposited 12 April 1842. Noted as "just published" in the *Boston Daily Advertiser,* 12 April 1842.

Locations: CEFC, CtY, NN, PSt.

Manuscript: Fragments of the manuscript preserved in Berg Collection, Clark Collection, Gratz Collection at the Historical Society of Pennsylvania, Houghton Library, and Rosenbach Foundation.

A 9.1.a2
First edition, first printing, second issue [1842]

For second issue, sheets of A 9.1.a1 were incorporated in vol. II of two-volume *Historical Tales for Youth* (see A 10).

Note: *Biographical Stories* was incorporated in collections entitled *True Stories* and *Grandfather's Chair* (see A 12). Also, "Samuel Johnson" section of *Biographical Stories* was issued separately as *The Sunday School Society's Gift* (see A 11).

LATER EDITIONS

A 9.2
Boston, New York: Houghton, Mifflin, 1883.

No. 10, *Riverside Literature Series*. Contents same as in first edition (A 9.1.a₁). 1,500 copies printed May 1883. Printed wrappers. Reprinted by H,M an unknown number of times.

A 9.3
London: W. Swan Sonnenschein, n.d.

[1883].

Reprinted: London: Swan Sonnenschein, 1898.

A 9.4
Cincinnati: The Phonographic Institute, 1912.

Printed wrappers.

A 10 HISTORICAL TALES FOR YOUTH

A 10.1

Collected issue: Grandfather's Chair, Famous Old People, Liberty Tree, Biographical Stories [*1842*]

2 vols. Made up of the sheets of the second edition of *GC* (A 6.2.a₁), the second edition of *FOP* (A 7.2.a₁), the third edition of *LT* (A 8.3.a₁), and the first edition of *BS* (A 9.1.a₁). No title page for the collection was prepared. Title appears only as a goldstamped spine imprint (see illustration, A 10 bindings).

I: [i–v] vi–vii [viii] [9]–139, ²[1], ³[i–v] vi–viii [9]–158, ⁴[1] 2

II: [i–v] vi–viii [9]–156, ²[i–iii] iv–v [vi] [7]–161 [162]

I: 1–12⁶ (×12₅₋₆), ²1–13⁶ 14²

II: 1–13⁶, ²1–12⁶ 13⁸ [14]¹

Contents: *I:* p. i: blank; p. ii: frontispiece cut of grandfather's chair; p. iii: title; p. iv: copyright; pp. v–vii: preface; p. viii: blank; pp. 9–139: text, headed 'GRANDFATHER'S CHAIR. | [rule] | CHAPTER I.'; p. ²1: ad. Room scene with Lady Arabella seated in grandfather's chair on p. 27. P. ³i: blank; p. ii: frontispiece cut of grandfather's chair; p. iii: title; p. iv: copyright; pp. v–viii: preface; pp. 9–158: text, headed 'FAMOUS OLD PEOPLE. | [rule] | CHAPTER I.'; pp. ⁴1–2: ads. Cut of Master Cheever's School on p. 31.

   II: p. i: blank; p. ii: frontispiece cut of grandfather's chair; p. iii: title; p. iv: copyright; pp. v–viii: preface; pp. 9–156: text, headed 'LIBERTY TREE. | [rule] | CHAPTER I.' Room scene with children before grandfather seated in his chair on p. 14. P. ²i: title; p. ii: copyright; pp. iii–v: preface; p. vi: blank; pp. 7–161: text, headed 'BIOGRAPHICAL STORIES. | [rule] | CHAPTER I.'; p. 162: blank.

Binding: Dark brown (62. d. gy. Br) bold-ribbed T cloth. Covers blindstamped with patterned and floral oval frame inside plain-rule rectangle; title goldstamped on spine (see illustration, A 10 bindings [at A 8]). Tan endpapers. All edges trimmed. Probably bound by Benjamin Bradley & Co., Boston.

Publication: Probably published April–May 1842.

Locations: Vol. I: CtY; vols. I and II: CEFC.

THE

Sunday School Society's Gift.

DEAR YOUNG FRIENDS,

The following beautiful story will we hope give you much pleasure. It is founded upon fact, and you will no doubt read it with more interest when you know that the circumstance related really took place. It is a circumstance also which is connected with the life of that remarkable man, Dr. Samuel Johnson, whose famous Dictionary you have probably seen, and whose valuable writings you may read at some future time. He was born 1709, and died 1784.

This story was written by Nathaniel Hawthorne, and he has given us the liberty of printing it for you. He has written some very interesting books both for young and old. Many have read his "Twice Told Tales," and the smaller volumes,

2

such as "Grandfather's Chair," "Liberty Tree," and "Biographical Stories," have been read with delight by thousands. If you have not read these we are glad of this opportunity to recommend them to you.

This little volume has been published, and is now placed in your hands, with the kindest wishes for your welfare by

THE SUNDAY SCHOOL SOCIETY.

BOSTON, 1842.

— — — — — — — — — —

A 11: Cover title, 5⁵/₈″ × 3¹³/₁₆″. Inside front cover. (Text page [not shown], 4⁵/₁₆″ [4⁵/₈″] × 2³/₁₆″)

A 11 THE SUNDAY SCHOOL SOCIETY'S GIFT
First edition, only printing [*1842*]

[1] 2 [3] 4–16

[1]⁸

Contents: pp. 1–2: title and introductory letter; pp. 3–16: text, headed 'SAMUEL JOHNSON. | [rule] | CHAPTER I.'

Self-cover pamphlet; cover title. Authorized reprint (Hawthorne to the Reverend R. C. Waterson, dated Concord, 1 September 1842). First separate printing, slightly cut, of the "Samuel Johnson" section of *Biographical Stories* (A 9.1.a1). Published by The Sunday School Society, Boston, 1842, after 1 September 1842.

Locations: CEFC, MB, MH, PDH.

Bindings for (1) A 12.1.a₁, "gift"; (2) A 12.1.a₁, trade; (3–6) A 12.2.a₁, with variant goldstamped designs on spine; (7) A 12.4.d

TRUE STORIES

FROM

HISTORY AND BIOGRAPHY.

BY

NATHANIEL HAWTHORNE.

BOSTON:
TICKNOR, REED, AND FIELDS.
MDCCCLI.

There is certainly no method, by which the shadowy outlines of departed men and women can be made to assume the hues of life more effectually, than by connecting their images with the substantial and homely reality of a fireside chair. It causes us to feel at once, that these characters of history had a private and familiar existence, and were not wholly contained within that cold array of outward action, which we are compelled to receive as the adequate representation of their lives. If this impression can be given, much is accomplished.

Setting aside Grandfather and his auditors, and excepting the adventures of the Chair, which form the machinery of the work, nothing in the ensuing pages can be termed fictitious. The author, it is true, has sometimes assumed the license of filling up the outline of history with details, for which he has none but imaginative authority, but which, he hopes, do not violate nor give a false coloring to the truth. He believes that, in this respect, his narrative will not be found to convey ideas and impressions, of which the reader may hereafter find it necessary to purge his mind.

The author's great doubt is, whether he has succeeded in writing a book which will be readable by the

A 12.1.a: Title page, 6^{9}/$_{16}$″ × 4″. Page format, 4^{15}/$_{16}$″ (5^{3}/$_{16}$″) × 3″

A 12 TRUE STORIES FROM HISTORY AND BIOGRAPHY

A 12.1.a₁
First edition, only printing, first state [1851]

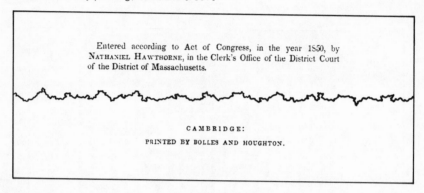

Entered according to Act of Congress, in the year 1850, by
NATHANIEL HAWTHORNE, in the Clerk's Office of the District Court
of the District of Massachusetts.

CAMBRIDGE:
PRINTED BY BOLLES AND HOUGHTON.

First edition has Bolles and Houghton imprint on copyright page.

A collection comprised of *Grandfather's Chair* (A 6), *Famous Old People* (A 7), *Liberty Tree* (A 8), and *Biographical Stories* (A 9). All previously published. No new material.

Note one: Two settings of preface (pp. iii–v), with following variants:

	PROBABLE FIRST STATE		PROBABLE SECOND STATE
iii.15	way, with	[	way with
iv.18	which, he	[	which he

[i–iii] iv–v [vi–viii] [1] 2–78 [79] 80–158 [159] 160–244 [245–247] 248–335 [336]. Frontispiece inserted facing title page, three plates inserted facing pages 90, 168, 328.

[a]⁴ 1–21⁸

Contents: p. i: title; p. ii: copyright; pp. iii–v: preface; p. vi: blank; p. vii: half title; p. viii: blank; pp. 1–244: text, headed: 'GRANDFATHER'S CHAIR. | [rule] | PART I. | CHAPTER I.'; p. 245: half title; p. 246: preface; pp. 247–335: text, headed 'BIO-GRAPHICAL STORIES. | [rule] | CHAPTER I.'; p. 336: blank.

Note two: Hawthorne made minor revisions in the text for this edition.

Typography and paper: See illustration, A 12.1.a₁ page format. Running heads: rectos and versos, pp. 2–244, 'GRANDFATHER'S CHAIR.'; pp. 248–335, 'BIOGRAPHICAL STORIES.' White wove paper.

Binding: In the style of Ticknor format B (see illustration, A 2.6 binding). Red (13. deep Red), blue (187. d. gy. B), green (151. d. gy. G) bold-ribbed T cloth. Spine goldstamped (see illustration, A 12 bindings). Most copies with blindstamped covers and plain edges. Also "gift" binding with central oval design on covers goldstamped and edges gilded. Pale yellow endpapers. White wove flyleaf inserted at front and rear. Edges trimmed.

Publication: 2,000 copies. Advertised for 16 November 1850 in *Literary World* of same date. Deposited 22 November 1850. Price 75¢, with a 10% royalty.

Printing: Printed from type metal by Bolles and Houghton, Cambridge, Mass. Probably bound by Benjamin Bradley & Co., Boston.

Locations: CEFC, LC, Lilly, MH, NN, OU.

A 12.1.a2
First edition, only printing, second state [1851]

Same as A 12.1.a1 except for probable second state of preface. See table under A 12.1.a1 for distinguishing characteristics.

Locations: CEFC, MH, NN, OU.

A 12.2.a1-A
Second edition, only printing, American issue–A [1851]

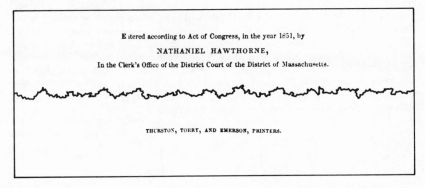

The second edition is a completely new setting of type with American issue A made up entirely of second edition sheets printed by Thurston, Torry, and Emerson (TT&E notice on copyright page). American issue B has sheets of the second edition TT&E text bound with a first edition Bolles and Houghton preliminary sheet (gathering [a]⁴ of A 12.1.a1 with B&H notice on copyright page).

[i–iii] iv–v [vi–viii] [1] 2–248 [249–251] 252–343 [344]. Frontispiece inserted facing title page, three plates inserted facing pages 90, 168, 328.

π^4 1–21⁸ 22⁴

Contents: p. i: title; p. ii: copyright; pp. iii–v: preface; p. vi: blank; p. vii: half title; p. viii: blank; pp. 1–248: text, headed 'GRANDFATHER'S CHAIR. | [rule] | PART I. | CHAPTER I.'; p. 249: half title; p. 250: preface; pp. 251–343: text, headed 'BIOGRAPH-ICAL STORIES. | [rule] | CHAPTER I.'; p. 344: blank.

Typography and paper: Page format same as A 12.1.a1. Running heads: rectos and versos, pp. 2–248, 'GRANDFATHER'S CHAIR.'; pp. 252–343, 'BIOGRAPHICAL STORIES.' White wove paper.

Binding: In the style of Ticknor format B—trade (see illustration, A 2.6 binding). Red (13. deep Red), blue (187. d. gy. B), green (151. d. gy. G), plum bold-ribbed T cloth. At least four styles of spine goldstamping (see illustration, A 12 bindings). A fifth style may be a later binding for remaindered sheets (see illustration, binding 6); two copies located (Location: CEFC), one with 1854 inscription, in which the last plate is inserted facing p. 336. Pale yellow endpapers. White wove flyleaf inserted at front and rear. Edges trimmed.

Publication: 2,500 copies published April 1851. Price 75¢, with a 10% royalty.

Printing: Printed from type metal by Thurston, Torry, and Emerson. Probably bound by Benjamin Bradley & Co., Boston.

Locations: CEFC, MH, NN, PSt.

A 12.2.a₁₋ʙ
Second edition, only printing, American issue–B [*1851*]

Same as American issue A, except that sheets of the second edition TT&E text are bound with a first edition Bolles and Houghton preliminary sheet (gathering [a]⁴ of A 12.1.a₁ with B&H notice on copyright page).

Locations: OU, Rosenbach Foundation Museum.

Note: The question exists as to whether American issue–B is in fact an issue (i.e., the result of deliberately binding the Bolles and Houghton preliminary sheet with the Thurston, Torry, and Emerson text), or simply represents binding sports. The B&H edition (A 12.1) was in the bindery in November 1850; the TT&E edition (A 12.2) was in the bindery in February 1851. Although different printers were involved, both editions were probably bound by Benjamin Bradley & Co., Boston, and it is possible that surplus B&H preliminary sheets could have been accidentally mixed with TT&E text during binding. That two copies with mixed sheets have survived would seem to argue in favor of a deliberately created issue, not an accident.

TRUE STORIES

FROM

HISTORY AND BIOGRAPHY.

BY

NATHANIEL HAWTHORNE.

LONDON:
SAMPSON LOW, SON, AND COMPANY.
M DCCC LIII.

There is certainly no method, by which the shadowy outlines of departed men and women can be made to assume the hues of life more effectually, than by connecting their images with the substantial and homely reality of a fireside chair. It causes us to feel at once, that these characters of history had a private and familiar existence, and were not wholly contained within that cold array of outward action, which we are compelled to receive as the adequate representation of their lives. If this impression can be given, much is accomplished.

Setting aside Grandfather and his auditors, and excepting the adventures of the Chair, which form the machinery of the work, nothing in the ensuing pages can be termed fictitious. The author, it is true, has sometimes assumed the license of filling up the outline of history with details, for which he has none but imaginative authority, but which, he hopes, do not violate nor give a false coloring to the truth. He believes that, in this respect, his narrative will not be found to convey ideas and impressions, of which the reader may hereafter find it necessary to purge his mind.

The author's great doubt is, whether he has succeeded in writing a book which will be readable by the

A12.2.aa: Title page, 6⁵/₈″ × 4¹/₈″. Page format, 4¹⁵/₁₆″ (5³/₁₆″) × 3″

A 12.2.a₂
Second edition, only printing, English issue [1853]

London: Sampson Low, M DCCC LIII.

Sheets of American issue—A (A 12.2.a1-A) with a cancel English title. 200 sets of American sheets were imported by Sampson Low (*Letter Books*, III, 199). Sampson Low ads bound in at rear.

Location: Bodleian.

A 12.3
First English edition [?]

London: J. Chapman, 1851.

Unlocated (see Browne).

PRINTINGS FROM THE T&F STEREOTYPE PLATES

A 12.4.a
Third American edition, first printing

Boston: Ticknor, Reed, and Fields, M DCCC LIV.

First stereotyped edition. Printed by Thurston, Torry, and Emerson from stereotype plates made by the Boston Type Foundry. Contents same as in the second edition (A 12.2.a1-A). See illustration, A 12 bindings. 500 copies printed April 1854. Price 75¢, with a 10% royalty.

A 12.4.b
Boston: Ticknor and Fields, M DCCC LV.

500 copies printed August 1855. See illustration, A 12 bindings. Price 75¢, with a 10% royalty.

A 12.4.c
Boston: Ticknor and Fields, M DCCC LVI.

1,500 copies printed April 1856. Price 75¢, with a 10% royalty.

A 12.4.d
Boston: Ticknor and Fields, M DCCC LVII.

500 copies printed April 1857. Price 75¢, with a 10% royalty.

A 12.4.e
Boston: Ticknor and Fields, M DCCC LIX.

500 copies printed March 1859. Price 75¢, with a 10% royalty.

A 12.4.f
Boston: Ticknor and Fields, M DCCC LX.

500 copies printed September 1860. Price 75¢, with a 10% royalty.

A 12.4.g
Boston: Ticknor and Fields, M DCCC LXIII.

350 copies printed August 1863. See illustration, A 12 bindings. Price 90¢, with a royalty of 8.75¢.

A 12.4.h
Boston: Ticknor and Fields, 1865.

Vol. 12 of untitled *"Tinted Edition"* on laid paper. 500 copies printed October 1864. Price $1.50, with a royalty of 12¢. See B 1[12] for reprintings of the *"Tinted Edition."*

A 12.4.i
Boston: Ticknor and Fields, 1865.

650 copies printed March 1865. Price $1.25, with a royalty of 10%.

A 12.4.j
Boston: Ticknor and Fields, 1866.

Note: Two printings with 1866 title-page date (see A 12.4.k), priority undetermined.

280 copies printed July 1866. Price $1.50, with a royalty of 12.5¢.

A 12.4.k
Boston: Ticknor and Fields, 1866.

300 copies printed August 1866. Price $1.50, with a royalty of 12.5¢.

A 12.4.l
Boston: Ticknor and Fields, 1868.

280 copies printed February 1868. Price $1.50, with a royalty of 12.5¢.

A 12.4.m
Boston: Ticknor and Fields, 1869.

500 copies printed October 1868. Price $1.50, with a royalty of 12.5¢.

A 12.4.n
Boston: Fields, Osgood, 1869.

280 copies printed April 1869. Price $2.00, with a royalty of 20¢.

A 12.4.o
Boston: Fields, Osgood, 1871.

280 copies printed November 1870. Price $2.00, with a royalty of 20¢.

A 12.4.p
Boston: Fields, Osgood, 1872.

280 copies printed December 1871. Price $1.50, with a royalty of 12.5¢.

A 12.4.q
Boston: James R. Osgood, 1873.

270 copies printed September 1872. Price $1.50, with a royalty of 12.5¢.

A 12.4.r
Boston: James R. Osgood, 1873.

500 copies printed July 1873. Price $1.50, with a royalty of 15¢.

A 12.4.s
Boston: James R. Osgood, 1875.

190 copies printed July 1875. Price $1.50, with a royalty of 15¢.

A 12.4.t
Boston: James R. Osgood, 1876.

280 copies printed March 1876.

A 12.4.u
Boston: James R. Osgood, 1876.

Parts I, II, and III of *Grandfather's Chair* combined with *A Wonder-Book* in four-volumes-in-one format and published as the tenth volume of the *Illustrated Library Edition; Biographical Stories* combined with *Tanglewood Tales* in two-volumes-in-one format and published as the eleventh volume of the *ILE*. 1,000 copies of each volume printed 23 May 1876. See B2 for reprintings of the *ILE*.

A 12.4.v
Boston: Houghton, Osgood, 1878.

174 copies printed August 1878.

A 12.4.w
Boston: Houghton, Osgood, 1879.

340 copies printed April 1879.

A 12.4.x
Boston: Houghton, Mifflin, 1880.

Grandfather's Chair and *Biographical Stories* combined with *A Wonder-Book* and *Tanglewood Tales* in four-volumes-in-one format and published as the fourth volume of the *Globe Edition*. 1,500 copies printed August 1880. See B3 for reprintings of the *Globe Edition*.

A 12.4.y
Boston: Houghton, Mifflin, 1881.

270 copies printed October 1880.

A 12.4.z
Boston: Houghton, Mifflin, 1881.

270 copies printed August 1881.

A 12.4.aa
Boston: Houghton, Mifflin, 1882.

270 copies printed June 1882

A 12.4.ab
Boston: Houghton, Mifflin, 1883.

270 copies printed August 1883.

A 12.4.ac
Boston: Houghton, Mifflin, 1884.

270 copies printed October 1883.

A 12.4.ad
Boston: Houghton, Mifflin, [1886].

Grandfather's Chair and *Biographical Stories* combined with *A Wonder-Book* and *Tanglewood Tales* in four-volumes-in-one format and published as the fourth volume of the *"New" Fireside Edition*. 1,000 copies printed May 1886. See B 4.

PRINTINGS FROM THE "LITTLE CLASSIC EDITION" PLATES

A 12.5.a

[All following within red and black double-rule frame] [red] TRUE STORIES | [black] FROM | HISTORY AND BIOGRAPHY. | BY | [red] NATHANIEL HAWTHORNE. | [black vignette of soldiers under elm] | [red] BOSTON: | [black] JAMES R. OSGOOD AND COMPANY, | Late Ticknor & Fields, and Fields, Osgood, & Co. | [red] 1876.

Vol. [XII], *"Little Classic Edition."* Contents same as in 1851 T&F edition (A 12.1). Sheets bound with James R. Osgood and, later, Houghton, Osgood spine stampings. 2,000 copies printed 29 March 1876. Price $1.25, royalty 12.5¢ per volume. See B 5[XII] for reprintings of the *"Little Classic Edition."*

Locations: CEFC, LC, OU.

A 12.5.b
Boston: Houghton, Osgood, 1879.

Parts I, II, and III of *Grandfather's Chair* combined with *A Wonder-Book* and published as vol. X of the *"Fireside Edition"*; *Biographical Stories* combined with *Tanglewood Tales* and published as vol. XI of the *"FE."* 500 copies of each volume printed 20 September 1879. See B 6 for reprintings of the *"FE."*

A 12.5.c
The Whole History of Grandfather's Chair Complete in Three Parts. Boston: Houghton, Mifflin, 1886.

Revised Copyright Edition. Omits *Biographical Stories*. Price 15¢. Printed wrappers. Reprinted by H,M in hard-cover format, 1891.

A 12.5.d
Boston: Houghton, Mifflin, [1891].

Combined with *A Wonder-Book* and *Tanglewood Tales* and published as vol. V of the *Popular Edition*. 1,000 copies printed June–August 1891. See B 7 for reprintings of the *Popular Edition*.

A 12.5.e
Boston: Houghton, Mifflin, [1899].

Vol. [XII], *Concord Edition.* See B 8.

PRINTINGS FROM THE RIVERSIDE EDITION PLATES

A 12.6.a₁
Riverside Edition (trade), first printing, American issue [1883]

[IV:] A WONDER BOOK | TANGLEWOOD TALES, AND | GRANDFATHER'S CHAIR |
BY | NATHANIEL HAWTHORNE | [vignette of head of Quicksilver] | BOSTON |
HOUGHTON, MIFFLIN AND COMPANY | New York: 11 East Seventeenth Street | The
Riverside Press, Cambridge | 1883

[XII:] TALES, SKETCHES, AND OTHER | PAPERS | BY | NATHANIEL HAWTHORNE |
WITH A BIOGRAPHICAL SKETCH | BY | GEORGE PARSONS LATHROP | [engraving
of the Wayside] | BOSTON | HOUGHTON, MIFFLIN AND COMPANY | New York: 11
East Seventeenth Street | The Riverside Press, Cambridge | 1883

2 vols. Parts I, II, and III of *Grandfather's Chair* combined with *A Wonder-Book* and
Tanglewood Tales in three-volumes-in-one format and published as vol. IV of the
Riverside trade printing. Also *Biographical Stories* combined with *Tales, Sketches,
and Other Papers* in omnibus volume and published as vol. XII of the Riverside trade
printing. Contents same as 1851 T&F edition (A 12.1), with the addition of introductory
notes by Lathrop. 1,500 copies of vol. IV printed January 1883; 3,000 copies of vol. XII
printed June 1883. See B 9 [IV, XII] for reprintings of the Riverside trade printing.

A 12.6.a₂
Riverside Edition (trade), first printing, English issue [1883]

London: Kegan Paul, Trench, 1883.

Sheets of vols. IV and XII, first printing (A 12.6.a₁), with cancel title, in a Kegan Paul
binding. 250 Kegan Paul title pages for each volume printed by Houghton, Mifflin,
June–July 1883. Later issues noted with dated and undated Kegan Paul, Trench,
Trübner title pages. See B 11.

A 12.6.b
Riverside Edition (large paper), second printing [1883]

[IV:] [red] A WONDER-BOOK | [black] TANGLEWOOD TALES, AND |
GRANDFATHER'S CHAIR | BY | NATHANIEL HAWTHORNE | [vignette of head of
Quicksilver] | [red] CAMBRIDGE | [black] Printed at the Riverside Press | 1883

[XII:] [red] TALES, SKETCHES | [black] AND | OTHER PAPERS | BY | NATHANIEL
HAWTHORNE | *WITH A BIOGRAPHICAL SKETCH* | BY | GEORGE PARSONS LATH-
ROP | [sepia vignette of Wayside] | [red] CAMBRIDGE | [black] Printed at the River-
side Press | 1883

Vols. IV and XII of the Riverside large-paper printing. 250 copies printed March 1883
and August 1883. See B 10.

A 12.6.c
Boston and New York: Houghton, Mifflin, 1884.

2 vols. Parts I, II, and III of *Grandfather's Chair* combined with the conclusion of

Tanglewood Tales in two-volumes-in-one format and published as vol. VIII of the *Wayside Edition*. *Biographical Stories* combined with *Tales and Sketches* and *Biographical Sketches* in an omnibus volume and published as vol. XXIII of the *Wayside Edition*. 500 copies printed September–October 1884. See B 12.

A 12.6.d
Boston and New York: Houghton, Mifflin, [1891].

Vols. IV and XII of the *Standard Library Edition* in the same volume makeup as the *Riverside Edition* (A 12.6.a₁). 500 copies printed October 1891. See B 13.

A 12.6.e
Boston and New York: Houghton, Mifflin, [1902].

Vols. IV and XII of the *"New" Wayside Edition* in the same volume makeup as the *Riverside Edition* (A 12.6.a₁). 500 copies printed September–October 1902. See B 14.

A 12.6.f
Boston and New York: [Houghton, Mifflin], MDCCCCIX.

Vols. IV and XII of the *Fireside Edition* in the same volume makeup as the *Riverside Edition* (A 12.6.a₁). See B 15.

A 12.6.g
Boston, New York: Jefferson Press, [1913].

2 vols. Parts I, II, and III of *Grandfather's Chair* combined with *A Wonder-Book* and *Tanglewood Tales* in three-volumes-in-one format and published as vol. [IV] of the *"Jefferson Press Edition."* *Biographical Stories* combined with *French and Italian Note-Books* and *Tales and Sketches* as an omnibus volume and published as vol. [X] of the *"Jefferson Press Edition."* See B 16.

PRINTINGS FROM THE MILLAR-ALDEN-LOVELL PLATES

A 12.7.a

GRANDFATHER'S CHAIR | A | *HISTORY FOR YOUTH.* | BY | NATHANIEL HAWTHORNE | [rule] | NEW YORK: | JAMES B. MILLAR & CO., PUBLISHERS. | 1884.

Omits *Biographical Stories*. Millar sheets also found with New York: John B. Alden undated cancel title.

A 12.7.b
New York: John W. Lovell, [n.d.].

No. 376, *Lovell's Library*, 6 May 1884. Printed wrappers. Price 20¢.

A 12.7.c
New York: United States Book Company Successors to John W. Lovell, [n.d.].

A 12.7.d
New York: United States Book Company, [n.d.].

OTHER EDITIONS

A 12.8
Printings from the Paterson-Scott plates

TRUE STORIES | FROM | HISTORY AND BIOGRAPHY | BY | NATHANIEL
HAWTHORNE. | [portrait of Hawthorne] | EDINBURGH: | WILLIAM PATERSON. |
1885.

No. 21, *Paterson's New England Novels*. Includes Parts I, II and III of *Grandfather's
Chair* and *Biographical Stories*. Published in cloth, top edges gilded, at 2s.; in ornamental paper covers at 1s. Also combined with *A Wonder-Book* in two-volumes-in-one
format and published as vol. [VI] of the *"Paterson Edition."* See B 17. Also reprinted
separately without date on title page. Also Paterson sheets found with cancel Walter
Scott title page. Also remanufactured from Paterson plates with Walter Scott title-page
imprint. Published in 1894 as vol. [VIII] of the *"Walter Scott Edition"* (gravure). See
B 18.

A 12.9
Printings from the Hurst plates

GRANDFATHER'S CHAIR | A | HISTORY FOR YOUTH. | BY | NATHANIEL
HAWTHORNE. | [rule] | NEW YORK: | HURST & CO., PUBLISHERS, | 122 NASSAU
ST.

[1889?]. *Arlington Edition*. Omits *Biographical Stories*. Reprinted an unknown number
of times with Hurst imprint. Later reprinted with Chicago: Thompson & Thomas imprint
in Hurst binding.

A 12.10
Grandfather's Chair. New York: F. M. Lupton, 1893.

No. 35, *The Arm Chair Library*, printed 2 September 1893. Prints only parts I and II of
Grandfather's Chair. Printed wrappers. Reprinted, with list of *Arm Chair Library* titles
on back cover expanded from 61 to 96 listings.

A 12.11
Philadelphia: David McKay, 1894.

Combined with *A Wonder-Book* in two-volumes-in-one format, *American Classic Series*.

A 12.12
Boston, New York, Chicago: Houghton, Mifflin, [1896].

Combines nos. 7, 8, and 9 of the *Riverside Literature Series*. Reprints A 6.3, A 7.3, and
A 8.4. Omits *Biographical Stories*.

A 12.13
Grandfather's Chair . . . and Biographical Stories. Boston, New York, Chicago: Houghton, Mifflin, 1896.

Riverside School Library.

A 12.14
Grandfather's Chair. Philadelphia: Henry Altemus, 1898.

Altemus' Young People's Library, with 60 illustrations. Omits *Biographical Stories*.

Reprinted. Also, same plates used to remanufacture title, omitting some illustrations, as no. 16 in *Altemus' Stories from History Series*. With dust jacket in color.

A 12.15
The Whole History of Grandfather's Chair. New York, Boston: Thomas Y. Crowell, n.d.

[ca. 1898]. Two printings, priority undetermined: on white wove paper with color frontispiece inserted; also on white laid paper with black and white frontispiece. Various bindings.

PRINTINGS FROM THE AUTOGRAPH PLATES

A 12.16.a
Boston and New York: Houghton, Mifflin, MDCCCC.

Vol. XII of the *Autograph Edition*. Contents same as in 1851 T&F edition (A 12.1), with editor's introductory note added. 500 copies. Deposited 20 December 1900. See B 20.

A 12.16.b
Boston and New York: Houghton, Mifflin, MDCCCC.

Vol. XII of the *Large-Paper (Autograph) Edition*. 500 copies printed 1900. See B 21.

A 12.16.c
Boston and New York: Houghton, Mifflin, 1903.

Vol. XII of the *Old Manse Edition*. See B 22.

OTHER EDITIONS

A 12.17
The Whole History of Grandfather's Chair. New York: Thomas Y. Crowell, [1902].

Introduction by Katharine Lee Bates. Includes *Biographical Stories*. Vol. [14] of the *Crowell "Lenox Edition."* See B 23.

A 12.18
Fanshawe, Grandfather's Chair, Biographical Stories. New York: Thomas Y. Crowell, [1902].

Introduction by Katharine Lee Bates. Omnibus volume published as vol. [I] of the *Crowell "Popular Edition."* See B 24.

A 12.19
[Columbus]: Ohio State University Press, [1972].

Vol. VI of the *Centenary Edition*. 2,526 copies published 1 November 1972. See B 32.

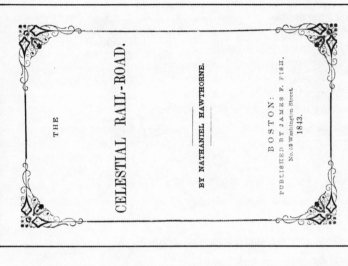

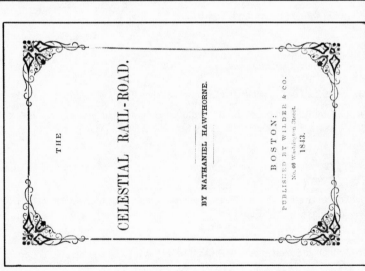

Printed wrappers for A 13.1.a and A 13.1.b (see also illustration at A 13.6)

amusement; while religion, though indubitably the main thing at heart, was thrown tastefully into the back-ground. Even an infidel would have heard little or nothing to shock his sensibility.

One great convenience of the new method of going on pilgrimage, I must not forget to mention. Our enormous burthens, instead of being carried on our shoulders, as had been the custom of old, were all snugly deposited in the baggage-car, and, as I was assured, would be delivered to their respective owners at the journey's end. Another thing, likewise, the benevolent reader will be delighted to understand. It may be remembered that there was an ancient feud between Prince Beelzebub and the keeper of the Wicket-Gate, and that the adherents of the former distinguished personage were accustomed to shoot deadly arrows at honest pilgrims, while knocking at the door. This dispute, much to the credit as well of the illustrious potentate above-mentioned, as of the worthy and enlightened Directors of the railroad, has been pacifically arranged, on the principle of mutual compromise. The Prince's subjects are now pretty numerously employed about the Station-house, some in taking care of the baggage, others in collecting fuel, feeding the engines, and such congenial occupations; and I can conscientious-

---

THE

CELESTIAL RAIL-ROAD:

BY NATHANIEL HAWTHORNE.

BOSTON:
PUBLISHED BY WILDER & CO.,
No. 46 Washington Street.
1843.

A 13.1.a: Title page, 4⅞″ × 3⅛″. Page format, 4⅛″ (4³/₈″) × 2½″

A 13 THE CELESTIAL RAIL-ROAD

A 13.1.a
First edition, first printing, a piracy [*1843*]

Exists with two imprints: Wilder & Co. (A 13.1.a) and James F. Fish (A 13.1.b). Probably two printings, with the priority assigned to the Wilder imprint (see Matthew J. Bruccoli, "Negative Evidence About 'The Celestial Rail-Road'," *Papers of the Bibliography Society of America*, 58 [Third Quarter 1964], 290–292). See also A 15.1, D 52.

Note: Collation has revealed no textural differences between the Wilder and Fish printings, other than the different imprints, and no significant type wear.

[1–3] 4–32

[1*]–2*⁸

Contents: p. 1: title; p. 2: blank; pp. 3–32: text, headed 'THE CELESTIAL RAIL-ROAD. | [rule]'.

Typography and paper: See illustration, A 13.1.a page format. White wove paper.

Binding: Buff (73. p. OY) printed wrappers (see illustration, A 13 wrappers). All edges trimmed.

Publication: Unknown number of copies published about October 1843. Advertised by Putnam, W & S. B. Ives, and Jewett in the Salem papers regularly during October–November 1843.

Locations: CEFC, CSmH, CtY, MH, MWA, NN, OU, PU, RPB.

amusement; while religion, though indubitably the main thing at heart, was thrown tastefully into the back-ground. Even an infidel would have heard little or nothing to shock his sensibility.

One great convenience of the new method of going on pilgrimage, I must not forget to mention. Our enormous burthens, instead of being carried on our shoulders, as had been the custom of old, were all snugly deposited in the baggage-car, and, as I was assured, would be delivered to their respective owners at the journey's end. Another thing, likewise, the benevolent reader will be delighted to understand. It may be remembered that there was an ancient feud between Prince Beelzebub and the keeper of the Wicket-Gate, and that the adherents of the former distinguished personage were accustomed to shoot deadly arrows at honest pilgrims, while knocking at the door. This dispute, much to the credit as well of the illustrious potentate above-mentioned, as of the worthy and enlightened Directors of the railroad, has been pacifically arranged, on the principle of mutual compromise. The Prince's subjects are now pretty numerously employed about the Station-house, some in taking care of the baggage, others in collecting fuel, feeding the engines, and such congenial occupations; and I can conscientious-

---

THE

CELESTIAL RAIL-ROAD:

BY NATHANIEL HAWTHORNE.

PUBLISHED BY JAMES F. FISH.
No. 52 Washington Street.
1843.

A 13.1.b: Title page, 5″ × 3¹/₈″. Page format, 4¹/₈″ (4³/₈″) × 2¹/₂″

A 13.1.b
Boston: James F. Fish, 1843.

Same as A 13.a except for title-page and wrapper imprints.

Locations: CEFC, MoSW.

4

"This," remarked Mr. Smooth-it-away, "is the famous Slough of Despond—a disgrace to all the neighbourhood; and the greater, that it might so easily be converted into firm ground."

"I have understood," said I, "that efforts have been made for that purpose, from time immemorial. Bunyan mentions that above twenty thousand cartloads of whole-some instructions had been thrown in here, without effect."

"Very probably!—and what effect could be anticipated from such unsubstantial stuff?" cried Mr. Smooth-it-away. "You observe this convenient bridge. We obtained a suffi-cient foundation for it by throwing into the Slough some editions of books of morality, volumes of French philosophy and German rationalism, tracts, sermons, and essays of modern clergymen, extracts from Plato, Confucius, and various Hindoo sages, together with a few ingenious com-mentaries upon texts of scripture; all of which, by some scientific process, have been converted into a mass like granite. The whole bog might be filled up with similar matter."

It really seemed to me, however, that the bridge vibrated and heaved up and down, in a very formidable manner; and, in spite of Mr. Smooth-it-away's testimony to the solidity of its foundation, I should be loth to cross it in a crowded omnibus, especially if each passenger were encumbered with as heavy luggage as that gentleman and myself. Never-theless, we got over without accident, and soon found our-selves at the stationhouse. This very neat and spacious edifice is erected on the site of the little Wicket-Gate, which formerly, as all old pilgrims will recollect, stood directly across the highway; and, by its inconvenient narrowness, was a great obstruction to the traveller of liberal mind and expansive stomach. The reader of John Bunyan will be glad to know, that Christian's old friend Evangelist, who was accustomed to supply each pilgrim with a mystic roll, now presides at the ticket-office. Some malicious persons, it is true, deny the identity of this reputable character with the Evangelist of old times, and even pretend to bring compe-tent evidence of an imposture. Without involving myself in the dispute, I shall merely observe, that, so far as my ex-perience goes, the square pieces of pasteboard now de-livered to passengers, are much more convenient and useful along the road than the antique roll of parchment. Whether

THE

CELESTIAL RAILROAD.

BY

NATHANIEL HAWTHORNE.

(Reprinted from the Baptist Magazine.)

LONDON:

HOULSTON AND STONEMAN, 65, PATERNOSTER ROW.

1844.

A 13.2: Title page: 6¹/₈" × 3³/₄". Page format, 4¹⁵/₁₆" (5³/₁₆') × 3¹/₁₆"

A 13.2

First English edition, only printing, a piracy [1844]

Reprinted from Houlston and Stoneman's *Baptist Magazine* (January, February 1844). See D 52.

[1–3] 4–16

π^8

Contents: p. 1: cover title; p. 2: printer's notice; pp. 3–16: text, headed 'THE CELES-TIAL RAILROAD. | [rule]'.

Typography and paper: See illustration, A 13.2 page format. White wove paper.

Binding: Pamphlet, cover title. All edges trimmed.

Publication: Unknown number of copies probably published shortly after February 1844.

Printing: Printed by J. Hadden, Castle Street, Finsbury.

Location: Berg.

A VISIT

TO THE

CELESTIAL CITY.

REVISED BY THE COMMITTEE OF PUBLICATION OF THE
AMERICAN SUNDAY-SCHOOL UNION.

PHILADELPHIA:
AMERICAN SUNDAY-SCHOOL UNION,
NO. 146 CHESTNUT STREET.

---

weight. On both sides lay an extensive quagmire, which could not have been more disagreeable either to sight or smell, had all the kennels of the earth emptied their pollution there.

"This," remarked Mr. Smooth-it-away, "is the famous Slough of Despond—a disgrace to all the neighbourhood; and the greater, that it might so easily be converted into firm ground."

"I have understood," said I, "that efforts have been made for that purpose, from time immemorial. Bunyan mentions that above twenty thousand cart loads of wholesome instructions had been thrown in here, without effect."

"Very probably!—and what effect could be anticipated from such unsubstantial stuff!" cried Mr. Smooth-it-away. "You observe this convenient bridge. We obtained a sufficient foun-

---

A 13.3.a: Title page, 5³/₄″ × 3⁵/₈″. Page format, 4⁹/₁₆″ (4⁷/₈″) × 2¹¹/₁₆″

A 13.3.a
Second American edition, first printing [1844]

PHILADELPHIA:
PRINTED BY KING & BAIRD.
No. 9 George street.

A slightly revised edition of *The Celestial Rail-Road* was published and distributed by the American Sunday-School Union under the title *A Visit to the Celestial City*. Omits three sentences in A 13.1.a concerning Beelzebub's purchase of a miser's soul (24.19–27, "Prince Beelzebub himself . . . a loser by the bargain."). Commencing in 1844 and continuing at least until 1897, numerous printings with the American Sunday-School Union imprint were made from the plates of this edition.

First printing has King & Baird notice on verso of title page.

[1–2] 3–54 [55–60] (See "Contents" for frontispiece and plate insertions.)

[1]⁶ 2–4⁶ 5² 5*² (5*₁ + 5*₂) [5**]², with singleton 5*₁ pasted to verso of leaf 5₂ and singleton 5*₂ pasted to recto of leaf [5**]₁; leaf [5**]₂ used as pastedown rear endpaper.

Contents: p. 1: title; p. 2: printer's notice; pp. 3–4: 'NOTE'; pp. 5–54: text, headed 'A VISIT | TO THE | CELESTIAL CITY. | [rule]'; pp. 55–60: blank. Frontispiece (' "I was amazed to discern Mr. Smooth-it-away, waving his hand in token of farewell." *Page 52'*) inserted facing title page; plate (' "Observe two dusty foot-travellers in the old pilgrim-guise." *Page 17'*) inserted facing p. 17; plate (' "Through the very heart of this rocky mountain a tunnel had been constructed." *Page 20'*) inserted facing p. 20; plate (' " 'Poh, nonsense!' Said Mr. Smooth-it-away taking my arm and leading me off." *Page 43'*) inserted facing p. 43. Also copies noted with three plates. Also noted with plates in different positions.

Typography and paper: See illustration, A 13.3.a page format. Running heads: versos, 'A VISIT TO THE'; rectos, 'CELESTIAL CITY.' White wove paper.

Binding: Marbled boards, black leather shelfback, title goldstamped on spine. Also plum, brown, blue bold-ribbed (some diagonal) T cloth with title and decoration goldstamped on spine. White wove endpapers. Single flyleaf inserted at front and rear. American Sunday-School Union ads inserted at rear in later printings. All edges trimmed.

Publication: Unknown number of copies published 1844. First advertised as item 1335, Thirteenth Series, Catalogue 27, for January 1845, American Sunday-School Union.

Location: CEFC, MH, OU.

REPRINTINGS WITHIN THE SECOND EDITION

Numerous reprintings were made from the American Sunday-School Union plates, all without printer's notice on verso of title page and all undated. Reprintings with "No.

146 Chestnut Street" as title-page imprint appeared prior to 1857. "1122 Chestnut St." as title-page imprint appeared not before 1857. As a result of plate-wear repair, page number on frontispiece was mistakenly recut from "52" to "12" in later version. Also page number on illustration facing p. 43 was mistakenly recut from "43" to "13" in later version. Also position of plates changed in later versions: p. 17 illustration was used for frontispiece in some later versions. Also new p. 17 illustration showing two dusty foot-travelers being threatened by devil riding fiery steam engine was used as frontispiece in some later printings. Also later printings have been noted with frontispiece only or without any illustrations. Last printing noted by compiler has title and author's name on decorated white cloth front cover, with fiery-devil frontispiece and owner inscription dated 1897.

OTHER EDITIONS

A 13.4

The Celestial Rail Road: or, Modern Pilgrim's Progress. After the Manner of Bunyan Vividly Representative of the Present-Day Professors of Religion. From the Original by Nathaniel Hawthorne. With Additions and Alterations. Philadelphia: Merrihew and Thompson, No. 7 Carter's Alley, 1844.

Printed wrappers.

A 13.5
Second English edition

London: Houlston and Stoneman, 1846.

[1–3] 4–16

A new setting of type from A 13.2. Cover title.

Location: CEFC.

A 13.6
Lowell: D. Skinner, 1847.

[1–3] 4–30 [31–32]. Pp. 31–32 blank.

Pamphlet, printed wrappers. Exists in two bindings: corner ornaments on decorative border of wrappers differ; titles on wrappers are different settings (see illustration, A 13.6 wrappers). Priority undetermined.

Locations: Wrapper A: CEFC, MSaE; Wrapper B: MSaE, NRU.

A 13.7
London: Houlston and Sons, n.d.

[1–3] 4–16

Complete resetting. *'TWELFTH THOUSAND'* slug on title page. Pamphlet, plain wrappers.

Location: CEFC.

A 13.8
Poona [India]: Chronicle Press, 1849.

Reprinted from the *Baptist Magazine.* See D 52. Pamphlet, cover title.

Location: Berg.

Wrappers for A13.6, two versions. Titles are different settings; corner ornaments differ; trim size varies from 4³/₄" × 3¹/₁₆" to 4⁵/₈" × 3¹/₈".

A 13.9
Poona [India]: Chronicle Press, by John William Sherlock, 1850.

Reprinted from the *Baptist Magazine*. See D 52. Includes 'MORAL', not by Hawthorne, dated 3 September 1850. Pamphlet, cover title.

Location: Berg.

A 13.10
Rochester, N.Y.: Advent Review Office, 1855.

Printed wrappers, cover title.

A 13.11
The Celestial Railroad: Or, Modern Pilgrim's Progress .... From the Original, By Nathaniel Hawthorne. With Additions and Alterations. Boston: J. V. Hines, 1860.

Pamphlet, cover title.

Location: NN.

A 13.12

ADVENT TRACTS (WESTERN SERIES)—NO. 16 | [rule] | CELESTIAL RAILROAD; | OR, | MODERN PILGRIM'S PROGRESS. | AFTER THE MANNER OF BUNYAN. | VIV-IDLY REPRESENTATIVE OF THE PRESENT | DAY PROFESSORS OF RELIGION. | FROM THE ORIGINAL, BY NATHANIEL HAWTHORNE. | WITH ADDITIONS AND AL-TERATIONS. | [rule] | BUCHANAN, MICHIGAN: | PUBLISHED BY THE W. A. C. P. ASSOCIATION. | 1867.

Pamphlet, cover title.

Location: Berg.

A 13.13
New York: Thomas Y. Crowell, n.d.

[c. 1904].

A 13.14
Boston and New York: Houghton Mifflin, 1927.

A 13.15
New York: American Tract Society, 1928.

Printed wrappers.

Bindings for (1) A 14.1.a$_1$, wrapper; (2) A 14.1.b$_1$; (3 & 4) A 14.1.a$_1$, two-in-one formats; (5) A 14.1.a$_2$; (6) A 14.1.a$_3$; (7 & 8) A 14.1.c$_1$; (9) A 14.2 (see also illustration at A 14.1.a$_1$)

JOURNAL

OF AN

AFRICAN CRUISER;

COMPRISING SKETCHES OF THE CANARIES, THE CAPE DE
VERDS, LIBERIA, MADEIRA, SIERRA LEONE, AND
OTHER PLACES OF INTEREST ON THE WEST
COAST OF AFRICA.

BY AN OFFICER OF THE U. S. NAVY.

EDITED BY

NATHANIEL HAWTHORNE.

NEW-YORK & LONDON.

WILEY AND PUTNAM.

1845.

---

as we seldom ask or find, in those of our own sex, on land! There, we leave the gentler humanities of life to woman; here, we are compelled to imitate her characteristics, as well as our sterner nature will permit.

22.—The sick man died last night, and was buried to-day. His history was revealed to no one. Where was his home, or whether he has left friends to mourn his death, are alike unknown. Dying, he kept his own counsel, and was content to vanish out of life, even as a speck of foam melts back into the ocean. At 11 A. M., for the first time, in a cruise likely to be fatal to many on board, the boatswain piped "all hands to bury the dead!" The sailor's corpse, covered with the union of his country's flag, was placed in the gangway. Two hundred and fifty officers and men stood around, uncovered, and reverently listened to the beautiful and solemn burial service, as it was read by one of the officers. The body was committed to the deep, while the ship dashed onward, and had left the grave far behind, even before the last words of the service were uttered. The boatswain "piped down," and all returned to their duties sadly, and with thoughtful countenances.

23.—At 4 A. M., the island of Palma and the Peak of Teneriffe are in full sight, though the lofty summit of the mountain is one hundred miles distant.

24.—At 5 A. M., anchored at Santa Cruz, capital of the island of Teneriffe. The health-officer informed us that we must ride out a quarantine of eight days. A fine precaution, considering that we are direct from New York! After break-fast, I went to the mole, to see the Consular Agent, on duty. While waiting in our boat, we were stared at by thirty or forty loafers (a Yankee phrase, but strictly applicable to these foreign vagabonds), of the most wretched kind. Some were dressed in coarse shirts and trowsers, and some had only one of these habiliments. None interested me, except a dirty, swarthy boy, with most brilliant black eyes, who lay flat on his stomach, and gazed at us in silence. His elf-like glance sparkles brightly in my memory.

One of the seamen in our boat spoke to the persons on shore in Spanish. I inquired whether that were his mother-tongue,

A 14 JOURNAL OF AN AFRICAN CRUISER

A 14.1.a₁
First edition, presumed first printing, American issue [1845]

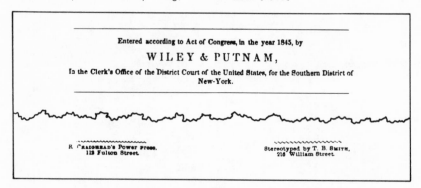

Has 4-line copyright notice, with printer's and stereotyper's notices present on copyright page. Contents precedes preface. (See note below.)

[A–B] [i–ii] [v] vi–viii [v] vi [1] 2–179 [180]

[1]⁶ (+1₂, ×1₃, +1₅) 2–12⁸ 13²

Contents: p. A: half title; p. B: blank; p. i: title; p. ii: copyright; pp. v–viii: contents; pp. v–vi: preface; pp. 1–179: text, headed 'JOURNAL | OF AN | AFRICAN CRUISER. | [rule] | CHAPTER I.'; p. 180: blank.

Note: Apparently problems requiring bindery correction were encountered in the printing of the preliminaries. Leaf 1₃ is excised. Leaves 1₂ (title) and 1₅, which ordinarily would be conjugate, are singletons, with the title (1₂) tipped to the stub of 1₃ and 1₅ tipped to 1₄. Two circumstances could have required these changes in the first gathering: some flaw in the original title or copyright imprint could have resulted in the removal of 1₃ and replacement with a cancel title; or misimposition could have required that parts of the first gathering be cut apart and rearranged. The overlapping of the pagination of the contents, [v] vi–viii, and the preface, [v] vi, could have contributed to a misimposition. The unanswered question is what was on leaf 1₃—a canceled title, blank pages, or pages that had to be reordered or replaced?

Lack of clear evidence makes the priorities assigned the presumed first and second printings of *African Cruiser* tentative. It seems certain that there were two Wiley and Putnam printings, the first published in June 1845 and the second, according to Duyckinck's letter to Hawthorne (2 September 1845), sometime in September or October 1845. LC has a deposit copy with this note on the title page: "Deposited in the Clerk's Office for the Southern District of New York June 20, 1845." Although this copy has been rebound and is not fully collatable, the verso of the title page has the 4-line copyright notice together with the printer's and stereotyper's notices. LC has a second copy, with the same presumed first printing form of the copyright page, presented by Horatio Bridge to Mrs. Polk in July 1845. Two other presentation copies from Bridge (Locations: Berg, ViU) and a presentation copy from Hawthorne (Location: Berg) are also in the presumed first-printing form. This evidence strongly suggests that copies with the 4-line copyright notice, the printer's and stereotyper's notices present on the copyright page, and the contents preceding the preface must have come from the first printing in June 1945. Also a sample collation on the Hinman machine suggests the possibility of progressive type batter in support of the priority tentatively assigned (e.g., broken "A" in running head, p. 7; missing second "7" in page number "77"; broken "R" in running head, p. 97).

Typography and paper: See illustration, A 14.1.a₁ page format. Running heads: versos, 'JOURNAL OF AN [CHAP. [no.].'; rectos, 'CHAP. [no.].] AFRICAN CRUISER.' White wove paper.

Binding: Buff (73. p. OY) printed wrappers noted in two states: wrapper A (see illustration, A 14.1.a₁ wrapper), with three titles in Wiley and Putnam's *Library of American Books* listed at top of outside rear wrapper, and wrapper B with seven titles listed. Inside of front and rear wrappers of state A lists titles in Wiley and Putnam's *Voyages and Travels;* inside of wrappers of state B lists W&P titles in *Library of Choice Literature, American Series,* and "In Press." Also dark brown (65. br Black) bold-ribbed T cloth with plain covers and gold-imprinted label pasted on spine. Also noted in plain gray and buff paper-covered boards with leather shelfback. Also LC has a presentation copy from Horatio Bridge to Mrs. Polk in contemporary leather binding with gilt edges. Clothbound copies have wove endpapers and single flyleaf inserted at front and rear of some copies. W&P catalogues inserted at rear of some copies. Ads used as rear endpapers in some copies. Also sheets of presumed first printing and presumed second printing have been found bound in two-volumes-in-one format with other titles in the Wiley and Putnam *Library of American Books* series, including George H. Calvert, *Scenes and Thoughts in Europe* (Locations: printing 1: OU, ViU; 2: CEFC, NN, OU); J. T. Headley, *Letters from Italy* (Locations: printing 2: CEFC, CtY, MH, MWA); Lady Duff Gordon, *The French in Algiers* (Location: PSt). Top edge untrimmed in most copies.

Publication: Hawthorne to Horatio Bridge 2 May 1845: "Duyckinck writes me that your book is stereotyped and about to go to press. The first edition will be of two thousand copies, five hundred of which will be sent to London." Deposited 20 June 1845. Advertised in the 20 June 1845 *New-York Daily Tribune* as "just published." Listed in *Appleton's Literary Bulletin,* July 1845. Listed in *Wiley & Putnam's Literary News-Letter,* July 1845.

Printing: Stereotype plates made by T. B. Smith, 216 William St., New York; printed by R. Craighead's Power Press, 112 Fulton St., New York.

Locations: Wrapper A: Berg 1 (Hawthorne presentation), Berg 2 (Bridge presentation), CEFC, CtY, OU, ViU (Bridge presentation); wrapper B: AT (two copies, both bound with presumed second-printing text—see A 14.1.b₁), Berg; cloth: CEFC, LC 1 (Bridge presentation), LC 2 (rebound deposit copy), OU.

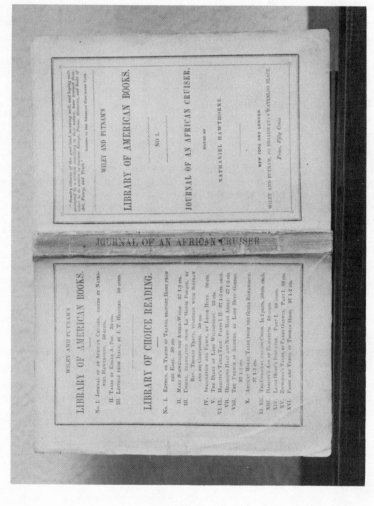

Wrapper A for A 14.1.a;, listing three titles under "LIBRARY OF AMERICAN BOOKS"

as we seldom ask or find, in those of our own sex, on land! There, we leave the gentler humanities of life to woman; here, we are compelled to imitate her characteristics, as well as our sterner nature will permit.

22.—The sick man died last night, and was buried to-day. His history was revealed to no one. Where was his home, or whether he has left friends to mourn his death, are alike unknown. Dying, he kept his own counsel, and was content to vanish out of life, even as a speck of foam melts back into the ocean. At 11 A. M., for the first time, in a cruise likely to be fatal to many on board, the boatswain piped "all hands to bury the dead!" The sailor's corpse, covered with the union of his country's flag, was placed in the gangway. Two hundred and fifty officers and men stood around, uncovered, and reverently listened to the beautiful and solemn burial service, as it was read by one of the officers. The body was committed to the deep, while the ship dashed onward, and had left the grave far behind, even before the last words of the service were uttered. The boatswain "piped down," and all returned to their duties sadly, and with thoughtful countenances.

23.—At 4 A. M., the island of Palma and the Peak of Teneriffe are in full sight, though the lofty summit of the mountain is one hundred miles distant.

24.—At 5 A. M., anchored at Santa Cruz, capital of the island of Teneriffe. The health-officer informed us that we must ride out a quarantine of eight days. A fine precaution, considering that we are direct from New York! After breakfast, I went to the mole, to see the Consular Agent, on duty. While waiting in our boat, we were stared at by thirty or forty loafers (a Yankee phrase, but strictly applicable to these foreign vagabonds), of the most wretched kind. Some were dressed in coarse shirts and trowsers, and some had only one of these habiliments. None interested me, except a dirty, swarthy boy, with most brilliant black eyes, who lay flat on his stomach, and gazed at us in silence. His elf-like glance sparkles brightly in my memory.

One of the seamen in our boat spoke to the persons on shore in Spanish. I inquired whether that were his mother-tongue,

---

JOURNAL

OF AN

AFRICAN CRUISER:

COMPRISING SKETCHES OF THE CANARIES, THE CAPE DE VERDS, LIBERIA, MADEIRA, SIERRA LEONE, AND OTHER PLACES OF INTEREST ON THE WEST COAST OF AFRICA.

BY AN OFFICER OF THE U. S. NAVY.

EDITED BY
NATHANIEL HAWTHORNE.

LONDON:
WILEY AND PUTNAM, 6, WATERLOO PLACE.
1845.

[ENTERED AT STATIONERS' HALL.]

A 14.1.aa: Title page, 7 9/16″ × 5 1/16″. Page format, 5 3/4″ (6″) × 3 7/16″

A 14.1.a₂
First edition, presumed first printing, English issue [1845]

Sheets of the presumed first printing with an English title leaf inserted. London binder cut apart first gathering, presumably to reorder the preliminary leaves so as to have the preface precede contents, with the result that the preliminary leaves are all singletons stabbed for binding.

[i–v] vi [v] vi–viii, [1] 2–179 [180]

[1]⁴ (1₁, ±1₂, +1₃, +1₄) 2–12⁸ 13²

Contents: p. i: half title; p. ii: blank; p. iii: title; p. iv: blank; pp. v–vi: preface; pp. v–viii: contents; pp. 1–179: text, headed 'JOURNAL | OF AN | AFRICAN CRUISER. | [rule] | CHAPTER I.'; p. 180: blank.

Binding: Bound in green (127. gy. Ol G) bold-ribbed T cloth. Covers with blind-stamped rectangular border panel enclosing central element, title goldstamped on spine (see illustration, A 14 bindings). Bound by Remnant & Edmonds, London.

Publication: 500 sets of imported sheets. Advertised in *Athenaeum*, 12 July 1845, as "now ready." Listed in *Publishers' Circular*, 15 July 1845, and *Athenaeum*, 19 July. Reviewed in the *Literary Gazette*, 2 August 1845.

Locations: BM (undated), CEFC.

A 14.1.a₃
First edition, presumed first printing, remainder issue [1848]

New York: John Wiley, 1848.

Remaindered presumed first-printing sheets with a tipped-in John Wiley title. Noted in cloth with 'Library of Choice Reading' blindstamped on covers and spine. It is probable that although not located, remaindered presumed second printing sheets, or mixed sheets, were issued in this format.

Location: CEFC.

A 14.1.b₁
First edition, presumed second printing, American issue [1845]

ENTERED according to Act of Congress, in the year 1845, by
WILEY & PUTNAM,
In the Clerk's Office of the District Court for the Southern District of New-York.

Has integral title, 3-line copyright notice, no printer's or stereotyper's notice on copyright page. Preface precedes contents.

Note: The 4-line copyright notice of the presumed first printing includes the phrase 'of the United States' which is omitted in the shorter 3-line copyright notice of the presumed second printing. Wiley and Putnam also used the 3-line form of the copyright notice in *Mosses from an Old Manse* (1846), Calvert's *Scenes and Thoughts in Europe* (1846), and Whittier's *Supernaturalism of New England* (1847), all later titles in the *Library of American Books* series.

[A–B] [i–v] vi [v] vi–viii, [1] 2–179 [180]

[1]⁶ 2–12⁸ 13²

Contents: pp. A–B: blank; p. i: half title; p. ii: blank; p. iii: title; p. iv: copyright; pp. v–vi: preface; pp. v–viii: contents; pp. 1–179: text, headed: 'JOURNAL | OF AN | AFRICAN CRUISER. | [rule] | CHAPTER I.'; p. 180: blank.

Binding: See A 14.1.a₁ bindings. Also noted in plum (260. v. d. p R) morocco L-like cloth with plain covers, red leather shelfback with 'Library of Choice Reading' and title goldstamped on spine (see illustration, A 14 bindings). Also noted with and without '20' goldstamped on spine (Locations: CEFC, OU).

Publication: Probably 1,000 copies published September–October 1845; Duyckinck to Hawthorne, 2 October 1845, "The *Journal of the Cruiser* has just gone to a second edition [i.e., printing] of one thousand copies, the first, I believe, having been two thousand."

Locations: Wrapper B: AT, Berg; cloth: CEFC, MH, OU.

A 14.1.b₂
First edition, presumed second printing, English issue [1845]

Sheets of the presumed second printing with original title canceled and English title tipped in.

[A–B] [i–v] vi [v] vi–viii, [1] 2–179 [180]

[1]⁶(±1₃) 2–12⁸ 13²

Contents: pp. A–B: blank; p. i: half title; p. ii: blank; p. iii: title; p. iv: blank; pp. v–vi: preface; pp. v–viii: contents; pp. 1–179: text, headed 'JOURNAL | OF AN | AFRICAN CRUISER. | [rule] | CHAPTER I.'; p. 180: blank.

Some portion of 1,000 sets of presumed second-printing sheets imported and bound by Remnant & Edmonds, London, in same format as first English issue.

Locations: CEFC, MH.

A 14.1.c₁
First edition, presumed third printing, first issue [1853]

New York: George P. Putnam, 1853.

Reprinted from repaired plates with integral title leaf, verso blank. With 'Putnam's Popular Library' blindstamped on covers.

Location: CEFC (E. T. Bridge presentation, dated 20 May 1853).

Note: What appear to be first-issue sheets with the Putnam title page intact, gathered in the same form as the Putnam publication, are also found in a typical Ticknor format A binding (see illustration, A 2.6 binding). (Location: CEFC.) When Ticknor and Fields bought the Putnam plates for *Mosses* and *Cruiser* at the Bangs Bros. Trade Sale in New York, March 1854, they may have acquired some Putnam sheets that were later bound up in Ticknor style and distributed in an effort to recover some of the purchase costs. The *Cost Books* record no printing of *Cruiser* and no use of the Putnam plates.

A 14.1.c₂
First edition, presumed third printing, second issue [1853]

New York: George P. Putnam, 1853.

Cancel Putnam title leaf pasted in; verso has Putnam copyright notice. Presumably original title was canceled to incorporate copyright notice.

Locations: CEFC, MH.

A 14.2
Second edition, first English printing, a piracy [1848]

Aberdeen: George Clark; London: S. Richardson, MDCCCXLVIII.

Combined with *The Narrative of the Hon. John Byron,* by Byron, in two-volumes-in-one format and published in various bindings.

Location: CEFC.

Bindings for (1 & 2) A 15.1.a₁, two states of spine imprint; (3 & 4) A 15.1.a₂; (5) A 15.1.a₁, two-in-one format; (6) A 15.1.c₁; (7) A 15.1.c₂; (8 & 9) A 15.3.a

MOSSES

from

AN OLD MANSE.

BY NATHANIEL HAWTHORNE.

IN TWO PARTS.

PART I.

NEW YORK:
WILEY AND PUTNAM.
1846.

---

to be no deadly error in holding theological libraries to be accumulations of, for the most part, stupendous impertinence.

Many of the books had accrued in the latter years of the last clergyman's lifetime. These threatened to be of even less interest than the elder works, a century hence, to any curious inquirer who should then rummage them, as I was doing now. Volumes of the Liberal Preacher and Christian Examiner, occasional sermons, controversial pamphlets, tracts, and other productions of a like fugitive nature, took the place of the thick and heavy volumes of past time. In a physical point of view, there was much the same difference as between a feather and a lump of lead; but, intellectually regarded, the specific gravity of old and new was about upon a par. Both, also, were alike frigid. The elder books, nevertheless, seemed to have been earnestly written, and might be conceived to have possessed warmth at some former period; although, with the lapse of time, the heated masses had cooled down even to the freezing point. The frigidity of the modern productions, on the other hand, was characteristic and inherent, and evidently had little to do with the writers' qualities of mind and heart. In fine, of this whole dusty heap of literature, I tossed aside all the sacred part, and felt myself none the less a Christian for eschewing it. There appeared no hope of either mounting to the better world on a Gothic staircase of ancient folios, or of flying thither on the wings of a modern tract.

Nothing, strange to say, retained any sap, except what had been written for the passing day and year, without the remotest pretension or idea of permanence. There were a few old newspapers, and still older almanacs, which re-produced, to my mental eye, the epochs when they had issued from the press, with a distinctness that was altogether unaccountable. It was as if I had found bits of magic looking-glass among the books, with the images of a vanished century in them. I turned my eyes towards the tattered picture, above-mentioned, and asked of the austere

A 15 MOSSES FROM AN OLD MANSE

A 15.1.a₁
First edition, first printing, American issue [1846]

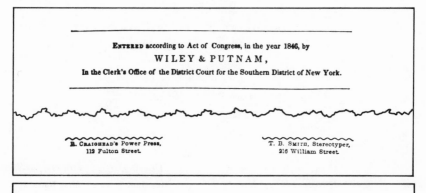

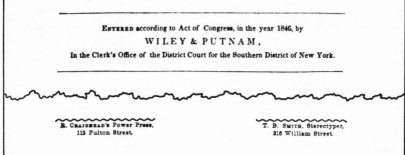

2 vols. First printing has Craighead and Smith imprints below copyright notice in both volumes and text can be distinguished from later printings on the basis of type batter (see table).

I: [i–vi] [1] 2–207 [208]

II: [i–vi] [1] 2–211 [212]

I: [1]² (1₂+1) 2–9¹² 10⁶ [11]²

II: [1]² (1₂+1) 2–9¹² 10⁶ [11–12]²

Note one: Contents leaf in each volume is tipped to verso of title leaf.

Contents: I: p. i: half title; p. ii: blank; p. iii: title; p. iv: copyright; p. v: contents; p. vi: blank; pp. 1–207: text, headed 'MOSSES FROM AN OLD MANSE. | [rule] THE OLD MANSE. | The Author makes the Reader acquainted with his Abode.'; p. 208: blank.
  II: p. i: half title; p. ii: blank; p. iii: title; p. iv: copyright; p. v: contents; p. vi: blank; pp. 1–211: text, headed 'MOSSES FROM AN OLD MANSE. | [rule] | THE NEW ADAM AND EVE. | [rule]'; p. 212: blank.

Tales and sketches: I: "The Old Manse,"# "The Birth-Mark,"† "A Select Party,"† "Young Goodman Brown,"† "Rappaccini's Daughter,"† "Mrs. Bullfrog,"† "Fire-

Type Batter Within the First Three Printings
of *Mosses from an Old Manse*

GATH.	PAGE.LINE	FIRST	SECOND	THIRD
Volume I				
[1]	[iii].5	IN TWO PARTS.	IN TWO PARTS	IN TWO PARTS
2	10.33	apophthegm,	apophthegm,	apophthegm
2	17.7	ser-	ser	ser
3	28.1	fire	fire	fire
4	61.30	made it	made it	made it
5	81.2	heart.	heart.	heart.
6	101.5	self-	self-	self
6	104.1	been	been	been
7	121.29	biscuits	b'scuits	b'scuits
7	125.13	Mrs. Bull-	Mrs. Bull-	Mrs. Bull
8	155.1	scrape	scrape	scrape
8	163.2	proverbial	proverbial	proverbial
9	172.4	had	had	hao
9	180.33	blasted	blasted	blasten
Volume II				
2	3.33	it is	it is	it is
3	36.29	heard	heard	heard
3	39.5	proba-	proba-	proba
4	50.33	it to	t to	t to
4	57.5	cur as	cur as	c ir as
5	72.33	than	han	han
5	88.29	tumult,	tumult,	tumult,
6	100.32	had	had	had
7	141.0	141	141	141
8	145.0	145	145	145
8	161.5	energetic,	energetic,	energetic,
9	169.33	school-	school-	school-

Worship,"† "Buds and Bird-Voices,"† "Monsieur du Miroir,"† "The Hall of Fantasy,"† "The Celestial Railroad,"† "The Procession of Life."†

II: "The New Adam and Eve,"† "Egotism; or the Bosom Friend [Serpent],"† "The Christmas Banquet,"† "Drowne's Wooden Image,"† "The Intelligence Office,"† "Roger Malvin's Burial,"† "P.'S Correspondence,"† "Earth's Holocaust,"† "The Old Apple Dealer,"† "The Artist of the Beautiful,"† "A Virtuoso's Collection."† Daggers (†) indicate first collected appearance. The number sign (#) indicates first appearance in print.

Typography and paper: See illustration, A 15.1.a₁ page format. Running heads: rectos, chapter titles; versos, 'MOSSES FROM AN OLD MANSE.' White wove paper.

Binding: Published in two volumes and bound in two formats: each volume separately bound in buff (73. p. OY) printed paper wrappers and sold individually or as a set; also two volumes combined in two-in-one format and sold as a single clothbound volume.

The wrappers were printed from stereotype plates and exist in various states as a result of new plates being introduced by the publisher in the process of updating the wrapper advertisements. Two states of the outside front wrapper have been noted. The illustrations of the two states show sufficient identification. State 1 of the front wrapper is more common (only 5 copies of state 2 have been noted out of some 70 copies examined). Five states of the outside rear wrapper have been noted:

State 1: Lists volumes I–X of Wiley and Putnam's *Library of American Books;* five titles "In Preparation."
State 2: Lists volumes I–XVI; five titles "In Immediate Preparation."
State 3: Lists volumes I–XVIII.
State 4: Lists volumes I–XX.
State 5: Lists volumes I–XXII.

State 1	State 2
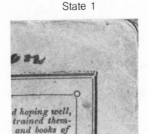	

Outside front wrapper

State 3 of the rear wrapper is the most common (one each only of states 1 and 2 have been reported). Spine imprint varies, with two states most common: state 1 has title imprint 4¹/₂" long; state 2 has title imprint 5¹/₁₆" long. No variant has been noted in the inside front wrapper. Two states of the inside rear wrapper have been found. The illustrations of the two states show sufficient identification.

Traditionally, the earliest printings of *MOSSES* have been identified on the basis of the state of the outside rear wrapper. This can be misleading. States of the wrappers are significant as binding variants only and should not be considered in assigning a priority to the printing of the text to which they are bound. The plates used to print the wrappers were paired up by the printer in various combinations as orders from the

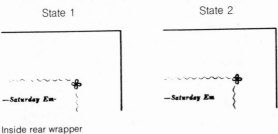

Inside rear wrapper

bindery for additional wrappers were filled, and no priority can be assigned to a particular combination with precision. Also, earliest printings of the text were not always bound with presumed earlier states of the wrappers. For example, copies of vols. I and II at Princeton University, which pair state 2 of the front wrappers with state 4 of the rear wrappers, are bound to second printings of the text, while a copy of vol. II in the Berg Collection, which pairs a state 2 front wrapper with a state 5 rear wrapper, is bound to a first printing of the text.

Separate volumes in two-in-one format bound in purple (234. d. p Gray), blue (187. d. gy. B), and green (136. m. y G) bold-ribbed T cloth with triple-rules frame enclosing eight-pointed center element blindstamped on front and rear covers. Title gold-stamped on spine (see illustration, A 15 bindings). White fibrous endpapers printed on one side with regular pattern of alternate red dots and small sunburst-like elements. Also buff endpapers. Also white wove endpapers coated pale yellow on one side. Top edges untrimmed in most copies examined.

Publication: Unknown number of copies published about 5 June 1846. Price 50¢ each for copies in wrappers; $1.25 for two-volumes-in-one clothbound issue.

Printing: Printed from stereotype plates made by T. B. Smith, 216 William Street, New York, and printed by R. Craighead's Power Press, 112 Fulton Street, New York.

Locations: Berg (I, 7 copies; II, 9 copies), CEFC (I, 1; II, 3), CtY (I, 4; II, 3), LC (deposited 5 June 1846) (I, 2; II, 1), MCo (I, 2; II, 1), MH (I, 5; II, 5), MoSW (I, 2; II, 2), MSaE (I, 1; II, 1), NN (I, 2; II, 2), OHi (I, 1; II, 1), PU (I, 1; II, 1), ViU (I, 2; II, 2); clothbound: CEFC, CtY, LC, OU.

Manuscripts: Hawthorne's manuscript of "The Old Manse" introduction located in the New York Public Library. Manuscript of "The Celestial Railroad" in the Parkman D. Howe collection. Manuscript of "Earth's Holocaust" in the Lilly Library, Indiana University. Manuscript of "Buds and Bird-Voices" in the C. E. Frazer Clark, Jr., collection.

Note two: E. T. Throop-Martin, Auburn, N.Y., collector, who had acquired the manuscript of "Buds and Bird-Voices," published anonymously an undated transcript of the manuscript. Probably published in the 1880s, the transcript was in the form of an 8-page pamphlet, with a facsimile of 'Buds and Bird-Voices. | By Nathaniel Hawthorne,' as it appeared at the head of the first page of the manuscript, together with a quotation from "A Book of Autographs," used as a cover title. No date, place, or publisher given. (Locations: ViU, CEFC, MJB.)

MOSSES

FROM

AN OLD MANSE.

BY NATHANIEL HAWTHORNE.

IN TWO PARTS.

PART I.

LONDON:

WILEY & PUTNAM, 6, WATERLOO PLACE.

1846.

[ENTERED AT STATIONERS' HALL.]

---

to be no deadly error in holding theological libraries to be accumulations of, for the most part, stupendous impertinence.

Many of the books had accrued in the latter years of the last clergyman's lifetime. These threatened to be of even less interest than the elder works, a century hence, to any curious inquirer who should then rummage them, as I was doing now. Volumes of the Liberal Preacher and Christian Examiner, occasional sermons, controversial pamphlets, tracts, and other productions of a like fugitive nature, took the place of the thick and heavy volumes of past time. In a physical point of view, there was much the same difference as between a feather and a lump of lead; but, intellectually regarded, the specific gravity of old and new was about upon a par. Both, also, were alike frigid. The elder books, nevertheless, seemed to have been earnestly written, and might be conceived to have possessed warmth at some former period; although, with the lapse of time, the heated masses had cooled down even to the freezing point. The frigidity of the modern productions, on the other hand, was characteristic and inherent, and evidently had little to do with the writers' qualities of mind and heart. In fine, of this whole dusty heap of literature, I tossed aside all the sacred part, and felt myself none the less a Christian for eschewing it. There appeared no hope of either mounting to the better world on a Gothic staircase of ancient folios, or of flying thither on the wings of a modern tract. Nothing, strange to say, retained any sap, except what had been written for the passing day and year, without the remotest pretension or idea of permanence. There were a few old newspapers, and still older almanacs, which re-produced, to my mental eye, the epochs when they had issued from the press, with a distinctness that was altogether unaccountable. It was as if I had found bits of magic looking-glass among the books, with the images of a vanished century in them. I turned my eyes towards the tattered picture, above-mentioned, and asked of the austere

A15.1.a2: Title page, 7½″ × 5″. Page format, 5⁹/₁₆″ (5¹³/₁₆″) × 3½″

A 15.1.a2
First edition, first printing, English issue [1846]

2 vols. Sheets of the first printing with a cancel English title in each volume.

I: [i–vi] [1] 2–207 [208]

II: [i–vi] [1] 2–211 [212]

I: [1]² (1₂+1) 2–9¹² 10⁶ [11]²

II: [1]² (1₂+1) 2–9¹² 10⁶ [11–12]²

Note: American title canceled and English title inserted between half title and contents in each volume.

Contents: *I:* p. i: half title; p. ii: blank; p. iii: title; p. iv: blank; p. v: contents; p. vi: blank; pp. 1–207: text, headed 'MOSSES FROM AN OLD MANSE. | [rule] | THE OLD MANSE. | The Author makes the Reader acquainted with his Abode.'; p. 208: blank.
II: p. i: half title; p. ii: blank; p. iii: title; p. iv: blank; p. v: contents; p. vi: blank; pp. 1–211: text, headed 'MOSSES FROM AN OLD MANSE. | [rule] | THE NEW ADAM AND EVE. | [rule]'; p. 212: blank.

Binding: Published in two clothbound volumes. Green (137. d. y G) bold-ribbed T cloth with wide decorative border panels enclosing central element blindstamped on front and rear covers. Title goldstamped on spine (see illustration, A 15 bindings). Buff wove endpapers yellow coated one side. Top and front edges untrimmed. Bound by Remnant & Edmonds, London.

Publication: Unknown number of sheets imported and bound for London distribution by Wiley and Putnam. Advertised in *Literary Gazette,* 11 July, and *Publishers' Circular,* 15 July 1846.

Locations: BM, 1154.h.15 (deposit-stamped, I: 25 Nov 47; II: 25 Nov 47), CEFC, NN, OU.

A 15.1.b
First edition, second American printing [1846]

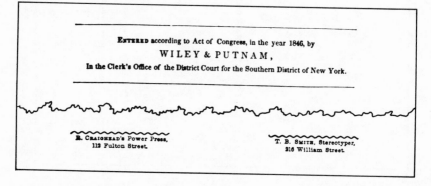

ENTERED according to Act of Congress, in the year 1846, by
WILEY & PUTNAM,
In the Clerk's Office of the District Court for the Southern District of New York.

R. CRAIGHEAD's Power Press,
112 Fulton Street.

T. B. SMITH, Stereotyper,
216 William Street.

2 vols. Second printing has Craighead and Smith imprints below copyright notice in vol. I, and verso of title page is blank in vol. 2. Text of second printing can be distinguished on the basis of type batter (see table under A 15.1.a1).

I: [i–vi] [1] 2–207 [208]

II: [i–vi] [1] 2–211 [212–216]

I: [1]² (1₂+1) 2–9¹² 10⁶ [11]²

II: [1]² (1₂+1) 2–10¹²

Contents: I: Same as in first printing. *II:*   p. i: half title; p. ii: blank; p. iii: title; p. iv: blank; p. v: contents; p. vi: blank; pp. 1–211: text, headed 'MOSSES FROM AN OLD MANSE. | [rule] | THE NEW ADAM AND EVE. | [rule]'; pp. 212–216: ads, headed 'NEW AND VALUABLE | BOOKS, | PUBLISHED BY | WILEY AND PUTNAM. | [rule] | NEW YORK: | [rule] | 1846.'

Binding: Same as on A 15.1.a₁. Also found as two volumes in wrappers and one cloth volume in two-in-one format. Some copies noted with final leaf or final two leaves of ads in vol. II removed. Top edge untrimmed in most copies examined.

Publication: Unknown number of copies printed not long after first printing. Some copies of two-volumes-in-one issue noted with first printing of vol. I bound with second printing of vol. II (Locations: CtY, DGU, LC).

Locations: CEFC, LC, MB, MdPB, MH, NjP, OCIW.

A 15.1.c₁
First edition, third printing, Wiley and Putnam issue [1846]

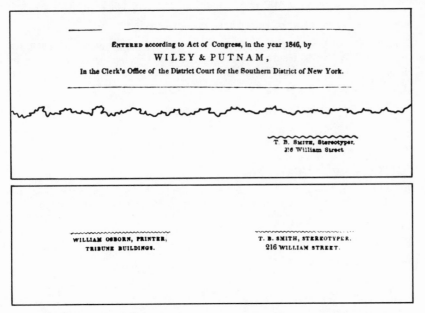

2 vols. Third printing, Wiley and Putnam issue, has W&P title pages with Smith imprint only below copyright notice in vol. I; vol. II has only Osborn and Smith imprints on verso of title page. Third printing can be distinguished on the basis of type batter (see table under A 15.1.a₁).

I: [i–vi] [1] 2–207 [208]

II: [i–vi] [1] 2–211 [212–216]

I: [1]² (1₂ + 1) 2–9¹² 10⁸

II: [1]² (1₂ + 1) 2–10¹²

Contents: I: Same as in first printing. *II:* Same as in second printing, except pp. 212–216 are blank.

Note: Final leaf of vol. II removed before binding in many copies examined.

A 15.1.c2
First edition, third printing, John Wiley issue [1849]

New York: John Wiley, 1849.

John Wiley issue has cancel title with third-printing sheets. Published in two-volumes-in-one format only.

[i–viii] [1] 2–207 [208], [1] 2–211 [212–216]

[1]^4 (1_1+1_2+1_3+1_4) 2–10^{12} 2–10^{12} (First gathering appears to consist of four single leaves.)

Contents: pp. i–ii: blank; p. iii: title; p. iv: blank; p. v: contents, vol. I; p. vi: blank; p. vii: contents, vol. II; p. viii: blank; pp. 1–207: text, headed 'MOSSES FROM AN OLD MANSE. | [rule] | THE OLD MANSE. | The Author makes the Reader acquainted with his Abode.'; p. 208: blank; pp. 1–211: text, headed 'MOSSES FROM AN OLD MANSE. | [rule] | THE NEW ADAM AND EVE. | [rule]'; pp. 212–216: blank.

Note: Final leaf or leaves may have been removed during binding.

Binding: Purple (234. d. p Gray) linen-like diagonal patterned cloth with 'LIBRARY OF CHOICE READING' blind embossed on covers and spine. Title goldstamped on spine (see illustration, A 15 bindings). Edges trimmed.

LATER PRINTINGS WITHIN THE FIRST EDITION

A 15.1.d
Fourth printing

New York: George P. Putnam, 1850.

Printed from the Wiley and Putnam plates and bound in cloth in two-volumes-in-one format. Published about July–August 1850. Price $1.25, with a probable 10% royalty.

A 15.1.e
Fifth printing

New York: George P. Putnam, 1851.

A 15.1.f
Sixth printing

New York: George P. Putnam, 1852.

MOSSES

FROM

AN OLD MANSE.

BY

NATHANIEL HAWTHORNE.

LONDON:

GEORGE ROUTLEDGE & CO., 36, SOHO SQUARE.

1851.

---

and deepest heart of a wood, which whispers it to be quiet, while the stream whispers back again from its sedgy borders, as if river and wood were hushing one another to sleep. Yes; the river sleeps along its course, and dreams of the sky, and of the clustering foliage; amid which fall showers of broken sunlight, imparting specks of vivid cheerfulness, in contrast with the quiet depth of the prevailing tint. Of all this scene, the slumbering river had a dream-picture in its bosom. Which, after all, was the most real—the picture, or the original?—the objects palpable to our grosser senses, or their spotlessness in the stream beneath? Surely, the disembodied images stand in closer relation to the soul. But both the original and the reflection had here an ideal charm; and had it been a thought more wild, I could have fancied that this river had strayed forth out of the rich scenery of my companion's inner world;—only the vegetation along its banks should then have had an oriental character.

Gentle and unobtrusive as the river is, yet the tranquil woods seem hardly satisfied to allow it passage. The trees are rooted on the very verge of the water, and dip their pendent branches into it. At one spot, there is a lofty bank, on the slope of which grow some hemlocks, declining across the stream, with outstretched arms, as if resolute to take the plunge. In other places, the banks are almost on a level with the water; so that the quiet congregation of trees set their feet in the flood, and are fringed with foliage down to the surface. Cardinal flowers kindle their spiral flames, and illuminate the dark nooks among the shrubbery. The pond-lily grows abundantly along the margin; that delicious flower which, as Thoreau tells me, opens its virgin bosom to the first sunlight, and perfects its being through the magic of that genial kiss. He has beheld beds of them unfolding in due succession, as the sunrise stole gradually from flower to flower; a sight not to be hoped for, unless when a poet adjusts his inward eye to a proper focus with the outward organ. Grape-vines, here and there, twine themselves around shrub and tree, and hang their clusters over the water, within reach of the boatman's hand. Oftentimes, they unite two trees of alien race in an inextricable twine, marrying the hemlock and the maple against their will, and enriching them with a purple offspring, of which neither is the parent. One of these ambitious parasites has climbed into the upper branches of a tall white pine, and is still ascending from bough to bough, unsatisfied, till it shall crown the tree's airy summit with a wreath of its broad foliage and a cluster of its grapes.

The winding course of the stream continually shut out the scene behind us, and revealed as calm and lovely a one before. We glided from depth to depth, and breathed new seclusion at every turn. The shy kingfisher flew from the withered branch close at hand, to another at a distance, uttering a shrill cry of anger or alarm. Ducks—that had been floating there since the preceding eve—were startled at our approach, and skimmed along the glassy river, breaking its dark surface with a bright streak.

ENGLISH PRINTINGS

A 15.2.a
First English edition, first printing, a piracy [1851]

[1–5] 6–256

[A]² B–I⁸ K–Q⁸ R⁶

Contents: p. 1: title; p. 2: blank; p. 3: contents; p. 4: blank; pp. 5–256: text, headed 'MOSSES FROM AN OLD MANSE. | [rule] | THE OLD MANSE. | The Author makes the Reader acquainted with his Abode.'

Tales and sketches: Includes in one volume same contents as in two-volume 1846 Wiley and Putnam edition (see A 15.1.a₁) except for "A Virtuoso's Collection," which was omitted.

Typography and paper: See illustration, A 15.2.a page format. Running heads: rectos, chapter titles; versos, 'MOSSES FROM AN OLD MANSE.' White wove paper.

Binding: Various issues bound by Routledge from the same sheets for marketing to various classes of trade: bound in fancy boards as no. 11 in *Routledge's Cheap Series* at 1s.; also bound in cloth and leather; also bound in various combinations with other titles. Copies noted bound with Bohn's *Snow-Image* (A 15.2.a). All edges trimmed.

Publication: Unknown number of copies probably published August–September 1851. Listed in *Athenaeum,* 13 September 1851.

Printing: Printed from stereotype plates by Savil & Edwards, 4 Chandos Street, Covent-Garden, London.

Location: CEFC (3).

A 15.2.b
Second printing

London: Routledge, 1852.

A 15.2.c
Third printing

London: Routledge, 1853. Reprint noted in 1873 (unlocated, see Browne).

MOSSES FROM AN OLD MANSE.

BY

NATHANIEL HAWTHORNE.

IN TWO VOLUMES.
VOL. I.

NEW EDITION,
CAREFULLY REVISED BY THE AUTHOR.

BOSTON:
TICKNOR AND FIELDS.
M.DCCC.LIV.

---

forth the ever-ready meal; but likewise almost as well by a man long habituated to city life, who plunges into such a solitude as that of the Old Manse, where he plucks the fruit of trees that he did not plant, and which therefore, to my heterodox taste, bear the closest resemblance to those that grew in Eden. It has been an apothegm these five thousand years, that toil sweetens the bread it earns. For my part, (speaking from hard experience, acquired while belaboring the rugged furrows of Brook Farm,) I relish best the free gifts of Providence.

Not that it can be disputed that the light toil requisite to cultivate a moderately-sized garden imparts such zest to kitchen vegetables as is never found in those of the market gardener. Childless men, if they would know something of the bliss of paternity, should plant a seed, — be it squash, bean, Indian corn, or perhaps a mere flower or worthless weed, — should plant it with their own hands, and nurse it from infancy to maturity altogether by their own care. If there be not too many of them, each individual plant becomes an object of separate interest. My garden, that skirted the avenue of the Manse, was of precisely the right extent. An hour or two of morning labor was all that it required. But I used to visit and revisit it a dozen times a day, and stand in deep contemplation over my vegetable progeny with a love that nobody could share or conceive of who had never taken part in the process of creation. It was one of the most bewitching sights in the world to observe a hill of beans thrusting aside the soil, or a row of early peas just peeping forth sufficiently to trace a line of delicate green. Later in the season

VOL. I.   2

A15.3.a: Title page, 7¹¹/₁₆″ × 4¹/₄″. Page format, 5¹/₈″ (5⁷/₁₆″) × 3″

PRINTINGS FROM THE T & F STEREOTYPE PLATES

A 15.3.a
Second American edition, first printing [1854]

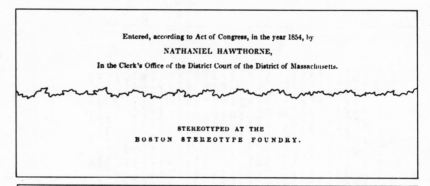

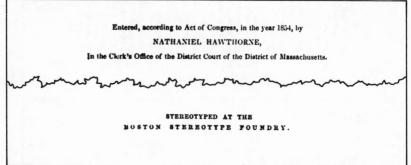

2 vols. Revised by Hawthorne, with a tale and two sketches added.

I: [1–2] 3 [4] 5–286 [287–288]

II: [1–2] 3 [4] 5–297 [298–300]

I: Signed [1]⁸ 2–18⁸; gathered in an alternating 8- and 4-leaf pattern [1]⁸ 2⁴ [3–24]⁸/₄

II: Signed [1]⁸ 2–18⁸ 19⁶; gathered in an alternating 8- and 4-leaf pattern [1]⁸ 2⁴ [3–24]⁸/₄ [25]⁶

Contents: I: p. 1: title; p. 2: copyright; p. 3: contents; p. 4: blank; pp. 5–286: text, headed 'MOSSES FROM AN OLD MANSE. | [rule] | THE OLD MANSE. | The Author makes the Reader acquainted with his Abode.'; pp. 287–288: blank.

   II: p. 1: title; p. 2: copyright; p. 3: contents; p. 4: blank; pp. 5–297: text, headed 'MOSSES FROM AN OLD MANSE. | [rule] | THE NEW ADAM AND EVE.'; pp. 298–300: blank.

Tales and sketches: I: Same as in vol. I of Wiley and Putnam first edition (A 15.1.a₁), with the addition of "Feathertop; a Moralized Legend."†

   II: Same as in vol. II of W&P first edition, with the addition of "Passages from a Relinquished Work"† and "Sketches from Memory."† Daggers (†) indicate first collected appearance.

Typography and paper: See illustration, A 15.3.a page format. Running heads: rectos, chapter titles; versos, 'MOSSES FROM AN OLD MANSE.' Wove paper.

Binding: Basic Ticknor trade binding (see illustration, A 2.6 binding, Ticknor format A). Brown (81. d. gy. y Br) bold-ribbed T cloth with title goldstamped on spines (see illustration, A 15 bindings). Pale yellow endpapers. Single white wove binder's leaf inserted front and rear. Eight-page catalogue of T&F books inserted between rear endpapers in some copies. All edges trimmed.

Publication: 1,000 copies of the 2-volume set published 18 September 1854. Price $1.50 per set, with a 10% royalty paid on 900 copies.

Printing: Stereotyped at the Boston Stereotype Foundry and printed by Thurston, Torry & Co., Boston. Probably bound by Benjamin Bradley & Co., Boston.

Locations: CEFC, CtY, LC, MB, NN.

Manuscript: Manuscript of "Feathertop" in the Morgan Library.

A 15.3.b
Boston: Ticknor and Fields, M DCCC LVII.

500 copies printed 19 June 1857. Price $1.50 per set, royalty 10%.

A 15.3.c
Boston: Ticknor and Fields, M DCCC LX.

280 copies printed 27 August 1860. Price $1.50 per set, royalty 10%.

A 15.3.d
Boston: Ticknor and Fields, 1863.

280 copies printed 21 October 1862. Price $2.00 per set, royalty 15¢.

A 15.3.e
Boston: Ticknor and Fields, 1864.

Note: Two printings with 1864 title-page date (see A 15.3.f), priority undetermined.

280 copies printed 13 May 1864. Price $2.50 per set, royalty 15¢.

A 15.3.f
Boston: Ticknor and Fields, 1864.

280 copies printed 20 September 1864. Price $3.00 per set, royalty 15¢ per set.

A 15.3.g
Boston: Ticknor and Fields, 1865.

Vols. 4 and 5 of untitled *"Tinted Edition"* on laid paper. 500 copies printed October 1864. Price $1.50 per volume, royalty 12¢ per volume. See B 1[4,5] for reprintings of the *"Tinted Edition."*

A 15.3.h
Boston: Ticknor and Fields, 1865.

500 Copies printed on wove paper 18 January 1865. Price $3.00 per set, royalty 25¢ per set.

A 15.3.i
Boston: Ticknor and Fields, 1866.

300 copies printed 14 August 1866. Price $3.00 per set, royalty 24¢ per set.

A 15.3.j
Boston: Ticknor and Fields, 1867.

280 copies printed 26 July 1867. Price $3.00 per set, royalty 24¢ per set.

A 15.3.k
Boston: Ticknor and Fields, 1871.

280 copies printed 13 September 1870. Price $4.00 per set, royalty 40¢ per set.

A 15.3.l
Boston: James R. Osgood, 1871.

Combined in two-volumes-in-one format and published as the second volume of the *Illustrated Library Edition*. 1,000 copies printed 3 June 1871. Price $2.00, royalty 20¢. See B 2 for reprintings of the *ILE*.

A 15.3.m
Boston: Houghton, Mifflin, 1880.

Combined with *The Scarlet Letter* and *The Blithedale Romance* in four-volumes-in-one format and published as the second volume of the *Globe Edition*. 1,500 copies printed August 1880. See B 3 for reprintings of the *Globe Edition*.

A 15.3.n
Boston: Houghton, Mifflin, [1886].

Combined with *The Scarlet Letter* and *The Blithedale Romance* in four-volumes-in-one format and published as the second volume of the *"New" Fireside Edition*. 1,000 copies printed May 1886. See B 4.

OTHER EDITIONS

A 15.4

MEMOIR OF | NATHANIEL HAWTHORNE | *WITH STORIES* | *NOW FIRST PUBLISHED IN THIS COUNTRY* | BY | H. A. PAGE | LONDON | HENRY S. KING & CO., 65 CORNHILL | 1872

Contains "Preface" and "Biographical Sketch" by Page (Alexander H. Japp), "Mother Rigby's Pipe" ("Feathertop"), "Passages from a Relinquished Work," "Sketches from Memory—The Notch of the White Mountains, The Canal Boat," "The Duston Family,"† "April Fools,"† "A Virtuoso's Collection," "A Prize from the Sea" ("The Sunken Treasure"). Daggers (†) indicate first collected appearance.

Locations: BM, 10882.bb.40 (deposit-stamp 11 JA 73); CEFC.

PRINTINGS FROM THE "LITTLE CLASSIC EDITION" PLATES

A 15.5.a

[All following within red and black double-rules frame] [red] Mosses from an Old Manse. | [black] BY | NATHANIEL HAWTHORNE. | VOL. I. [VOL. II.] | [vignette of manse] | [red] BOSTON: | [black] JAMES R. OSGOOD AND COMPANY, | Late Ticknor & Fields, and Fields, Osgood, & Co. | [red] 1876.

Vols. [IV] and [V], *"Little Classic Edition."* Contents same as in 1854 T&F edition (A 15.3.a). Sheets bound with James R. Osgood and, later, Houghton, Osgood spine imprints. 3,000 copies of each of the two volumes printed November–December 1875. Price $1.25 per volume, royalty 12.5¢ per volume. See B 5[IV,V] for reprintings of the *"Little Classic Edition."*

A 15.5.b
Boston: Houghton, Osgood, 1879.

Two volumes in one combined as vol. II of the *"Fireside Edition."* 500 copies printed 20 September 1879. See B 6[II] for reprintings of the *"Fireside Edition."*

A 15.5.c
Boston: Houghton, Mifflin, [1891].

Combined with *The Blithedale Romance* in three-volumes-in-one format and published as vol. II of the *Popular Edition.* 1,000 copies printed June–August 1891. See B 7 for reprintings of the *Popular Edition.*

A 15.5.d
Boston: Houghton, Mifflin, 1893.

Two-volumes-in-one format with *'SALEM EDITION'* slug on title page. Reprinted with 1894 title-page date and also an unknown number of times in various bindings with undated title page.

A 15.5.e
Boston: Houghton, Mifflin, [1899].

Vols. [IV] and [V], *Concord Edition.* See B 8.

OTHER EDITION

A 15.6

A Virtuoso's Collection, | AND OTHER TALES. | BY | NATHANIEL HAWTHORNE. | [cut of urn] | BOSTON: | JAMES R. OSGOOD AND COMPANY, | *Late Ticknor & Fields, and Fields, Osgood, & Co.* | 1877.

Contains "A Virtuoso's Collection," "The Celestial Railroad," "A Select Party." 1,500 copies printed 27 June 1877.

PRINTINGS FROM THE RIVERSIDE EDITION PLATES

A 15.7.a₁
Riverside Edition (trade), first printing, American issue [1883]

MOSSES FROM AN OLD MANSE | BY | NATHANIEL HAWTHORNE | [vignette of men fishing] | BOSTON | HOUGHTON, MIFFLIN AND COMPANY | New York: 11 East Seventeenth Street | The Riverside Press, Cambridge | 1883

Two volumes in one published as vol. II of the Riverside trade printing. Contents same as in vols. I and II of T&F edition (A 15.3.a), with "Introductory Note" by George

Parsons Lathrop added. 1,500 copies printed January 1883. Price $2.00. See B 9 for reprintings of the Riverside trade printing.

A 15.7.a2
Riverside Edition (trade), first printing, English issue [1883]

London: Kegan Paul, Trench, 1883.

Sheets of vol. II, first printing (A 15.7.a₁), with cancel title, in a Kegan Paul binding. 250 Kegan Paul title pages printed by Houghton, Mifflin, June–July 1883. Later issues noted with dated and undated Kegan Paul, Trench, Trübner title pages. See B 11.

A 15.7.b
Riverside Edition, (large paper), second printing [1883]

[red] MOSSES FROM AN OLD MANSE | [black] BY | NATHANIEL HAWTHORNE | [sepia vignette of men fishing] | [red] CAMBRIDGE | [black] Printed at the Riverside Press | 1883

Combined in two-volumes-in-one format and published as vol. II of the Riverside large-paper printing. 250 copies printed January 1883. See B 10.

A 15.7.c
Boston and New York: Houghton, Mifflin, 1884.

Vols. III and IV of the *Wayside Edition*. 500 copies printed September–October 1884. See B 12.

A 15.7.d
Boston and New York: Houghton, Mifflin, [1891].

Combined in two-volumes-in-one format and published as vol. II of the *Standard Library Edition*. 500 copies printed October 1891. See B 13.

A 15.7.e
Boston and New York: Houghton, Mifflin, [1902].

Combined in two-volumes-in-one format and published as vol. II of the *"New" Wayside Edition*. 500 copies printed September–October 1902. See B 14.

A 15.7.f
Boston and New York: [Houghton, Mifflin], MDCCCCIX.

Combined in two-volumes-in-one format and published as vol. II of the *Fireside Edition*. See B 15.

A 15.7.g
Boston, New York: Jefferson Press, [1913].

Combined in two-volumes-in-one format and published as vol. [II] of the *"Jefferson Press Edition."* See B 16.

OTHER EDITIONS

A 15.8
Printings from the Paterson-Scott plates

2 vols.

[I:] MOSSES | FROM AN OLD MANSE. | BY | NATHANIEL HAWTHORNE. | [portrait of Hawthorne] | EDINBURGH: | WILLIAM PATERSON. | 1883.

[II:] THE | NEW ADAM AND EVE, | ETC. | BEING THE SECOND SERIES OF | MOSSES FROM AN OLD MANSE. | BY | NATHANIEL HAWTHORNE. | [portrait of Hawthorne] | EDINBURGH: | WILLIAM PATERSON. | 1883.

Nos. 9 and 10, *Paterson's New England Novels.* Contents same as in 1854 T&F edition (A 15.3.a). Published in cloth, top edge gilded, at 2s. per volume; in ornamental paper covers at 1s. Also combined in two-in-one format and published as vol. [II] of the *"Paterson Edition."* See B 17. Also Paterson sheets found with cancel Walter Scott title. Also remanufactured from Paterson plates with Walter Scott title-page imprints. Later published as vols. [V] and [X] of the *"Walter Scott Edition"* (gravure). See B 18.

A 15.9
London: Frederick Warne, [1884].

Two volumes in one published as no. 115 in the *Chandos Classics.* Contents same as in 1854 T&F edition (A 15.3.a). Reprinted an unknown number of times.

Location: BM, 12204.ff.1/45 (deposit-stamp 17 DE 84).

A 15.10
New York: Hurst & Co., [n.d.].

[ca. 1888]. Two volumes in one, *Arlington Edition.* Contents same as in 1846 W&P edition (A 15.1.a1). Reprinted an unknown number of times in various bindings. Same plates used for 1895 F. M. Lupton printing, no. 213 in *The Elite Series* in wrappers. Also reprinted by Lupton in cloth.

A 15.11
Philadelphia: David McKay, 1889.

Two volumes in one, *American Classic Series.* Contents same as in 1854 T&F edition (A 15.3.a). Reprinted with 1893 imprint.

A 15.12

MOSSES | FROM | AN OLD MANSE | BY | NATHANIEL HAWTHORNE | [rule] | PHILADELPHIA | HENRY ALTEMUS | 1893

Two volumes in one published as no. 29 in *The Altemus Library.* Contents same as in 1854 T&F edition (A 15.3.a), omitting "Passages from a Relinquished Work" and "Sketches from Memory." Reprinted 1894 and 1895. Also reprinted without date on title page in various bindings. Also published as no. 12 in the *Altemus' New Illustrated Vademecum Series.*

A 15.13
London: Richard Edward King, [n.d.].

[ca. 1893]. Printings on different grades of paper, apparently for different classes of trade, in various bindings. Customized booksellers' titles inserted replacing King title in some copies.

A 15.14
London: George Bell, 1894.

Two volumes in one published as vol. IV, *Hawthorne's Novels and Tales,* in the *Bohn's Standard Library.* Contents same as in 1854 T&F edition (A 15.3.a).

A 15.15
The Old Manse and a Few Mosses. Boston, New York, Chicago, San Francisco: Houghton, Mifflin, [1894].

No. 69, *Riverside Literature Series*. Contains "Introductory Note," "The Old Manse," "Drowne's Wooden Image," "Feathertop: a Moralized Legend," "The Old Apple Dealer." Wrappers.

A 15.16
The New Adam and Eve. London, New York, Chicago: F. Tennyson Neely, 1899.

No. 25, *Neely's Booklet Library*. Prints title story only. Printed wrappers.

PRINTINGS FROM THE AUTOGRAPH EDITION PLATES

A 15.17.a
Boston and New York: Houghton, Mifflin, MDCCCC.

Vols. IV and V of the *Autograph Edition*. Contents same as in 1854 T&F edition (A 15.3.a), with addition of new "Introductory Note" and "Bibliographical Note" at front of vol. IV. 500 copies. Deposited 20 December 1900. See B 20.

A 15.17.b
Boston and New York: Houghton, Mifflin, MDCCCC.

Vols. IV and V of the *Large-Paper (Autograph) Edition*. 500 copies. See B 21.

A 15.17.c
Boston and New York: Houghton, Mifflin, 1903.

Vols. IV and V of the *Old Manse Edition*. See B 22.

OTHER EDITIONS

A 15.18
New York: Thomas Y. Crowell, [1900].

[c. 1900]. 2 vols. *Crowell Handy Volume Classics Series*. Introduction by Katherine Lee Bates. Contents same as in 1854 T&F edition (A 15.3.a). Also reprinted as vols. [3] and [4] of the *Crowell "Lenox Edition."* See B 23.

A 15.19
New York: Thomas Y. Crowell, n.d.

[c. 1902]. Combined in two-volumes-in-one format and published as vol. [3] of the *Crowell "Popular Edition."* See B 24.

A 15.20
New York: P. F. Collier, MCMIII.

Contents same as in 1854 T&F edition (A 15.3.a), omitting "Passages from a Relinquished Work."

A 15.21
The Old Manse. [Cambridge, Mass.]: The Riverside Press, 1904.

Prints title story only. Boards, cloth shelfback, boxed. 530 numbered copies.

A 15.22
A Virtuoso's Collection. With an Introduction by J. Christian Bay. Cedar Rapids, Iowa: Friends of the Torch Press, Nineteen Forty-Nine.

Boards, cloth shelfback, printed paper label on front cover. 400 copies.

A 15.23
[Columbus]: Ohio State University Press, [1974].

Vol. X of the *Centenary Edition.* 2,506 copies published 1 November 1974. See B 32.

Bindings for (1) A16.1; (2) A16.4.a; (3) A16.2; (4) A16.3.a; (5) A16.4.b, *Bohn's Cheap Series*; (6) A16.3.c; (7) A16.4.d; (8) A16.5.a, format B; (9) A16.7; (10) A16.10; (11) A16.13.g (see also illustration at A16.4.b)

THE

SCARLET LETTER,

A ROMANCE.

BY

NATHANIEL HAWTHORNE.

BOSTON:
TICKNOR, REED, AND FIELDS.
M DCCC L.

---

he casts his leaves forth upon the wind, the author addresses, not the many who will fling aside his volume, or never take it up, but the few who will understand him, better than most of his schoolmates and lifemates. Some authors, indeed, do far more than this, and indulge themselves in such confidential depths of revelation as could fitingly be addressed, only and exclusively, to the one heart and mind of perfect sympathy; as if the printed book, thrown at large on the wide world, were certain to find out the divided segment of the writer's own nature, and complete his circle of existence by bringing him into communion with it. It is scarcely decorous, however, to speak all, even where we speak impersonally. But — as thoughts are frozen and utterance benumbed, unless the speaker stand in some true relation with his audience — it may be pardonable to imagine that a friend, a kind and apprehensive, though not the closest friend, is listening to our talk; and then, a native reserve being thawed by this genial consciousness, we may prate of the circumstances that lie around us, and even of ourself, but still keep the inmost Me behind its veil. To this extent and within these limits, an author, methinks, may be autobiographical, without violating either the reader's rights or his own.

It will be seen, likewise, that this Custom-House sketch has a certain propriety, of a kind always recognized in literature, as explaining how a large portion of the following pages came into my possession, and as offering proofs of the authenticity of a narrative therein contained. This, in fact, — a desire to put myself in

A16.1: Title page, 7¹/₈″ × 4³/₈″; 'SCARLET LETTER,' in red in A16.1, A16.2, A16.3.a. Page format, 5″ (5³/₈″) × 2¹⁵/₁₆″

A 16 THE SCARLET LETTER

A 16.1
First edition, only printing [1850]

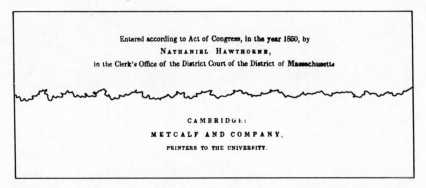

First edition has contents listed on pp. iii–iv and no preface. Preface first appears in second edition on pp. iii–iv with contents listed on pp. v–vi. See table for variants between first and second editions.

Variants Between the First and Second Editions

The first edition reading is given to the left of the bracket; the second edition reading is to the right of the bracket. All variants are given. Variants listed on pp. 238 through 301 are variants in standing type.

6.23   door, [door
9.26   Charter Street [Charter-Street
17.4   pleasant, [pleasant
21.20 reduplicate [repudiate
26.14 distance, [distance
31.7   for a [fora
31.20 me [me,
41.5   characterss [characters
46.25 convulsives [convulsive
46.27 that, [that
48.8   or the [or in the
50.22 altogether [although
51.21 Meanwhile, [Meanwhile
61.5   Madam [Madame
61.31 into the sunshine [into sunshine
62.12 free-will [free will
64.10 of the [of her
68.1   concentred [concentrated
74.25 But, [But
76.3   Prynne! [Prynne,
84.12 patient," [patient,
88.18 "True!" ["True,"
90.10 life, . . . fame; [life; . . . fame,
99.17 stedfast [steadfast

102.22 t obelieve [or] tobelieve [to believe
103.6 Sometimes, [Sometimes
105.6 became [become
106.3 be for good [be good
106.28 cottage-floor [cottage floor
107.16 being, [being
107.22 then, [then
108.20 strict, [strict
108.28 whether addressed [whethera dressed
113.26 out, [out
115.13 malice, [malice
117.4 she, [she
117.22 mothers' [mother's
121.31 occurrences [occurrences,
124.6 deep [keep
129.20 that this [thatthis
132.29 Chatechism [Catechims
137.6 is weighty [is a weighty
143.30 roots [roots,
163.24 minister [minister,
169.3 token, [token
171.2 their [the
183.10 which, [which
188.23 there, [there
189.1 oath, [oath
189.23 said [answered
191.3 minister [minister,
193.10 come, [come
198.16 circumstance [circumstance,
199.4 known of it [known it
203.6 there, [there
208.19 all? [all!
209.21 m ust [must
211.1 but, [but
218.9 stedfast [steadfast
224.8 her, [her
228.2 time [or] time! [time,
238.31 grown [prown
253.23 stedfastly [steadfastly
279.12 looks, [looks
279.21 But, [But
280.5 -time, [-time
300.10 harrassed [harassed
300.13 roundabout [round about
301.16 painfully [painfully,

[i–iii] iv [1] 2–54 [55] 56–322 [323–324]

[a]² 1–20⁸ 21²

Contents: p. i: title; p. ii: copyright; pp. iii–iv: contents; pp. 1–54: text, headed 'THE CUSTOM-HOUSE. | INTRODUCTORY TO "THE SCARLET LETTER." | [rule]'; pp. 55–322: text, headed 'THE SCARLET LETTER. | [rule] | I. [THE PRISON-DOOR.'; pp. 323–324: blank.

Typography and paper: See illustration, A 16.1 page format. Running heads: rectos, titles of introductory essay and chapters; versos, 'THE SCARLET LETTER.' White wove paper.

Binding: In style of Ticknor format A (see illustration, A 2.6 bindings). Brown (81. d. gy. y Br) bold-ribbed T cloth with blindstamped floral device inside ruled panels on both covers. Spine goldstamped (see illustration, A 16 bindings). Cream-colored wove endpapers. Flyleaf inserted at front and rear. 4 pp. of T&F ads with various dates inserted between front endpapers in most copies. All edges trimmed. Dates on ads have no bibliographical significance for the printing of the text bound with them.

Note one: Advertisements in the 2, 9, and 16 March 1850 *New York Literary World* announced that *The Scarlet Letter* would be available in cloth and paper bindings. No evidence has yet been found that paperbound copies appeared in 1850. One copy made up of 1851 stereotyped-edition sheets bound in a stiff paper cover dated 1850 survives in the Berg Collection (Location: NN). However, the back cover of the Berg copy carries an ad for *The House of the Seven Gables* (published 9 April 1851). An entry in the *Cost Books* (A 217c) for "Covers for Scarlet Letter" notes that four quires of paper were sent to I. R. Butts on 15 April 1851 for two-color printing. The covers of the Berg copy are printed in red and black. On 24 April 1851, Ticknor & Fields wrote Bangs Bros., the New York trade-sale dealers, to expect 25 copies of the paperbound *Scarlet Letter* (*Letter Books,* III, 33, 51–52).

Publication: 2,500 copies published 16 March 1850. Price 75¢, with a 25 percent discount to the trade. Hawthorne received a 15% royalty on 2,400 copies.

Printing: Composed and printed from type metal by Metcalf & Co., Cambridge, Mass. Probably bound by Benjamin Bradley & Co., Boston.

Note two: Gathering 21, which consists of two leaves (pp. 321–322, text; pp. 323–324, blank), was set up by the printer in duplicate, presumably for production economy. There is no textual variation in the duplicate settings of pp. 321–322, and since the two settings were machined simultaneously, no priority can be assigned to either. The two settings represent states that can be easily differentiated (see table for states x^1 and x^2). Also lines 9–11 on p. 321 of state x^1 were reset creating two substates, as

	P. 321	P. 322
State x^1	simple slab of s may still discern ort — there appea 21	motto and brief des egend; so sombre r-glowing point of LETTER A, GULES."
State x^2	simple slab of s may still discern ort — there appea 21	motto and brief des egend; so sombre r-glowing point of LETTER A, GULES."

can be distinguished by the presence or absence of work-up in line 10 after the word "that."

Also, in gathering a the type used to print the copyright notice appears to have loosened since there are two settings for the second and third lines of the copyright notice: in state a¹ the first limb of the "N" is under the "o" in "according," in state a² the "N" is beneath the "r" in "according." Also, the "1" of "192" on p. iii loosened and moved out of position (see table for states a¹ and a²).

Note three: Ticknor & Fields sent sheets of the first edition to Richard Bentley, London, with whom they had a half-profits arrangement, in an effort to secure English publication. Bentley refused the project because two other English publishers were pirating the work. Hawthorne received no royalty on the many English printings of *The Scarlet Letter.*

Locations: CEFC, MH, NN, OU, ViU; x¹: CEFC, OU, ViU; x²: CEFC, OU, ViU; a¹: CEFC, ViU; a²: CEFC, OU, ViU.

Manuscript: The leaf with the title on the recto and the table of contents on the verso is all that survives of *The Scarlet Letter* manuscript (Location: NNMP). See Mathew J. Bruccoli, "Notes on the Destruction of *The Scarlet Letter* Manuscript," *Studies in Bibliography,* 20 (1967), 257–259.

Note four: Collector interest in the first edition of *The Scarlet Letter* has encouraged the manufacture of "sophisticated" copies of this rare book. Because of the similarity between the first and second editions, a common form of sophistication is the removal of the preface leaf from the second edition. Also, various techniques have been used to improve the condition of a "first edition," including recasing.

	P. ii	P. iii
		154
	ed according to Act of Congress, i	167
State a¹	NATHANIEL HAWTH(	177
	Office of the District Court of the	192
		203
		154
	ed according to Act of Congress, i	167
State a²	NATHANIEL HAWTH(	177
	Office of the District Court of the	192
		203

A 16.2
Second edition, only printing [1850]

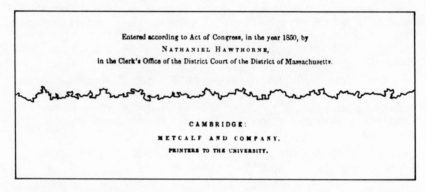

Boston: Ticknor, Reed, and Fields, M DCCC L.

Second edition has first appearance of Hawthorne's 'PREFACE | TO THE SECOND EDITION' on pp. iii–iv, contents on pp. v–vi.

Note one: P. 9 missing the numeral "9" in some copies, apparently as a result of loosened type.

[A–B] [i–iii] iv [v] vi [1] 2–54 [55] 56–322 [323–324]

[a]² b² 1–20⁸ 21²

Contents: pp. A–B: blank; p. i: title; p. ii: copyright; pp. iii–iv: preface; pp. v–vi: contents; pp. 1–54: text, headed 'THE CUSTOM HOUSE. | INTRODUCTORY TO "THE SCARLET LETTER." | [rule]'; pp. 55–322: text, headed 'THE SCARLET LETTER. | [rule] | I. | THE PRISON-DOOR.'; pp. 323–324: blank.

Typography and paper: Same as in first edition.

Binding: Same as in first edition.

Publication: 2,500 copies published 22 April 1850. Price 75¢, with a royalty of 15% on 2,500 copies.

Printing: Partly reset and printed from type metal by Metcalf & Co., Cambridge, Mass., and probably bound by Benjamin Bradley & Co., Boston.

Note two: First-edition type was partially distributed before work was begun on the second edition. Type was completely reset through gathering 13; some standing type from the first edition was salvaged for use in gatherings 14–15; gatherings 16–21 were printed largely from first edition standing type. *Centenary* distinguished a total of 226 reset type pages in the second edition and 96 pages of standing type. Variants between the first and second editions are given in the list under A 16.1 (see pages 142–143).
   No first-edition standing type was used to print preliminary gatherings a and b of the second edition. Both preliminary gatherings were set in duplicate and probably

printed in one 16-page form. The two settings of each gathering can easily be differentiated (see table for states y^1 and y^2).

P. ii   P. iv

State y^1

CAMBRIDGE:
METCALF AND COMPANY,
PRINTERS TO THE UNIVERSITY.

State z^1

sclaims
s, have
public,
under-
uld not

State y^2

CAMBRIDGE:
METCALF AND COMPANY,
PRINTERS TO THE UNIVERSITY.

State z^2

sclaims
s, have
public
under-
uld not

There is no consistency in the way the gatherings are bound up, and all four possible combinations (y^1z^1, y^1z^2, y^2z^1, y^2z^2) of substates have been noted. No priority can be assigned.

Locations: y^1z^1: ViU; y^1z^2: CEFC, OU, ViU; y^2z^1: CEFC, OU; y^2z^2: CEFC, ICU, ViU.

A 16.3.a
Third edition, first printing (first plated edition) [1850]

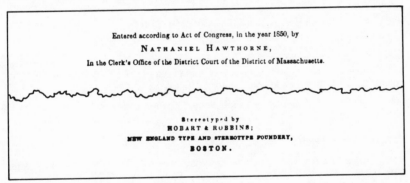

Boston: Ticknor, Reed, and Fields, M DCCC L.

Third edition has Hobart & Robbins imprint on copyright page, and last page of text is numbered 307.

[A–B] [i–iii] iv [v] vi [1] 2–51 [52–53] 54–307 [308]

[A]^4 1–19^8 20^2

Contents: pp. A–B: blank; p. i: title; p. ii: copyright; pp. iii–iv: preface; pp. v–vi: contents; pp. 1–51: text, headed 'THE CUSTOM-HOUSE. | INTRODUCTORY TO "THE SCARLET LETTER." | [rule].'; p. 52: blank; pp. 53–307: text, headed 'THE SCARLET LETTER. | [rule] | I. | THE PRISON-DOOR.'; p. 308: blank.

Publication: 1,000 copies printed 9 September 1850. Price 75¢, with a 15% royalty.

Printing: Entirely reset, with stereotype plates made by Hobart & Robbins, New England Type & Stereotype Foundry, Boston, and printed by Wier and White, Boston. Probably bound by Benjamin Bradley & Co., Boston.

Locations: CEFC, CtY, MH, NN.

REPRINTS FROM THE T&F STEREOTYPE PLATES

A 16.3.b
Second printing

Boston: Ticknor, Reed, and Fields, M DCCC LI.

[A–B] [i–iii] iv [v] vi [1] 2–51 [52–53] 54–307 [308]

[A]⁴ 1–19⁸ 20²

Note: Second and third printings of the stereotyped edition both have an 1851 title-page date. Third printing has two additional leaves (all blank) in gathering 20 (see A 16.3.c).

800 copies published June 1851. Price 75¢, royalty 15%.

A 16.3.c
Third printing

Boston: Ticknor, Reed, and Fields, M DCCC LI.

[A–B] [i–iii] iv [v] vi [1] 2–51 [52–53] 54–307 [308–312]

[A]⁴ 1–19⁸ 20⁴

Note: The priority of the two 1851 printings is confirmed by the *Cost Books* entries, which show a slightly greater per-copy amount of paper used for the later printing, as accounted for in the two additional leaves in gathering 20 (see A 16.3.b).

500 copies printed 23 September 1853. Price 75¢, royalty 15%.

A 16.3.d
Boston: Ticknor, Reed, and Fields, M DCCC LII.

Note: Three printings with 1852 title-page date (see A 16.3.e, A 16.3.f), priority undetermined.

T&F ads on pp. 309–312. 500 copies printed April 1852. Price 75¢, royalty 15%.

A 16.3.e
Boston: Ticknor, Reed, and Fields, M DCCC LII.

500 copies printed 28 August 1852. Price 75¢, royalty 15%.

A 16.3.f
Boston: Ticknor, Reed, and Fields, M DCCC LII.

500 copies printed 16 October 1852. Price 75¢, royalty 15%.

A 16.3.g
Boston: Ticknor, Reed, and Fields, M DCCC LIII.

Note: Two printings with 1853 title-page date (see A 16.3.h), priority undetermined.

500 copies printed 14 April 1853. Price 75¢, royalty 15%.

A 16.3.h
Boston: Ticknor, Reed, and Fields, M DCCC LIII.

500 copies printed October 1853. Price 75¢, royalty 15%.

A 16.3.i
Boston: Ticknor and Fields, M DCCC LIV.

500 copies printed 30 June 1854. Price 75¢, royalty 15%.

A 16.3.j
Boston: Ticknor and Fields, M DCCC LV.

500 copies printed 12 September 1855. Price 75¢, royalty 15%.

A 16.3.k
Boston: Ticknor and Fields, M DCCC LVI.

500 copies printed 29 September 1856. Price 75¢, royalty 15%.

A 16.3.l
Boston: Ticknor and Fields, M DCCC LVIII.

500 copies printed 2 June 1858. Price 75¢, royalty 15%.

A 16.3.m
Boston: Ticknor and Fields, M DCCC LX.

Note: Two printings with 1869 title-page date (see A 16.3.n), priority undetermined.
Stereotyper's slug removed from copyright page.

500 copies printed 19 March 1860. Price 75¢, royalty 15%.

A 16.3.n
Boston: Ticknor and Fields, M DCCC LX.

500 copies printed August 1860. Price 75¢, royalty 15%.

A 16.3.o
Boston: Ticknor and Fields, 1862.

500 copies printed 10 May 1862. Price 75¢, royalty 15%.

A 16.3.p
Boston: Ticknor and Fields, 1864.

500 copies printed 1 August 1864. Price $1.50, royalty 11.25¢.

A 16.3.q
Boston: Ticknor and Fields, 1865.

Vol. 6 of untitled *"Tinted Edition"* on laid paper. 500 copies printed 31 October 1864.

Price $1.50, royalty 12¢. Welch, Bigelow imprint added to copyright page. See B 1 for reprintings of the *"Tinted Edition."*

A 16.3.r
Boston: Ticknor and Fields, 1865.

Note: Two printings on wove paper with 1865 title-page date (see A 16.3.s), priority undetermined.

525 copies printed 11 November 1864. Price $1.50, royalty 11.25¢.

A 16.3.s
Boston: Ticknor and Fields, 1865.

500 copies, on wove paper, printed June 1865. Price $1.50, royalty 12¢.

A 16.3.t
Boston: Ticknor and Fields, 1866.

Note: Two printings with 1866 title-page date (see A 16.3.u), priority undetermined.

550 copies printed 25 July 1866. Price $1.50, royalty 12¢.

A 16.3.u
Boston: Ticknor and Fields, 1866.

270 copies printed August 25, 1866. Price $1.50, royalty 12¢.

A 16.3.v
Boston: Fields, Osgood, 1871.

280 copies printed 24 March 1871. Price $2.00, royalty 20¢.

A 16.3.w
Boston: James R. Osgood, 1871.

Combined with *The Blithedale Romance* in two-volumes-in-one format and published as the third volume of the *Illustrated Library Edition.* 1,000 copies printed 25 June 1871. Price $2.00, royalty 20¢. See B 2 for reprintings of the *ILE.*

A 16.3.x
Boston: James R. Osgood, 1871.

A 16.3.y
Boston: James R. Osgood, 1872.

140 copies printed 19 June 1872. Price $2.00, royalty 20¢.

A 16.3.z
Boston: James R. Osgood, 1878.

174 copies printed 7 May 1878. Royalty 15¢.

A 16.3.aa
Boston: Houghton, Mifflin, 1880.

Combined with *The Blithedale Romance* and *Mosses from an Old Manse* in four-volumes-in-one format and published as the second volume of the *Globe Edition.* 1,500 copies printed August 1880. See B 3 for reprintings of the *Globe Edition.*

A 16.3.ab
Boston: Houghton, Mifflin, [1886].

Combined with *The Blithedale Romance* and *Mosses from an Old Manse* in four-volumes-in-one format and published as the second volume of the *"New" Fireside Edition*. 1,000 copies printed May 1886. See B 4.

THE

SCARLET LETTER:

A Romance.

BY

NATHANIEL HAWTHORNE.

LONDON:
(PUBLISHED FOR J. WALKER)
DAVID BOGUE, FLEET STREET;
HAMILTON AND CO.; JOHNSTONE AND HUNTER; H. WASHBOURNE.
EDINBURGH: JOHNSTONE AND HUNTER; OLIVER AND BOYD.
DUBLIN: JAMES M'GLASHAN.
1851.

and forms the type whereby I recognise the man. As most of these old Custom-house officers had good traits, and as my position in reference to them, being paternal and protective, was favourable to the growth of friendly sentiments, I soon grew to like them all. It was pleasant in the summer forenoons,—when the fervent heat, that almost liquefied the rest of the human family, merely communicated a genial warmth to their half-torpid systems,—it was pleasant to hear them chatting in the back entry, a row of them all tipped against the wall, as usual; while the frozen witticisms of past generations were thawed out, and came bubbling with laughter from their lips. Externally, the jollity of aged men has much in common with the mirth of children; the intellect, any more than a deep sense of humour, has little to do with the matter; it is, with both, a gleam that plays upon the surface, and imparts a sunny and cheery aspect alike to the green branch, and grey, mouldering trunk. In one case, however, it is real sunshine; in the other, it more resembles the phosphorescent glow of decaying wood.

It would be sad injustice, the reader must understand, to represent all my excellent old friends as in their dotage. In the first place, my coadjutors were not invariably old; there were men among them in their strength and prime, of marked ability and energy, and altogether superior to the sluggish and dependent mode of life on which their evil stars had cast them. Then, moreover, the white locks of age were sometimes found to be the thatch of an intellectual tenement in good repair. But, as respects the

OTHER EDITIONS

A 16.4.a
First English edition, first printing, a piracy [*1851*]

[i–iii] iv [5] 6–320

[B]⁸ C–I⁸ K–U⁸ X⁸

Contents: p. i: title; p. ii: printer's imprint; pp. iii–iv: contents; pp. 5–320: text, headed 'THE SCARLET LETTER. | [rule] | The Custom-House. | INTRODUCTORY.'

Typography and paper: See illustration, A 16.4.a page format. Running heads: rectos, chapter titles; versos, 'THE SCARLET LETTER.' White wove paper.

Binding: Red (13. deep Red) bold-ribbed T cloth; faded rose (19. gy. Red) bold-ribbed T cloth. Covers with blindstamped double-rules frame and corner elements. Spine goldstamped (see illustration, A 16 bindings). White wove endpapers cream coated one side. Top edge untrimmed in most copies. Bound by Remnant & Edmonds, London. Also noted in faded olive (111. d. gy. Ol) smooth V-like cloth with blind-embossed floral pattern overall. Gilt-imprinted black leather label on spine. White wove endpapers. Single flyleaf inserted at front and rear. Top edge untrimmed in most copies.

Publication: Unknown number of copies. Listed in the London *Athenaeum,* 17 May 1851; *Publishers' Circular,* 2 June 1851.

Printing: Printed by Knight and Son, Clerkenwell Close, London.

Locations: BM, 12705.aa.63 (deposit-stamp 8 JY 51); CEFC.

A 16.4.b
First English edition, second printing, a piracy [*1852*]

THE | SCARLET LETTER. | A Romance. | BY | NATHANIEL HAWTHORNE. | LONDON: | HENRY G. BOHN, YORK STREET, COVENT GARDEN. | 1852.

Same pagination and collation as in first English printing (A 16.4.a). Contents same as in first printing except that Harrison and Son imprint replaces Knight and Son imprint on verso of title page and at foot of p. 320 (later printings omit Harrison and Son imprint at foot of p. 320).

Note: Various binding issues produced by Bohn from the same sheets for marketing to various classes of trade, priority uncertain:
   A. *Bohn's Cheap Series.* No. 38 in *BCS.* Green (135. l. y G) paper-covered boards (see illustration, A 16.4.b binding A). Price 1s. Location: CEFC.
   B. *Uniform With Bohn's Standard Library.* Combined with *The House of the Seven Gables* (A 17.2) and published in two-volumes-in-one format as vol. II, *Nathaniel Hawthorne's Tales.* Price 3s. 6d. Location: CEFC.
   C. Cloth, at 1s. 6d., and custom leather-bound volumes in various formats. Location: CEFC.

A 16.4.c
London: Bell & Daldy, 1866.

Combined with *The House of the Seven Gables* in two-volumes-in-one format and published as vol. II, *Nathaniel Hawthorne's Tales* (see A 17.2.c), with volume title added. Each part paged separately. Noted with separate titles for each part preserved, both with London: Bell & Daldy, 1870 title-page imprint.

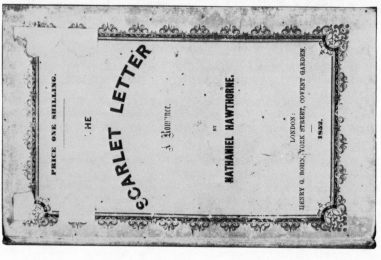

Front cover for A16.4.b, *Bohn's Cheap Series*, and A16.5.a, *The Railway Library*

A 16.4.d
London: Bell & Daldy, 1871.

Published as a separate volume. Also combined with *The House of the Seven Gables* in two-volumes-in-one format and published as vol. II, *Nathaniel Hawthorne's Tales* (see A 16.4.c), with volume title only. Each part paged separately. Reprinted with London: Bell & Daldy, 1873 title-page imprint. Also new edition in similar format published 1877 (see A 16.9).

A 16.5.a
Second English edition, first printing, a piracy [1851]

THE | SCARLET LETTER: | A Romance | BY | NATHANIEL HAWTHORNE. | [rule] | LONDON: | GEORGE ROUTLEDGE AND CO., SOHO SQUARE. | 1851.

Note: Various binding issues produced by Routledge from the same sheets for marketing to different classes of trade in competition with Bohn, priority undetermined:

A. *The Railway Library.* No. 30 in Routledge's *RL.* Bound in green (135. l. y G) paper-covered boards, imprinted in blue ink (see illustration, A 16.5.a binding [A]). Price 1s. Location: CEFC. Also in cloth at 1s. 6d. Location: CEFC.

B. *Routledge's Standard Novels.* Combined with *The House of the Seven Gables* and published in two-volumes-in-one format in *RSN* series. Price 2s. 6d. Volume title leaf inserted to replace *Scarlet Letter* title, frontispiece added. Location: CEFC.

C. Also combined with *The House of the Seven Gables* in two-volumes-in-one format with the original title and contents leaves for each title preserved. Location: CEFC.

A 16.5.b
London: G. Routledge, 1852.

A 16.5.c
London: G. Routledge, 1853.

A 16.5.d
London: G. Routledge, 1854.

'THIRTY-FIFTH THOUSAND' slug on title page.

A 16.5.e
London: G. Routledge, 1856.

'THIRTY-SEVENTH THOUSAND' slug on title page.

A 16.5.f
London: George Routledge, 1865.

'NEW EDITION' slug on title page. Reprint. New edition noted in 1887 (see A 16.16).

LATER EDITIONS

A 16.6

THE | SCARLET LETTER, | A ROMANCE. | BY | NATHANIEL HAWTHORNE. | COPYRIGHT EDITION. | LEIPZIG | BERNHARD TAUCHNITZ | 1852.

Vol. 226, *Tauchnitz Collection of British Authors.* In cloth and printed wrappers. Reprinted using same plates. Later printings advertise Hawthorne titles published after 1860.

A 16.7
London: Charles H. Clarke, n.d.

1859. Illustrations by Miss M. E. Dear.

Locations: BM, 12704.g.17 (deposit-stamp 18 NO 59); CEFC.

PRINTINGS FROM THE ''LITTLE CLASSIC EDITION'' PLATES

A 16.8.a

[All following within red and black double-rules frame] THE | [red] Scarlet Letter. | [black] BY | NATHANIEL HAWTHORNE. | [vignette of graveyard] | [red] BOSTON: | [black] JAMES R. OSGOOD AND COMPANY, | Late Ticknor & Fields, and Fields, Osgood, & Co. | [red] 1875.

Vol. [VI], *"Little Classic Edition."* Contents same as in third T&F edition (A 16.3.a). Sheets bound with James R. Osgood and, later, Houghton, Osgood spine imprints. 3,000 copies printed 5 October 1875. Deposited 22 October 1874. Price $1.25, royalty 12.5¢. See B 5[VI] for reprintings of the *"Little Classic Edition."*

A 16.8.b
Boston: Houghton, Osgood, 1879.

Combined with *The Blithedale Romance* in two-volumes-in-one format and published as vol. III of the *"Fireside Edition."* 500 copies printed 20 September 1879. See B 6[III] for reprintings of the *"Fireside Edition."*

A 16.8.c
Boston: Houghton, Mifflin, [1891].

Combined with *The Marble Faun* in three-volumes-in-one format and published as vol. III of the *Popular Edition*. 1,000 copies printed June–August 1891. See B 7 for reprintings of the *Popular Edition*.

A 16.8.d
Boston and New York: Houghton, Mifflin, 1892.

'*SALEM EDITION*' slug on title page. "Introduction" by George Parsons Lathrop. Reprinted with 1893 title-page date. Also issued with London: Gay & Bird, 1893 title bound with *Salem Edition* sheets (unlocated, see Browne).

Note: This *Salem Edition* printing of the *"Little Classic Edition"* plates is not to be confused with the *Salem Edition* printing of the *Riverside Edition* plates (see A 16.13.f).

A 16.8.e
Boston: Houghton, Mifflin, [1899].

Vol. [VI], *Concord Edition*. See B 8.

OTHER EDITIONS

A 16.9
London: George Bell and Sons, 1877.

Combined with *The House of the Seven Gables* in two-volumes-in-one format and published as vol. II, *Nathaniel Hawthorne's Tales* (see A 16.4.d and A 17.2.e), with volume title only. Volume paged continuously. Reprinted 1881, 1884. Also reprinted 1886 and 1892 in *Bohn's Standard Library.*

A 16.10
Boston: James R. Osgood, 1878.

Illustrated by Mary Hallock Foote. 3,650 copies printed 16 October 1877. Reprinted with undated Houghton, Mifflin title-page imprint. 5,000 copies of 2-page H,M promotional circular printed June 1883 with price $4.00 in cloth, $9.00 in morocco or tree calf.

A 16.11

COMPOSITIONS in OUTLINE | FROM | HAWTHORNE'S [in decorative floral and type panel] SCARLET LETTER | BY | F. O. C. DARLEY | BOSTON | HOUGHTON, OS-GOOD & COMPANY | The Riverside Press, Cambridge. | Copyright, 1879, by F. O. C. DARLEY. THE HELIOTYPE PRINTING CO. 220 DEVONSHIRE ST. BOSTON.

Prints 12 plates each accompanied by a page extract from the text of *Scarlet Letter.* $16^{1}/_{2}'' \times 21^{1}/_{2}''$. Printed paper-covered boards. Price $10.00 in printed stiff covers. Reprinted with 1884 Houghton, Mifflin title-page imprint as *Hawthorne's Scarlet Letter.* 500 copies of Darley's "text" printed August 1883, 500 copies of text printed June 1884, 300 copies September 1884.

A 16.12
Toronto: Belfords, Clark, MDCCCLXXIX.

PRINTINGS FROM THE RIVERSIDE EDITION PLATES

A 16.13.a1
Riverside Edition (trade), first printing, American issue [1883]

THE SCARLET LETTER | AND | THE BLITHEDALE ROMANCE | BY | NATHANIEL HAWTHORNE | [vignette of Pearl] | BOSTON | HOUGHTON, MIFFLIN AND COM-PANY | New York: 11 East Seventeenth Street [The Riverside Press, Cambridge | 1883.

Two volumes in one published as vol. V of the Riverside trade printing. Contents same as in *"Little Classic Edition"* (A 16.8), with "Introductory Note" by George Parsons Lathrop added. 1,500 copies printed March 1883. Price $2.00. See B 9 for reprintings of the Riverside trade printing.

A 16.13.a2
Riverside Edition (trade), first printing, English issue [1883]

London: Kegan Paul, Trench, 1883.

Sheets of vol. V, first printing (A 16.13.a1), with cancel title, in a Kegan Paul binding.

250 Kegan Paul title pages printed by Houghton, Mifflin, June–July 1883. Later issues noted with dated and undated Kegan Paul, Trench, Trübner title pages. See B 11.

A 16.13.b
Riverside Edition (large paper), second printing [*1883*]

[red] THE SCARLET LETTER | [black] AND | THE BLITHEDALE ROMANCE | BY | NATHANIEL HAWTORNE | [vignette of Pearl] | [red] CAMBRIDGE | [black] Printed at the Riverside Press | 1883

Two volumes in one published as vol. V of the Riverside large-paper printing. 250 copies printed April 1883. See B 10.

A 16.13.c
Boston and New York: Houghton, Mifflin, 1884.

Vol. IX of the *Wayside Edition*. 500 copies printed September–October 1884. See B 12.

A 16.13.d
Boston: Houghton, Mifflin, 1885.

"Popular Edition." Reprinted with and without date on title.

Note: This *"Popular Edition"* is not to be confused with the *Popular Edition* of Hawthorne's works (B 7).

A 16.13.e
Boston and New York: Houghton, Mifflin, [1891].

Combined with *The Blithedale Romance* in two-volumes-in-one format and published as vol. V of the *Standard Library Edition*. 500 copies printed October 1891. See B 13.

A 16.13.f
Boston and New York: Houghton, Mifflin, 1892.

'SALEM EDITION' slug on title page. Regularly reprinted with and without date on title page.

Note: This *Salem Edition* printing of the *Riverside Edition* plates is not to be confused with the *Salem Edition* printing of the *"Little Classic Edition"* plates (see A 16.8.d).

A 16.13.g
Boston and New York: Houghton, Mifflin, MDCCCXCII.

Illustrations by F. O. C. Darley. Trade printing, with separate printed red cloth wrapper. Also large-paper printing (see A 16.13.h).

A 16.13.h
Cambridge: [Houghton, Mifflin], MDCCCXCII.

Illustrations by F. O. C. Darley. Large-paper printing of A 16.13.g, limited to 200 numbered copies in vellum binding.

A 16.13.i
Boston and New York: Houghton, Mifflin, [1902].

Combined with *The Blithedale Romance* in two-volumes-in-one format and published as vol. V of the *"New" Wayside Edition*. 500 copies printed September–October 1902. See B 14.

A 16.13.j
Boston and New York: [Houghton, Mifflin], MDCCCCIX.

Combined with *The Blithedale Romance* in two-volumes-in-one format and published as vol. V of the *Fireside Edition.* See B 15.

A 16.13.k
Boston, New York: Jefferson Press, [1913].

Combined with *The Blithedale Romance* in two-volumes-in-one format and published as vol. [V] of the *"Jefferson Press Edition."* See B 16.

A 16.13.l
Boston and New York: Houghton, Mifflin, 1929.

The Riverside Library. With printed dust jacket.

OTHER EDITIONS

A 16.14
Printings from the Paterson-Scott plates
Edinburgh: William Paterson, 1883.

No. 2, *Paterson's New England Novels.* Contents same as in third American T&F edition (A 16.3.a). Published in cloth, top edges gilded, at 2s.; in ornamental paper covers at 1s. Also combined with *The House of the Seven Gables* in two-volumes-in-one format and published as vol. [I] of the *"Paterson Edition."* See B 17. Also Paterson sheets found with cancel Walter Scott title. Also remanufactured from Paterson plates with Walter Scott title-page imprint. Published in 1894 as vol. [I] of the *"Walter Scott Edition"* (gravure). See B 18.

A 16.15.a1
London, Paris, New York & Melbourne: Cassell, n.d.

[1886]. *Cassell's Red Library.* London issue. Also Toronto issue with cancel title (see A 16.15.a2).

A 16.15.a2
Toronto: Hart & Riddell, 1892.

Toronto issue, A 16.15.a1 sheets with cancel Hart & Riddell title.

A 16.16
London: George Routledge, n.d.

[1887]. Reprinted with 1893 Routledge title page.

A 16.17
New York, Boston: Thomas Y. Crowell, n.d.

[c. 1891]. Contents same as in third American T&F edition (A 16.3.a). Same plates used to manufacture vol. [5] of the *Crowell "Lennox" Edition,* with the addition of an introduction by Katherine Lee Bates. See B 23. Also reprinted as Crowell separate [1902]. Also 1902 Crowell sheets issued with cancel title, London: S. C. Brown, [1904].

A 16.18
New York: Worthington, 1892.

A 16.19
Boston: Samuel E. Cassino, n.d.

[c. 1892]. Illustrated by H. P. Barnes. Reprinted with undated Philadelphia: Altemus title-page imprint [ca. 1892], with Cassino Art Co. on verso of title.

A 16.20
Philadelphia: Henry Altemus, 1892.

No. 17 in *The Altemus Library*. Contents same as in third American T&F edition (A 16.3.a). Reprinted with 1893 title page. Also reprinted with undated title page. Noted in various binding formats. Also published as no. 184 in the *Altemus' New Illustrated Vademecum Series*.

A 16.21
New York: John B. Alden, 1892.

Omits Hawthorne's "Preface."

A 16.22
Manchester, England: W. H. White, 1892.

The Manchester Library. Printed wrappers. Also combined with *The House of the Seven Gables, Ivanhoe,* and the *Legend of Montrose* in four-volumes-in-one format, with original title pages retained.

A 16.23
New York: F. M. Lupton, 1893.

No. 1, *The Arm Chair Library*. Omits Hawthorne's "Preface" and Custom-House introduction. Wrappers.

A 16.24
New York: Frederick A. Stokes, [1893].

Illustrated by Frederick C. Gordon. Also issued with undated cancel title, London: Griffith, Farran.

A 16.25
Baltimore: R. H. Woodward, [1893].

Omits Hawthorne's "Preface." Reprinted with undated New York: Hurst title-page imprint.

A 16.26
New York: Home Book Company, [1893].

No. 11, *The Premium Library,* printed 17 June 1893. Omits Hawthorne's "Preface." Printed wrappers. Also issued with undated cancel title, New York: Lovell. Also issued with undated cancel title, Boston: Joseph Knight. Also reprinted with undated Chicago: M. A. Donohue and with Donohue, Henneberry title-page imprints.

A 16.27
London: Richard Edward King, n.d.

[1893]. Omits preface. Reprinted on different grades of paper, with and without inserted frontispiece, in various bindings designed for different classes of trade. Customized booksellers' titles inserted replacing King titles in what are probably special-order trade issues.

A 16.28
London: Bliss Sands, MDCCCXCVI.

Omits preface. Reprinted with title page dated MDCCCXCVII. Also with London: Sands & Co., MDCCCXCIX, title-page imprint.

A 16.29
London: Service and Paton, 1897.

Introduction by Moncure D. Conway. Omits preface. Reprinted with London: James Nisbet, 1901, title-page imprint.

A 16.30
New York: Woman's World, [1897].

No. 9, *Woman's World Series,* printed April 1897. Omits preface. Printed wrappers.

A 16.31
The Custom House and Main Street. Boston, New York, and Chicago: Houghton, Mifflin, 1899.

Combines Custom-House introduction with "Main Street" in two-volumes-in-one format as no. 138, *Riverside Literature Series,* printed 6 December 1899. Printed wrappers.

A 16.32
London: The Gresham Publishing Co., [1900].

Combined with *The House of the Seven Gables* in two-volumes-in-one format. Introduction by J. A. Nicklin. Omits preface.

A 16.33
New York: Dodd Mead, MDCCCC.

Omits preface.

PRINTINGS FROM THE AUTOGRAPH EDITION PLATES

A 16.34.a
Boston and New York: Houghton, Mifflin, MDCCCC.

Vol. VI of the *Autograph Edition.* Contents same as in the *Riverside Edition* (A 16.13.a₁), with a new introductory note. 500 copies. Deposited 20 December 1900. See B 20.

A 16.34.b
Boston and New York: Houghton, Mifflin, MDCCCC.

Vol. VI of the *Large-Paper (Autograph) Edition.* 500 copies. See B 21.

A 16.34.c
Boston and New York: Houghton, Mifflin, 1903.

Vol. VI of the *Old Manse Edition.* See B 22.

OTHER EDITIONS

A 16.35
New York: Thomas Y. Crowell, [1902].

Introduction by Katherine Lee Bates. *Astor Prose Series.* Also same plates used to manufacture *Crowell "Popular Edition": The Scarlet Letter* and *The House of the Seven Gables* combined in two-volumes-in-one format and published as vol. [4] of the edition. See B 24. Priority undetermined.

A 16.36
London: Grant Richards, 1903.

No. XXVI, *The World's Classics.* Price 1s. in cloth; 2s. in leather. Reprinted with undated Henry Frowde title-page imprint. Also noted with Humphry Milford spine imprint.

A 16.37
London and New York: John Lane, MDCCCCIV.

A 16.38

NATHANIEL HAWTHORNE | The | [red] Scarlet Letter | [black] A Romance | Literally Reprinted from the First Edition. | WITH FIFTEEN ORIGINAL COLORED ILLUSTRA-TIONS | BY | A. ROBAUDI | AND | C. GRAHAM. | NEW YORK | [red] PRIVATELY PRINTED | [black] 1904.

Each plate in color and in black and white. 125 copies on Japanese imperial paper and one copy on vellum. Stiff printed wrappers.

A 16.39
London: J. M. Dent; New York: E. P. Dutton, [1906].

No. 122, *Everyman's Library.* Reprinted 1909, 1910, 1913, 1916, 1917, 1919, 1925, 1927, 1930, 1967.

A 16.40

[red] THE SCARLET | LETTER | [black] BY NATHANIEL HAWTHORNE | ILLUS-TRATED BY | GEORGE H. BOUGHTON | [red Grolier seal] | [black] THE GROLIER CLUB | OF THE CITY OF NEW YORK | 1908

Contents same as in T&F second edition (A 16.2). 300 copies on French handmade paper and three copies on imperial Japanese paper. Glassine dust cover. Boxed.

A 16.41
New York: Modern Library, [1927].

Introduction by William Lyon Phelps. contents same as in T&F second edition (A 16.2). First ML printing has slug on copyright page: '*First Modern Library Edition* | 1927'.

A 16.42
New York: Random House, 1928.

Illustrated by Valenti Angelo, printed by Edwin and Robert Grabhorn. Omits preface. 980 numbered copies.

A 16.43
New York: Cheshire House, 1931.

Illustrated by Joanne Pursell. Glassine dust cover. Boxed. 1,200 numbered copies.

A 16.44
New York: Heritage Press, [1935].

Illustrated by W. A. Dwiggins. Omits preface. Boxed.

A 16.45
New York: The Limited Editions Club, 1941.

Illustrated by Henry Varnum Poor. Introduction by Dorothy Canfield. Omits preface. Boxed. 1,500 numbered copies, signed by the illustrator.

A 16.46
The Scarlet Letter and Other Tales of the Puritans. Edited with an introduction and notes by Harry Levin. Boston: Houghton, Mifflin, [1960].

No. A56 of H,M *Riverside Editions.* Includes eight tales. Published simultaneously in paperback format.

A 16.47
New York: Libra, [1960].

Illustrated by Jacob Landau. Foreword by Louise Bogan. Omits preface and Custom-House introduction. Boxed.

A 16.48
[Columbus]: Ohio State University Press, [1962].

Vol. I of the *Centenary Edition.* 1,942 copies published 1 February 1963. See B 32.

FACSIMILE EDITIONS

A 16.49
San Francisco: Chandler Publishing Company, [1968].

Introduction, note on the text, bibliography, and chronology by Hyatt H. Waggoner and George Monteiro. Facsimile of the first edition (A 16.1). Printed wrappers.

A 16.50
New York and London: Fleet Press, [1969].

Commentary by Van Allen Bradley. Facsimile of the first edition [A 16.1].

DRAMATIZATIONS

A 16.51
The Scarlet Letter. A Drama in Three Acts By George H. Andrews. Boston: Charles H. Spencer, Agent, 1871.

No. LXI, *Spencer's Universal Stage.* Pamphlet.

A 16.52
A Romantic Drama, in Four Acts, Entitled, The Scarlet Letter. Dramatized from Nathaniel Hawthorne's Masterly Romance. By Gabriel Harrison. Brooklyn: Harry M. Gardner, Jr., 1876.

Printed wrappers. Limited to 100 copies.

A 16.53
Nathaniel Hawthorne's Scarlet Letter, Dramatized. A Play in Five Acts. By Elizabeth Weller Peck. Boston: Franklin Press; Rand, Avery, & Co., 1876.

A 16.54
The Scarlet Letter. Dramatic Poem. By George Parsons Lathrop. Music by Walter Damrosch. N.p.: n.p., 1894.

Copyright 1894, by George Parsons Lathrop. Printed wrappers.

A 16.55
The Scarlet Letter. A Dramatic Composition. By George Parsons Lathrop. Music by Walter Damrosch. New York and London: The Transatlantic Publishing Company, MDCCCXCVI.

New edition of A 16.54. Printed wrappers.

A 16.56
The Scarlet Stigma. A Drama in Four Acts. By James Edgar Smith. Washington, D.C.: James J. Chapman, 1899.e3000

Noted in two bindings, priority undetermined: (A) red cloth with title giltstamped on front cover, and (B) gray cloth with title printed in red.

Bindings for (1) A17.1.a, format A; (2) A17.1.a, format E; (3) A17.1.a, format C; (4) A17.2.a, format C; (5) A18.1.a, trade; (6) A18.1.b; (7) A18.1.t; (8) A18.2.a; (9) A19.1.a; (10) A19.2.a, *Bohn's Cheap Series*; (11) A19.2.a, format C; (12 & 13) A20.1; (14) A20.2.a, trade (see also illustrations at A17.2.a and A19.2.a)

THE HOUSE

OF

THE SEVEN GABLES,

A ROMANCE.

BY

NATHANIEL HAWTHORNE.

BOSTON:
TICKNOR, REED, AND FIELDS.
M DCCC LI.

---

the moment, a single bitter thought against the world at large, or one individual man or woman. She wished them all well, but wished, too, that she herself were done with them, and in her quiet grave.

The applicant, by this time, stood within the door-way. Coming freshly, as he did, out of the morning light, he appeared to have brought some of its cheery influences into the shop along with him. It was a slender young man, not more than one or two and twenty years old, with rather a grave and thoughtful expression, for his years, but like-wise a springy alacrity and vigor. These qualities were not only perceptible, physically, in his make and motions, but made themselves felt almost immediately in his character. A brown beard, not too silken in its texture, fringed his chin, but as yet without completely hiding it; he wore a short moustache, too, and his dark, high-featured counte-nance looked all the better for these natural ornaments. As for his dress, it was of the simplest kind; a summer sack of cheap and ordinary material, thin, checkered panta-loons, and a straw hat, by no means of the finest braid. Oak Hall might have supplied his entire equipment. He was chiefly marked as a gentleman — if such, indeed, he made any claim to be — by the rather remarkable whiteness and nicety of his clean linen.

He met the scowl of old Hepzibah without apparent alarm, as having heretofore encountered it, and found it harmless.

"So, my dear Miss Pyncheon," said the daguerreotypist, — for it was that sole other occupant of the seven-gabled mansion, — "I am glad to see that you have not shrunk from your good purpose. I merely look in to offer my best wishes, and to ask if I can assist you any further in your preparations."

People in difficulty and distress, or in any manner at

A 17 THE HOUSE OF THE SEVEN GABLES

A 17.1.a
First edition, first printing [*1851*]

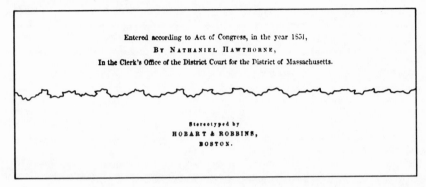

First printing is distinguished by type batter (see table).

[i–iii] iv–vi [vii–viii] [9] 10–344

[1]⁸ 2–21⁸ 22⁴

Contents: p. i: title; p. ii: copyright; pp. iii–vi, preface; p. vii: contents; p. viii: blank; pp. 9–344: text, headed 'THE HOUSE | OF | THE SEVEN GABLES. | [rule] | I. | THE OLD PYNCHEON FAMILY.'

Typography and paper: See illustration, A 17.1.a page format. Running heads: rectos, chapter titles; versos, 'THE HOUSE OF THE SEVEN GABLES.' White wove paper.

Binding: In style of Ticknor format A (see illustration, A 2.6 binding). Brown (81. d. gy. y Br) bold-ribbed T cloth with blindstamped floral device inside ruled panels on both covers. Spine goldstamped (see illustration, A 17 bindings). Cream-colored wove endpapers. Flyleaf inserted at front and rear. 4 pp. of T&F ads with various dates inserted between front endpapers in most copies. (Dates on ads have no bibliographical significance.) All edges trimmed.

Publisher's name goldstamped on spine in at least five forms (see illustration, A 17 bindings): (A) "TICKNOR & CO." in roman caps, line 1¹/₄″ wide; (B) "TICKNOR & CO." in roman caps, line 1¹/₁₆″ wide, stamped in a face ³/₃₂″ high; (C) "TICKNOR & Co." with italic ampersand and small "o" in "Co.," line 1¹/₈″ wide; (D) "TICKNOR & CO." with italic ampersand and large "O" in "CO.," line 1³/₁₃″ wide; (E) "TICKNOR & CO." in roman caps, line 1¹/₁₆″ wide, stamped in a face ¹/₈″ (scant) high. Priority undetermined. Form of spine stamping without bibliographical significance in establishing priority of text.

Publication: 1,690 copies printed 6–24 March 1851, published 9 April 1851. 190 review copies were distributed. Price $1.00. Hawthorne received a royalty of 15¢ per copy paid on 1,500 copies.

Printing: Composition and stereotype plates by Hobart & Robbins, Boston; presswork by Metcalf & Co., Boston. Probably bound by Benjamin Bradley & Co., Boston.

Locations: CEFC, LC (deposited 7 May 1851), MH, NN, OU, ViU.

Type Batter Within the 1851 Printings of *The House of the Seven Gables*

	FIRST (April 1851, 1,690 copies)	SECOND (April 1851, 1,969 copies)	THIRD (May 1851, 2,051 copies)	FOURTH (Sept. 1851, 1,000 copies)	FIFTH [5] (Oct. 1852, 1,000 copies)
50.25	apparent	apparent / or ; apparen / or ; apparen / o [2]	apparen	apparen	apparen
278.25	or		o	o	o
149.1–3	e tha⁄ [1] ; brusb ; ıunted	e that [1] ; brush ; ıunted	e that ; brush ; ıunted	e that ; brush ; ıunted	e that ; brush ; ıunted
58.16–17	ʼn lady, ; door ?"	ʼn lady, ; door ?"	ʼn lady, [3] ; door ?"	ʼn lady, ; door ?"	ʼn lady, ; door ?"
57.32–33	for the ; child,	for the ; child,	for the ; child,	for the [4] ; child,	for the ; child,

1. In the first printing, lines 1–3 on page 149 show type batter along the right-hand margin. The battered type was reset for the second printing. Although the point at which the damage occurred has not been established, all copies of the first printing so far examined show batter. The reset type is slightly out of line.

2. Batter on pp. 50 and 278 occurred progressively during the second printing—three states have been identified, all within the second printing.

3. Page 58 was completely reset for the third printing.

4. The last three lines of p. 57 were reset for the fourth printing.

5. According to the *Cost Books* (A 258c), a fifth printing was ordered in September 1852. Matthew J. Bruccoli has determined that the fifth printing is dated 1851, has the characteristics of the fourth printing, and can be differentiated by gutter measurements (see "Concealed Printings in Hawthorne," *Papers of the Bibliographical Society of America*, LVII [1963], 42–45).

Manuscript: Manuscript that served as printer's copy located in the Houghton Library, Harvard University (MS AM 121.26).

Note: The Centenary Edition of *Seven Gables* (see B 32) identifies two states present in all printings from the first edition stereotype plates: a comma is present or absent following the word "solitude" in 343.31. The states resulted from the use of duplicate plates to print gathering 22.

A 17.1.b
Second printing

Boston: Ticknor, Reed, and Fields, M DCCC LI.

For distinguishing features see table under A 17.1.a. 1,969 copies printed March 1851, published 9 April 1851. Price $1.00, royalty 15¢.

A 17.1.c
Third printing

Boston: Ticknor, Reed, and Fields, M DCCC LI.

For distinguishing features see table under A 17.1.a. 2,051 copies printed April, published May 1851. Price $1.00, royalty 15¢.

A 17.1.d
Fourth printing

Boston: Ticknor, Reed, and Fields, M DCCC LI.

For distinguishing features see table under A 17.1.a. 1,000 copies printed 14 August, published September 1851. Price $1.00, royalty 15¢.

A 17.1.e
Fifth printing

Boston: Ticknor, Reed, and Fields, M DCCC LI.

For distinguishing features see table under A 17.1.a. 1,000 copies printed September 1852 (see note 5 of table). Price $1.00, royalty 15¢.

LATER PRINTINGS WITHIN THE FIRST EDITION

A 17.1.f
Boston: Ticknor, Reed, and Fields, M DCCC LIII.

1,000 copies printed 4 October 1853. Price $1.00, royalty 15¢.

A 17.1.g
Boston: Ticknor and Fields, M DCCC LV.

500 copies printed 12 September 1855 by T. R. Marvin, Boston. Price $1.00, royalty 15¢.

A 17.1.h
Boston: Ticknor and Fields, M DCCC LVII.

500 copies printed 14 August 1855 by T. R. Marvin, Boston. Price $1.00, royalty 15¢.

A 17.1.i
Boston: Ticknor and Fields, M DCCC LX.

500 copies printed 19 March 1860. Price $1.00, royalty 15¢.

A 17.1.j
Boston: Ticknor and Fields, M DCCC LXI.

280 copies printed 23 August 1861. Price $1.00, royalty 15¢.

A 17.1.k
Boston: Ticknor and Fields, 1863.

280 copies printed 25 April 1863. Price $1.25, royalty 15¢.

A 17.1.l
Boston: Ticknor and Fields, 1864.

Note: Two printings with 1864 title-page date (see A 17.1.m), priority undetermined.

280 copies printed 7 May 1864. Price $1.50, royalty 15¢.

A 17.1.m
Boston: Ticknor and Fields, 1864.

500 copies printed 12 September 1864. Price $1.50, royalty 15¢.

A 17.1.n
Boston: Ticknor and Fields, 1865.

Vol. 7 of untitled *"Tinted Edition"* on laid paper. 500 copies printed 31 October 1864.
Price $1.50, royalty 12¢. See B 1[7] for reprintings of the *"Tinted Edition."*

A 17.1.o
Boston: Ticknor and Fields, 1865.

550 copies on wove paper printed 17 May 1865. Price $1.50, royalty 12.5¢.

A 17.1.p
Boston: Ticknor and Fields, 1866.

Note: Two printings with 1866 title-page date (see A 17.1.q), priority undetermined.
Copies noted with Ticknor & Co. spine imprint (Location: CEFC) and Fields, Osgood &
Co. spine imprint (Location: OU).

312 copies printed 30 August 1866. Price $1.50, royalty 12¢.

A 17.1.q
Boston: Ticknor and Fields, 1866.

600 copies printed 31 October 1866. Price $1.50, royalty 12¢.

A 17.1.r
Boston: Fields, Osgood, 1869.

280 copies printed 28 April 1869. Price $2.00, royalty 20¢.

A 17.1.s
Boston: Fields, Osgood, 1870.

A 17.1.t
Boston: James R. Osgood, 1871.

Combined with *The Snow Image* in two-volumes-in-one format and published as the
fourth volume of the *Illustrated Library Edition*. 1,000 copies printed 15 July 1871.
Price $2.00, royalty 20¢. See B 2 for reprintings of the *ILE*.

A 17.1.u
Boston: James R. Osgood, 1872.

Note: Two printings with 1872 title-page date (see A 17.1.v), priority undetermined.

280 copies printed 8 November 1871. Price $2.00, royalty 20¢.

A 17.1.v
Boston: James R. Osgood, 1872.

150 copies printed 19 January 1872.

A 17.1.w
Boston: Houghton, Mifflin, 1880.

Combined with *Twice-Told Tales* and *The Snow Image* in four-volumes-in-one format and published as the first volume of the *Globe Edition*. 1,500 copies printed August 1880. See B 3 for reprintings of the *Globe Edition*.

A 17.1.x
Boston: Houghton, Mifflin, [1886].

Combined with *Twice-Told Tales* and *The Snow Image* in four-volumes-in-one format and published as the first volume of the *"New" Fireside Edition*. 1,000 copies printed May 1886. See B 4.

busy Yankees never have found out how to put him to any use? Upon my word, Miss Hepzibah, I doubt whether I've ever been so comfortable as I mean to be at my farm, which most folks call the workhouse. But you,—you're a young woman yet,—you never need go there? Something still better will turn up for you. I'm sure of it!"

Hepzibah fancied that there was something peculiar in her venerable friend's look and tone; insomuch, that she gazed into his face with considerable earnestness, endeavoring to discover what secret meaning, if any, might be lurking there. Individuals whose affairs have reached an utterly desperate crisis almost invariably keep themselves alive with hopes, so much the more airily magnificent, as they have the less of solid matter within their grasp, whereof to mould any judicious and moderate expectation of good. Thus, all the while Hepzibah was perfecting the scheme of her little shop, she had cherished an unacknowledged idea that some harlequin trick of fortune would intervene in her favor. For example, an uncle—who had sailed for India fifty years before, and never been heard of since—might yet return, and adopt her to be the comfort of his very extreme and decrepit age, and adorn her with pearls, diamonds, and oriental shawls and turbans, and make her the ultimate heiress of his unreckonable riches. Or the member of parliament, now at the head of the English branch of the family,—with which the elder stock, on this side of the Atlantic, had held little or no intercourse for the last two centuries,—this eminent gentleman might invite Hepzibah to quit the ruinous House of the Seven Gables, and come over to dwell with her kindred at Pyncheon Hall. But, for reasons the most imperative, she could not yield to his request. It was more probable, therefore, that the descendants of a Pyncheon who had emigrated to Virginia, in some past generation, and became a great planter there,—hearing of Hepzibah's destitution, and impelled by the splendid generosity of character with which their Virginian mixture must have enriched the New England blood,—would send her a remittance of a thousand dollars, with a hint of repeating the favor annually. Or—and surely anything so undeniably just could not be beyond the limits of reasonable anticipation—the great claim to the heritage of Waldo County might finally be decided in favor of the Pyncheons; so that, instead of keeping a cent-shop, Hepzibah would build a

---

THE HOUSE

OF

THE SEVEN GABLES.

A ROMANCE.

BY NATHANIEL HAWTHORNE.

LONDON:
HENRY G. BOHN, YORK STREET, COVENT GARDEN.
1851.

A 17.2.a: Title page, 6³/₁₆″ × 4¹/₄″. Page format, 5³/₈″ (5⁵/₈″) × 3³/₁₆″

PRINTINGS FROM THE BOHN EDITION PLATES

A 17.2.a
First English edition, first printing, a piracy [*1851*]

[i–iii] iv–vi [vii–viii] [1] 2–255 [256]

[A]⁴ B–I⁸ K–R⁸

Contents: p. i: title; p. ii: printer's imprint; pp. iii–vi: preface; p. vii: contents; p. viii: blank; pp. 1–255: text, headed 'THE HOUSE | OF | THE SEVEN GABLES. | [rule] | I.—THE OLD PYNCHEON FAMILY.'; p. 256: colophon.

Typography and paper: See illustration, A 17.2.a page format. Running heads: rectos, chapter titles; versos, 'THE HOUSE OF THE SEVEN GABLES.' White wove paper.

Binding: Various binding issues produced by Bohn from the same sheets for marketing to various classes of trade, priority uncertain:
 A. *Bohn's Cheap Series.* No. 31 in *BCS.* Green (135. 1. y G) paper-covered boards, imprinted in blue (see illustration, A 17.2.a cover). Price 1s. Location: CEFC.
 B. *Uniform with Bohn's Standard Library.* Combined with *The Scarlet Letter* (A 16.4.b) and published in two-volumes-in-one format as vol. II, *Nathaniel Hawthorne's Tales.* Price 3s. 6d. Location: CEFC.
 C. Cloth, at 1s. 6d., and custom leather-bound volumes in various formats. Location: CEFC.

Publication: Unknown number of copies. Listed in the London *Athenaeum,* 31 May 1851.

Printing: Printed by Harrison and Son, London Gazette Office, St. Martin's Lane and Orchard Street, Westminster.

Locations: CEFC; binding C: BM, 12206.h.6 (deposit-stamp 9 MR 1853).

A 17.2.b
London: Bohn, 1861.

A 17.2.c
London: Bell & Daldy, 1866.

Combined with *The Scarlet Letter* in two-volumes-in-one format and published as vol. II, *Nathaniel Hawthorne's Tales* (see A 16.4.c), with volume title added. Each part paged separately. Noted with separate titles for each part retained, both with London: Bell & Daldy, 1870 title-page imprint.

A 17.2.d
London: Bell & Daldy, 1871.

Combined with *The Scarlet Letter* in two-volumes-in-one format and published as vol. II, *Nathaniel Hawthorne's Tales* (see A 17.2.c), with volume title only. Each part paged separately. Reprinted with London: Bell & Daldy, 1873 title-page imprint.

A 17.2.e
London: George Bell and Sons, 1877.

Combined with *The Scarlet Letter* in two-volumes-in-one format and published as vol. II, *Nathaniel Hawthorne's Tales* (see A 16.9), with volume title only. Volume paged continuously. Reprinted 1881, 1884. Also reprinted 1886 and 1892 in *Bohn's Standard Library.*

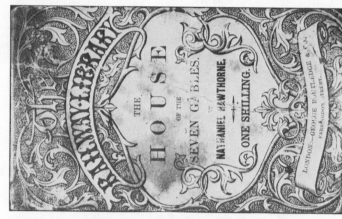

Front cover for A 17.2.a, *Bohn's Cheap Series*, and A.17.3.a, *The Railway Library*

OTHER EDITIONS

A 17.3.a
Second English edition, first printing, a piracy [1851]

THE HOUSE | OF | THE SEVEN GABLES: | A Romance. | BY | NATHANIEL HAWTHORNE. | [rule] | LONDON: | GEORGE ROUTLEDGE AND CO., SOHO SQUARE. | 1851.

Note: Various binding issues produced by Routledge from the same sheets for marketing to different classes of trade in competition with Bohn, priority undetermined:
   A. *The Railway Library.* No. 31 in Routledge's *RL.* Bound in green (135. l. y G) paper-covered boards, imprinted in blue ink (see illustration, A 17.3.a cover [at A 17.2.a]). Price 1s. Also in cloth with 'RAILWAY LIBRARY' blindstamped on covers. Price 1s. 6d. Location: CEFC.
   B. *Routledge's Standard Novels.* Combined with *The Scarlet Letter* and published in two-volumes-in-one format in *RSN* series. Price 2s. 6d. Volume title leaf inserted, frontispiece added. Location: CEFC.
   C. Also combined with *The Scarlet Letter* in two-volumes-in-one format with original title and contents leaves for each title preserved. Location: CEFC.

A 17.3.b
London: Geo. Routledge, 1852.

A 17.3.c
London: G. Routledge, 1853.

A 17.3.d
London: G. Routledge, 1854.

'Twenty-sixth Thousand.' slug added to title page.

A 17.4

Halifax, [England]: Milner & Sowerby, 1856[?].

Advertised in the London *Publishers' Circular and Booksellers' Record,* 1 December 1856. (Unlocated.)

PRINTINGS FROM THE ''LITTLE CLASSIC EDITION'' PLATES

A 17.5.a

[All following within red and black double-rules frame] THE | [red] House of the Seven Gables. | [black] A ROMANCE. | BY | [red] NATHANIEL HAWTHORNE. | [black vignette of house] | [red] BOSTON: | [black] JAMES R. OSGOOD AND COMPANY, | Late Ticknor & Fields, and Fields, Osgood, & Co. | [red] 1876.

Vol. [VII], *"Little Classic Edition."* Contents same as in first T&F edition (A 17.1.a). Sheets bound with James R. Osgood and, later, Houghton, Osgood spine imprints. 3,000 copies printed 11 October 1875. Price $1.25, royalty 12.5¢. See B 5[VII] for reprintings of the *"Little Classic Edition."*

A 17.5.b
Boston: Houghton, Osgood, 1879.

Combined with *The Snow-Image* in two-volumes-in-one format and published as vol.

IV of the *"Fireside Edition."* 500 copies printed 20 September 1879. See B 6[IV] for reprintings of the *"Fireside Edition."*

A 17.5.c
Boston: Houghton, Mifflin, [1891].

Combined with *Twice-Told Tales* in three-volumes-in-one format and published as vol. I of the *Popular Edition.* 1,000 copies printed June—August 1891. See B 7 for reprintings of the *Popular Edition.*

A 17.5.d
Boston and New York: Houghton, Mifflin, 1892.

'*Salem Edition*' slug on title page. Reprinted with 1893, 1894, and undated title pages. Not to be confused with A 17.12. Also issued with London: Gay & Bird 1893 title page bound with *Salem Edition* sheets (unlocated, see Browne).

A 17.5.e
Boston: Houghton, Mifflin, [1899].

Vol. [VII], *Concord Edition.* See B 8.

OTHER EDITION

A 17.6
London: Goubaud, 1877.

(Unlocated, see Browne.) Reprinted without date on title page as no. 42, *Daisy Books.*

PRINTINGS FROM THE RIVERSIDE EDITION PLATES

A 17.7.a₁
Riverside Edition (trade), first printing, American issue [1883]

THE | HOUSE OF THE SEVEN GABLES | AND | THE SNOW IMAGE | *AND OTHER TWICE-TOLD TALES* | BY | NATHANIEL HAWTHORNE | [vignette of child] | BOS-TON | HOUGHTON, MIFFLIN AND COMPANY | New York: 11 East Seventeenth Street | The Riverside Press, Cambridge | 1883

Two volumes in one published as vol. III of the Riverside trade printing. Contents same as in *"Little Classic"* edition (A 17.5.a), with "Introductory Note" by George Parsons Lathrop. 1,500 copies printed January 1883. Price $2.00. See B 9 for reprintings of the Riverside trade printing.

A 17.7.a₂
Riverside Edition (trade), first printing, English issue [1883]

London: Kegan Paul, Trench, 1883.

Sheets of vol. III, first printing (A 17.7.a₁), with cancel title, in a Kegan Paul binding. 250 Kegan Paul title pages printed by Houghton, Mifflin, June—July 1883. Later issues noted with dated and undated Kegan Paul, Trench, Trübner title pages. See B 11.

A 17.7.b
Riverside Edition (large paper), second printing [1883]

THE | [red] HOUSE OF THE SEVEN GABLES | [black] AND | THE SNOW IMAGE |

AND OTHER TWICE-TOLD TALES | BY | NATHANIEL HAWTHORNE | [red] CAM-
BRIDGE | [black] Printed at the Riverside Press | 1883

Two volumes in one published as vol. III of the Riverside large-paper printing. 250
copies printed March 1883. See B 10.

A 17.7.c
Boston and New York: Houghton, Mifflin, 1884.

Vol. V of the *Wayside Edition*. 500 copies printed September–October 1884. See B 12.

A 17.7.d
Boston and New York: Houghton, Mifflin, [1891].

Combined with *The Snow Image* in two-volumes-in-one format and published as vol.
III of the *Standard Library Edition*. 500 copies printed October 1891. See B 13.

A 17.7.e
Boston and New York: Houghton, Mifflin, [1902].

Combined with *The Snow Image* in two-volumes-in-one format and published as vol.
III of the *"New" Wayside Edition*. 500 copies printed September–October 1902. See
B 14.

A 17.7.f
Boston and New York: [Houghton, Mifflin], MDCCCCIX.

Combined with *The Snow Image* in two-volumes-in-one format and published as vol.
III of the *Fireside Edition*. See B 15.

A 17.7.g
Boston, New York: Jefferson Press, [1913].

Combined with *The Snow Image* in two-volumes-in-one format and published as vol.
III of the *"Jefferson Press Edition."* See B 16.

OTHER EDITIONS

A 17.8
Printings from the Paterson-Scott plates

Edinburgh: William Paterson, 1883.

No. 1, *Paterson's New England Novels*. Contents same as in first T&F edition (A 17.1).
Published in cloth, top edges gilded, at 2s.; in ornamental paper covers at 1s. Also
combined with *The Scarlet Letter* in two-volumes-in-one format and published as vol.
[I] of the *"Paterson Edition."* See B 17. Also Paterson sheets found with cancel Walter
Scott title. Also remanufactured from Paterson plates with Walter Scott title-page im-
prints. Published in 1894 as vol. [II] of the *"Walter Scott Edition"* (gravure). See B 18.

A 17.9
Manchester, England: W. H. White, 1891.

No. IX, *The Manchester Library*. Printed wrappers. Also combined with *The Scarlet
Letter, Ivanhoe,* and the *Legend of Montrose* in four-volumes-in-one format, with original title pages preserved.

A 17.10
Philadelphia: Henry Altemus, [1892].

Copyright, 1892, The Cassino Art Company. Illustrated by Hiram Putnam Barnes. Two parts in one volume. Reprinted [1899?] as no. 79 in the *Altemus' New Illustrated Vademecum Series*.

A 17.11
Philadelphia: Henry Altemus, 1893.

No. 21, *The Altemus Library*. Reprinted 1894, 1895.

A 17.12
Boston and New York: Houghton, Mifflin, 1893.

Introduction by George Parsons Lathrop. '*SALEM EDITION*' slug on title page. Reprinted 1894, later reprinted without date on title page. Not to be confused with A 17.5.d

A 17.13
New York: Home Book Company, [1893].

No. 4, *The Premium Library*, printed 29 April 1893. Printed wrappers. Also issued with undated H. M. Caldwell title and frontispiece inserted. Reprinted in Caldwell *Pastel Edition*. Reprinted with M. A. Donohue and with Donohue, Henneberry title-page imprints.

A 17.14
New York: Hurst and Company, [1893].

No. 92, *The Universal Library*, printed 15 May 1893. Printed wrappers. Also reprinted with undated Hurst and F. M. Lupton title pages, in cloth. Also reprinted with Chicago, New York: F. Tennyson Neely, 1895, title page. No. 32, *Neely's Popular Library*, printed December 1894. Printed wrappers. Also reprinted with undated Cleveland: Arthur Westbrook Company title page. No. 44, *The All Star Series*. Printed wrappers.

A 17.15
London: Richard Edward King, [1895].

Reprinted in King's *Imperial Library* and *Sun-Dial Library*.

A 17.16
Chicago: Scott, Foresman and Company, 1898.

The Lake English Classics. Reprinted with undated title page.

A 17.17
London: Service and Paton, 1898.

Introduction by Moncure D. Conway. Reprinted with London: James Nisbet, 1901, title-page imprint.

A 17.18.a
Boston and New York: Houghton, Mifflin, MDCCCXCIX.

2 vols. Illustrated by Maude and Genevieve Cowles. Also large-paper printing (see A 17.18.b).

A 17.18.b

Boston and New York: Houghton, Mifflin, 1899.

2 vols. Illustrated by Maude and Genevieve Cowles. Large-paper printing of A 17.18.a, limited to 250 numbered copies.

A 17.19

New York: Thomas Y. Crowell, [1899].

Deposited 17 August 1899. Reprinted in various formats. Also plates used to manufacture vol. [6] of the *Crowell "Lenox Edition,"* with added introduction. See B 23.

PRINTINGS FROM THE AUTOGRAPH EDITION PLATES

A 17.20.a

Boston and New York: Houghton, Mifflin, MDCCCC.

Vol. VII of the *Autograph Edition.* Contents same as in the *Riverside Edition* (A 17.7.a1), with a new introductory note provided. 500 copies. Deposited 20 December 1900. See B 20.

A 17.20.b

Boston and New York: Houghton, Mifflin, MDCCCC.

Vol. VII of the *Large-Paper (Autograph) Edition.* 500 copies. See B 21.

A 17.20.c

Boston and New York: Houghton, Mifflin, 1903.

Vol. VII of the *Old Manse Edition.* See B 22.

OTHER EDITIONS

A 17.21

New York: Thomas Y. Crowell, [1902].

Introduction by Katharine Lee Bates. *Astor Prose Series.* Also same plates used to manufacture *Crowell "Popular Edition": The Scarlet Letter* and *The House of the Seven Gables* combined in two-volumes-in-one format and published as vol. [4] of the edition. See B 24. Priority undetermined.

A 17.22

London: J. M. Dent; New York: E. P. Dutton, [1907].

No. 176, *Everyman's Library.* Last reprinted 1967.

A 17.23

New York: The Limited Editions Club, 1935.

Illustrated by Valenti Angelo. Introduction by Van Wyck Brooks. Boxed. 1,500 numbered copies, signed by the illustrator. Also reprinted with undated Heritage Press title-page imprint. Spine imprint in two forms, giltstamped or silverstamped. Boxed.

A 17.24

Boston: Houghton, Mifflin, [1964].

Introduction and newly edited text by Hyatt H. Waggoner. No. A89 of the *Riverside Editions.* Published simultaneously in paperback format.

A 17.25
[Columbus]: Ohio State University Press, [1965].

Vol. II of the *Centenary Edition*. 2,000 copies published 27 December 1965. See B 32.

A 17.26
Barre, Mass.: Imprint Society, [1970].

Introduction by James Franklin Beard. Uses the *Centenary Edition* text (see B 32). Boxed. 1,950 numbered copies signed by Beard.

A

WONDER-BOOK

FOR

GIRLS AND BOYS.

BY

NATHANIEL HAWTHORNE.

WITH ENGRAVINGS BY BAKER FROM DESIGNS BY BILLINGS.

BOSTON:
TICKNOR, REED, AND FIELDS.
MDCCCLII.

---

least, without so much as a glance at the enemy with whom he was contending. Else, while his arm was lifted to strike, he would stiffen into stone, and stand with that uplifted arm for centuries, until time, and the wind and weather, should crumble him quite away. This would be a very sad thing to befall a young man, who wanted to perform a great many brave deeds, and to enjoy a great deal of happiness, in this bright and beautiful world.

So disconsolate did these thoughts make him, that Perseus could not bear to tell his mother what he had undertaken to do. He therefore took his shield, girded on his sword, and crossed over from the island to the main land, where he sat down in a solitary place, and hardly refrained from shedding tears.

But, while he was in this sorrowful mood, he heard a voice close beside him.

"Perseus," said the voice, "why are you sad?"

He lifted his head from his hands, in which he had hidden it, and, behold! all alone as Perseus had supposed himself to be, there was a stranger in the solitary place. It was a brisk, intelligent, and remarkably shrewd-looking young man, with a cloak over his shoulders, an odd sort of cap on his head, a strangely-twisted staff in his hand, and a short and very crooked sword

A18.1.a: Title page, 6⅝" × 4¼". Page format, 4¹¹⁄₁₆" (5¹⁄₁₆") × 3"

A 18 A WONDER-BOOK FOR GIRLS AND BOYS

A 18.1.a
First edition, first printing [*1852*]

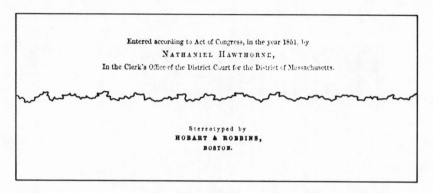

All printings of the first edition of *Wonder-Book* were made from stereotype plates with the first two printings dated MDCCCLII. The first printing has "lifed" at 21.3. This was corrected to "lifted" in the second printing.

[i–iii] iv [v] vi [7] 8–14 [15] 16–53 [54] 55–56 [57] 58–61 [62] 63–88 [89] 90–92 [93] 94–97 [98] 99–124 [125] 126–127 [128] 129–135 [136] 137–168 [169] 170–172 [173] 174–176 [177] 178–207 [208] 209 [210] 211–213 [214] 215–250 [251] 252–256. Frontispiece inserted facing title page, six plates inserted facing pages 15, 62, 98, 136, 177, 214.

[1]⁸ 2–16⁸

Contents: p. i: title; p. ii: copyright; pp. iii–iv: preface; pp. v–vi: contents; pp. 7–256: text, headed 'TANGLEWOOD PORCH. | INTRODUCTORY TO "THE GORGON'S HEAD." '.

Includes "Preface," "Tanglewood Porch, Introductory . . . ," " 'The Gorgon's Head,' Tanglewood Porch, After . . . ," "Shadow Brook, Introductory . . . ," "The Golden Touch," "Shadow Brook, After . . . ," "Tanglewood Play-room, Introductory . . . ," "The Paradise of Children," "Tanglewood Play-room, After . . . ," "Tanglewood Fireside, Introductory . . . ," "The Three Golden Apples," "Tanglewood Fireside, After . . . ," "The Hill-side, Introductory . . . ," "The Miraculous Pitcher," "The Hill-side, After . . . ," "Bald-summit, Introductory . . . ," "The Chimaera," "Bald-summit, After the Story."

Typography and paper: See illustration, A 18.1.a page format. Running heads: rectos and versos, chapter titles. White wove paper.

Binding: In the style of Ticknor format A (see illustration, A 2.6 binding). Red (16. d. Red), greenish yellow-olive (113. 01 Gy), blue (187. d. gy. B) and (188. blackish B), black, and lavender bold-ribbed T cloth. Spine goldstamped (see illustration, A 18 bindings [at A 17]). Most copies with blindstamped covers and edges plain. Also "gift" binding in style of Ticknor format B, with covers goldstamped and edges gilded. Ornament on spine separating title from author's name found in various forms. Pale yellow wove endpapers. White wove flyleaf inserted at front and rear. All edges trimmed. Bound by Benjamin Bradley & Co., Boston.

Publication: 3,067 copies published 8 November 1851. 100 review copies distributed. Price 75¢. Hawthorne received a royalty of 15% against 2,967 copies.

Printing: Composition and stereotype plates by Hobart & Robbins, Boston; printed by Thurston, Torry and Company, Boston. Engravings by William J. Baker from designs by Hammatt Billings.

Locations: Trade: CEFC, LC (deposited 22 December 1851), MH, NN, ViU; gift: CEFC.

Manuscript: The author's manuscript that served as printer's copy located in Barrett Collection at the University of Virginia Library.

LATER PRINTINGS WITHIN THE FIRST EDITION

A 18.1.b
Second printing
Boston: Ticknor, Reed, and Fields, MDCCCLII.

1,600 copies printed 4 December 1851. Price 75¢, royalty 15%.

A 18.1.c
Third printing
Boston: Ticknor, Reed, and Fields, MDCCCLIII.

Imprint of Geo. C. Rand added to copyright page. Printed on paper thinner than A 18.1.b. 500 copies printed 16 September 1853. Price 75¢, royalty 10.75¢.

A 18.1.d
Boston: Ticknor and Fields, MDCCCLIV.

1,000 copies printed 1 December 1853. Price 75¢, royalty 15%.

A 18.1.e
Boston: Ticknor and Fields, M DCCC LV.

672 copies printed 7 August 1855. Price 75¢, royalty 15%.

A 18.1.f
Boston: Ticknor and Fields, M DCCC LVII.

500 copies printed April 1857. Price 75¢, royalty 12.5¢.

A 18.1.g
Boston: Ticknor and Fields, M DCCC LVIII.

1,000 copies printed 3 September 1858. Price 75¢, royalty 7.5¢.

A 18.1.h
Boston: Ticknor and Fields, M DCCC LIX.

Note: Two printings with 1859 title-page date (see A 18.1.i), priority undetermined.

500 copies printed 8 February 1859. Price 75¢, royalty 7.5¢.

A 18.1.i
Boston: Ticknor and Fields, M DCCC LIX.

500 copies printed 20 September 1859. Price 75¢, royalty 7.5¢.

A 18.1.j
Boston: Ticknor and Fields, M DCCC LX.

500 copies printed 19 December 1859. Price 75¢, royalty 7.5¢.

A 18.1.k
Boston: Ticknor and Fields, 1863.

500 copies printed 21 September 1863. Price 90¢, royalty 7.5¢.

A 18.1.l
Boston: Ticknor and Fields, 1865.

Vol. 13 of untitled *"Tinted Edition"* on laid paper. 500 copies printed 31 October 1864. Price $1.50, royalty 12¢. See B 1[13] for reprintings of the *"Tinted Edition."*

A 18.1.m
Boston: Ticknor and Fields, 1865.

500 copies printed 30 January 1865. Price $1.25, royalty 12¢.

A 18.1.n
Boston: Ticknor and Fields, 1866.

Note: Two printings with 1866 title-page date (see A 18.1.o), priority undetermined.

280 copies printed 1 July 1866. Price $1.50, royalty 12¢.

A 18.1.o
Boston: Ticknor and Fields, 1866.

280 copies printed 31 August 1866. Price $1.50, royalty 12¢.

A 18.1.p
Boston: Ticknor and Fields, 1867.

Note: Two printings with 1867 title-page date (see A 18.1.q), priority undetermined.

280 copies printed December 1866. Price $1.50, royalty 15¢.

A 18.1.q
Boston: Ticknor and Fields, 1867.

280 copies printed 29 October 1867. Price $1.50, royalty 12¢.

A 18.1.r
Boston: Ticknor and Fields, 1868.

280 copies printed 28 April 1868. Price $1.50, royalty 12¢.

A 18.1.s
Boston: Fields, Osgood, 1869.

500 copies printed 10 November 1868. Price $1.50, royalty 15¢.

A 18.1.t
Boston: Fields, Osgood, 1871.

150 copies printed 15 December 1870. Price $1.50, royalty 12.5¢.

A 18.1.u
Boston: James R. Osgood, 1872.

280 copies printed 17 May 1872. Price $1.50, royalty 12.5¢.

A 18.1.v
Boston: James R. Osgood, 1873.

Note: Two printings with 1873 title-page date (see A 18.1.w), priority undetermined.

275 copies printed November–December 1872. Price $1.50, royalty 12.5¢.

A 18.1.w
Boston: James R. Osgood, 1873.

280 copies printed 1873. Price $1.50, royalty 15¢.

A 18.1.x
Boston: James R. Osgood, 1874.

280 copies printed 30 June 1874. Price $1.50, royalty 15¢.

A 18.1.y
Boston: James R. Osgood, 1875.

500 copies printed 9 December 1874. Price $1.50, royalty 15¢.

A 18.1.z
Boston: James R. Osgood, 1876.

Combined with *Grandfather's Chair* in two-volumes-in-one format and published as the tenth volume of the *Illustrated Library Edition*. 1,000 copies printed 21 May 1876. Price $2.00, royalty 20¢. See B 2 for reprintings of the *ILE*.

A 18.1.aa
Boston: James R. Osgood, 1877.

150 copies printed 23 February 1877. Price $1.50, royalty 15¢.

A 18.1.ab
Boston: James R. Osgood, 1878.

150 copies printed 7 February 1878. Price $1.50, royalty 15¢.

A 18.1.ac
Boston: Houghton, Osgood, 1878.

292 copies printed 7 November 1878. Price $1.50, royalty 15¢.

A 18.1.ad
Boston: Houghton, Osgood, 1879.

286 copies printed 14 March 1879. Price $1.50, royalty 15¢.

A 18.1.ae
Boston: Houghton, Mifflin, 1880.

Combined with *Tanglewood Tales, Grandfather's Chair,* and *Biographical Stories* in four-volumes-in-one format and published as the fourth volume of the *Globe Edition*. 1,500 copies printed August 1880. See B 3 for reprintings of the *Globe Edition*.

A 18.1.af
Boston: Houghton, Mifflin, 1880.

270 copies printed October 1880. Reprintings, probably with undated title pages: 270 copies, January 1881; 270 copies, August 1882; 270 copies, August 1883; 500 copies, October 1883; 500 copies, August 1884.

A 18.1.ag
Boston: Houghton, Mifflin, [1886].

Combined with *Tanglewood Tales, Grandfather's Chair,* and *Biographical Stories* in four-volumes-in-one format and published as the fourth volume of the *"New" Fireside Edition.* 1,000 copies printed May 1886. See B 4.

A

WONDER-BOOK

FOR

GIRLS AND BOYS.

BY NATHANIEL HAWTHORNE.

WITH ILLUSTRATIVE ENGRAVINGS.

LONDON:
HENRY G. BOHN, YORK STREET, COVENT GARDEN.
1852.

But, before they reached the clump of bushes, one of the Three Grey Women spoke:

"Sister! Sister Scarecrow!" cried she, "you have had the eye long enough. It is my turn now!"

"Let me keep it a moment longer, Sister Nightmare," answered Scarecrow. "I thought I had a glimpse of something behind that thick bush."

"Well, and what of that?" retorted Nightmare, peevishly. "Can't I see into a thick bush as easily as yourself? The eye is mine, as well as yours; and I know the use of it as well as you, or may be a little better. I insist upon taking a peep immediately!"

But here the third sister, whose name was Shakejoint, began to complain, and said it was her turn to have the eye, and that Scarecrow and Nightmare wanted to keep it all to themselves. To end the dispute, old Dame Scarecrow took the eye out of her forehead, and held it forth in her hand.

"Take it, one of you," cried she, "and quit this foolish quarrelling. For my part, I shall be glad of a little thick darkness. Take it quickly, however, or I must clap it into my own head again!"

Accordingly, both Nightmare and Shakejoint stretched out their hands, groping eagerly to snatch the eye out of the hand of Scarecrow. But, being both alike blind, they could not easily find where Scarecrow's hand was; and Scarecrow, being now just as much in the dark as Shakejoint and Nightmare, could not at once meet either of their hands, in order to put the eye into it.

PRINTINGS FROM THE BOHN EDITION PLATES

A 18.2.a
First English edition, first printing, [1852]

[a–b] [i–iii] iv [v] vi [1] 2–6 [7] 8–39 [40] 41–45 [46] 47–69 [70] 71–73 [74] 75–77 [78]
79–99 [100] 101 [102] 103–108 [109] 110–136 [137] 138–140 [141] 142–144 [145]
146–171 [172] 173 [174] 175–177 [178] 179–208 [209] 210–213 [214–216]. Frontispiece inserted facing title page, seven plates inserted facing pages 7, 46, 78, 109,
141 or 146, 145, 178.

[A]⁴ B–I⁸ K–O⁸ P⁴

Contents: p. a: half title; p. b: blank; p. i: title; p. ii: printer's imprint; pp. iii–iv:
preface; v–vi: contents; pp. 1–213: text, headed 'TANGLEWOOD PORCH. | INTRO-
DUCTORY TO "THE GORGON'S HEAD." '; p. 214: printer's imprint; pp. 215–216:
blank.

Contents same as in T&F first edition (A 18.1), with the addition of one new plate
'HILL-SIDE WOOD'.

Typography and paper: See illustration, A 18.2.a page format. Running heads: rectos
and versos, chapter titles. White wove paper.

Binding: Trade binding in green (146. d. G) pebble-grain P cloth. Spine goldstamped (see illustration, A 18 bindings [at A 17]). Covers have triple-rules frame
blindstamped, inside rule with floral elements at intervals facing center. Edges plain.
White wove endpapers creamcoated one side. "Gift" binding in red (13. deep Red)
and blue (194. v. p. B) coarse-ribbed morocco AR-like cloth or pebble-grain P cloth.
Spine goldstamped (see illustration, A 18 bindings). Covers blindstamped with floral
pattern inside outer rule, or blindstamped with oriental panel design inside double
rules. Elaborate decorative frame containing title goldstamped on front cover. Edges
gilded. White wove endpapers coated pale yellow or cream one side. All edges
gilded. Bound by Bone & Son, 76 Fleet Street, London.

Note: 'HILL-SIDE WOOD' plate inserted facing p. 146 in trade copies and facing p.
141 in "gift" copies.

Publication: Unknown number of copies published December 1851. Listed in *Publishers' Circular* among books published between 13–29 December 1851.

Printing: Type set from sheets of the American first edition supplied by Ticknor,
Reed, and Fields for a fee of less than £40, including copyright and electrotypes of
the woodcuts.

Locations: Trade: CEFC; gift: CEFC, OU.

A 18.2.b₁
First English edition, second printing, first issue [1868]

A | WONDER-BOOK | FOR | GIRLS AND BOYS. | BY | NATHANIEL HAWTHORNE. |
With Illustrations. | LONDON: | GEORGE ROUTLEDGE & SONS, | THE BROADWAY,
LUDGATE. | 1868.

First issue includes *Wonder-Book* only. Published in 1867 using the Bohn plates. Title
leaf inserted. Four of the Bohn engravings used in a slightly modified format. Reprinted with undated title page in the Routledge *Every Boy's Library.*

A 18.2.b2
First English edition, second printing, second issue [1868]

A | WONDER-BOOK | FOR | GIRLS & BOYS, | (INCLUDING "TANGLEWOOD TALES.") | BY | NATHANIEL HAWTHORNE. | With Illustrations. | LONDON: | GEORGE ROUTLEDGE & SONS, | THE BROADWAY, LUDGATE. | 1868.

Second issue combined with Routledge *Tanglewood Tales* in two-volumes-in-one format with volume title inserted. Reprinted with undated title page (see A 22.4).

LATER EDITION

A 18.3
Tanglewood Tales: A Wonder-Book for Girls and Boys. London: Knight and Son, n.d.

[1855]. Although titled *Tanglewood Tales*, prints *Wonder-Book* only. A piracy. Reprinted in 1860 combined with *Tanglewood Tales* in two-volumes-in-one format.

PRINTINGS FROM THE "LITTLE CLASSIC EDITION" PLATES

A 18.4.a
[All following within red and black double-rules frame] [red] A Wonder-Book | [black] *FOR GIRLS AND BOYS.* | BY | [red] NATHANIEL HAWTHORNE. | [black vignette of Pegasus] | [red] Boston: | [black] JAMES R. OSGOOD AND COMPANY, | Late Ticknor & Fields, and Fields, Osgood, & Co. | [red] 1876.

Vol. [XIII], *"Little Classic Edition."* Contents same as in first T&F edition (A 18.1.a). Sheets bound with James R. Osgood and, later, Houghton, Osgood spine imprints. 2,000 copies printed 28 March 1876. Price $1.25, royalty 12.5¢. See B 5[XIII] for reprintings of the *"Little Classic Edition."*

A 18.4.b
Boston: Houghton, Osgood, 1879.

Combined with *Grandfather's Chair* in two-volumes-in-one format and published as vol. X of the *"Fireside Edition."* 500 copies printed 20 September 1879. See B 6[X] for reprintings of the *"Fireside Edition."*

A 18.4.c
Boston: Houghton, Mifflin, [1891].

Combined with *True Stories from History and Biography* and *Tanglewood Tales* in three-volumes-in-one format and published as vol. V of the *Popular Edition.* 1,000 copies printed June–August 1891. See B 7 for reprintings of the *Popular Edition.*

A 18.4.d
Boston and New York: Houghton, Mifflin, 1893.

'SALEM EDITION' slug on title page. Reprinted with 1894 title-page date. Also reprinted with undated title page. Also later reprinted with undated Boston: Charles E. Brown title-page imprint. Not to be confused with A 18.11.

A 18.4.e
Boston: Houghton, Mifflin, [1899].

Vol. [XIII], *Concord Edition.* See B 8.

A 18.5
Louisville: American Printing House for the Blind, 1878.

Printed in line letter. (Unlocated, see Browne.)

A 18.6
Tanglewood Tales: A Wonder-Book for Girls and Boys. London: Frederick Warne, [1882].

Combined with *Tanglewood Tales* in two-volumes-in-one format and published as no. 107 in the *Chandos Classics.* Contents same as in first T&F edition (A 18.1.a). Reprinted with undated title page 1883, 1884, 1885.

PRINTINGS FROM THE RIVERSIDE EDITION PLATES

A 18.7.a1
Riverside Edition (trade), first printing, American issue [1883]

A WONDER-BOOK | TANGLEWOOD TALES, AND | GRANDFATHER'S CHAIR | BY | NATHANIEL HAWTHORNE | [vignette of head of Quicksilver] | BOSTON | HOUGH-TON, MIFFLIN AND COMPANY | New York: 11 East Seventeenth Street | The River-side Press, Cambridge | 1883

Three volumes in one published as vol. IV of the Riverside trade printing. Contents same as in *"Little Classic Edition"* (A 18.4.a), with "Introductory Note" by George Parsons Lathrop added. 1,500 copies printed January 1883. Price $2.00. See B 9 for reprintings of the Riverside trade printing.

A 18.7.a2
Riverside Edition (trade), first printing, English issue [1883]

London: Kegan Paul, Trench, 1883.

Sheets of vol. IV, first printing (A 18.7.a1) with cancel title, in a Kegan Paul binding. 250 Kegan Paul title pages printed by Houghton, Mifflin, June–July 1883. Later issues noted with dated and undated Kegan Paul, Trench, Trübner title pages. See B 11.

A 18.7.b
Riverside Edition (large paper), second printing [1883]

[red] A WONDER-BOOK | [black] TANGLEWOOD TALES, AND | GRANDFATHER'S CHAIR | BY | NATHANIEL HAWTHORNE | [vignette of head of Quicksilver] | [red] CAMBRIDGE | [black] Printed at the Riverside Press | 1883

Three volumes in one published as vol. IV of the Riverside large-paper printing. 250 copies printed March 1883. See B 10.

A 18.7.c
Boston and New York: Houghton, Mifflin, 1884.

Combined with the first portion of *Tanglewood Tales* in two-volumes-in-one format and published as vol. VII of the *Wayside Edition.* 500 copies printed September–October 1884. See B 12.

A 18.7.d
Boston, New York, Chicago: Houghton, Mifflin, [1886].

In two parts as nos. 17 and 18 of the *Riverside Literature Series*. Printed wrappers. Unknown number of reprintings. Also later reprinted in combined format, nos. 17 and 18 in one cloth volume.

A 18.7.e
Boston and New York: Houghton, Mifflin, [1891].

Combined with *Tanglewood Tales* and *Grandfather's Chair* in three-volumes-in-one format and published as vol. IV of the *Standard Library Edition*. 500 copies printed October 1891. See B 13.

A 18.7.f
A Wonder-Book for Girls and Boys and Tanglewood Tales. Boston and New York: Houghton, Mifflin, 1898.

Combined with *Tanglewood Tales* and published in two-volumes-in-one format, with Walter Crane *Wonder-Book* illustrations reproduced in halftone.

A 18.7.g
Boston and New York: Houghton, Mifflin, [1902].

Combined with *Tanglewood Tales* and *Grandfather's Chair* in three-volumes-in-one format and published as vol. IV of the *"New" Wayside Edition*. 500 copies printed September–October 1902. See B 14.

A 18.7.h
Boston and New York: [Houghton, Mifflin], MDCCCCIX.

Combined with *Tanglewood Tales* and *Grandfather's Chair* in three-volumes-in-one format and published as vol. IV of the *Fireside Edition*. See B 15.

A 18.7.i
Boston, New York: Jefferson Press, [1913].

Combined with *Tanglewood Tales* and *Grandfather's Chair* in three-volumes-in-one format and published as vol. [IV] of the *"Jefferson Press Edition."* See B 16.

OTHER EDITIONS

A 18.8
Printings from the Paterson-Scott plates

Edinburgh: William Paterson, 1885.

No. 22, *Paterson's New England Novels*. Contents same as in first T&F edition (A 18.1.a). Published in cloth, top edges gilded, at 2s.; in ornamental paper covers at 1s. Also combined with *True Stories* in two-volumes-in-one format and published as vol. [VI] of the *"Paterson Edition."* See B 17. Also Paterson sheets found with cancel Walter Scott title page. Also remanufactured from Paterson plates with Walter Scott title-page imprint. Later published as vol. [IV] in the *"Walter Scott Edition"* (gravure). See B 18.

A 18.9
Boston: Houghton, Mifflin, 1885.

Illustrations by F. S. Church. Regularly reprinted with slugs designating later edition on title page. Published in England with London: John C. Nimmo, 1885 title.

A 18.10.a₁
First printing, American issue

Boston: Houghton, Mifflin, MDCCCXCII.

With designs by Walter Crane. Contents same as in first T&F edition (A 18.1.a). Inserted title leaf. H,M spine imprint. Reprinted with MDCCCXCIII title-page date.

A 18.10.a₂
First printing, English issue

London: Osgood, McIlvaine & Co., MDCCCXCII.

Bound from American sheets by Houghton, Mifflin with English title inserted. Has Osgood, McIlvaine spine imprint.

A 18.10.b
Boston: Houghton, Mifflin, MDCCCXCIII.

Large-paper printing. "Edition de luxe" binding, printed cloth jacket, boxed. 250 numbered copies, with limitation notice on copyright page.

A 18.11
Boston and New York: Houghton, Mifflin, 1893.

Introduction by George Parsons Lathrop. 'SALEM EDITION' slug on title page. Reprinted 1894, later reprinted without date on title page. Not to be confused with A 18.4.d.

A 18.12
New York: Hurst & Company, [1894].

No. 66, *The Useful Knowledge Series*, printed April 9, 1894. Printed wrappers. Reprinted in clothbound format with undated title page.

A 18.13
Philadelphia: David McKay, 1894.

Combined with *True Stories* in two-volumes-in-one format and published in *American Classic Series*.

A 18.14
The Golden Touch. Boston, New York, Chicago, San Francisco: Educational Publishing Company, [1894].

Vol. II, no. 22, *Young Folk's Library of Choice Literature*, printed February 1, 1895. Prints title story only. Printed wrappers.

A 18.15
The Paradise of Children. Boston, New York, Chicago, San Francisco: Educational Publishing Company, [1895].

Vol. II, no. 34, *Young Folk's Library of Choice Literature*, printed August 1, 1895. Prints title story only. Printed wrappers.

A 18.16
New York: Thomas Y. Crowell, [1896].

A 18.17
New York and New Orleans: University Publishing Company, 1896.

No. 16, *Standard Literature Series,* printed October 16, 1896. Includes only "Preface" and four stories: "The Golden Touch," "The Paradise of Children," "The Three Golden Apples," "The Miraculous Pitcher." Printed wrappers.

A 18.18
Philadelphia: Henry Altemus, [1899].

No. 234, *Altemus' New Illustrated Vademecum Series.*

PRINTINGS FROM THE AUTOGRAPH EDITION PLATES

A 18.19.a
Boston and New York: Houghton, Mifflin, MDCCCC.

Vol. XIII of the *Autograph Edition.* Contents same as in the *Riverside Edition* (A 18.7), with new introductory note added. 500 copies. Deposited 20 December 1900. See B 20.

A 18.19.b
Boston and New York: Houghton, Mifflin, MDCCCC.

Vol. XIII of the *Large-Paper (Autograph) Edition.* 500 copies. See B 21.

A 18.19.c
Boston and New York: Houghton, Mifflin, 1903.

Vol. XIII of the *Old Manse Edition.* See B 22.

OTHER EDITIONS

A 18.20
The Three Golden Apples. Chicago: Orville Brewer Publishing Co., 1901.

Vol. 2, no. 24, Student's Series of *Four Penny Classics,* printed April 15, 1901. Prints sketch of Hawthorne and title story only. Printed wrappers, cover title. Later published by F. A. Owen, Danville, N.Y., as no. 24, *Instructor Literature Series.* Printed wrappers.

A 18.21
The Miraculous Pitcher. Chicago: Orville Brewer Publishing Co., 1901.

Vol. 2, no. 25, Student's Series of *Four Penny Classics,* printed May 1, 1901. Prints sketch of Hawthorne and title story only. Printed wrappers, cover title. Later published by F. A. Owen, Danville, N.Y., as no. 25, *Instructor Literature Series.* Printed wrappers.

A 18.22
New York: Thomas Y. Crowell, [1902].

Introduction by Katharine Lee Bates. Vol. [7] of the *Crowell "Lenox Edition."* See B 23.

A 18.23
New York: Thomas Y. Crowell, [1902].

Combined with *Tanglewood Tales* in two-volumes-in-one format and published as vol. [7] of the *Crowell "Popular Edition."* See B 24.

A 18.24
London, New York, and Melbourne: Ward, Lock & Co., 1903.

Reprinted with undated title page.

A 18.25
London: J. M. Dent; New York: E. P. Dutton, 1903.

With 12 illustrations by H. Grenville Fell. Contents same as in first T&F edition (A 18.1.a). Same plates combined with repaged plates of 1903 Dent *Tanglewood Tales* in continuously paged two-volumes-in-one format and published as no. 5 of *Everyman's Library,* printed 6 February 1906. Illustrations omitted. Reprinted 1906, 1907, 1908, 1909, 1911, 1914, 1917, 1919, 1921. Reset 1924; reprinted 1926, 1929. Also new Dent/Dutton edition combining *Wonder-Book* and *Tanglewood Tales* in two-volumes-in-one format, incorporating Fell's illustrations for both titles, published 1910. Also new edition of Dent/Dutton *Wonder-Book* separately published 1937 with illustrations by S. Van Abbé. Reprinted 1949, 1952. Last reprinting 1968.

A 18.26
New York: Frederick A. Stokes, [1908].

Illustrated by Lucy Fitch Perkins.

A 18.27
A Wonder Book and Tanglewood Tales. New York: Duffield & Company, MCMX.

Illustrated by Maxfield Parrish.

A 18.28
Chicago, New York: Rand McNally & Company, [1913].

Illustrated by Milo Winter. *The Windermere Series.* Reprinted an unknown number of times. Variant publisher's imprints on copyright page, priority undetermined. Noted with and without series title on front cover.

A 18.29
London, New York, and Toronto: Hodder & Stoughton, [1922].

Contents same as in first T&F edition (A 18.1.a). 600 copies signed by Rackham and specially bound in white buckram, boxed. Also trade printing. Also reprinted, New York: George H. Doran, [1922], with front matter renumbered and list of illustrations revised and renumbered. Hodder & Stoughton plates inserted or tipped to plate leaves in different locations. Also reprinted with undated Garden City, N.Y.: Garden City Publishing Co., title page. List of illustrations revised: only 6 of original 24 reprinted.

A 18.30
A Wonder-Book and Tanglewood Tales. London, Bombay, Sidney: George G. Harrap, [1925].

Illustrated by Gustaf Tenggren and Stephen Reid. Two-volumes-in-one format. Reprinted January 1929.

A 18.31
The Golden Touch. [San Francisco]: The Grabhorn Press, Mcmxxvii.

Illustrated by Valenti Angelo. 240 copies printed April 1927. Prints title story only. Boxed.

A 18.32
Akron, Ohio; New York: The Saalfield Publishing Company, [MCMXXIX].

Illustrated by Fern Bisel Peat. Reprinted in various formats.

A 18.33
A Wonder Book and Tanglewood Tales. Chicago, Philadelphia, Toronto: The John C. Winston Company, [1930].

Illustrated by Frederick Richardson. Introduction and notes by Katherine G. Carpenter. Two-volumes-in-one format.

A 18.34
London, New York: Standard Book Company, [MCMXXXI].

A 18.35
Pegasus the Winged Horse. New York: Macmillan; London: Collier-Macmillan, 1963.

Illustrated by Herschel Levit. Introduction by Robert Lowell. Prints title story only.

A 18.36
A Wonder Book and Tanglewood Tales. [Columbus]: Ohio State University Press, [1972].

Vol. VII of the *Centenary Edition.* 2,435 copies published 1 November 1972. See B 32.

"O no, Peony!" answered Violet, with grave wisdom. "That will not do at all. Warm milk will not be wholesome for our little snow-sister. Little snow-people, like her, eat nothing but icicles. No, no, Peony; we must not give her anything warm to drink!"

There was a minute or two of silence; for Peony, whose short legs were never weary, had gone on a pilgrimage again to the other side of the garden. All of a sudden, Violet cried out, loudly and joyfully,

"Look here, Peony! Come quickly! A light has been shining on her cheek out of that rose-colored cloud! and the color does not go away! Is not that beautiful?"

"Yes; it is beau-ti-ful," answered Peony, pronouncing the three syllables with deliberate accuracy. "O, Violet, only look at her hair! It is all like gold!"

"O, certainly," said Violet, with tranquillity, as if it were very much a matter of course. "That color, you know, comes from the golden clouds, that we see up there in the sky. She is almost finished now. But her lips must be made very red,— redder than her cheeks. Perhaps, Peony, it will make them red, if we both kiss them!"

Accordingly, the mother heard two smart little smacks, as if both her children were kissing the snow-image on its frozen mouth. But, as this did not seem to make the lips quite red enough, Violet next proposed that the snow-child should be invited to kiss Peony's scarlet cheek.

"Come, 'ittle snow-sister, kiss me!'" cried Peony.

"There! she has kissed you," added Violet, "and

THE

SNOW-IMAGE,

AND

OTHER TWICE-TOLD TALES.

BY

NATHANIEL HAWTHORNE.

BOSTON:

TICKNOR, REED, AND FIELDS.

M DCCC LII.

A19.1.a: Title page. 7″ × 4¹/₄″. Page format, 5³/₁₆″ (5⁷/₁₆″) × 3″

A 19 THE SNOW-IMAGE, AND OTHER TWICE-TOLD TALES

A 19.1.a
First edition, first printing [1852]

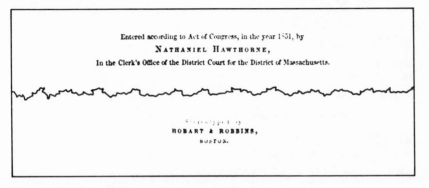

All printings of the first edition of *The Snow-Image* were made from stereotype plates.

Note: Although the first printing of the first American edition bears a title-page date of M DCCC LII and the first printing of the first English edition has an 1851 title-page date, they were intended for simultaneous publication and both editions appeared in December 1851. American publication probably preceded by several days.

[3–7] 8–10 [11–13] 14–35 [36] 37–62 [63] 64–101 [102] 103–124 [125] 126–133 [134] 135–144 [145] 146–158 [159] 160–192 [193] 194–202 [203] 204–212 [213] 214–220 [221] 222–227 [228] 229–236 [237] 238–246 [247] 248–273 [274]

[1]⁸ 2–17⁸

Contents: pp. 3–4: blank; p. 5: title; p. 6: copyright; pp. 7–10: preface; p. 11: contents; p. 12: blank; pp. 13–273: text, headed 'THE SNOW-IMAGE: | A CHILDISH MIRACLE.'; p. 274: blank.

Tales: "The Snow-Image: A Childish Miracle,"† "The Great Stone Face,"† "Main-Street,"† "Ethan Brand,"† "A Bell's Biography,"† "Sylph Etherege,"† "The Canterbury Pilgrims,"† "Old News. I,"† "II.—The Old French War,"† "III.—The Old Tory,"† "The Man of Adamant: An Apologue,"† "The Devil in Manuscript,"† "John Inglefield's Thanksgiving,"† "Old Ticonderoga: A Picture of the Past,"† "The Wives of the Dead,"† "Little Daffydowndilly,"† "Major Molineux."† Also first printing of Hawthorne's "Preface." Daggers (†) indicate first collected appearance.

Typography and paper: See illustration, A 19.1.a page format. Running heads: rectos and versos, story titles. White wove paper.

Binding: In the style of Ticknor format A (see illustration, A 2.6 binding). Brown (81. d. gy. y Br) bold-ribbed T cloth with blindstamped floral device inside ruled panels on both covers. Spine goldstamped (see illustration, A 19 bindings [at A 17]). Pale yellow wove endpapers. Flyleaf inserted at front and rear. Bottom edge untrimmed. 4 pp. of T&F ads with various dates inserted between front endpapers in some copies.

Publication: 2,425 copies printed 11 December 1851. Advertised as "just published" in the *New York Literary World,* 20 December 1851. Also listed in the *Literary World* as published during the period 13–27 December 1851. MH has copy inscribed by owner "Dec. 25, 1851." Price 75¢. Hawthorne received a 10% royalty on 2,300 copies.

Printing: Composition and stereotype plates by Hobart & Robbins, Boston, printed by C. Hickling, Boston. Bound by Benjamin Bradley & Co., Boston.

Locations: CEFC, CtY, MH, NN, OU, ViU.

Manuscript: Only manuscript for title story, "The Snow-Image," has been located (in the Huntington Library).

LATER PRINTINGS WITHIN THE FIRST EDITION

A 19.1.b
Second Printing

Boston: Ticknor, Reed, and Fields, M DCCC LIII.

1,000 copies printed 1 December 1852. Price 75¢, royalty 7.5¢.

A 19.1.c
Boston: Ticknor and Fields, M DCCC LVII.

500 copies printed 28 August 1857. Price 75¢, royalty 7.5¢.

A 19.1.d
Boston: Ticknor and Fields, M DCCC LXI.

280 copies printed 21 August 1861. Price 75¢, royalty 7.5¢.

A 19.1.e
Boston: Ticknor and Fields, 1863.

280 copies printed 25 July 1863. Price $1.00, royalty 7.5¢.

A 19.1.f
Boston: Ticknor and Fields, 1865.

Vol. 3 of untitled *"Tinted Edition"* on laid paper. 500 copies printed 31 October 1864. Price $1.50, royalty 12¢. See B 1[3] for reprintings of the *"Tinted Edition."*

A 19.1.g
Boston: Ticknor and Fields, 1865.

Note: Two printings with 1865 title-page dates, on wove paper (see A 19.1.h), priority undetermined.

280 copies printed 19 November 1864. Price $1.50, royalty 7.5¢.

A 19.1.h
Boston: Ticknor and Fields, 1865.

500 copies printed 4 May 1865. Price $1.50, royalty 13.5¢.

A 19.1.i
Boston: Ticknor and Fields, 1866.

270 copies printed 25 August 1866. Price $1.50, royalty 12¢.

A 19.1.j
Boston: Fields, Osgood, 1869.

280 copies printed 10 November 1868. Price $2.00, royalty 20¢.

A 19.1.k
Boston: James R. Osgood, 1871.

Combined with *The House of the Seven Gables* in two-volumes-in-one format and published as the fourth volume of the *Illustrated Library Edition*. 1,000 copies printed 15 July 1871. Price $2.00, royalty 20¢. See B 2 for reprintings of the *ILE*.

A 19.1.l
Boston: James R. Osgood, 1872.

140 copies printed 1872. Price $2.00, royalty 20¢.

A 19.1.m
Boston: James R. Osgood, 1876.

140 copies printed 30 August 1876.

A 19.1.n
Boston: Houghton, Mifflin, 1880.

Combined with *Twice-Told Tales* and *The House of the Seven Gables* in four-volumes-in-one format and published as the first volume of the *Globe Edition*. 1,500 copies printed August 1880. See B 3 for reprintings of the *Globe Edition*.

A 19.1.o
Boston: Houghton, Mifflin, [1886].

Combined with *Twice-Told Tales* and *The House of the Seven Gables* in four-volumes-in-one format and published as the first volume of the *"New" Fireside Edition*. 1,000 copies printed May 1886. See B 4.

THE SNOW-IMAGE,

AND

OTHER TALES.

BY

NATHANIEL HAWTHORNE.

LONDON:

HENRY G. BOHN, YORK STREET, COVENT GARDEN.

1851.

of beneficence, and assume a control over human affairs as wise and benignant as the smile of the Great Stone Face. Full of faith and hope, Ernest doubted not that what the people said was true, and that now he was to behold the living likeness of those wondrous features on the mountain side. While the boy was still gazing up the valley, and fancying, as he always did, that the Great Stone Face returned his gaze and looked kindly at him, the rumbling of wheels was heard swiftly approaching along the winding road.

"Here he comes!" cried a group of people who were assembled to witness the arrival. "Here comes the great Mr. Gathergold!"

A carriage, drawn by four horses, dashed round the turn of the road. Within it, thrust partly out of the window, appeared the physiognomy of a little old man, with a skin as yellow as if his own Midas-hand had transmuted it. He had a low forehead, small, sharp eyes, puckered about with innumerable wrinkles, and very thin lips, which he made still thinner by pressing them forcibly together.

"The very image of the Great Stone Face!" shouted the people. "Sure enough, the old prophecy is true; and here we have the great man come at last!"

And, what greatly perplexed Ernest, they seemed actually to believe that here was the likeness which they spoke of. By the road-side there chanced to be an old beggar-woman and two little beggar-children, stragglers from some far-off region, who, as the carriage rolled onward, held out their hands and lifted up their doleful voices, most piteously beseeching charity. A yellow claw—the very same that had clawed together so much wealth—poked itself out of the coach-window, and dropt some copper coins upon the ground; so that, though the great man's name seems to have been Gathergold, he might just as suitably have been nicknamed Scattercopper. Still, nevertheless, with an earnest about, and evidently with as much good faith as ever, the people bellowed:

"He is the very image of the Great Stone Face!"

But Ernest turned sadly from the wrinkled shrewdness of that sordid visage, and gazed up the valley, where, amid a gathering mist, gilded by the last sunbeams, he could still distinguish those glorious features which had impressed themselves into his soul. Their aspect cheered him. What did the benign lips seem to say?

A19.2.a: Title page. 7¹/₈″ × 4⁷/₁₆″. Page format, 5³/₈″ (5⁵/₈″) × 3⁵/₁₆″

PRINTINGS FROM THE BOHN EDITION PLATES

A 19.2.a
First English edition, first printing [1851]

Although the first printing of the first American edition bears a title-page date of M DCCC LII and the first printing of the first English edition has an 1851 title-page date, they were intended for simultaneous publication and both editions appeared in December 1851. American publication probably preceded by several days.

[i–iii] iv–vi [vii–viii] [1] 2–176

[A]⁴ B–I⁸ K–M⁸

Contents: p. i: title; p. ii: printer's imprint; pp. iii–vi: preface; p. vii: contents; p. viii: blank; pp. 1–176: text, headed 'THE SNOW-IMAGE: | A CHILDISH MIRACLE.'

Tales: Same as in first American edition (A 19.1.a).

Typography and paper: See illustration, A 19.2.a page format. Running heads: rectos and versos, story titles. White wove paper.

Binding: Various binding issues produced by Bohn from the same sheets for marketing to various classes of trade, priority uncertain:
   A. *Bohn's Cheap Series.* No. 37 in *BCS*. Green (135. 1. y G) paper-covered boards, imprinted in blue (see illustration, A 19.2.a cover). Price 1s. Location: CEFC.
   B. *Uniform with Bohn's Standard Library.* Combined with parts I and II, *Twice-Told Tales* (A 2.9.a) in three-volumes-in-one format and published as vol. I, *Nathaniel Hawthorne's Tales.* Price 3s. 6d. Location: CEFC.
   C. Issued in rose (19. gy. Red) linen-like T cloth with broad blindstamped border panel. Probably sold for 1s. 6d. 32 pp. Bohn catalogue bound in at rear in many copies. Also found in custom leather bindings. Location: CEFC.

Note: Copies found bound with Routledge's *Mosses* (A 15.2.a).

Publication: Unknown number of copies published late in December 1851. Advertised for December publication in *Athenaeum,* 27 December 1851. Also listed in *Athenaeum,* 27 December 1851; *Literary Gazette,* 27 December; *Publishers' Circular,* 1 January 1852.

Printing: Set from advance sheets of the American first edition first printing supplied under agreement with Ticknor, Reed, and Fields. Printed by Harrison and Son, London Gazette Office, St. Martin's Lane and Orchard Street, Westminster.

Locations: Cloth: BM, 12206.h.7 (deposit-stamp 9 MR 53), CEFC, MH, NN; paper: CEFC.

A 19.2.b
London: Bell & Daldy, 1866.

Combined with the First and Second Series of *Twice-Told Tales* in three-volumes-in-one format and published as vol. I, *Nathaniel Hawthorne's Tales,* with omnibus volume title added (see A 2.9.b). First and Second Series of *TTT* paged consecutively, *Snow-Image* paged independently. Three secondary titles preserved; *SI* secondary title with London: Bell & Daldy, 1868 title-page imprint. Other *SI* secondary title imprints are probable.

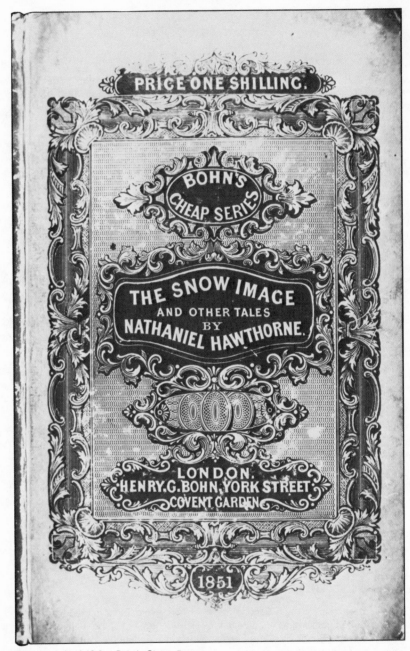

Front cover for A 19.2.a, *Bohn's Cheap Series*

A 19.2.c
London: George Bell, 1875.

Same three-in-one format as A 19.2.b. Second Series *TTT* secondary title omitted (see A 2.9.c). *SI* secondary title with London: Bell & Daldy, 1871 title-page imprint. Other *SI* secondary title imprints are probable.

LATER EDITIONS

A 19.3
The Canterbury Pilgrims, and Other Twice-Told Tales. London: Knight & Son, n.d.

[ca. 1852]. A piracy of *The Snow-Image.*

A 19.4
The Snow-Image: A Childish Miracle. New York: James G. Gregory, M DCCC LXIV.

Prints title story only. Illustrations by Marcus Waterman. Reprinted with New York: Hurd and Houghton, 1866; Boston: E. P. Dutton, 1866; and New York: Hurd and Houghton, 1868, title-page imprints. Also a London (Sampson Low) "edition" (probably an issue of American sheets) advertised for "next week" in the 26 November 1865 *Athenaeum,* also listed in the 26 November 1865 *Athenaeum* (unlocated).

A 19.5
Boston: Ticknor and Fields, 1865.

Combined with the conclusion of the second part of *Twice-Told Tales* and published as vol. II of the *"Blue & Gold Edition"* (see A 2.14.a). 1,500 two-volume set published 28 October 1864. Price $3.00 per set, royalty 20¢. Reprinted 1865, 1866, 1879.

PRINTINGS FROM THE "LITTLE CLASSIC EDITION" PLATES

A 19.6.a
[All following within red and black double-rules frame] THE | [red] Snow-Image, | [black] AND | *OTHER TWICE-TOLD TALES.* | BY | [red] NATHANIEL HAWTHORNE. | [black] [vignette of great stone face] | [red] BOSTON: | JAMES R. OSGOOD AND COMPANY, | Late Ticknor & Fields, and Fields, Osgood, & Co. | [red] 1876.

Vol. [III], *"Little Classic Edition."* Contents same as in 1852 T&F edition (A 19.1). Sheets bound with James R. Osgood and, later, Houghton, Osgood spine imprints. 3,000 copies printed 13 November 1875. Price $1.25, royalty 12.5¢. See B 5[III] for reprintings of the *"Little Classic Edition."*

A 19.6.b
Boston: Houghton, Osgood, 1879.

Combined with *The House of the Seven Gables* in two-volumes-in-one format and published as vol. IV of the *"Fireside Edition."* 500 copies printed 20 September 1879. See B 6[IV] for reprintings of the *"Fireside Edition."*

A 19.6.c
Boston: Houghton, Mifflin, [1891].

Combined with *Septimius Felton, Fanshawe,* and *The Dolliver Romance* in four-volumes-in-one format and published as vol. IV of the *Popular Edition.* 1,000 copies printed June–August 1891. See B 7 for reprintings of the *Popular Edition.*

A 19.6.d
Boston and New York: Houghton, Mifflin, 1893.

'SALEM EDITION' slug on title page. Reprinted without date on title page. Not to be confused with A 19.11.

A 19.6.e
Boston: Houghton, Mifflin, [1899].

Vol. [III], *Concord Edition.* See B 8.

PRINTINGS FROM THE RIVERSIDE EDITION PLATES

A 19.7.a₁
Riverside Edition (trade), first printing, American issue [1883]

THE | HOUSE OF THE SEVEN GABLES | AND | THE SNOW IMAGE | *AND OTHER TWICE-TOLD TALES* | BY | NATHANIEL HAWTHORNE | [vignette of child] | BOSTON | HOUGHTON, MIFFLIN AND COMPANY | New York: 11 East Seventeenth Street | The Riverside Press, Cambridge | 1883

Two volumes in one published as vol. III of the Riverside trade printing. Contents same as in *"Little Classic"* edition (A 19.6.a), with "Introductory Note" by George Parsons Lathrop. 1,500 copies printed January 1883. Price $2.00. See B 9 for reprintings of the Riverside trade printing.

A 19.7.a₂
Riverside Edition (trade), first printing, English issue [1883]

London: Kegan Paul, Trench, 1883.

Sheets of vol. III, first printing (A 19.7.a₁), with cancel title, in a Kegan Paul binding. 250 Kegan Paul title pages printed by Houghton, Mifflin, June–July 1883. Later issues noted with dated and undated Kegan Paul, Trench, Trübner title pages. See B 11.

A 19.7.b
Riverside Edition (large paper), second printing [1883]

THE | [red] HOUSE OF THE SEVEN GABLES | [black] AND | THE SNOW IMAGE | *AND OTHER TWICE-TOLD TALES* | BY | NATHANIEL HAWTHORNE | [red] CAMBRIDGE | [black] Printed at the Riverside Press | 1883

Two volumes in one published as vol. III of the Riverside large-paper printing. 250 copies printed March 1883. See B 10.

A 19.7.c
Boston and New York: Houghton, Mifflin, 1884.

Vol. VI of the *Wayside Edition.* 500 copies printed September–October 1884. See B 12.

A 19.7.d
Boston and New York: Houghton, Mifflin, [1891].

Combined with *The House of the Seven Gables* in two-volumes-in-one format and published as vol. III of the *Standard Library Edition.* 500 copies printed October 1891. See B 13.

A 19.7.e

Boston and New York: Houghton, Mifflin, [1902].

Combined with *The House of the Seven Gables* in two-volumes-in-one format and published as vol. III of the *"New" Wayside Edition.* 500 copies printed September–October 1902. See B 14.

A 19.7.f

Boston and New York: [Houghton, Mifflin], MDCCCCIX.

Combined with *The House of the Seven Gables* in two-volumes-in-one format and published as vol. III of the *Fireside Edition.* See B 15.

A 19.7.g

Boston, New York: Jefferson Press, [1913].

Combined with *The House of the Seven Gables* in two-volumes-in-one format and published as vol. III of the *"Jefferson Press Edition."* See B 16.

OTHER EDITIONS

A 19.8

Printings from the Paterson-Scott plates

Edinburgh: William Paterson, 1883.

No. 13, *Paterson's New England Novels.* Contents same as in first T&F printing (A 19.1.a). Published in cloth, top edges gilded, at 2s.; in ornamental paper covers at 1s. Also combined with *Our Old Home* in two-volumes-in-one format and published as vol. [IV] of the *"Paterson Edition."* See B 17. Also Paterson sheets found with cancel Walter Scott title. Also remanufactured from Paterson plates with Walter Scott title-page imprints. Published in 1894 as vol. [XII] of *"Walter Scott Edition"* (gravure). See B 18. Also noted with undated London and Melbourne: John G. Murdoch, title page in *The Farringdon Library* series.

A 19.9

Ethan Brand. Chicago and New York: Belford, Clarke & Co., 1884.

Caxton Edition. A collection, with the lead story "Ethan Brand" the only item in the collection by Hawthorne. Spine imprint 'ETHAN BRAND | Hawthorne'. Volume produced to capitalize on Hawthorne's name. Reprinted 1888. Also reprinted as no. 109, *The Ideal Library,* Chicago: Donohue, Henneberry, October 26, 1894. Printed wrappers.

A 19.10

Little Daffydowndilly and Other Stories. Boston, New York, Chicago: Houghton, Mifflin, [1887].

Number 29 of the *Riverside Literature Series,* printed October 1887. Contains "A Sketch of the Life of Nathaniel Hawthorne," "Little Daffydowndilly," "Little Annie's Ramble," "The Snow-Image," "A Rill from the Town Pump," "David Swan," "The Vision of the Fountain," "The Threefold Destiny." Printed wrappers. Reprinted without date on front wrapper. Also joined with *Biographical Stories* as combined nos. 29 and 10 of the *Riverside Literature Series,* cloth.

A 19.11
Boston: Houghton, Mifflin, 1893.

'SALEM EDITION' slug on title page. Reprinted unknown number of times with and without date on title page. Not to be confused with A 19.6.d.

A 19.12
The Blithedale Romance—The Snow Image and Other Twice-Told Tales. Philadelphia: David McKay, 1894.

A 19.13
The Great Stone Face. New York, Boston, Chicago, San Francisco: Educational Publishing Co., n.d.

[ca. 1898]. No. 93, *Young Folk's Library of Choice Literature.* Prints title story only. Printed wrappers, cover title.

A 19.14
The Snow-Image. New York, Boston, Chicago, San Francisco: Educational Publishing Co., 1898.

Vol. V., no. 94, *Young Folk's Library of Choice Literature,* printed February 1, 1898. Prints title story only. Printed wrappers, cover title.

A 19.15
The Snow-Image, The Great Stone Face, Little Daffydowndilly. New York: Charles E. Merrill, [1898].

No. 203, *Maynard's English Classic Series.* Prints title stories only. Printed wrappers.

A 19.16
New York: Thomas Y. Crowell, [1899].

Introduction by Richard Burton. Deposited 14 July 1899. Contents same as in first T&F printing (A 19.1.a). Also same plates used to manufacture vol. [12] of the *Crowell "Lenox Edition,"* with new introduction by Katharine Lee Bates. See B 23. Also undated London: S. C. Brown, Langham issue with cancel title page.

A 19.17
Philadelphia: Henry Altemus, [1899].

No. 192, *Altemus' New Illustrated Vademecum Series.*

A 19.18
The Great Stone Face. Chicago: Orville Brewer Publishing Co., 1900.

Vol. 1, no. 5, Student's Series of *Four Penny Classics,* printed April 1, 1900. Prints sketch of Hawthorne and title story only. Printed wrappers, cover title.

A 19.19
The Snow Image. Chicago: Orville Brewer Publishing Co., 1900.

Vol. 1, no. 16, Student's Series of *Four Penny Classics,* printed December 15, 1900. Prints sketch of Hawthorne and title story only. Printed wrappers, cover title.

PRINTINGS FROM THE AUTOGRAPH EDITION PLATES

A 19.20.a
Boston and New York: Houghton, Mifflin, MDCCCC.

Vol. III of the *Autograph Edition*. Contents same as in the *Riverside Edition* (A 19.7.a), with a new introductory note provided. 500 copies. Deposited 20 December 1900. See B 20.

A 19.20.b
Boston and New York: Houghton, Mifflin, MDCCCC.

Vol. III of the *Large-Paper (Autograph) Edition*. 500 copies. See B 21.

A 19.20.c
Boston and New York: Houghton, Mifflin, 1903.

Vol. III of the *Old Manse Edition*. See B 22.

OTHER EDITIONS

A 19.21
Main-Street. Canton, Pa.: Lewis Buddy 3rd, The Kirgate Press, MCM&I.

Preface by Julian Hawthorne. Prints title story only. 950 copies, 75 of which were on Japan vellum. Deposited 20 December 1901.

A 19.22
New York: Thomas Y. Crowell, [1902].

Combined with *The Blithedale Romance* in two-volumes-in-one format and published as vol. [5] of the *Crowell "Popular Edition."* See B 24.

A 19.23
The Great Stone Face. London: A. L. Humphreys, 1903.

Prints title story only.

A 19.24
The Great Stone Face, and Other Stories. Topeka: Crane & Company, 1907.

Biography and notes by Margaret Hill McCarter. Includes "Sketch of Nathaniel Hawthorne," "The Great Stone Face," "The Snow-Image," "A Bell's Biography." No. 30, *The Crane Classics*. Printed wrappers.

A 19.25
The Great Stone Face. London: L. N. Fowler & Co.; Chicago: The Progress Company, 1908.

Prints title story only.

A 19.26
The Snow-Image a Childish Miracle. Portland, Maine: The Bradford Press, 1934.

Prefatory note by Herbert Ross Brown. Prints title story only. Boards. 300 numbered copies.

A 19.27
The Great Stone Face. Lunenburg, Vt.: The Stinehour Press, [1957].

Foreword by Stearns Morse. Drawings by John Nash. Prints title story only. Printed wrappers.

A 19.28
The Great Stone Face & Two Other Stories. New York: Franklin Watts, [1967].

Illustrations by Leonard Everett Fisher. Includes "The Great Stone Face," "Feathertop: A Moralized Legend," "The Minister's Black Veil."

A 19.29
The Snow-Image and Uncollected Tales. [Columbus]: Ohio State University Press, [1974].

Vol. XI of the *Centenary Edition*. Includes 13 previously uncollected tales: "The Battle-Omen," "An Old Woman's Tale," "The Haunted Quack," "Alice Doane's Appeal," "My Visit to Niagara," "Graves and Goblins," "Sketches from Memory," "A Visit to the Clerk of the Weather," "Fragments from the Journal of a Solitary Man," "Time's Portraiture," "The Antique Ring," "A Good Man's Miracle," "A Book of Autographs." 2,388 copies published 7 December 1974. See B 32.

THE

BLITHEDALE ROMANCE.

BY

NATHANIEL HAWTHORNE,

AUTHOR OF "THE SCARLET LETTER," "THE HOUSE OF THE SEVEN GABLES," &c.

IN TWO VOLUMES

VOL. I.

LONDON:
CHAPMAN AND HALL, 193, PICCADILLY.
1852.

come. The greater, surely, was my heroism, when, puffing out a final whiff of cigar-smoke, I quitted my cosey pair of bachelor-rooms,—with a good fire burning in the grate, and a closet right at hand, where there was still a bottle or two in the champagne-basket, and a residuum of claret in a box,—quitted, I say, these comfortable quarters, and plunged into the heart of the pitiless snow-storm, in quest of a better life.

The better life! Possibly it would hardly look so, now; it is enough if it looked so then. The greatest obstacle to being heroic is the doubt whether one may not be going to prove one's self a fool; the truest heroism is, to resist the doubt; and the profoundest wisdom, to know when it ought to be resisted, and when to be obeyed.

Yet, after all, let us acknowledge it wiser, if not more sagacious, to follow out one's day-dream to its natural consummation, although,

A20.1: Title page. 7¹/₂" × 4¹/₄". Page format, 5³/₁₆" (5⁷/₁₆") × 3"

A 20 THE BLITHEDALE ROMANCE

A 20.1
First English edition, only printing [1852]

> *⁎⁎ The English Copyright of this Romance is the property of*
> MESSRS. CHAPMAN *and* HALL.

> *⁎⁎ The English Copyright of this Romance is the property of*
> MESSRS. CHAPMAN *and* HALL.

2 vols. To protect the English copyright, Ticknor and Fields held up American publication to allow Chapman and Hall to publish first.

I: [i–iii] iv [1] 2–7 [8–9] 10–17 [18] 19–28 [29] 30–48 [49] 50–67 [68] 69–83 [84] 85–106 [107] 108–125 [126] 127–151 [152] 153–179 [180] 181–196 [197] 198–216 [217] 218–233 [234] 235–259 [260]

II: [i–iii] iv [1] 2–25 [26] 27–44 [45] 46–62 [63] 64–80 [81] 82–95 [96] 97–114 [115] 116–126 [127] 128–143 [144] 145–169 [170] 171–191 [192] 193–211 [212] 213–230 [231] 232–245 [246] 247–265 [266] 267–280 [281] 282–287 [288]. II.64 is misnumbered as 46.

I: [A]² B–I⁸ K–R⁸ S²

II: [A]² B–I⁸ K–T⁸

Contents: I: p. i: title; p. ii: copyright; pp. iii–iv: contents; pp. 1–7: preface; p. 8: blank; pp. 9–259: text, headed 'THE BLITHEDALE ROMANCE. | [rule] | I. | OLD MOODIE.'; p. 260: blank.

   II: p. i: title; p. ii: copyright; pp. iii–iv: contents; pp. 1–287: text, headed 'THE BLITHEDALE ROMANCE. | [rule] | I. | ELIOT'S PULPIT.'; p. 288: blank.

Typography and paper: See illustration, A 20.1 page format. Running heads: rectos, chapter titles; versos, 'THE BLITHEDALE ROMANCE.' White wove paper.

Binding: Brown (81. d. gy. y Br) coarse-ribbed morocco AR-like cloth. Covers blind-stamped with design incorporating triple-rules border frame containing elaborate floral frame. Spine goldstamped (see illustration, A 20 bindings [at A 17]). White wove endpapers coated pale yellow one side. Chapman and Hall ads printed on some endpapers. 36 pp. of C&H catalogue inserted at rear in some copies. Top and front edges untrimmed in most copies. Bound by Bone & Son, 76 Fleet Street, London.

Publication: Unknown number of copies published shortly before 7 July 1852. Price for two-volume set 21s. C&H purchased the British rights to *Blithedale* for £200 ($1,000 at the then current rate of exchange).

Printing: Set from proof sheets of the American typesetting. Printed by Whiting, Beaufort House, Strand, London.

Locations: BM, 12705.d.10 (deposit-stamp 1 JY 52), CEFC, MB, MH, NN.

THE

BLITHEDALE ROMANCE.

BY

NATHANIEL HAWTHORNE.

BOSTON:
TICKNOR, REED, AND FIELDS.
M DCCC LII.

---

very sorry, for you will certainly hear me singing them, sometimes, in the summer evenings."

"Of all things," answered I, "that is what will delight me most."

While this passed, and while she spoke to my companions, I was taking note of Zenobia's aspect; and it impressed itself on me so distinctly, that I can now summon her up, like a ghost, a little warmer than the life, but otherwise identical with it. She was dressed as simply as possible, in an American print (I think the dry goods people call it so), but with a silken kerchief, between which and her gown there was one glimpse of a white shoulder. It struck me as a great piece of good fortune that there should be just that glimpse. Her hair, which was dark, glossy, and of singular abundance, was put up rather soberly and primly, without curls or other ornament, except a single flower. It was an exotic, of rare beauty, and as fresh as if the hot-house gardener had just clipt it from the stem. That flower has struck deep root into my memory. I can both see it and smell it, at this moment. So brilliant, so rare, so costly, as it must have been, and yet enduring only for a day, it was more indicative of the pride and pomp which had a luxuriant growth in Zenobia's character than if a great diamond had sparkled among her hair.

Her hand, though very soft, was larger than most women would like to have, or than they could afford to have, though not a whit too large in proportion with the spacious plan of Zenobia's entire development. It did one good to see a fine intellect (as hers really was, although its natural tendency lay in another direction than towards literature) so fitly cased. She was, indeed, an

A 20.2.a: Title page, 7¹/₁₆" × 4¹/₄." Page format, 5¹/₈" (5⁷/₁₆") × 3"

A 20.2.a
First American edition, first printing [1852]

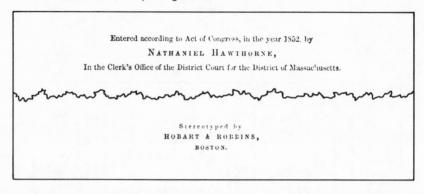

Entered according to Act of Congress, in the year 1852, by
NATHANIEL HAWTHORNE,
In the Clerk's Office of the District Court for the District of Massachusetts.

Stereotyped by
HOBART & ROBBINS,
BOSTON.

All printings of the first American edition of *Blithedale* were made from stereotype plates, with the first two printings dated M DCCC LII on the title page. The first printing may be distinguished by the position of the copyright-page notices (see illustrations of type batter in the 1852 printings of *Blithedale,* pp. 214–215). An examination of type-batter confirms the priority of printings. For a discussion of the evidence establishing the first printing, see my article "Distinguishing the First Printing of *The Blithedale Romance,*" in *The Nathaniel Hawthorne Journal 1973* (Englewood, Colo.: Microcard Editions Books, 1973), pp. 172–176. Found in trade binding (see illustration, A 20 bindings [at A 17]) and in Ticknor format B "gift" binding (see illustration, A 2.6 binding). Publisher's spine stamping noted with both capital "O" and small "o" in "CO."

[i–iii] iv–vi [vii] viii [9] 10–288

[1]⁸ 2–18⁸

Contents: p. i: title; p. ii: copyright; pp. iii–vi: preface; pp. vii–viii: contents; pp. 9–288: text, headed 'THE BLITHEDALE ROMANCE. | [rule] | I. | OLD MODIE.'

Typography and paper: See illustration, A 20.2.a page format. Running heads: rectos, chapter titles; versos, 'THE BLITHEDALE ROMANCE.' White wove paper.

Binding: In the style of Ticknor format A (see illustration, A 2.6 binding). Brown (81. d. gy. y Br) bold-ribbed T cloth with blindstamped floral device inside ruled panels on both covers. Spine goldstamped, with publisher's imprint in two variant forms (see illustration, A 20 bindings [at A 17]). Pale yellow endpapers. Flyleaf inserted front and rear. 8 pp. of T&F catalogue inserted front or rear, with various dates (see Introduction), in some copies. Edges trimmed. Also "gift" binding in style of Ticknor format B (see illustration, A 2.6 binding), with central designs on covers goldstamped and edges gilded. Red (13. deep Rose) bold-ribbed T cloth. Spine goldstamped. Edges trimmed and gilded.

Publication: 5,090 copies published 14 July 1852. 90 review copies distributed. Price 75¢. Hawthorne received a 15% royalty on 5,000 copies.

Printing: Composition and stereotype plates by Hobart & Robbins, Boston; printed by Thurston, Torry & Co., Boston. Probably bound by Benjamin Bradley & Co., Boston.

Locations: CEFC, MH, NN.

Manuscript: The author's holograph manuscript that served as printer's copy located in the Pierpont Morgan Library. Also a single page from an early draft preserved at OU.

LATER PRINTINGS WITHIN THE FIRST AMERICAN EDITION

A 20.2.b
Second printing

Boston: Ticknor, Reed, and Fields, M DCCC LII.

See illustrations of the type batter in the 1852 printings under A 20.2.a for distinguishing characteristics. 2,350 copies published 12 August 1852. Price 75¢, royalty 5¢.

A 20.2.c
Boston: Ticknor and Fields, M DCCC LV.

536 copies printed 5 September 1855. Price 75¢, with a 15% royalty on 500 copies.

A 20.2.d
Boston: Ticknor and Fields, M DCCC LIX.

277 copies printed 1 February 1859. Price 75¢, royalty 11.25¢.

A 20.2.e
Boston: Ticknor and Fields, M DCCC LX.

280 copies printed 18 August 1860. Price 75¢, royalty 11.25¢.

A 20.2.f
Boston: Ticknor and Fields, M DCCC LXII.

280 copies printed 24 June 1862. Price 75¢, royalty 11.25¢.

A 20.2.g
Boston: Ticknor and Fields, M DCCC LXIII.

280 copies printed 30 July 1863. Price $1.00, royalty 11.25¢.

A 20.2.h
Boston: Ticknor and Fields, 1865.

Vol. 8 of untitled *"Tinted Edition"* on laid paper. 500 copies printed 31 October 1864. Price $1.50, royalty 12¢. See B 1[8] for reprintings of the *"Tinted Edition."*

A 20.2.i
Boston: Ticknor and Fields, M DCCC LXV.

280 copies printed 19 November 1864. Price $1.50, royalty 11.25¢.

A 20.2.j
Boston: Ticknor and Fields, 1865.

520 copies printed 11 April 1865. Price $1.50, royalty 12.5¢.

A 20.2.k
Boston: Ticknor and Fields, 1866.

315 copies printed 20 August 1866. Price $1.50, royalty 12¢.

PREFACE.

IN the " BLITHEDALE" of this volume many read-ers will, probably, suspect a faint and not very faith-ful shadowing of BROOK FARM, in Roxbury, which (now a little more than ten years ago) was occupied and cultivated by a company of socialists. The author does not wish to deny that he had this community in his mind, and that (having had the good fortune, for a time, to be personally connected with it) he has occa-sionally availed himself of his actual reminiscences, in the hope of giving a more life-like tint to the fancy-sketch in the following pages. He begs it to be understood, however, that he has considered the insti-tution itself as not less fairly the subject of fictitious handling than the imaginary personages whom he has introduced there. His whole treatment of the affair is altogether incidental to the main purpose of the romance ; nor does he put forward the slightest pre-tensions to illustrate a theory, or elicit a conclusion, favorable or otherwise, in respect to socialism.

In short, his present concern with the socialist

Entered according to Act of Congress, in the year 1852, by
NATHANIEL HAWTHORNE,
In the Clerk's Office of the District Court for the District of Massachusetts.

Stereotyped by
HOBART & ROBBINS,
BOSTON.

HOLLING

97.1	**better kind of sha**	108.28	Especially does the
	on this bare slope		out that latent hostili
			sects, and those who

First 1852 Printing of *The Blithedale Romance*

A 20.2.l
Boston: Fields, Osgood, 1870.

280 copies printed 5 September 1870. Price $2.00, royalty 20¢.

A 20.2.m
Boston: James R. Osgood, 1871.

Combined with *The Scarlet Letter* in two-volumes-in-one format and published as the third volume of the *Illustrated Library Edition*. 1,000 copies printed 25 June 1871. Price $2.00, royalty 20¢. See B 2 for reprintings of the *ILE*.

A 20.2.n
Boston: Houghton, Mifflin, 1880.

Combined with *The Scarlet Letter* and *Mosses from an Old Manse* in four-volumes-in-one format and published as the second volume of the *Globe Edition*. 1,500 copies printed August 1880. See B 3 for reprintings of the *Globe Edition*.

PREFACE.

In the "BLITHEDALE" of this volume many readers will, probably, suspect a faint and not very faithful shadowing of BROOK FARM, in Roxbury, which (now a little more than ten years ago) was occupied and cultivated by a company of socialists. The author does not wish to deny that he had this community in his mind, and that (having had the good fortune, for a time, to be personally connected with it) he has occasionally availed himself of his actual reminiscences, in the hope of giving a more life-like tint to the fancy-sketch in the following pages. He begs it to be understood, however, that he has considered the institution itself as not less fairly the subject of fictitious handling than the imaginary personages whom he has introduced there. His whole treatment of the affair is altogether incidental to the main purpose of the romance ; nor does he put forward the slightest pretensions to illustrate a theory, or elicit a conclusion, favorable or otherwise, in respect to socialism.

In short, his present concern with the socialist

HOLLING

97.1	**better kind of sha** **on this bare slope**	108.28	Especially does the out that latent hostili sects, and those who

Second 1852 Printing of *The Blithedale Romance*

A 20.2.o
Boston: Houghton, Mifflin, [1886].

Combined with *The Scarlet Letter* and *Mosses from an Old Manse* in four-volumes-in-one format and published as the second volume of the *"New" Fireside Edition.* 1,000 copies printed May 1886. See B 4.

OTHER EDITION

A 20.3
Second English edition

London: Chapman and Hall, MDCCCLIV.

'SECOND EDITION' slug on title page. In Chapman and Hall's *Select Library of Fiction.* Yellow printed paper-covered boards. Price 2s. Sheets also bound with other titles in the series and issued in two-volumes-in-one format in various bindings.

PRINTINGS FROM THE "LITTLE CLASSIC EDITION" PLATES

A 20.4.a

[All following within red and black double-rules frame] THE | [red] Blithedale Romance. | [black] BY | NATHANIEL HAWTHORNE. | [vignette of brook scene] | [red] BOSTON: | [black] JAMES R. OSGOOD AND COMPANY, | Late Ticknor & Fields, and Fields, Osgood, & Co. | [red] 1876.

Vol. [VIII], *"Little Classic Edition."* Contents same as in first American edition (A 20.2.a). Sheets bound with James R. Osgood and, later, Houghton, Osgood spine imprints. 3,000 copies printed 18 November 1875. Price $1.25, royalty 12.5¢. See B 5 [VIII] for reprintings of the *"Little Classic Edition."*

A 20.4.b
Boston: Houghton, Osgood, 1879.

Combined with *The Scarlet Letter* in two-volumes-in-one format and published as vol. III of the *"Fireside Edition."* 500 copies printed 20 September 1879. See B 6[III] for reprintings of the *"Fireside Edition."*

A 20.4.c
Boston: Houghton, Mifflin, [1891].

Combined with *Mosses from an Old Manse* in three-volumes-in-one format and published as vol. II of the *Popular Edition.* 1,000 copies printed June–August 1891. See B 7 for reprintings of the *Popular Edition.*

A 20.4.d
Boston and New York: Houghton, Mifflin, 1893.

'SALEM EDITION' slug on title page. Introduction by George Parsons Lathrop. Reprinted 1894; also reprinted without title-page date.

A 20.4.e
Boston: Houghton, Mifflin, [1899].

Vol. [VIII], *Concord Edition.* See B 8.

PRINTINGS FROM THE RIVERSIDE EDITION PLATES

A 20.5.a1
Riverside Edition (trade), first printing, American issue [1883]

THE SCARLET LETTER | AND | THE BLITHEDALE ROMANCE | BY | NATHANIEL HAWTHORNE | [vignette of Pearl] | BOSTON | HOUGHTON, MIFFLIN AND COMPANY | New York: 11 East Seventeenth Street | The Riverside Press, Cambridge | 1883

Two volumes in one published as vol. V of the Riverside trade printing. Contents same as in *"Little Classic Edition"* (A 20.4.a), with "Introductory Note" by George Parsons Lathrop added. 1,500 copies printed March 1883. Price $2.00. See B 9 for reprintings of the Riverside trade printing.

A 20.5.a₂
Riverside Edition (trade), first printing, English issue [1883]

London: Kegan Paul, Trench, 1883.

Sheets of vol. V, first printing (A 20.5.a₁), with cancel title, in a Kegan Paul binding. 250 Kegan Paul title pages printed by Houghton, Mifflin, June–July 1883. Later issues noted with dated and undated Kegan Paul, Trench, Trübner title pages. See B 11.

A 20.5.b
Riverside Edition (large paper), second printing [1883]

[red] THE SCARLET LETTER | [black] AND | THE BLITHEDALE ROMANCE | BY | NATHANIEL HAWTHORNE | [vignette of Pearl] | [red] CAMBRIDGE | [black] Printed at the Riverside Press | 1883

Two volumes in one published as vol. V of the Riverside large-paper printing. 250 copies printed April 1883. See B 10.

A 20.5.c
Boston and New York: Houghton, Mifflin, 1884.

Vol. X of the *Wayside Edition.* 500 copies printed September–October 1884. See B 12.

A 20.5.d
Boston and New York: Houghton, Mifflin, [1891].

Combined with *The Scarlet Letter* in two-volumes-in-one format and published as vol. V of the *Standard Library Edition.* 500 copies printed October 1891. See B 13.

A 20.5.e
Boston and New York: Houghton, Mifflin, [1902].

Combined with *The Scarlet Letter* in two-volumes-in-one format and published as vol. V of the *"New" Wayside Edition.* 500 copies printed September–October 1902. See B 14.

A 20.5.f
Boston and New York: [Houghton, Mifflin], MDCCCCIX.

Combined with *The Scarlet Letter* in two-volumes-in-one format and published as vol. V of the *Fireside Edition.* See B 15.

A 20.5.g
Boston, New York: Jefferson Press, [1913].

Combined with *The Scarlet Letter* in two-volumes-in-one format and published as vol. [V] of the *"Jefferson Press Edition."* See B 16.

OTHER EDITIONS

A 20.6
London: George Bell, 1884.

Combined with *Transformation* in three-volumes-in-one format and published as vol. III, *Nathaniel Hawthorne's Tales,* in the *Bohn's Standard Library.* Reprinted 1886.

A 20.7
London, New York: Ward, Lock, [n.d.].

[1884.] 'SEVENTH EDITION' slug on title page.

Location: BM, 12622.1.16 (deposit-stamp 6 NO 84).

Note: No earlier Ward, Lock "editions" located.

A 20.8
Printings from the Paterson-Scott plates

Edinburgh: William Paterson, 1885.

No. 20, *Paterson's New England Novels.* Contents same as in first American edition
(A 20.2.a). Published in cloth, top edges gilded, at 2s.; in ornamental paper covers at
1s. Also combined with *Tanglewood Tales* in two-volumes-in-one format and published as vol. [V] of the *"Paterson Edition."* See B 17. Also Paterson sheets found with
cancel Walter Scott title. Also remanufactured from Paterson plates with Walter Scott
title-page imprints. Published in 1894 as vol. [III] of the *"Walter Scott Edition"* (gravure). See B 18.

A 20.9
New York: Hurst and Company, [1894].

No. 414, *The Universal Library,* printed 15 June 1894. Printed wrappers. Reprinted
with undated title page, in cloth.

A 20.10
Philadelphia: David McKay, 1894.

Combined with *The Snow Image* in two-volumes-in-one format and published in
American Classic Series.

A 20.11
London: Service and Paton, 1899.

Introduction by Moncure D. Conway. Reprinted with London: James Nisbet, 1901,
title-page imprint.

A 20.12
New York: T. Y. Crowell, [1899].

Introduction by Andrew J. George. Deposited 20 July 1899. Also plates used to manufacture vol. [9] of the *Crowell "Lenox Edition,"* with new introduction by Katharine Lee
Bates, 1902. See B 23.

A 20.13
Philadelphia: Henry Altemus, [n.d.].

[ca. 1899]. No. 18 in the *Altemus' New Illustrated Vademecum Series.* Reprinted in
various undated formats.

A 20.14.a
Boston and New York: Houghton, Mifflin, MDCCCC.

Vol. VIII of the *Autograph Edition*. Contents same as in the *Riverside Edition* (A 20.5.a₁), with a new introductory note provided. 500 copies. Deposited 20 December 1900. See B 20.

A 20.14.b
Boston and New York: Houghton, Mifflin, MDCCCC.

Vol. VIII of the *Large-Paper (Autograph) Edition*. 500 copies. See B 21.

A 20.14.c
Boston and New York: Houghton, Mifflin, 1903.

Vol. VIII of the *Old Manse Edition*. See B 22.

OTHER EDITIONS

A 20.15
New York: Thomas Y. Crowell, [1902].

Combined with *The Snow-Image* in two-volumes-in-one format and published as vol. [5] of the *Crowell "Popular Edition."* See B 24.

A 20.16
The Blithedale Romance and Fanshawe. [Columbus]: Ohio State University Press, [1965].

The Blithedale Romance and *Fanshawe* combined in two-volumes-in-one format and published as vol. III of the *Centenary Edition*. 1,000 copies published 27 December 1965. See B 32 for reprintings of the *Centenary Edition*.

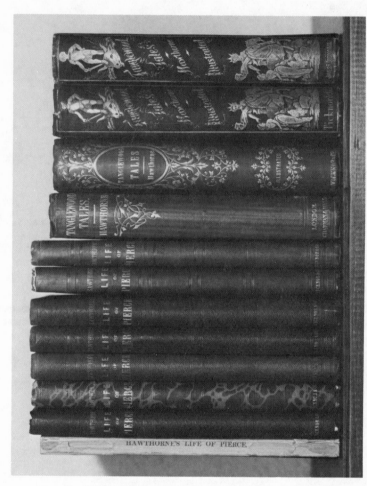

Bindings for (1–8) A21.1, some of a wide variety; (9) A22.1; (10) A22.2.a; (11) A22.2.d; (12) A22.2.t (see also illustration at A21.2)

LIFE

OF

FRANKLIN PIERCE.

BY

NATHANIEL HAWTHORNE.

BOSTON:
TICKNOR, REED, AND FIELDS.
M DCCC LII.

The opponents of the measure ridiculed him as the " baby judge;" but his conduct in that high office showed the prescient judgment of the friend who had known him from a child, and had seen in his young manhood already the wisdom of ripened age. It was some years afterwards when Franklin Pierce entered the office of Judge Woodbury as a student. In the interval, the judge had been elected governor, and, after a term of office that thoroughly tested the integrity of his democratic principles, had lost his second election, and returned to the profession of the law.

The last two years of Pierce's preparatory studies were spent at the law school of Northampton, in Massachusetts, and in the office of Judge Parker at Amherst. In 1827, being admitted to the bar, he began the practice of his profession at Hillsborough. It is an interesting fact, considered in reference to his subsequent splendid career as an advocate, that he did not, at the outset, give promise of distinguished success. His first case was a failure, and perhaps a somewhat marked one. But it is remembered that this defeat, however mortifying at the moment, did but serve to make him aware of the latent resources of his mind, the full command of which he was far from having yet attained. To a friend, an older practitioner, who addressed him with some expression of condolence and encouragement, Pierce replied,—and it was a kind of self-assertion which no triumph would

A21.1: Title page, 7¹/₁₆" × 4⁵/₁₆". Text page, 5¹/₁₆" (5⁵/₁₆") × 3¹/₁₆"

A 21 LIFE OF FRANKLIN PIERCE

A 21.1.a,b,c
First edition, three printings [1852]

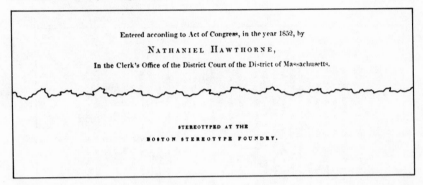

The *Cost Books* record three printings of the first edition, all with title-page date M DCCC LII (31 August, 30 September, 4 October), from stereotype plates. Priority undetermined.

[1–3] 4 [5–7] 8–144. Frontispiece portrait of Pierce inserted facing title page.

[A]⁸ B–I⁸; also signed [1]⁶ 2–12⁶

Contents: p. 1: title; p. 2: copyright; pp. 3–4: preface; p. 5: contents; p. 6: blank; pp. 7–144: text, headed 'LIFE | OF | FRANKLIN PIERCE. | [rule] | CHAPTER I. | HIS PARENTAGE AND EARLY LIFE.'

Typography and paper: See illustration, A 21.1 page format. Running heads: versos, 'LIFE OF'; rectos, 'FRANKLIN PIERCE'. White wove paper.

Binding: In the style of Ticknor format A (see illustration, A 2.6 binding). Brown (81. d. gy. y Br) bold-ribbed T cloth with blindstamped floral device inside ruled panels on both covers. Also noted in a wide variety of cloth in basic Ticknor binding A format, including blue-marbled brown, red-marbled brown, black, and green—any bindery cloth that was available was probably used as expedient for this campaign biography. Spine goldstamped, with publisher's imprint in various forms (see illustration, A 21 bindings). Pale yellow wove endpapers. Flyleaf inserted front and rear. Bottom edges untrimmed in most copies. 4 pp. of T&F ads with various dates inserted at front. Also issued in buff printed wrappers in two forms: (A) with 'Price 37-1/2¢' on front cover; (B) without price slug (see illustration). Wrappers probably printed from duplicate sets of plates, with variation in positioning of spine imprint. Inside front wrapper and inside and outside rear wrapper carry ads for Hawthorne titles.

Note one: The *Cost Books* entry is confusing, but it appears as if 3,110 copies were bound in cloth and 9,790 copies in paper wrappers. 995 of the wrappered copies apparently differed in some way as they cost more than twice as much to bind as the balance of the wrappered copies. The fact that the print runs and the binding totals do not coincide suggests that sheets of each print run were bound both in cloth and in paper wrappers.

Publication: 4,762 copies printed 31 August 1852, 6,190 copies printed 30 September, 2,000 copies printed 4 October. *Cost Books* list a royalty of $300 against 12,000 copies. Listed in the *Boston Daily Advertiser,* 11 September 1852, as "published this day."

Note two: The publisher made an effort to secure the widest possible distribution of this title. Discounts to the trade were raised to 40% and more. On 2 October 1852 Hawthorne wrote W. D. Ticknor supporting a plan by the Democratic party for gratuitous distribution of the *Life* in New York City. 5,000 copies were bought by the Democratic Committee at a discount of 62.5%.

Printing: Composition ad stereotype plates by the Boston Stereotype Foundry. Frontispiece portrait engraved and printed by Joseph Andrews and C. E. Wagstaff.

Locations: Cloth: CEFC, CtY, LC, Lilly, MB, MH, NN, PSt; wrappers A and B: CEFC.

Manuscript: Manuscript located in the Huntington Library.

Wrapper A

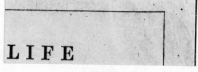

Wrapper B

LIFE

OF

FRANKLIN PIERCE,

PRESIDENT OF THE UNITED STATES.

BY

NATHANIEL HAWTHORNE

LONDON:

GEORGE ROUTLEDGE AND CO., FARRINGDON STREET.
1853.

---

spring of the succeeding year, he built himself a log hut, and began the clearing and cultivation of his tract. Another year beheld him married to his first wife, Elizabeth Andrews, who died within a twelvemonth after their union, leaving a daughter, the present widow of General John McNeil. In 1789, he married Anna Kendrick, with whom he lived about half a century, and who bore him eight children, of whom Franklin was the sixth.

Although the revolutionary soldier had thus betaken himself to the wilderness for a subsistence, his professional merits were not forgotten by those who had witnessed his military career. As early as 1786, he was appointed brigade-major of the militia of Hillsborough county, then first organized and formed into a brigade. And it was a still stronger testimonial to his character as a soldier, that, nearly fifteen years afterwards, during the presidency of John Adams, he was offered a high command in the northern division of the army which was proposed to be levied in anticipation of a war with the French republic. Inflexibly democratic in his political faith, however, Major Pierce refused to be implicated in a policy which he could not approve. " No, gentlemen," said he to the delegates, who urged his acceptance of the commission, " poor as I am, and acceptable as would be the position under other circumstances, I would sooner go to yonder mountains, dig me

---

A 21.2: Title page, 6⁷/₁₆″ × 4″. Page format, 5″ (5¹/₄″) × 3¹/₁₆″

A 21.2
First English edition, only printing [*1853*]

[i–viii] [1]–135 [136]

[A]⁴ B–I⁸ K⁴

Contents: p. i: title; p. ii: blank; pp. iii–v: preface; p. vi: blank; p. vii: contents; p. viii: blank; pp. 1–135: text, headed 'LIFE | OF | FRANKLIN PIERCE. | [rule] | CHAPTER I. | HIS PARENTAGE AND EARLY LIFE.'; p. 136: blank.

Omits notes A and B at end of T&F edition. Also omits frontispiece portrait of Pierce.

Typography and paper: See illustration, A 21.2 page format. Running heads: versos, 'THE LIFE OF'; rectos, 'FRANKLIN PIERCE.' White wove paper.

Binding: Orange paper-covered boards, imprinted in black ink (see illustration, A 21.2 cover). Endpapers imprinted with Routledge advertisements.

Publication: Unknown number of copies published in December 1852 as part of *The Railway Library*. Price 1s. Listed in *Athenaeum,* 11 December 1852, and *Publishers' Circular,* 1 January 1853.

Printing: Printed by Cox (Brothers) and Wyman, Printers, Great Queen Street, [London].

Locations: BM (rebound), 12705.bb.19 (deposit-stamp 29 DE 52), LC, PSt.

PRINTINGS FROM THE RIVERSIDE EDITION PLATES

A 21.3.a₁
Riverside Edition (trade), first printing, American issue [*1883*]

Boston: Houghton, Mifflin, 1883.

Combined with other works in *Tales, Sketches, and Other Papers* and published as vol. XII of the Riverside trade printing. Contents same as in first T&F edition (A 21.1.a), except for omission of note B. 3,000 copies printed June 1883. Price $2.00. See B 9 for reprintings of the Riverside trade printing.

A 21.3.a₂
Riverside Edition (trade), first printing, English issue [*1883*]

London: Kegan Paul, Trench, 1883.

Sheets of vol. XII, first printing (A 21.3.a₁), with cancel title, in a Kegan Paul binding. 250 Kegan Paul title pages printed by Houghton, Mifflin, June–July 1883. Later issues noted with dated and undated Kegan Paul, Trench, Trübner title pages. See B 11.

A 21.3.b
Riverside Edition (large paper), second printing [*1883*]

Cambridge: Riverside Press, 1883.

Combined with *Tales, Sketches, and Other Papers* and published as vol. XII of the Riverside large-paper printing. 250 copies printed August 1883. See B 10.

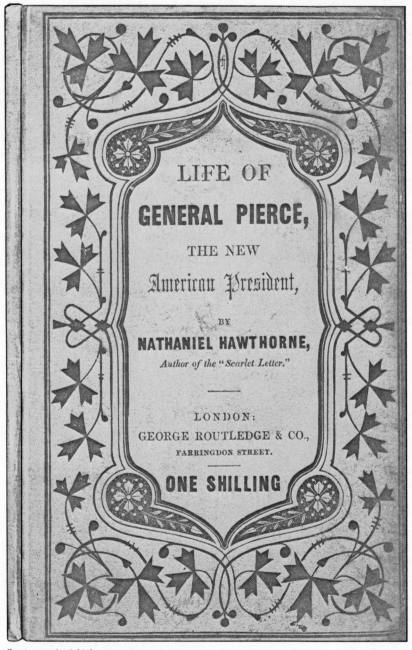

Front cover for A 21.2

A 21.3.c
Boston and New York: Houghton, Mifflin, 1884.

Combined with the second part of *Tales, Sketches, and Other Papers* and published as vol. XXIII of the *Wayside Edition*. 500 copies printed September–October 1884. See B 12.

A 21.3.d
Boston and New York: Houghton, Mifflin, [1891].

Combined with other works in *Tales, Sketches, and Other Papers* and published as vol. XII of the *Standard Library Edition*. 500 copies printed October 1891. See B 13.

A 21.3.e
Boston and New York: Houghton, Mifflin, [1902].

Combined with other works in *Tales, Sketches, and Other Papers* and published as vol. XII of the *"New" Wayside Edition*. 500 copies, printed September–October 1902. See B 14.

A 21.3.f
Boston and New York: [Houghton, Mifflin], MDCCCCIX.

Combined with other works in *Tales, Sketches, and Other Papers* and published as vol. XII of the *Fireside Edition*. See B 15.

PRINTINGS FROM "LITTLE CLASSIC EDITION" PLATES

A 21.4.a
Boston: Houghton, Mifflin, [1883].

Combined with other works in *Sketches and Studies* and published as vol. [XXIV] of the *"Little Classic Edition."* Contents same as in first T&F edition (A 21.1.a), except for omission of notes A and B. 1,000 copies printed September 1883. See B 5.

A 21.4.b
Boston: Houghton, Mifflin, [1891].

Combined with *Passages from the French and Italian Note-Books* and other works in *Sketches and Studies* in three-volumes-in-one format and published as vol. VIII of the *Popular Edition*. 1,000 copies printed June–August 1891. See B 7.

A 21.4.c
Boston: Houghton, Mifflin, [1899].

Combined with other works in *Sketches and Studies* and published as vol. [XXIV] of the *"Concord Edition."* See B 8.

PRINTINGS FROM THE AUTOGRAPH EDITION PLATES

A 21.5.a
Boston and New York: Houghton, Mifflin, MDCCCC.

Combined with other works in *Miscellanies* and published as vol. XVII in the *Autograph Edition*. Contents same as in first T&F edition (A 21.1.a), except for omission of note B. 500 copies. Deposited 5 March 1901. See B 20.

A 21.5.b
Boston and New York: Houghton, Mifflin, MDCCCC.

Combined with other works in *Miscellanies* and published as vol. XVII in the *Large-Paper (Autograph) Edition*. 500 copies. See B 21.

A 21.5.c
Boston and New York: Houghton, Mifflin, 1903.

Combined with other works in *Miscellanies* and published as vol. XVII in the *Old Manse Edition*. See B 22.

"Leave that to me, please your majesty," she replied. "Only admit this evil-minded young man to your presence, treat him civilly, and invite him to drink a goblet of wine. Your majesty is well aware that I sometimes amuse myself with distilling very powerful medicines. Here is one of them in this small phial. As to what it is made of, that is one of my secrets of state. Do but let me put a single drop into the goblet, and let the young man taste it ; and I will answer for it, he shall quite lay aside the bad designs with which he comes hither."

As she said this, Medea smiled ; but, for all her smiling face, she meant nothing less than to poison the poor innocent Theseus, before his father's eyes. And King Ægeus, like most other kings, thought any punishment mild enough for a person who was accused of plotting against his life. He therefore made little or no objection to Medea's scheme, and as soon as the poisonous wine was ready, gave orders that the young stranger should be admitted into his presence. The goblet was set on a table beside the king's throne ; and a fly, meaning just to sip a little from the brim, immediately tumbled into it, dead. Observing this, Medea looked round at the nephews and smiled again.

When Theseus was ushered into the royal apartment, the only object that he seemed to behold was the white-bearded old king. There he sat on his magnificent throne, a dazzling crown on his head, and a sceptre in his hand. His aspect was stately and

TANGLEWOOD TALES,

FOR

GIRLS AND BOYS :

Being a Second Wonder-Book.

BY

NATHANIEL HAWTHORNE.

WITH ILLUSTRATIONS.

LONDON:
CHAPMAN AND HALL, 193, PICCADILLY.
1853.

A22.1: Title page, 6⅝" × 4⅛". Page format, 5³/₁₆" (5⁷/₁₆") × 3"

A 22 TANGLEWOOD TALES, FOR GIRLS AND BOYS; BEING A SECOND
WONDER-BOOK

A 22.1
First English edition, only printing [1853]

To protect the English copyright, Ticknor and Fields held up American publication to
allow Chapman and Hall to publish first.

[i–vi] [1] 2–10 [11] 12–49 [50] 51–76 [77] 78–117 [118] 119–157 [158] 159–201 [202]
203–251 [252]. Frontispiece illustration on verso of first leaf of a two-leaf fold on plate
paper facing engraved title page on recto of second leaf, each obverse blank. This
two-leaf fold inserted between half-title leaf (A1) and printed title leaf (A1+1). Printed
title is on plate paper also and tipped in. Plates inserted facing pp. 44, 72, 141, 162,
202.

[A]² (A1+1) B–I⁸ K–Q⁸ R⁶

Note: Engraved title page is same as in first American edition (A 22.2.a); engraved
illustrations are taken from the American edition but incorporate story captions and
page references instead of quotations used in the T&F edition.

Contents: p. i: half title; p. ii: blank; p. iii: printed title; p. iv: blank; p. v: contents; p.
vi: blank; pp. 1–251: text, headed 'TANGLEWOOD TALES. | [double rules] | THE
WAYSIDE. | [rule] | INTRODUCTORY.'; p. 252: blank.

Includes "The Wayside—Introductory," "The Minotaur," "The Pygmies," "The Dragon's
Teeth," "Circe's Palace," "The Pomegranate Seeds," "The Golden Fleece."

Typography and paper: See illustration, A 22.1 page format. Running heads: rectos
and versos, chapter titles. White wove paper.

Binding: Green (126. d. Ol G) herringbone-patterned cloth. Covers blindstamped
with decorative lattice-framed window-like panel with central floral element, all inside
single-edge rule. Spine goldstamped (see illustration, A 22 bindings [at A 21]). White
wove endpapers coated pale yellow one side. Top edge untrimmed. Bound by Bone &
Son, 76 Fleet Street, London.

Publication: Unknown number of copies published August 1853. Advertised for "this
day" in *Athenaeum,* 13 August 1853. C&H purchased the British rights to *Tanglewood
Tales* for £50, including copyright. Casts of American engravings offered for an
additional £14.

Printing: Type set from sheets of the American first edition supplied by Ticknor,
Reed, and Fields.

Locations: BM, 4505.a.18 (deposit-stamp 24 AU 53), CEFC, CtY, MH, OU.

The little fellow had a great opinion of his own strength. So, grasping the rough protuberances of the rock, he tugged and toiled amain, and got himself quite out of breath, without being able to stir the heavy stone. It seemed to be rooted into the ground. No wonder he could not move it; for it would have taken all the force of a very strong man to lift it out of its earthy bed.

His mother stood looking on, with a sad kind of a smile on her lips and in her eyes, to see the zealous and yet puny efforts of her little boy. She could not help being sorrowful at finding him already so impatient to begin his adventures in the world.

"You see how it is, my dear Theseus," said she. "You must possess far more strength than now before I can trust you to go to Athens, and tell King Ægeus that you are his son. But when you can lift this rock, and show me what is hidden beneath it, I promise you my permission to depart."

Often and often, after this, did Theseus ask his mother whether it was yet time for him to go to Athens; and still his mother pointed to the

---

TANGLEWOOD TALES,

FOR

GIRLS AND BOYS;

BEING

A SECOND WONDER-BOOK.

BY

NATHANIEL HAWTHORNE.

WITH FINE ILLUSTRATIONS.

BOSTON:

TICKNOR, REED, AND FIELDS.

M DCCC LIII.

A22.2.a: Title page, 6⁹/₁₆″ × 4³/₁₆″. Page format, 4¹⁵/₁₆″ (5¹/₄″) × 3″

A 22.2.a
First American edition, first printing [1853]

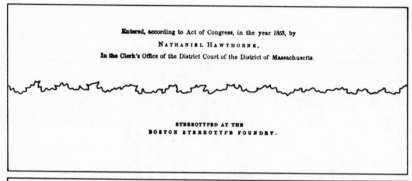

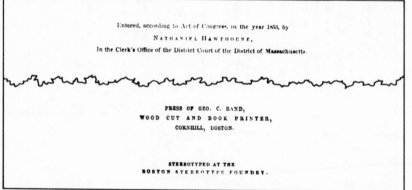

All printings of the first American edition of *Tanglewood Tales* were made from stereo-type plates, with the first two printings dated M DCCC LIII. The first printing has only the stereotyper's imprint at the bottom of the copyright page. The printer's imprint was added in the second printing.

[1–4] 5 [6] 7–336. Engraved title on plate paper inserted before printed title. Six plates inserted facing pp. 64, 85, 114, 191, 220, 272.

[1]⁸ 2–21⁸

Contents: pp. 1–2: blank; p. 3: printed title; p. 4: copyright; p. 5: contents; p. 6: blank; pp. 7–336: text, headed 'THE WAYSIDE. | INTRODUCTORY.'

Includes "The Wayside—Introductory," "The Minotaur," "The Pygmies," "The Dragon's Teeth," "Circe's Palace," "The Pomegranate Seeds," "The Golden Fleece."

Typography and paper: See illustration, A 22.2.a page format. Running heads: rectos and versos, chapter titles. White wove paper.

Note one: A heavier paper (.006 vs. .004) was used in the first printing resulting in an appreciably bulkier book than the second printing. (Sheets of first printing bulk about 1″ vs. ³/₄″ for second printing.)

Binding: In the style of Ticknor format A (see illustration, A 2.6 binding). Red (16. d. Red), green (147. v. d. G), purplish blue (196. s. p B) reddish brown (47. d. gy. r Br) bold-ribbed T cloth. Most copies with blindstamped covers and plain edges. Spine goldstamped (see illustration, A 22 bindings [at A 21]). Pale yellow wove endpapers. White wove flyleaf inserted front and rear. 8 pp. of T&F ads with various dates inserted between front endpapers in most copies. Also "gift" binding in style of Ticknor format B (see illustration, A 2.6 binding), with covers goldstamped and edges gilded. White wove endpapers coated pale rose one side. Bound by Benjamin Bradley & Co., Boston.

Publication: 3,000 copies published 20 September 1853, but copies were on hand at least a month earlier. 200 review copies distributed. Price 87.5¢. Hawthorne received a royalty of 15% against 2,800 copies.

Note two: Extract entitled, "Antaeus and the Pygmies" printed in *The Evening Post* (New York), LII (24 August 1853), in advance of book publication (see D 81).

Printing: Composition and stereotype plates by the Boston Stereotype Foundry; printed by T. R. Marvin, Boston. Engravings by Baker, Smith & Andrew, Boston, from illustrations by Hammatt Billings.

Locations: CEFC, NN, OU; "gift": CEFC.

Manuscript: Manuscript that served as printer's copy located in the Pierpont Morgan Library.

LATER PRINTINGS WITHIN THE FIRST AMERICAN EDITION

A 22.2.b
Second printing

Boston: Ticknor, Reed, and Fields, M DCCC LIII.

First appearance of Geo. C. Rand imprint on copyright page. A lighter weight paper (.004 vs. .006) was used in the second printing resulting in an appreciably thinner book than the first printing (see "Note one" at A 22.2.a). Trade and "gift" bindings as in first printing. 800 copies printed 16 September 1853. Price 88¢, royalty 15%.

A 22.2.c
Boston: Ticknor, Reed, and Fields, M DCCC LIV.

Rand imprint dropped from copyright page. 1,000 copies printed 5 January 1854. Price 88¢, royalty 15%.

A 22.2.d
Boston: Ticknor, Reed, and Fields, M DCCC LVI.

500 copies printed 22 March 1856. Price 88¢, royalty 10%.

A 22.2.e
Boston: Ticknor, Reed, and Fields, M DCCC LVII.

500 copies printed 10 June 1857. Price 87^1/2¢, royalty 10%.

A 22.2.f
Boston: Ticknor and Fields, M DCCC LIX.

500 copies printed 21 September 1859. Price 87.5¢, royalty 8.75¢.

A 22.2.g
Boston: Ticknor and Fields, M DCCC LXII.

280 copies printed 10 February 1862. Price 88¢, royalty 8.75¢.

A 22.2.h
Boston: Ticknor and Fields, 1863.

350 copies printed 21 August 1863. Price 90¢, royalty 8.75¢.

A 22.2.i
Boston: Ticknor and Fields, 1864.

500 copies printed 12 July 1864. Price $1.25, royalty 8.75¢.

A 22.2.j
Boston: Ticknor and Fields, 1865.

Vol. 14 of untitled *"Tinted Edition"* on laid paper. 500 copies printed 31 October 1864. Price $1.50, royalty 12¢. See B 1[14] for reprintings of the *"Tinted Edition."*

A 22.2.k
Boston: Ticknor and Fields, 1865.

650 copies printed 16 March 1865. Price $1.25, royalty 12¢.

A 22.2.l
Boston: Ticknor and Fields, 1866.

278 copies printed 13 July 1866. Price $1.50, royalty 12¢.

A 22.2.m
Boston: Ticknor and Fields, 1867.

280 copies printed 29 October 1867. Price $1.50, royalty 12¢.

A 22.2.n
Boston: Ticknor and Fields, 1868.

500 copies printed 1 April 1868. Price $1.50, royalty 12¢.

A 22.2.o
Boston: Fields, Osgood, 1870.

280 copies printed March 1870. Price $1.50, royalty 12.5¢.

A 22.2.p
Boston: Fields, Osgood, 1871.

150 copies printed 15 December 1870. Price $1.50, royalty 12.5¢.

A 22.2.q
Boston: James R. Osgood, 1872.

Note: Two printings with 1872 title-page date (see A 22.2.r), priority undetermined.

280 copies printed 29 December 1871. Price $1.50, royalty 12.5¢.

A 22.2.r
Boston: James R. Osgood, 1872.

270 copies printed 25 September 1872. Price $1.50, royalty 12.5¢.

A 22.2.s
Boston: James R. Osgood, 1873.

Note: Two printings with 1873 title-page date (see A 22.2.t), priority undetermined.

150 copies printed 30 April 1873. Price $1.50, royalty 15¢.

A 22.2.t
Boston: James R. Osgood, 1873.

500 copies printed 23 June 1873. Price $1.50, royalty 15¢.

A 22.2.u
Boston: James R. Osgood, 1875.

280 copies printed 3 February 1875. Price $1.50, royalty 15¢.

A 22.2.v
Boston: James R. Osgood, 1876.

280 copies printed 24 December 1875. Price $1.50, royalty 15¢.

A 22.2.w
Boston: James R. Osgood, 1876.

Combined with *Biographical Stories* in two-volumes-in-one format and published as the eleventh volume of the *Illustrated Library Edition*. 1,000 copies printed 23 May 1876. Price $2.00, royalty 20¢. See B 2 for reprintings of the *ILE*.

A 22.2.x
Boston: James R. Osgood, 1878.

150 copies printed 4 February 1878. Price $1.50, royalty 15¢.

A 22.2.y
Boston: Houghton, Osgood, 1878.

292 copies printed 8 November 1878. Price $1.50, royalty 15¢.

A 22.2.z
Boston: Houghton, Osgood, 1879.

316 copies printed 20 March 1879. Price $1.50, royalty 15¢.

A 22.2.aa
Boston: Houghton, Mifflin, 1880.

Combined with *A Wonder-Book, Grandfather's Chair,* and *Biographical Stories* in four-volumes-in-one format and published as the fourth volume of the *Globe Edition*. 1,500 copies printed August 1880. See B 3 for reprintings of the *Globe Edition*.

A 22.2.ab
Boston: Houghton, Mifflin, 1880.

270 copies printed October 1880. Reprintings, probably with undated title pages: 270

copies, August 1881; 270 copies, March 1882; 270 copies, September 1882; 270 copies, August 1883; 270 copies, October 1883; 500 copies, August 1884.

A 22.2.ac
Boston: Houghton, Mifflin, [1886].

Combined with *A Wonder-Book, Grandfather's Chair,* and *Biographical Stories* in four-volumes-in-one format and published as the fourth volume of the *"New" Fireside Edition.* 1,000 copies printed May 1886. See B 4.

LATER EDITIONS

A 22.3
Tanglewood Tales for Girls and Boys. Being a Second Wonder Book. London: Knight and Son, n.d.

[1856]. Prints *Tanglewood Tales* only. A piracy. Reprinted in 1860 combined with *Wonder-Book* in two-volumes-in-one format.

A 22.4
London: George Routledge, 1868.

Two issues: (A) *Tanglewood Tales* only published as separate volume, inserted title leaf. Reprinted in Routledge *Every Boy's Library.* (B) Combined with *Wonder-Book* (see A 18.2.b2) in two-volumes-in-one format with volume title inserted. Reprinted with undated title page.

PRINTINGS FROM THE "LITTLE CLASSIC EDITION" PLATES

A 22.5.a

[All following within red and black double-rules frame] [red] Tanglewood Tales, | [black] FOR GIRLS AND BOYS. | BEING [red] A SECOND WONDER-BOOK. | [black] BY | NATHANIEL HAWTHORNE. | [vignette of centaur] | [red] BOSTON: | [black] JAMES R. OSGOOD AND COMPANY, | Late Ticknor & Fields, and Fields, Osgood, & Co. | [red] 1876.

Vol. [XIV], *"Little Classic Edition."* Contents same as in first American edition (A 22.2.a). Sheets bound with James R. Osgood and, later, Houghton, Osgood spine imprints. 2,000 copies printed 27 April 1876. Price $1.25, royalty 12.5¢. See B 5 [XIV] for reprintings of the *"Little Classic Edition."*

A 22.5.b
Boston: Houghton, Osgood, 1879.

Combined with *Biographical Stories* in two-volumes-in-one format and published as vol. XI of the *"Fireside Edition."* 500 copies printed 20 September 1879. See B 6 [XI] for reprintings of the *"Fireside Edition."*

A 22.5.c
Boston: Houghton, Mifflin, [1891].

Combined with *True Stories from History and Biography* and *Wonder-Book* in three-volumes-in-one format and published as vol. V of the *Popular Edition.* 1,000 copies printed June–August 1891. See B 7 for reprintings of the *Popular Edition.*

A 22.5.d
Boston: Houghton, Mifflin, [1899].

Vol. [XIV], *Concord Edition.* See B 8.

LATER EDITIONS

A 22.6
Boston: Howe Memorial Press, 1881–1882.

2 vols. In raised letters for the use of the blind (unlocated, see Browne).

A 22.7
Tanglewood Tales: A Wonder-Book for Girls and Boys. London: Frederick Warne,
[1882].

Combined with *The Wonder-Book* in two-volumes-in-one format and published as no.
107 of the *Chandos Classics.* Contents same as in first American edition (A 22.2.a).
Reprinted with undated title page 1883, 1884, 1885.

PRINTINGS FROM THE RIVERSIDE EDITION PLATES

A 22.8.a1
Riverside Edition (trade), first printing, American issue [1883]

A WONDER-BOOK | TANGLEWOOD TALES, AND | GRANDFATHER'S CHAIR | BY |
NATHANIEL HAWTHORNE | [vignette of head of Quicksilver] | BOSTON | HOUGH-
TON, MIFFLIN AND COMPANY | New York: 11 East Seventeenth Street | The River-
side Press, Cambridge | 1883.

Three volumes in one published as vol. IV of the Riverside trade printing. Contents
same as in *"Little Classic Edition"* (A 22.5.a), with "Introductory Note" by George
Parsons Lathrop added. 1,500 copies printed January 1883. Price $2.00. See B 9 for
reprintings of the Riverside trade printing.

A 22.8.a2
Riverside Edition (trade), first printing, English issue [1883]

London: Kegan Paul, Trench, 1883.

Sheets of vol. IV, first printing (A 22.8.a1) with cancel title, in a Kegan Paul binding.
250 Kegan Paul title pages printed by Houghton, Mifflin, June–July 1883. Later issues
noted with dated and undated Kegan Paul, Trench, Trübner title pages. See B 11.

A 22.8.b
Riverside Edition (large paper), second printing [1883]

[red] A WONDER-BOOK | [black] TANGLEWOOD TALES, AND | GRANDFATHER'S
CHAIR | BY | NATHANIEL HAWTHORNE | [vignette of head of Quicksilver] | [red]
CAMBRIDGE | [black] Printed at the Riverside Press | 1883

Three volumes in one published as vol. IV of the Riverside large-paper printing. 250
copies printed March 1883. See B 10.

A 22.8.c
Boston and New York: Houghton, Mifflin, 1884.

2 vols. First part combined with *Wonder-Book* in two-volumes-in-one format and published as vol. VII of the *Wayside Edition*. Second part combined with *Grandfather's Chair* in two-volumes-in-one format and published as vol. VIII of the *Wayside Edition*. 500 copies of each of the two volumes printed September–October 1884. See B 12.

A 22.8.d
Boston, New York, Chicago: Houghton, Mifflin, [1886–1887].

In two parts as nos. 22 and 23 of the *Riverside Literature Series*. Printed wrappers. Regularly reprinted. Also later reprinted in combined format, nos. 22 and 23 in one cloth volume.

A 22.8.e
Boston and New York: Houghton, Mifflin, [1891].

Combined with *Wonder-Book* and *Grandfather's Chair* in three-volumes-in-one format and published as vol. IV of the *Standard Library Edition*. 500 copies printed October 1891. See B 13.

A 22.8.f
Boston and New York: Houghton, Mifflin, 1893.

Advertised as separate "Illustrated' work at $1.25. Reprinted with later dated and undated title pages.

A 22.8.g
A Wonder-Book for Girls and Boys and Tanglewood Tales. Boston and New York: Houghton, Mifflin, 1898.

Combined with *Tanglewood Tales* and published in two-volumes-in-one format, with Walter Crane *Wonder-Book* illustrations reproduced in halftone.

A 22.8.h
Boston and New York: Houghton, Mifflin, [1902].

Combined with *The Wonder-Book* and *Grandfather's Chair* in three-volumes-in-one format and published as Vol. IV of the *"New" Wayside Edition*. 500 copies printed September–October 1902. See B 14.

A 22.8.i
Boston and New York: [Houghton, Mifflin], MDCCCCIX.

Combined with *Wonder-Book* and *Grandfather's Chair* in three-volumes-in-one format and published as vol. IV of the *Fireside Edition*. See B 15.

A 22.8.j
Boston, New York: Jefferson Press, [1913].

Combined with *Wonder-Book* and *Grandfather's Chair* in three-volumes-in-one format and published as vol. [IV] of the *"Jefferson Press Edition."* See B 16.

OTHER EDITIONS

A 22.9
London and Edinburgh: William Blackwood, 1884.

Blackwoods' Educational Series.

A 22.10
Printings from the Paterson-Scott plates

Edinburgh: William Paterson, 1885.

No. 18, *Paterson's New England Novels.* Contents same as in first American edition (A 22.2.a). Published in cloth, top edges gilded, at 2s.; in ornamental paper covers at 1s. Also combined with *The Blithedale Romance* in two-volumes-in-one format and published as vol. [V] of the *"Paterson Edition."* See B 17. Also Paterson sheets found with cancel Walter Scott title page. Also remanufactured from Paterson plates with Walter Scott title-page imprint. Later published as vol. [VII] in the *"Walter Scott Edition"* (gravure). See B 18.

A 22.11
Boston and New York: Houghton, Mifflin, 1887.

Illustrated by George Wharton Edwards. Reprinted unknown number of times. Also English issue with London: Chatto and Windus, 1888, cancel title and American sheets.

A 22.12
New York: Hurst & Company, [1897].

No. 181, *The Universal Library,* printed April 1, 1897. Contents same as in first American edition (A 22.2.a). Printed wrappers. Reprinted in clothbound format with undated title page. Also noted with undated F. M. Lupton title page inserted.

A 22.13
New York: Thomas Y. Crowell, [1897].

Contents same as in first American edition (A 22.2.a).

A 22.14
Philadelphia: Henry Altemus, [1898].

No. 200, *Altemus' New Illustrated Vademecum Series.*

A 22.15
Two Tanglewood Tales: The Dragon's Teeth, The Minotaur. New York: Maynard, Merrill, 1899.

No. 217, *Maynard's English Classic Series.* Prints two title stories with biographical sketch and notes.

PRINTINGS FROM THE AUTOGRAPH EDITION PLATES

A 22.16.a
Boston and New York: Houghton, Mifflin, MDCCCC.

Vol. XIII of the *Autograph Edition.* Contents same as in the *Riverside Edition* (A 22.8.a), with new introductory note added. 500 copies. Deposited 20 December 1900. See B 20.

A 22.16.b
Boston and New York: Houghton, Mifflin, MDCCCC.

Vol. XIII of the *Large-Paper (Autograph) Edition.* 500 copies. See B 21.

A 22.16.c
Boston and New York: Houghton, Mifflin, 1903.

Vol. VI of the *Old Manse Edition*. See B 22.

OTHER EDITIONS

A 22.17
The Minotaur. Chicago: Orville Brewer Publishing Co., 1901.

Vol. II, no. 21, Student's Series of *Four Penny Classics*, printed March 1, 1901. Prints sketch of Hawthorne and title story only. Printed wrappers, cover title. Later published by F. A. Owen, Danville, N.Y., as no. 26, *Instructor Literature Series*. Printed wrappers.

A 22.18
Circe's Palace. Chicago: Orville Brewer Publishing Co., 1901.

Vol. 2, no. 28, Student's Series of *Four Penny Classics*, printed June 15, 1901. Prints title story only. Printed wrappers, cover title.

A 22.19
New York: Thomas Y. Crowell, [1902].

Introduction by Katherine Lee Bates. Vol. [8] of the *Crowell "Lenox Edition."* See B 23.

A 22.20
New York: Thomas Y. Crowell, [1902].

Combined with *Wonder-Book* in two-volumes-in-one format and published as vol. [7] of the *Crowell "Popular Edition."* See B 24.

A 22.21
London: J. M. Dent; New York: E. P. Dutton, 1903.

With 12 illustrations by H. Grenville Fell. Contents same as in first American edition (A 22.2.a). Also Dent *Tanglewood Tales* plates repaged, combined with plates of 1903 Dent *Wonder-Book* in continuously paged two-volumes-in-one format, and published as no. 5 of *Everyman's Library*, printed 6 February 1906. Illustrations omitted. Reprinted 1906, 1907, 1908, 1909, 1911, 1914, 1917, 1919, 1921. Reset 1924; reprinted 1926, 1929. Also new Dent/Dutton edition combining *Wonder-Book* and *Tanglewood Tales* in two-volumes-in-one format, incorporating Fell's illustrations for both titles, published 1910. Also new edition of Dent/Dutton *Tanglewood Tales* separately published about 1937 with illustrations by S. Van Abbé. Last reprinted 1966.

A 22.22
A Wonder Book and Tanglewood Tales. New York: Duffield & Company, MCMX.

Illustrated by Maxfield Parrish. Contents same as in first American edition (A 22.2.a).

A 22.23
Chicago, New York: Rand McNally & Company, [1913].

Illustrated by Milo Winter. *The Windermere Series*. Reprinted an unknown number of times. Also English issue with London: Duckworth & Co., [1914], cancel title and American sheets.

A 22.24
Philadelphia: Penn Publishing Company, [1921].

Illustrated by Virginia Frances Sterrett. Large-paper format. Also issued in trade format with New York: Hampton Publishing Company, [MCMXXI], title inserted.

A 22.25
A Wonder Book and Tanglewood Tales. London, Bombay, Sidney: George G. Harrap, [1925].

Illustrated by Gustaf Tenggren and Stephen Reid. Reprinted January 1929 in two-volumes-in-one format.

A 22.26
A Wonder Book and Tanglewood Tales. Chicago, Philadelphia, Toronto: The John C. Winston Company, [1930].

Illustrated by Frederick Richardson. Introduction and notes by Katherine G. Carpenter. Two-volumes-in-one format.

A 22.27
London, New York: Standard Book Company, [MCMXXXI].

Contents same as in first American edition (A 22.2.a).

A 22.28
[London]: Hodder and Stoughton, [1938].

Illustrated by Edmund Dulac. Also deluxe format, signed by Dulac, limited to 500 numbered copies. Priority uncertain.

A 22.29
A Wonder Book and Tanglewood Tales. [Columbus]: Ohio State University Press, [1972].

Vol. VII of the *Centenary Edition*. 2,435 copies published 1 November 1972. See B 32.

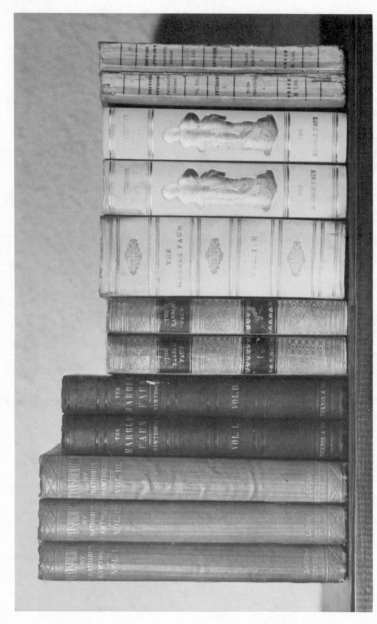

Bindings for (1–3) A23.1.a; (4 & 5) A23.3.a; (6 & 7) A 23.4; (8) A 23.5; (9 & 10) A 23.6; (11 & 12) A 23.7 (Nos. 6–12 are some of a wide variety of binding formats for the Tauchnitz editions.)

TRANSFORMATION:

OR, THE
ROMANCE OF MONTE BENI.

BY

NATHANIEL HAWTHORNE,
AUTHOR OF "THE SCARLET LETTER," ETC. ETC.

IN THREE VOLUMES.

VOL. I.

LONDON:
SMITH, ELDER AND CO., 65, CORNHILL.
M.DCCCLX.

---

pression, "that Rome—mere Rome—will crowd everything else out of my heart."

"Heaven forbid!" ejaculated the sculptor.

They had now reached the grand stairs that ascend from the Piazza di Spagna to the hither brow of the Pincian Hill. Old Beppo, the millionaire of his ragged fraternity—it is a wonder that no artist paints him as the cripple whom St. Peter heals at the Beautiful Gate of the Temple—was just mounting his donkey to depart, laden with the rich spoil of the day's beggary.

Up the stairs, drawing his tattered cloak about his face, came the model, at whom Beppo looked askance, jealous of an encroacher on his rightful domain. The figure passed away, however, up the Via Sistina. In the piazza below, near the foot of the magnificent steps, stood Miriam, with her eyes bent on the ground, as if she were counting those little, square, uncomfortable paving stones, that make it a penitential pilgrimage to walk in Rome. She kept this attitude for several minutes, and when, at last, the importunities of

A23.1.a: Title page. 7³/₁₆″ × 4³/₄″. Page format, 5¹/₄″ (5¹/₂″) × 3″

A 23 THE MARBLE FAUN/TRANSFORMATION

Note: Unless otherwise noted, all English editions have the title *"Transformation: or, The Romance of Monte Beni"* and all American editions have the title *"The Marble Faun: or, The Romance of Monte Beni."*

A 23.1.a
First English edition, first printing [*1860*]

[The right of Translation is reserved.]

This notice appears on verso of title page of each volume of A 23.1.a.

3 vols.

First and second printings can be distinguished by the *'SECOND EDITION'* slug added to title page of all three volumes of the second printing (A 23.1.b). Also "Postscript" added at the end of vol. III in the second printing.

I: [i–v] vi–xiv [xv–xvi] [1] 2–273 [274–276]

II: [i–iv] [1] 2–294 [295–296]

III: [i–iv] [1] 2–285 [286–288]

I: π^8 1—17^8 18^2

II: π^2 19–36^8 37^4

III: π^2 38–55^8

Contents: I: p. i: half title; p. ii: blank; p. iii: title; p. iv: '[The right of Translation is reserved.]'; pp. v–xiv: preface; p. xv: contents; p. xvi: blank; pp. 1–273: text, headed 'THE | ROMANCE OF MONTE BENI. | [double rule] | CHAPTER I. | MIRIAM, HILDA, KENYON, DONATELLO.'; p. 274: blank; p. 275: colophon; p. 276: blank.

II: p. i: title; p. ii: translation notice; p. iii: contents; p. iv: blank; pp. 1–294: text, headed 'THE | ROMANCE OF MONTE BENI. | [double rule] | CHAPTER I. | MIRIAM's TROUBLE.'; p. 295: colophon; p. 296: blank.

III: p. i: title; p. ii: translation notice; p. iii: contents; p. iv: blank; pp. 1–285: text, headed 'THE | ROMANCE OF MONTE BENI. | [double rule] | CHAPTER I. | MARKET-DAY IN PERUGIA.'; p. 286: colophon; pp. 287–288: ads.

Typography and paper: See illustration, A 23.1.a page format. Running heads: rectos, chapter titles; versos, 'ROMANCE OF MONTE BENI.' White wove paper.

Binding: Primary trade binding red (19. gy. Red) wavy-grain TR cloth. Covers blind embossed with decorative border composed of double outer rules and inner floral-patterned strip. Spine goldstamped (see illustration, A 23 bindings). White wove endpapers coated pale yellow one side. 32-page Smith, Elder catalogue inserted at rear of vol. III in most trade sets. Top edges untrimmed in most copies. Bound by Leighton Son and Hodge, London. Also copies in custom leather bindings.

Publication: Unknown number of copies published 28 February 1860. Price for three-volume set 31/6. Hawthorne received £600 for the English rights.

Printing: Printed from type metal by Smith, Elder and Co., Little Green Arbour Court, Old Bailey, London, E.C.

Note: The first English edition was set directly from the manuscript supplied by Hawthorne while in England. In London in July 1859, James T. Fields personally negotiated the sale of the English rights to Smith, Elder, who agreed to supply T&F advance sheets from which the American edition could be set. To protect copyright, simultaneous publication was planned, but in actuality the English edition preceded the American by a week.

Locations: BM, 12705.f.11 (deposit-stamp 14 APR 60), CEFC, OU, PSt, ViU.

Manuscript: Hawthorne's manuscript, lacking the second-printing "Postscript," located in British Museum (2 vols., Add. MSS. 44889, 44890).

A 23.1.b
First English edition, second printing [1860]

3 vols. Second printing was made from standing type used for first printing, with *'SECOND EDITION'* slug appearing between volume designation and publisher's imprint on title pages of all three volumes. Hawthorne's "Postscript" first appears at end of vol. III of second printing. Two minor corrections were made in standing type for this printing:

	FIRST PRINTING		SECOND PRINTING
I, 197.7	millionaire	[	millionnaire
III, 223.running head	CONTADINO.	[	CONTADINA.

Collation of vols. I and II same as first printing; vol. III: [i–iv] [1] 2–294 [295–296]

π^2 38–55^8 56^4

Contents: *III:* p. i: title; p. ii: translation notice; p. iii: contents; p. iv: blank; pp. 1–285: text, headed 'THE | ROMANCE OF MONTE BENI. | [double rule] | CHAPTER I. | MARKET-DAY IN PERUGIA.'; pp. 286–294, postscript, subscribed *'Leamington, March 14th, 1860.'*; pp. 295–296: ads.

Publication: Unknown number of copies published shortly after 16 March 1860.

Locations: BM, 12705.f.12 (deposit-stamp 14 APR 60), CEFC, OU.

A 23.2
Second English edition: London: Smith, Elder & Co., M.DCCC.LX.

3 vols. Vols. I and II of the second English edition are line-for-line resettings of first two volumes of second printing of the first English edition (A 23.1.b). Vol. III was printed from standing type of first edition, second printing. All three volumes have *'THIRD EDITION'* slug appearing between volume designation and publisher's imprint on title pages. Frontispiece inserted facing title page in vol. I.

Note: On reading the printed book, Hawthorne noted several errors and wrote Smith, Elder (7 March 1860), asking that 'with foot' (II, 9.6–7) and 'literary' (II, 30.19) be changed to 'with her foot' and 'literally'. At what point the publisher made these corrections is uncertain. Although it is possible that Hawthorne's changes were introduced by stop-press during the manufacture of the second printing of the first English edition, no copy of the second printing showing these changes has been located. The corrections are present in some copies of the second English edition, but only four copies have been located (see "Locations"). These four copies show two states of each of the two gatherings involved. Also, the gatherings are in different combinations:

	STATE A	STATE B	STATE C
II, 9.6–7			
(gathering 19)	with | foot	with | foot	with | her foot
II, 30.29			
(gathering 20)	literary	literally	literally

The second English edition followed soon after the second printing of the first edition, and it is possible that some gatherings from each printing were intermixed in the bindery. It is also possible that sheets of the corrected gatherings were ready soon enough to have been used in a late binding-up of copies of the second printing, and surplus original gatherings may have been used to piece out the second edition.

Publication: Unknown number of copies published sometime between 14 and 21 April 1860.

Locations: State A: CEFC; state B: OU; state C: Berg, PSt.

THE MARBLE FAUN:

OR, THE

ROMANCE OF MONTE BENI.

BY

NATHANIEL HAWTHORNE,

AUTHOR OF "THE SCARLET LETTER," ETC., ETC.

IN TWO VOLUMES.

VOL. I.

BOSTON:
TICKNOR AND FIELDS.
M DCCC LX.

---

ual lives. Romance and poetry, ivy, lichens, and wall-flowers need ruin to make them grow.

In re-writing these volumes, the author was somewhat surprised to see the extent to which he had introduced descriptions of various Italian objects, antique, pictorial, and statuesque. Yet these things fill the mind everywhere in Italy, and especially in Rome, and cannot easily be kept from flowing out upon the page when one writes freely, and with self-enjoyment. And, again, while reproducing the book, on the broad and dreary sands of Redcar, with the gray German Ocean tumbling in upon me, and the northern blast always howling in my ears, the complete change of scene made these Italian reminiscences shine out so vividly that I could not find it in my heart to cancel them.

An act of justice remains to be performed towards two men of genius with whose productions the author has allowed himself to use a quite unwarrantable freedom. Having imagined a sculptor in this Romance, it was necessary to provide him with such works in marble as should be in keeping with the artistic ability which he was supposed to possess. With this view, the author laid felonious hands upon a certain bust

1*

A 23.3.a: Title page, 7¹/₁₆″ × 4³/₈″. Page format, 5³/₁₆″ (5⁷/₁₆″) × 3¹/₁₆″

A 23.3.a
First American edition, first printing [1860]

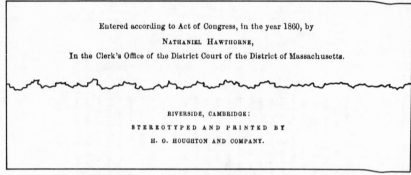

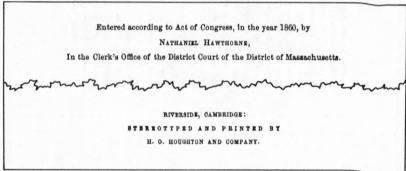

2 vols. First printing is distinguished by plate variants (see table).

I: [i–v] vi–xi [xii–xiv] [15] 16–283 [284–288]

II: [i–vi] [7] 8–284 [285–288]

I: [1–18]⁸ (signed in 12's as 1–12¹², with 1₅ signed 1*)

II: [1–18]⁸ (signed in 12's as 1–12¹², with 1₅ signed 1*)

Contents: I: p. i: half title; p. ii: blank; p. iii: title; p. iv: copyright; pp. v–xi: preface; p. xii: blank; p. xiii: contents; p. xiv: blank; pp. 15–283: text, headed 'THE ROMANCE OF MONTE BENI. | [rule] | CHAPTER I. | MIRIAM, HILDA, KENYON, DONATELLO.'; pp. 284–288: blank.

II: p. i: half title; p. ii: blank; p. iii: title; p. iv: copyright; p. v: contents; p. vi: blank; pp. 7–284: text, headed 'THE ROMANCE OF MONTE BENI. | [rule] | CHAPTER I. | THE PEDIGREE OF MONTE BENI.'; pp. 285–288: blank.

Typography and paper: See illustration, A 23.3.a page format. Running heads: rectos, chapter titles; versos, 'ROMANCE OF MONTE BENI.' White wove paper.

Binding: In the style of Ticknor format A (see illustration, A 2.6 binding). Brown (81. d. gy. y Br) bold-ribbed T cloth with blindstamped floral device inside ruled panels on both covers. Spine goldstamped (see illustration, A 23 bindings). White wove endpapers brown coated one side. Flyleaf inserted at front and rear. All edges trimmed. 16 pp. of T&F catalogue inserted at rear of vol. I in most copies.

Plate Variants Within the First American Edition of *The Marble Faun*[1]

	A	B	C	D²	E
Volume I					
Order of prelims	Pref.-Cont.	Cont.-Pref.	Pref.-Cont.	Pref.-Cont.	Pref.-Cont.
Gathered/signed	8/12	12/12	12/12/	12/12	12/12
Copyright page	—	—	—	—	SEVENTEENTH THOUSAND
vii	1*	1*	—	—	—
ix	—	—	—	—	—
17.17	gaily	gaily	gaily	?	gayly
56.21	nature	nature	nature	?	Nature
225.22	for	for	on	on	on
252.30	there	there	them	them	them
Volume II					
Gathered/signed	8/12	12/12	12/12	12/12	12/12
Copyright page	—	—	—	—	SEVENTEENTH THOUSAND
9.27	friend	friend	friend	friend	friend,
92.23	Etrucean	Etrucean	Etruscan	Etruscan	Etruscan
98.3	strangely	strangely	strangely	strangelg	strangelg
197	4*	9*	—	—	—
Conclusion	No	No	No	Yes	Yes

1. The *Cost Books* record seven printings in 1860, each with the title-page date 'M DCCC LX': This table of plate variants shows enough examples to identify the five basic forms of the plates. A complete listing of plate variants is given in the *Centenary Edition* of *Marble Faun*.
The first three printings coincide with plate forms A, B, and C. The fourth printing probably coincides with plate form D, in which the Conclusion first appears. Printings five and six probably intervene between plate forms D and E. The seventh printing probably coincides with plate form E.
2. Plate form D for vol. I to match plate form D for vol. II has not been confirmed. It is not necessary for there to have been a special D form of vol. I. See Matthew J. Bruccoli, "Concealed Printings in Hawthorne," *Papers of the Bibliographical Society of America*, LVII (1963), 42–49.

Note: There was a remainder issue of at least the first-printing sheets bound in green (151. d. gy. G) bead-grain BD cloth without a publisher's imprint on the spine. Inserted at the back of vol. II is a 4-pp. catalogue of ads for books offered for sale by T. O. H. P. Burnham, Boston (Locations: Two volumes: PDH, ViU; vol. I only: CEFC). See Matthew J. Bruccoli, "Burnham Marble Faun," *The Centenary Hawthorne News-Sheet,* 1 (1962), 1–2.

Publication: The *Cost Books* list three printings in advance of publication, 20, 23, 27 February 1860. These printings totaled 8,000 two-volume sets, presumably published Wednesday, 7 March 1860. Price $1.50 per set, with a 15% royalty (22.5¢ per set).

Printing: Stereotyped and printed by H. O. Houghton at the Riverside Press, Cambridge, Mass.

Locations: CEFC, CtY, Lilly, MH, NN, OU, ViU.

REPRINTINGS FROM THE T&F STEREOTYPE PLATES (IN 2 VOLS.)

A 23.3.b
Second printing

Boston: Ticknor and Fields, M DCCC LX.

2 vols.

I: [i–iv] [xiii–xiv] [v] vi–xi [xii] [15] 16–283 [284–288]

II: [i–vi] [7] 8–284 [285–288]

I: [1]¹² 2–12¹²

II: [1]¹² 2–12¹²

Both volumes gathered in 12's as signed. In this printing the contents leaf in vol. I precedes the preface, with the result that p. vii is signed 1* (see table of plate variants under A 23.3.a). First, second, and third printings, totaling 8,000 two-volume sets, published 7 March 1860. Price $1.50 per set, royalty 15%.

A 23.3.c
Third printing

Boston: Ticknor and Fields, M DCCC LX.

2 vols.

I: [i–v] vi–xi [xii–xiv] [15] 16–283 [284–288]

II: [i–vi] [7] 8–284 [285–288]

I: [1]¹² 2–12¹²

II: [1]¹² 2–12¹²

Both volumes gathered in 12's as signed. In this and all following printings of the first American edition, the preface precedes the contents leaf in vol. I, and the signing notation 1* is eliminated (see table of plate variants under A 23.3.a). First, second, and third printings, totaling 8,000 two-volume sets, published 7 March 1860. Price $1.50 per set, royalty 15%.

A 23.3.d
Fourth printing

Boston: Ticknor and Fields, M DCCC LX. See table of plate variants under A 23.3.a. 3,000 copies printed 3 April 1860. Price $1.50 per set, royalty 15%.

A 23.3.e
Fifth printing

Boston: Ticknor and Fields, M DCCC LX.

See table of plate variants under A 23.3.a. 1,500 copies printed 25 May 1860. Price $1.50 per set, royalty 15%.

A 23.3.f
Sixth printing

Boston: Ticknor and Fields, M DCCC LX.

See table of plate variants under A 23.3.a. 1,000 copies printed 23 July 1860. Price $1.50 per set, royalty 15%.

A 23.3.g
Seventh printing

Boston: Ticknor and Fields, M DCCC LX.

See table of plate variants under A 23.3.a. 1,000 copies printed September 1861. Price $1.50 per set, royalty 15%.

A 23.3.h
Boston: Ticknor and Fields, 1864.

Note: Two printings with 1864 title-page date (see A 23.3.i), priority undetermined.

280 copies printed 4 June 1864. Price $3.00 per set, royalty 22.5¢ per set.

A 23.3.i
Boston: Ticknor and Fields, 1864.

280 copies printed 20 September 1864. Price $3.00 per set, royalty 22.5¢ per set.

A 23.3.j
Boston: Ticknor and Fields, 1865.

Vols. 9 and 10 of untitled *"Tinted Edition"* on laid paper. 500 copies printed 31 October 1864. Price $1.50 per volume, royalty 12¢ per volume. See B 1[9,10] for reprintings of the *"Tinted Edition."*

A 23.3.k
Boston: Ticknor and Fields, 1865.

500 copies printed 11 April 1865. Price $3.00 per set, royalty 25¢ per set.

A 23.3.l
Boston: Ticknor and Fields, 1866.

Note: Two printings with 1866 title-page date (see A 23.3.m), priority undetermined.

500 copies printed 23 July 1866. Price $3.00 per set, royalty 24¢ per set.

A 23.3.m
Boston: Ticknor and Fields, 1866.

320 copies printed 13 August 1866. Price $3.00 per set, royalty 24¢ per set.

A 23.3.n
Boston: Fields, Osgood, 1870.

Note: Two printings with 1870 title-page date (see A 23.3.o), priority undetermined. 280 copies printed 7 April 1870. Price $4.00 per set, royalty 20¢ per set.

A 23.3.o
Boston: Fields, Osgood, 1870.

280 copies printed 5 September 1870. Price $4.00 per set, royalty 20¢ per set.

A 23.3.p
Boston: James R. Osgood, 1871.

A 23.3.q
Boston: James R. Osgood, 1871.

Vols. I and II combined in two volumes in one and published as the fifth volume of the *Illustrated Library Edition*. 500 copies printed 27 August 1871. Price $2.00, royalty 20¢. See B 2 for reprintings of the *ILE*.

A 23.3.r
Boston: Houghton, Mifflin, 1880.

Combined with *French and Italian Note Books* in four-volumes-in-one format and published as the fifth volume of the *Globe Edition*. 1,500 copies printed July 1880. See B 3 for reprintings of the *Globe Edition*.

A 23.3.s
Boston: Houghton, Mifflin, [1886].

Combined with *French and Italian Note Books* in four-volumes-in-one format and published as the fifth volume of the *"New" Fireside Edition*. 1,000 copies printed May 1886. See B 4.

TAUCHNITZ EDITIONS

A 23.4
First Tauchnitz edition

TRANSFORMATION: | OR, THE | ROMANCE OF MONTE BENI. | BY | NATHANIEL HAWTHORNE, | AUTHOR OF "THE SCARLET LETTER," ETC. ETC. | *COPYRIGHT EDITION.* | IN TWO VOLUMES. | VOL. I. [VOL. II] | LEIPZIG | BERNHARD TAUCHNITZ | 1860.

Vols. 515 and 516 of the *Tauchnitz Collection of British Authors.*

Confusion has resulted from the Tauchnitz practice of preserving the 1860 title page unchanged through at least four editions and an untold number of printings extending

Plate Variants Within the *Tauchnitz Editions*

	A	B	C	D
Volume I				
ii	—	—	—	TAUCHNITZ EDITION. By the same Author. THE SCARLET LETTER . . . . . 1 vol. ENGLISH NOTE-BOOKS . . . . . 2 vols.
x	*Leamington, December 15, 1859.*	*Leamington, December 15, 1859.*	*Leamington, December 15, 1859.*	*Leamington, December 15, 1859.*
xi	CHAPTER I.	CHAPTER I.	CHAPTER I.	CHAPTER I.
25.28–29	d fear- attrac-	fearfully attractive	fearfully attractive	d fear- attrac-
19.4–6	and joy- afford to nd make	joyous, to have e toler-	joyous, to have ce toler-	and joy- afford to nd make
5.18–19	ne, and forlorn	ne, and forlorn	erine, the for-	ne, and forlorn
21.16	redden-	redden-	reddening;	reddening;
92.20–21	Italian med to	Italian med to	Italian to hang	Italian med to
Volume II				
.11	voice,	voice,—	voice,—	voice,
5.27	emin-	emin-	emin-	emi-
7.23–25	it — shall to educate dedicate	ss it — ll try to ply de-	it—shall ll try to I solely	ess it— ll try to lely de-
280	*Leamington, March 14th, 1860.*	*Leamington, March 14th, 1860.*	*Leamington, March 14th, 1860.*	*Leamington, March 14th, 1860.*

well into the twentieth century. Four different settings of type have been identified on the basis of a 30-copy sample; more may exist. The first Tauchnitz edition is probably setting A; copies with owner inscriptions dated 1860 exist (Location: CEFC). Settings B, C, and D are virtually line-for-line resettings with minor variants, primarily end-of-line word breaks and type spacings. The table of plate variants in the Tauchnitz editions provides samples of these variants sufficient to distinguish the four settings.

Tauchnitz secured rights for Continental distribution under arrangements with Hawthorne and Smith, Elder. Bound in two volumes in printed wrappers. Also bound in a wide variety of custom bindings both in two volumes and in two-volumes-in-one format. Also distributed with special attention to the tourist trade in Italy; copies with illustrations are found in a profusion of elaborate formats in special bindings many of which were cutsom-made by booksellers in Rome and Florence. Customers could purchase ready-made copies embellished by photographs of the scenes Hawthorne described, select from large offerings of loose photographs and have them bound to order, or provide their own photographs for preparing a personalized copy. The absence, presence, or sequence of inserted photographs has no significance in determining textual priority.

A 23.5
Second Tauchnitz edition

Leipzig: Bernhard Tauchnitz, 1860.

See table under A 23.4. Unknown number of reprintings.

A 23.6
Third Tauchnitz edition

Leipzig: Bernhard Tauchnitz, 1860.

See table under A 23.4. Unknown number of reprintings.

A 23.7
Fourth Tauchnitz edition

Leipzig: Bernhard Tauchnitz, 1860.

See table under A 23.4. List of other Hawthorne titles appears on verso of half title. Unknown number of reprintings. Issued in two volumes in printed wrappers as late as 1907.

LATER EDITION

A 23.8
Third English edition

London: Smith, Elder, M.DCCC.LXI.

One-volume *Popular Library* format ($6^3/4''$ × $4^3/16''$) in limp cloth at 2s. 6d. Printed from stereotype plates made from a new setting of type. Reprinted in limp cloth and, later, hard back, 1867, 1872, 1878, 1881, 1888, 1897, 1906, all with 'A NEW EDITION' slug on title page. Also same plates used to publish a one-volume, large-paper ($7^1/2''$ × $4^7/8''$) "Illustrated Edition": London: Smith, Elder, 1865. Price 3s. 6d, with four illustrations. Reprinted 1878, 1890.

PRINTINGS FROM THE "LITTLE CLASSIC EDITION" PLATES

A23.9.a

[All following within red and black double-rules frame] THE | [red] Marble Faun; | [black] OR, | *THE ROMANCE OF MONTE BENI.* | BY | [red] NATHANIEL HAWTHORNE. | [black] VOL. I. [II.] | [vignette of statue's head] | [red] BOSTON: | [black] JAMES R. OSGOOD AND COMPANY, | Late Ticknor & Fields, and Fields, Osgood, & Co. | [red] 1876.

Vols. [IX] and [X], *"Little Classic Edition."* Contents same as in first T&F edition (A23.3.a). Sheets bound with James R. Osgood and, later, Houghton, Osgood spine imprints. 3,000 copies of each volume printed 12 November 1875. Price $1.25 per volume, royalty 12.5¢ per volume. See B5[IX,X] for reprintings of the *"Little Classic Edition."*

A23.9.b
Boston: Houghton, Osgood, 1879.

Combined in two-volumes-in-one format and published as vol. V of the *"Fireside Edition."* 500 copies printed 20 September 1879. See B6[V] for reprintings of the *"Fireside Edition."*

A23.9.c
Boston: Houghton, Mifflin, [1891].

Combined with *The Scarlet Letter* in three-volumes-in-one format and published as vol. III of the *Popular Edition.* 1,000 copies printed June–August 1891. See B7 for reprintings of the *Popular Edition.*

A23.9.d
Boston: Houghton, Mifflin, [1899].

Vols. [IX] and [X], *Concord Edition.* See B8.

A23.9.e
Boston and New York: Houghton, Mifflin, 1901.

Combined in two-volumes-in-one format and published with 'Wayside Edition' slug on title page.

Note: This printing not to be confused with A23.10.c.

PRINTINGS FROM THE RIVERSIDE EDITION PLATES

A23.10.a₁
Riverside Edition (trade), first printing, American issue [1883]

THE MARBLE FAUN | OR | THE ROMANCE OF MONTE BENI | BY | NATHANIEL HAWTHORNE | [vignette of girl with doves] | BOSTON | HOUGHTON, MIFFLIN AND COMPANY | New York: 11 East Seventeenth Street | The Riverside Press, Cambridge | 1883

Two volumes in one published as vol. VI of the Riverside trade printing. Contents same as in the *"Little Classic Edition"* (A23.9.a), with "Introductory Note" by George Parsons Lathrop added. 1,500 copies printed March 1883. Price $2.00. See B9 for reprintings of the Riverside trade printing.

A 23.10.a2
Riverside Edition (trade), first printing, English issue [1883]

London: Kegan Paul, Trench, 1883.

Sheets of vol. VI, first printing (A 23.10.a1), with cancel title, in a Kegan Paul binding. 250 Kegan Paul title pages printed by Houghton, Mifflin, June–July 1883. Later issues noted with dated and undated Kegan Paul, Trench, Trübner title pages. See B 11.

A 23.10.b
Riverside Edition (large paper), second printing [1883]

[red] THE MARBLE FAUN | [black] OR | THE ROMANCE OF MONTE BENI | BY | NATHANIEL HAWTHORNE | [vignette of girl and doves] | [red] CAMBRIDGE | [black] Printed at the Riverside Press | 1883

Combined in two-volumes-in-one format and published as vol. VI of the Riverside large-paper printing. 250 copies printed April 1883. See B 10.

A 23.10.c
Boston and New York: Houghton, Mifflin, 1884.

Vols. XI and XII of the *Wayside Edition*. 500 copies printed September–October 1884. See B 12.

A 23.10.d
Boston and New York: Houghton, Mifflin, M DCCC LXXXIX.

2 vols. Illustrated with photogravures executed by A. W. Elson & Co., Boston. Trade printing, gilt top, issued in cloth, full polished calf, full vellum in box. Also English issue with American sheets and London: Kegan Paul, Trench, MDCCCLXXXIX, cancel title. Also special printing on laid paper limited to 150 numbered copies and designated "Large-Paper Edition" on half title. Full vellum, printed linen boxed. Trade printing advertised as the "Holiday Edition" and reprinted in 1890 and regularly thereafter.

A 23.10.e
Boston and New York: Houghton, Mifflin, [1891].

Combined in two-volumes-in-one format and published as vol. VI of the *Standard Library Edition*. 500 copies printed October 1891. See B 13.

A 23.10.f
Boston and New York: Houghton, Mifflin, [1902].

Combined in two-volumes-in-one format and published as vol. VI of the *"New" Wayside Edition*. 500 copies printed September–October 1902. See B 14.

A 23.10.g
Boston and New York: [Houghton, Mifflin], MDCCCCIX.

Combined in two-volumes-in-one format and published as vol. VI of the *Fireside Edition*. See B 15.

A 23.10.h
Boston, New York: Jefferson Press, [1913].

Combined with *Doctor Grimshawe's Secret* in three-volumes-in-one format and published as vol. [VI] of the *"Jefferson Press Edition."* See B 16.

OTHER EDITIONS

A 23.11

Transformation [The Marble Faun] and The Blithedale Romance. London: George Bell, 1884.

Combined with *The Blithedale Romance* in three-volumes-in-one format and published as vol. III, *Nathaniel Hawthorne's Tales*, in the *Bohn's Standard Library*. Reprinted 1886.

A 23.12

Boston and New York: Houghton, Mifflin, M dccc xcix.

2 vols. Advertised as *"The Roman Edition,"* with 48 illustrations. Top edges gilded. In cloth, with printed cloth wrappers, and in half calf.

PRINTINGS FROM THE AUTOGRAPH EDITION PLATES

A 23.13.a

Boston and New York: Houghton, Mifflin, MDCCCC.

Vols. IX and X of the *Autograph Edition*. Contents same as in the *Riverside Edition* (A 23.10.a), with a new introductory note provided. 500 copies. Deposited 5 March 1901. See B 20.

A 23.13.b

Boston and New York: Houghton, Mifflin, MDCCCC.

Vols. IX and X of the *Large-Paper (Autograph) Edition*. 500 copies. See B 21.

A 23.13.c

Boston and New York: Houghton, Mifflin, 1903.

Vols. IX and X of the *Old Manse Edition*. See B 22.

OTHER EDITIONS

A 23.14

New York: Thomas Y. Crowell, [1902].

2 vols. Introduction by Katharine Lee Bates. Also issued as vols. [10] and [11] of the *Crowell "Lenox Edition."* See B 23.

A 23.15

New York: Thomas Y. Crowell, [1902].

Combined in two-volumes-in-one format and published as the *"Luxembourg Edition."* Designated 'Luxembourg Edition' on front cover of dust jacket. Introduction by Katharine Lee Bates. Same plates used to manufacture vol. [2] of the *Crowell "Popular Edition"*; also in two-volumes-in-one format. See B 24.

A 23.16

London: J. M. Dent; New York: E. P. Dutton, [1910].

Everyman's Library. Reprinted 1912, 1915, 1920.

A 23.17
[New York]: The Limited Editions Club, 1931.

2 vols. Illustrated by Carl Strauss. Introduction by Herbert Gorman. Boxed. 1,500 numbered copies, signed by the illustrator.

A 23.18
[Columbus]: Ohio State University Press, [1968].

Vol. IV of the *Centenary Edition*. 1,969 copies published 1 July 1968. See B 32.

Bindings for (1) A 24.1.a; (2–7) A 24.2; (8 & 9) A 26.1.a, with Ticknor & Co. imprint; (10 & 11) A 26.1.a, with Fields, Osgood & Co. imprint; (12 & 13) A 26.1.c; (14 & 15) A 26.2, format A(1); (16 & 17) A 26.2, format A(2); (18) A 26.2, formats B and C

OUR OLD HOME:

A SERIES OF ENGLISH SKETCHES.

BY

NATHANIEL HAWTHORNE.

BOSTON:

TICKNOR AND FIELDS.

1863.

---

many other Americans, had long cherished a fantastic notion that he was one of the rightful heirs of a rich English estate; and on the strength of Her Majesty's letter and the hopes of royal patronage which it inspired, he had shut up his little country-store and come over to claim his inheritance. On the voyage, a German fellow-passenger had relieved him of his money on pretence of getting it favorably exchanged, and had disappeared immediately on the ship's arrival; so that the poor fellow was compelled to pawn all his clothes except the remarkably shabby ones in which I beheld him, and in which (as he himself hinted, with a melancholy, yet good-natured smile) he did not look altogether fit to see the Queen. I agreed with him that the bobtailed coat and mixed trousers constituted a very odd-looking court-dress, and suggested that it was doubtless his present purpose to get back to Connecticut as fast as possible. But no! The resolve to see the Queen was as strong in him as ever; and it was marvellous the pertinacity with which he clung to it amid raggedness and starvation, and the earnestness of his supplication that I would supply him with funds for a suitable appearance at Windsor Castle.

I never had so satisfactory a perception of a complete booby before in my life; and it caused me to feel kindly towards him, and yet impatient and exasperated on behalf of common sense, which could not possibly tolerate that such an unimaginable donkey should exist. I laid his absurdity before him in the very plainest terms, but without either exciting his anger or slaking his resolution. "Oh, my dear man," quoth he, with good-natured placid, simple, and tearful stubbornness, "if you could but enter into my feelings and see the matter from beginning

A 24 OUR OLD HOME

A 24.1.a
First American edition, first printing [1863]

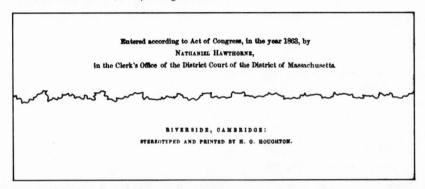

First printing has T&F ads on p. 399. Second printing has p. 399 blank. Published simultaneously with first English edition 19 September 1863.

[i–ix] x–xi [xii] [9] 10–48 [49] 50–76 [77] 78–105 [106] 107–140 [141] 142–162 [163] 164–194 [195] 196–224 [225] 226–247 [248] 249–281 [282] 283–319 [320] 321–357 [358] 359–398 [399–400]

[1]² [2]⁴ [3]⁸ [4–18]¹² [19]⁸; but signed 2–25⁸.

Contents: p. i: half title; p. ii: blank; p. iii: title; p. iv: copyright; p. v: dedication; p. vi: blank; p. vii: contents; p. viii: blank; pp. ix–xi: 'TO A FRIEND.'; p. xii: blank; pp. 9–398: text, headed 'OUR OLD HOME. | [rule] | CONSULAR EXPERIENCES.'; p. 399: ads; p. 400: blank.

Includes prefatory letter to Franklin Pierce and a following collection of sketches of English life, only one of which first appears in this collection: "To a Friend,"# "Consular Experiences,"# "Leamington Spa,"† "About Warwick,"† "Recollections of a Gifted Woman,"† "Lichfield and Uttoxeter,"† "Pilgrimage to Old Boston,"† "Near Oxford,"† "Some of the Haunts of Burns,"† "A London Suburb,"† "Up the Thames,"† "Outside Glimpses of English Poverty,"† "Civic Banquets."† Daggers (†) indicate first collected appearance. Number signs (#) indicate first appearance in print.

Typography and paper: See illustration, A 24.1.a page format. Running heads: rectos and versos, chapter titles. White wove paper.

Binding: In the style of Ticknor format A (see illustration, A 2.6 binding). Brown (81. d. gy. y Br) bold-ribbed T cloth with blindstamped floral device inside ruled panels on both covers. Spine goldstamped (see illustration, A 24 bindings). White wove endpapers brown coated one side. Flyleaf inserted at front and rear. All edges trimmed.

Printing: Composition, stereotyping, and printing by H. O. Houghton, Riverside Press, Cambridge, Mass. Since *Cost Books* list stereotyping and printing by Welch, Bigelow, & Co., Houghton may have jobbed out the plating. Probably bound by Benjamin Bradley & Co., Boston.

Publication: 3,500 copies printed 22 July 1863, published 19 September. Price $1.25, with a 12% royalty (15¢ per copy).

Locations: CEFC, Lilly, MH, NN, OU, PSt.

Manuscript: "To a Friend": CSmH; "Consular Experiences": ViU; "Leamington Spa": NCaS; "About Warwick" broken up by James T. Fields, fragments at: Berg, CSt, MH, ViU, Walter P. Chrysler, Jr.; "Recollections of a Gifted Woman": MH; "Lichfield and Uttoxeter": Robert Taylor; "Pilgrimage to Old Boston": NNC; "Near Oxford": Berg; "A London Suburb": OU; "Up the Thames": MH; "Civic Banquets": NNPM.

A 24.1.b
Second printing

Boston: Ticknor and Fields, 1863.

Omits ads from p. 399. 2,000 copies printed September 1863. Price $1.25, royalty 12%.

A 24.1.c
Third printing

Boston: Ticknor and Fields, 1864.

Misprint 'myterious' corrected to 'mysterious' at 145.23. Ads restored on p. 399. Printed on thinner paper stock. 1,000 copies printed 15 March 1864.

A 24.1.d
Boston: Ticknor and Fields, 1865.

Vol. 11 of untitled *"Tinted Edition"* on laid paper. 500 copies printed 31 October 1864. Price $1.50, royalty 12¢. See B 1[11] for reprintings of the *"Tinted Edition."*

A 24.1.e
Boston: Ticknor and Fields, 1865.

280 copies printed 7 November 1865. Price $1.50.

A 24.1.f
Boston: Ticknor and Fields, 1866.

Note: Two printings with 1866 title-page date (see A 24.1.g), priority undetermined.

500 copies printed 21 July 1866. Price $1.50, royalty 12¢.

A 24.1.g
Boston: Ticknor and Fields, 1866.

318 copies printed 25 August 1866.

A 24.1.h
Boston: James R. Osgood, 1871.

175 copies printed 28 October 1871. Price $2.00, royalty 20¢.

A 24.1.i
Boston: James R. Osgood, 1872.

150 copies printed. Price $2.00, royalty 20¢.

A 24.1.j
Boston: James R. Osgood, 1873.

Combined with *Septimius Felton* in two-volumes-in-one format and published as the ninth volume of the *Illustrated Library Edition*. 1,500 copies printed 7 August 1873. Price $2.00, royalty 20¢. See B 2 for reprintings of the *ILE*.

A 24.1.k
Boston: Houghton, Mifflin, 1880.

Combined with *Septimius Felton, Fanshawe,* and *The Dolliver Romance* in four-volumes-in-one format and published as the third volume of the *Globe Edition*. 1,500 copies printed August 1880. See B 3 for reprintings of the *Globe Edition*.

A 24.1.l
Boston: Houghton, Mifflin, [1886].

Combined with *Septimius Felton, Fanshawe,* and *The Dolliver Romance* in four-volumes-in-one format and published as the third volume of the *"New" Fireside Edition*. 1,000 copies printed May 1886. See B 4.

OUR OLD HOME.

BY

NATHANIEL HAWTHORNE,

AUTHOR OF "TRANSFORMATION," "THE SCARLET LETTER,"
ETC. ETC.

IN TWO VOLUMES.

VOL. I.

LONDON:
SMITH, ELDER AND CO., 65, CORNHILL.

M.DCCC.LXIII.

---

an interview with Queen Victoria had haunted his
poor foolish mind; and now, when he really stood
on English ground, and the palace-door was
hanging ajar for him, he was expected to turn
back, a penniless and bamboozled simpleton,
merely because an iron-hearted Consul refused
to lend him thirty shillings (so low had his demand
ultimately sunk) to buy a second-class ticket on
the rail for London!

He visited the Consulate several times afterwards, subsisting on a pittance that I allowed him
in the hope of gradually starving him back to
Connecticut, assailing me with the old petition at
every opportunity, looking shabbier at every visit,
but still thoroughly good-tempered, mildly stub-
born, and smiling through his tears, not without
a perception of the ludicrousness of his own
position. Finally, he disappeared altogether, and
whither he had wandered, and whether he ever
saw the Queen, or wasted quite away in the
endeavour, I never knew; but I remember unfolding the *Times*, about that period, with a daily
dread of reading an account of a ragged Yankee's
attempt to steal into Buckingham Palace, and how
he smiled tearfully at his captors, and besought

A 24.2: Title page, 7½" × 4½". Page format, 5⅛" (5⅜") × 3"

A 24.2
First English edition [1863]

2 vols. Published simultaneously with the first American edition 19 September 1863.

Note: Possibly as many as four printings according to advertisements. A "second edition" was advertised in the 17 October 1863 *Athenaeum;* a "third edition," in the 31 October 1863 *Reader;* a "new edition," in the 28 November 1863 *Athenaeum.* Variants, type batter, and loosened type tend to confirm more than one printing. First printing possibly conforms to the following variant schedule:

	FIRST PRINTING		LATER PRINTINGS
Volume I			
27.25	archipelagos	[	archipelagoes
Volume II			
13.19	conducted	[	condu cted
13.21	apartments	[	apart ments
18.25	trhee	[	three
56 (folio)	56	[	56 ("5" battered)
129 (folio)	129	[	129 ("9" battered)
133 (folio)	133	[	13 (last "3" dropped)
151.22	Englishman,	[	Englishman ("n" battered, final comma dropped)
151.23	with	[	with ("h" battered)

Centenary has surveyed six copies and CEFC has surveyed six without clear pattern of variants emerging. Sheets may have been mixed. BM deposit copy of vol. I received 14 October 1863 has 'archipelagos' at 27.25, which suggests first printing, but book could be second printing as easily as first. There is not enough evidence to establish with certainty the priority of printing.

I: [i–vii] viii–xii [1] 2–272

II: [i–iv] [1] 2–299 [300]

I: [A]⁶ B–I⁸ K–S⁸

II: [A]² B–I⁸ K–T⁸ U⁶

Contents: I: p. i: half title; p. ii: blank; p. iii: title; p. iv: blank; p. v: dedication; p. vi: blank; pp. vii–xii: 'TO A FRIEND. | [rule]'; pp. 1–272: text, headed 'OUR OLD HOME. | [rule] | CONSULAR EXPERIENCES.'

II: p. i: half title; p. ii: blank; p. iii: title; p. iv: blank; pp. 1–299: text, headed 'OUR OLD HOME. | [rule] | NEAR OXFORD.'; p. 300: colophon.

Combined contents of vols. I and II include same material as in T&F edition.

Typography and paper: See illustration, A 24.2 page format. Running heads: rectos and versos, 'OUR OLD HOME.' White wove paper.

Binding: Primary trade binding green (126. d. 0l G) wavy-grain TR cloth. Covers blind embossed with elaborate floral panel inside bold border rule. Spine gold-stamped, with volume imprint in variant forms (see illustration, A 24 bindings). White wove endpapers cream-coated one side. 4-page Smith, Elder catalogue inserted at rear of vol. II in most trade sets. Edges untrimmed in most copies. Also copies in custom leather bindings. Also custom bound in two-volumes-in-one format.

Publication: Unknown number of copies of first printing published 19 September 1863. Smith, Elder paid £150 for English rights. Price 1 guinea.

Printing: Probably printed from type metal by Smith, Elder and Co., Little Green Arbour Court, Old Bailey, London, E.C.

Locations: BM, 10348.C.18 (deposit-stamp 14 OC 63), CEFC, Lilly, OU.

A 24.3
Second English edition

London: Smith, Elder, 1864.

Vol. I and II combined in two-volumes-in-one format in a new typesetting published November 1864. Price 5s.

PRINTINGS FROM THE "LITTLE CLASSIC EDITION" PLATES

A 24.4.a

[All following within red and black double-rules frame] [red] Our Old Home: | [black] *A SERIES OF ENGLISH SKETCHES.* | BY | [red] NATHANIEL HAWTHORNE. | [black] [vignette of castle] | [red] BOSTON: | [black] JAMES R. OSGOOD AND COMPANY, | Late Ticknor & Fields, and Fields, Osgood, & Co. | [red] 1876.

Vol. [XI], *"Little Classic Edition."* Contents same as in first T&F edition (A 24.1.a). Sheets bound with James R. Osgood and, later, Houghton, Osgood spine imprints. 3,000 copies printed November–December 1875. Price $1.25, royalty 12.5¢. See B 5 [XI] for reprintings of the *"Little Classic Edition."*

A 24.4.b
Boston: Houghton, Osgood, 1879.

Combined with *Septimius Felton* in two-volumes-in-one format and published as vol. IX of the *"Fireside Edition."* 500 copies printed 20 September 1879. See B 6[IX] for reprintings of the *"Fireside Edition."*

A 24.4.c
Boston: Houghton, Mifflin, [1891].

Combined with *Passages from the American Note-Books* in three-volumes-in-one format and published as vol. VI of the *Popular Edition.* 1,000 copies printed June–August 1891. See B 7 for reprintings of the *Popular Edition.*

A 24.4.d
Boston: Houghton, Mifflin, [1899].

Vol. [XI], *Concord Edition.* See B 8.

PRINTINGS FROM THE RIVERSIDE EDITION PLATES

A 24.5.a₁
Riverside Edition (trade), first printing, American issue [1883]

OUR OLD HOME, AND ENGLISH | NOTE-BOOKS | BY | NATHANIEL HAWTHORNE | VOL. I. | [vignette of harbor scene] | BOSTON | HOUGHTON, MIFFLIN AND COM-PANY | New York: 11 East Seventeenth Street | The Riverside Press, Cambridge | 1883

Two volumes in one published as vol. VII of the Riverside trade printing (see A 27.5.a₁). Contents same as in *"Little Classic" Edition* (A 24.4.a), with "Introductory Note" by George Parsons Lathrop added. 2,000 copies printed April 1883. Price $2.00. See B 9 for reprintings of the Riverside trade printing. Also sheets of later printings with dated and undated title pages and with Riverside half title preserved issued in a two-volume set in H,M trade binding.

A 24.5.a₂
Riverside Edition (trade), first printing, English issue [1883]

London: Kegan Paul, Trench, 1883.

Sheets of vol. VII, first printing (A 24.5.a₁), with cancel title, in a Kegan Paul binding. 250 Kegan Paul title pages printed by Houghton, Mifflin, June–July 1883. Later issues noted with dated and undated Kegan Paul, Trench, Trübner title pages. See B 11.

A 24.5.b
Riverside Edition (large paper), second printing [1883]

[red] OUR OLD HOME | [black] AND | ENGLISH NOTE-BOOKS | BY | NATHANIEL HAWTHORNE | VOL. I. | [sepia vignette of harbor scene] | [red] CAMBRIDGE | [black] Printed at the Riverside Press | 1883

Combined with first part of *English Note-Books* in two-volumes-in-one format and published as vol. VII of the Riverside large-paper printing. 250 copies printed May 1883. See B 10.

A 24.5.c
Boston and New York: Houghton, Mifflin, 1884.

Vols. XIII and XIV of the *Wayside Edition.* (Vol. XIV in combination with *English Note-Books.*) 500 copies printed September–October 1884. See B 12.

A 24.5.d
Boston and New York: Houghton, Mifflin, [1891].

Combined with first part of *English Note-Books* in two-volumes-in-one format and published as vol. VII of the *Standard Library Edition.* 500 copies printed October 1891. See B 13.

A 24.5.e
Boston and New York: Houghton, Mifflin, [1902].

Combined with first part of *English Note-Books* in two-volumes-in-one format and published as vol. VII of the *"New" Wayside Edition.* 500 copies printed September–October 1902. See B 14.

A 24.5.f
Boston and New York: [Houghton, Mifflin], MDCCCCIX.

Combined with first part of *English Note-Books* in two-volumes-in-one format and published as vol. VII of the *Fireside Edition.* See B 15.

A 24.5.g
Boston, New York: Jefferson Press, [1913].

Combined with first part of *English Note-Books* in two-volumes-in-one format and published as vol. [VII] of the *"Jefferson Press Edition."* See B 16.

A 24.6
Printings from the Paterson-Scott plates

Edinburgh: William Paterson, 1884.

No. 17, *Paterson's New England Novels*. Contents same as in first American T&F edition (A 24.1.a) except dedication and 'TO A FRIEND' omitted. Published in cloth, top edges gilded, at 2s.; in ornamental paper covers at 1s. Also combined with *The Snow-Image* in two-volumes-in-one format and published as vol. [IV] of the *"Paterson Edition."* See B 17. Also Paterson sheets found with cancel Walter Scott title. Also remanufactured from Paterson plates with Walter Scott title-page imprint. Published in 1894 as vol. [VI] of the *"Walter Scott Edition"* (gravure). See B 18.

A 24.7
Boston and New York: Houghton, Mifflin, M DCCC XCI.

2 vols. Illustrated with photogravures. Omits dedication and 'TO A FRIEND'. Trade printing on wove paper. Limited printing of 250 copies on laid paper. Also English issue with trade sheets and cancel London: Chatto and Windus, 1890, title page, printed by Houghton, Mifflin. Also one-volume impression from same plates: Boston and New York, Houghton, Mifflin, 1901. Also one-volume impression from same plates: Boston and New York: Houghton Mifflin, 1907, with dedication and 'To A Friend' restored.

A 24.8.a
Boston and New York: Houghton, Mifflin, MDCCCC.

Vol. XI of the *Autograph Edition*. Contents same as in *Riverside Edition* (A 24.5.a), with a new introductory note provided. 500 copies. Deposited 5 March 1901. See B 20.

A 24.8.b
Boston and New York: Houghton, Mifflin, MDCCCC.

Vol. XI of the *Large-Paper (Autograph) Edition*. 500 copies. See B 21.

A 24.8.c
Boston and New York: Houghton, Mifflin, 1903.

Vol. XI of the *Old Manse Edition*. See B 22.

A 24.9
Warwick, England: Henry H. Lacy, [n.d.].

[ca. 1920]. An extract, prints only "Leamington Spa," "[About] Warwick," and "Stratford-on-Avon" ["Recollections of a Gifted Woman"]. Printed wrappers.

A 24.10
[Columbus]: Ohio State University Press, [1970].

Vol. V of the *Centenary Edition*. 2,458 copies published 1 September 1970. See B 32.

Wrappers for (1) A 25.1, setting A, and (2) A 25.1, setting B

PANSIE:

A Fragment.

——✻——

THE LAST LITERARY EFFORT OF

NATHANIEL HAWTHORNE.

LONDON:
JOHN CAMDEN HOTTEN, PICCADILLY.

---

suppose, remain unwritten, and perhaps it is just as well that it should be so. Men of sensibility and genius hate to have their infirmities dragged out of them by the roots in exhaustive series of cross-questionings and harassing physical explorations, and he who has enlarged the domain of the human soul may perhaps be spared his contribution to the pathology of the human body. At least, I was thankful that it was not my duty to sound all the jarring chords of this sensitive organism, and that a few cheering words and the prescription of a not ungrateful sedative and cordial or two could not lay on me the reproach of having given him his "final bitter taste of this world, perhaps doomed to be a recollected nauseousness in the next."

There was nothing in Mr. Hawthorne's aspect that gave warning of so sudden an end as that which startled us all. It seems probable that he died by the gentlest of all modes of release,—fainting,—without the

A 25.1: Title page, 6⅛″ × 4⅛″. Page format, 4¾″ (5⅛″) × 2⅞″

A 25 PANSIE

A 25.1
Only edition, a piracy [*1864*]

[1–3] 4–14 [15] 16–48

[A]⁸ B–C⁸

Contents: p. 1: title; p. 2: blank; pp. 3–14: 'NATHANIEL HAWTHORNE.'; pp. 15–48: text, headed 'PANSIE | AND | DOCTOR DOLLIVER. | [rule]'.

Includes "NATHANIEL HAWTHORNE," tribute by Oliver Wendell Holmes, reprinted in slightly modified form from first appearance in *Atlantic Monthly*, LXXXI (July 1864), 98–101. *Pansie* text same as first appearance, also in *AM*, 101–109. (*Pansie* later included in A 30.1.a as "A Scene from the Dolliver Romance.")

Typography and paper: See illustration, A 25.1, page format. Running heads: rectos and versos, pp. 3–14, '*Nathaniel Hawthorne.*'; pp. 16–48, rectos, '*Doctor Dolliver.*'; versos, '*Pansie and*'. White wove paper.

Binding: Printed wrappers, white wove stock with outer surface yellow coated. Wrapper imprint exists in at least two settings, priority undetermined (see illustration, A 25.1 wrapper imprints A and B). Top edge untrimmed. 16-page John Camden Hotten catalogue inserted at rear.

Publication: Unknown number of copies. Advertised in *Bookseller* (London), 30 July 1864, for "this day," but possibly premature. Reviewed in *Athenaeum*, 10 September 1864. Listed in *Publishers' Circular*, 15 September 1864, and in *Bookseller*, 30 September 1864.

Note: Collation of a three-copy sample reveals only one variant, which affects the publisher's title-page imprint. The variant is probably the result of type movement (see illustration, variants A and B).

Printing: Probably printed from type metal by John Camden Hotten, Printer, 74 and 75 Piccadilly, London.

Locations: BM, 12706.aaa.8 (deposit-stamp 31 OC 64), CEFC, CtY, MH, NN, PSt.

A	B
LONDON:	**LONDON:**
JOHN CAMDEN HOTTEN, PICCADILLY.	JOHN CAMDEN HOTTEN, PICCADILLY.

he is never seen to clap his wings to his sides. He seems to govern his movements by the inclination of his wings and tail to the wind, as a ship is propelled by the action of the wind on her sails.

In old country-houses in England, instead of glass for windows, they used wicker, or fine strips of oak disposed checkerwise. Horn was also used. The windows of princes and great noblemen were of crystal; those of Studley Castle, Holinshed says, of beryl. There were seldom chimneys; and they cooked their meats by a fire made against an iron back in the great hall. Houses, often of gentry, were built of a heavy timber frame, filled up with lath and plaster. People slept on rough mats or straw pallets, with a round log for a pillow; seldom better beds than a mattress, with a sack of chaff for a pillow.

October 25. — A walk yesterday through Dark Lane, and home through the village of Danvers. Landscape now wholly autumnal. Saw. an elderly man laden with two dry, yellow, rustling bundles of Indian corn-stalks, — a good personification of Autumn. Another man hoeing up potatoes. Rows of white cabbages lay ripening. Fields of dry Indian corn. The grass has still considerable greenness. Wild rose-bushes devoid of leaves, with their deep, bright red seed-vessels. Meeting-house in Danvers seen at a distance, with the sun shining through the windows of its belfry. Barberry-bushes, — the leaves now of a brown red, still juicy and healthy; very few berries remaining, mostly frost-bitten and wilted. All among the yet green grass,

PASSAGES

FROM THE

AMERICAN NOTE-BOOKS

OF

NATHANIEL HAWTHORNE

VOL. I.

BOSTON:
TICKNOR AND FIELDS.
1868.

A26.1.a: Title page. 7" × 4½". Page format, 5³/₁₆" (5⁷/₁₆") × 3"

A 26 PASSAGES FROM THE AMERICAN NOTE-BOOKS

A 26.1.a
First edition, first printing [*1868*]

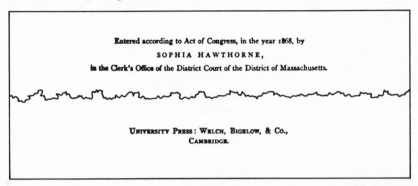

Entered according to Act of Congress, in the year 1868, by
SOPHIA HAWTHORNE,
in the Clerk's Office of the District Court of the District of Massachusetts.

UNIVERSITY PRESS: WELCH, BIGELOW, & CO.,
CAMBRIDGE.

2 vols. First and second printings have 1868 title-page date. See table of distinguishing characteristics.

Note one: The plate change at II, 6.4 and the different signings of vol. II make the distinction between the first and second printings of vol. II sheets certain. However, the distinguishing characteristics for vol. I are not definitive and must be used with caution. Only 19 days separated the two printings, and copies with mixed sheets from both printings are likely. Also anomalies exist, e.g., a second printing of vol. II was found in a T&Co. binding (Location: ViU), a first printing of vol. I and a second printing of vol. II were found in F,O&Co. bindings (Location: MCo), and Lilly has second-printing sheets of vols. I and II in T&Co. bindings. Other binding and flyleaf variants have been noted.

I: [i–ii] [1] 2–222

II: [i–iv] [1] 2–228

I: [1–9]^{12} [10]^4; signed π^1 1–9^{12} 10^3; also signed π^1 A–M^8 N^7

II: π^2 1–9^{12} 10^6; signed π^2 A–N^8 O^2

Contents: I: p. i: title; p. ii: copyright; pp. 1–222: text, headed 'PASSAGES | FROM | HAWTHORNE'S AMERICAN NOTE-BOOKS. | [rule]'.
II: pp. i–ii: blank; p. iii: title; p. iv: copyright; pp. 1–228: text, headed 'PASSAGES | FROM | HAWTHORNE'S AMERICAN NOTE-BOOKS. | [rule] | EXTRACTS FROM HIS PRIVATE LETTERS'.

Note two: Large sections of *American Note-Books*, totaling approximately 75,000 words, were first serialized in *Atlantic Monthly*. See D 98. In preparing the book for publication, Mrs. Hawthorne cut some 15,000 words from the magazine version and added close to 65,000 words of new material.

Typography and paper: See illustration, A 26.1.a page format. Running heads: rectos and versos, 'AMERICAN NOTE-BOOKS.' with year added. Parchment-tinted, unwatermarked, laid paper with horizontal chain lines from 1^1/$_8$" to 1^1/$_4$" apart.

Binding: In the style of Ticknor format D (see illustration, B 1 binding), without classical male figure blindstamped on covers. Binding uniform with *"Tinted Edition"* but

Distinguishing Characteristics of the First and Second Printings

of *The American Note-Books*

	FIRST	SECOND
Volume I		
Spine imprint	'TICKNOR & CO.'	'Fields, Osgood & Co.'
Flyleaves	chain lines vertical	chain lines horizontal
20.26-27	**Meeting-house** sun shining	**Meeting-house** sun shining
167.17	commis-	commis
173.31	horse	horse
221.21-24	yesterday with had given me y thankful. The sun shines	yesterday with had given me y thankful. The sun shines
Volume II		
Spine imprint	'TICKNOR & CO.'	'Fields, Osgood & Co.'
Flyleaves	chain lines vertical	chain lines horizontal
6.4	thick ; fog	thick fog ;
51.25	**Ameri-**	**Ameri**
141.1	with	with
collation	[i-iv] [1] 2-228	[i-ii] [1] 2-228 [229-230]

without volume number immediately below 'WORKS' imprint (see B 1). Green (146. d. G) pebble-grain P cloth with blindstamped-rules panel on cover. Spine goldstamped (see illustration, A 26 bindings [at A 24]). Noted with publisher's spine imprint in two forms: 'TICKNOR & CO.' and the later 'Fields, Osgood & Co.' White wove endpapers brown coated one side. Laid-paper flyleaf inserted at front and rear. All edges trimmed.

Publication: 1,500 copies of two-volume set printed 9 October 1868. Published 11 November. Price $4.00 per set, with Mrs. Hawthorne receiving a royalty of 40¢ per set.

Printing: Stereotyped and printed by Welch, Bigelow, & Co., Cambridge, Mass.

Locations: CEFC, CtY, CSmH, MH, MSaE, NN, OU, ViU.

Manuscript: Five manuscript notebooks located in the Pierpont Morgan Library. A sixth manuscript notebook with 330 entries dating from 28 May 1835 to 29 June 1841 located by Mrs. Frank E. Mouffe, Boulder, Colo.

A 26.1.b
Second printing

Boston: Ticknor and Fields, 1868.

2 vols. See table of distinguishing characteristics of first and second printings under A 26.1.a.

I: [1–ii] [1] 2–222

II: [i–ii] [1] 2–228 [229–230]

I: [1–9^{12} [10]^4; signed π^1 1–9^{12} 10^3; also signed π^1 A–M^8 N^7

II: [1–9]^{12} [10]^8; signed π^1 1–9^{12} 10^7; also signed π^1 A–N^8 O^3

Contents: I: p. i: title; p. ii: copyright; pp. 1–222: text, headed 'PASSAGES | FROM | HAWTHORNE'S AMERICAN NOTE-BOOKS. | [rule]'.

II: p. i: title; p. ii: copyright; pp. 1–228: text, headed 'PASSAGES | FROM | HAWTHORNE'S AMERICAN NOTE-BOOKS. | [rule] | EXTRACTS FROM HIS PRIVATE LETTERS.'; pp. 229–230: blank.

500 copies printed 28 October 1868. Published with the first printing 11 November. Price $4.00 per set, royalty 40¢ per set.

REPRINTINGS FROM THE T&F STEREOTYPE PLATES

A 26.1.c
Boston: Fields, Osgood, 1870.

Vols. 15 and 16 of untitled *"Tinted Edition"* on laid paper. Spine goldstamped with 'VOL. 15 [VOL. 16]' imprint immediately below 'WORKS' imprint. 280 copies printed 4 October 1869. Price $4.00 per set, royalty 40¢ per set. See B 1[15,16] for reprintings of the *"Tinted Edition."*

A 26.1.d
Boston: James R. Osgood, 1871.

Vols. I and II combined in two-volumes-in-one format and published as the seventh volume of the *Illustrated Library Edition.* 1,000 copies printed 26 October 1871. Price $2.00, royalty 20¢. See B 2 for reprintings of the *ILE.*

A 26.1.e
Boston: James R. Osgood, 1872.

280 copies of each of two volumes printed 27 August 1872. Price $4.00 per set, royalty 40¢ per set.

A 26.1.f
Boston: Houghton, Mifflin, 1880.

Vols. I and II combined with the *English Note-Books* in four-volumes-in-one format and published as the sixth volume of the *Globe Edition.* 1,500 copies printed July 1880. See B 3 for reprintings of the *Globe Edition.*

A 26.1.g
Boston: Houghton, Mifflin, [1886].

Vols. I and II combined with the *English Note-Books* in four-volumes-in-one format and published as the sixth volume of the *"New" Fireside Edition*. 1,000 copies printed May 1886. See B 4.

great deal of linen, much of my brass, some of my pewter, and now I am come to eat iron ; and what will come next I know not."

A scold and a blockhead,—brimstone and wood,—a good match.

To make one's own reflection in a mirror the subject of a story.

In a dream to wander to some place where may be heard the complaints of all the miserable on earth.

Some common quality or circumstance that should bring together people the most unlike in all other respects, and make a brotherhood and sisterhood of them, — the rich and the proud finding themselves in the same category with the mean and the despised.

A person to consider himself as the prime mover of certain remarkable events, but to discover that his actions have not contributed in the least thereto. Another person to be the cause, without suspecting it.

PASSAGES

FROM

THE AMERICAN NOTE-BOOKS

OF

NATHANIEL HAWTHORNE,

AUTHOR OF "TRANSFORMATION," "OUR OLD HOME," ETC. ETC.

IN TWO VOLUMES.

VOL. I.

LONDON: SMITH, ELDER AND CO.
1868.

A26.2: Title page, 7³/₈" × 4¹³/₁₆". Page format, 5¹/₈" (5⁷/₁₆") × 3⁵/₁₆"

A 26.2
First English edition [*1868*]

Note one: Smith, Elder, who had negotiated with Ticknor and Fields for the English rights to the *American Note-Books,* produced a two-volume edition to be sold at 15s. On the eve of publication, threatened by a competing piracy by John Camden Hotten (see A 26.4), Smith, Elder reduced the price of the work to 5s. and took an ad in the 21 November 1868 *Athenaeum* explaining the situation and announcing its own one-volume "edition." Smith, Elder countered the Hotten threat by marketing what appear to be the same sheets in at least three formats:
   A. Bound as a two-volume set.
   B. Combined in two-volumes-in-one format and bound as one volume with original volume titles retained.
   C. Combined in two-volumes-in-one format and bound as one volume with original titles omitted and new undated combined-volume title added, with *'NEW EDITION'* slug on title page.
   Smith, Elder further countered the Hotten threat by publishing a cheap, completely reset, one-volume edition (A 26.3).

I: [a–b] [i–iii] iv [1] 2–295 [296]

II: [i–iv] [1] 2–304

I: π^2 $(1+1_1)$ $1–18^8$ 19^4

II: π^2 $20–38^8$

Note two: Vol. I half title is a singleton tipped to recto of title leaf and is omitted in some copies examined. Vol. II half title is omitted in some copies.

Contents: I: p. a: half title; p. b: blank; p. i: title; p. ii: blank; pp. iii–iv: 'ADVERTISE-MENT.'; pp. 1–295: text, headed 'PASSAGES | FROM | HAWTHORNE'S AMERICAN NOTE-BOOKS. | [double rule]'; p. 296: colophon.
   II: p. i: half title; p. ii: blank; p. iii: title; p. iv: blank; pp. 1–304: text, headed 'PASSAGES | FROM | HAWTHORNE'S AMERICAN NOTE-BOOKS. | [double rule] | EXTRACTS FROM HIS PRIVATE LETTERS.'

Contents same as T&F 2-vol. edition (A 26.1.a), with addition of 2-page prefatory editorial note titled 'ADVERTISEMENT.'

Typography and paper: See illustration, A 26.2 page format. Running heads: rectos and versos, 'AMERICAN NOTE-BOOKS.' with year added. White wove paper.

Binding: Two-volume format A noted in two bindings: (1) Reddish brown (43. m. r Br) V-like smooth cloth with blindstamped triple-rules frame along outer edge of covers. Covers beveled. Spine goldstamped (see illustration, A 26 bindings [at A 24]). (2) Same as (1) except triple rules on front cover and at top and base of spine imprinted in black. Combined two-volumes-in-one formats B and C in same style as (1). White wove endpapers brown coated one side. Edges untrimmed.

Publication: Unknown number of copies. Two-volume set advertised in the 21 November 1868 *Athenaeum* as "ready this day."

Printing: Printed by Smith, Elder and Co., Old Bailey, London, E.C.

Locations: Format A (2-vol. set): BM, 10882.b.13 (deposit-stamp 22 MH 69), CEFC, Lilly; formats B, C (2 vols. in one): CEFC.

A 26.3
Second English edition [1868]

PASSAGES | FROM | THE AMERICAN NOTE-BOOKS | OF | NATHANIEL HAWTHORNE. | AUTHOR OF "TRANSFORMATION," "OUR OLD HOME," | ETC. ETC. | *SECOND EDITION.* | LONDON: SMITH, ELDER AND CO. | 1868.

A cheap, completely reset, one-volume edition. Advertised in the 5 December 1868 *Athenaeum* as ready. Published in cloth at 1s. 6d. Noted in two styles of bindings (see illustration, A 26 bindings), in purple or yellow cloth. Spine goldstamped.

A 26.4
Third English edition, a piracy [1869]

PASSAGES FROM THE | NOTE-BOOKS OF | THE LATE | NATHANIEL HAWTHORNE. | *WITH AN INTRODUCTION BY* | MONCURE D. CONWAY. | [quotation from Persius] | LONDON: | JOHN CAMDEN HOTTEN, PICCADILLY. | 1869.

Includes a section of the *English Note-Books* plus ten of the twelve installments of the *American Note-Books* from *Atlantic Monthly*, with a few excisions. Advertised in *Athenaeum*, 5 December and 12 December 1869, and in *Publishers' Circular*, 16 January 1870 as "just published." Issued in cloth at 1s. 6d. and in "stiff cover" paperback at 1s. Also found bound with other Hotten titles in omnibus volumes. Also found in custom leather bindings.

Location: Cloth, paper, omnibus: CEFC.

PRINTINGS FROM THE "LITTLE CLASSIC EDITION" PLATES

A 26.5.a

[All following within red and black double-rules frame] PASSAGES | FROM | [red] The American Note-Books | [black] OF | NATHANIEL HAWTHORNE. | VOL. I. [VOL. II.] | [I: vignette of Custom House] [II: vignette of lakeshore scene] | [red] BOSTON: | [black] JAMES R. OSGOOD AND COMPANY, | Late Ticknor & Fields, and Fields, Osgood, & Co. | [red] 1876.

Vols. [XV] and [XVI], *"Little Classic Edition."* Contents same as in T&F edition (A 26.1.a). Sheets bound with James R. Osgood and, later, Houghton, Osgood spine imprints. 2,000 copies of each of two volumes printed 10 February 1876. Price $1.25 per volume, royalty 12.5¢ per volume. See B 5[XV,XVI] for reprintings of the *"Little Classic Edition."*

A 26.5.b
Boston: Houghton, Osgood, 1879.

Vols. I and II combined in two-volumes-in-one format and published as vol. VII of the *"Fireside Edition."* 500 copies printed 20 September 1879. See B 6[VII] for reprintings of the *"Fireside Edition."*

A 26.5.c
Boston: Houghton, Mifflin, [1891].

Vols. I and II combined with *Our Old Home* in three-volumes-in-one format and published as vol. VI of the *Popular Edition.* 1,000 copies printed June–August 1891. See B 7 for reprintings of the *Popular Edition.*

A 26.5.d
Boston: Houghton, Mifflin, [1899].

Vols. [XV] and [XVI], *Concord Edition*. See B 8.

PRINTINGS FROM THE RIVERSIDE EDITION PLATES

A 26.6.a₁
Riverside Edition (trade), first printing, American issue [1883]

PASSAGES FROM THE AMERICAN | NOTE-BOOKS | OF | NATHANIEL HAWTHORNE | [vignette of woodland scene] | BOSTON | HOUGHTON, MIFFLIN AND COMPANY | New York: 11 East Seventeenth Street | The Riverside Press, Cambridge | 1883

Two volumes in one published as vol. IX of the Riverside trade printing. Contents same as in *"Little Classic" Edition* (A 26.5.a), with "Introductory Note" by George Parsons Lathrop added. 2,000 copies printed May 1883. Price $2.00. See B 9 for reprintings of the Riverside trade printing.

A 26.6.a₂
Riverside Edition (trade), first printing, English issue [1883]

London: Kegan Paul, Trench, 1883.

Sheets of vol. IX, first printing (A 26.6.a₁), with cancel title, in a Kegan Paul binding. 250 Kegan Paul title pages printed by Houghton, Mifflin, June–July 1883. Later issues noted with dated and undated Kegan Paul, Trench, Trübner title pages. See B 11.

A 26.6.b
Riverside Edition (large paper), second printing [1883]

PASSAGES | FROM | [red] THE AMERICAN NOTE-BOOKS | [black] OF | NATHAN-IEL HAWTHORNE | [sepia vignette of woodland scene] | [red] CAMBRIDGE | [black] Printed at the Riverside Press | 1883

Two volumes in one published as vol. IX of the Riverside large-paper printing. 250 copies printed June 1883. See B 10.

A 26.6.c
Boston and New York: Houghton, Mifflin, 1884.

Vols. XVII and XVIII of the *Wayside Edition*. 500 copies printed September–October 1884. See B 12.

A 26.6.d
Boston and New York: Houghton, Mifflin, [1891].

Two volumes in one published as vol. IX of the *Standard Library Edition*. 500 copies printed October 1891. See B 13.

A 26.6.e
Boston and New York: Houghton, Mifflin, [1902].

Two volumes in one published as vol. IX of the *"New" Wayside Edition*. 500 copies printed September–October 1902. See B 14.

A 26.6.f

Boston and New York: [Houghton, Mifflin], MDCCCCIX.

Two volumes in one published as vol. IX of the *Fireside Edition.* See B 15.

A 26.6.g

Boston, New York: Jefferson Press, [1913].

Combined with *The Dolliver Romance, Fanshawe,* and *Septimius Felton* in five-volumes-in-one format and published as vol. [IX] of the *"Jefferson Press Edition."* See B 16.

PRINTINGS FROM THE AUTOGRAPH EDITION PLATES

A 26.7.a

Boston and New York: Houghton, Mifflin, MDCCCC.

Two volumes in one published as vol. XVIII of the *Autograph Edition.* Contents same as in the *Riverside Edition* (A 26.6.a₁), with a new introductory note provided. 500 copies. Deposited 5 March 1901. See B 20.

A 26.7.b

Boston and New York: Houghton, Mifflin, MDCCCC.

Two volumes in one published as vol. XVIII of the *Large-Paper (Autograph) Edition.* 500 copies. See B 21.

A 26.7.c

Boston and New York: Houghton, Mifflin, 1903.

Two volumes in one published as vol. XVIII of the *Old Manse Edition.* See B 22.

OTHER EDITIONS

A 26.8

The Heart of Hawthorne's Journals. Edited by Newton Arvin. Boston and New York: Houghton Mifflin, 1929.

Prints selections from the *American Note-Books* combined in one volume with selections from Hawthorne's other journals. Issued in two formats: trade printing in black-green T cloth; also 250 uncut copies in red V cloth with paper label on spine. Deposited 24 April 1929.

A 26.9

The American Notebooks. Edited by Randall Stewart. New Haven: Yale University Press, 1932.

A reediting of the five surviving manuscript journals in which Stewart attempted to restore as much of Hawthorne's original text as possible. Printed dust jacket. Second printing June 1933, with 'Second Printing' noted on dust jacket.

A 26.10

[Columbus]: Ohio State University Press, [1972].

Vol. VIII of the *Centenary Edition.* 3,000 copies in cloth published 1 May 1973. Also a paperback reprint of 1,880 copies published 1 May 1973. See B 32.

Bindings for (1 & 2) A27.1.a; (3 & 4) A27.2, format A; (5 & 6) A27.2, format B; (7 & 8) A28.1, format A; (9 & 10) A28.1, format B; (11 & 12) A28.2.a

son, and myself, in the black-plumed coach, and the landlady, her daughter, and a female friend, in the coach behind. Previous to this, however, everybody had taken some wine or spirits; for it seemed to be considered disrespectful not to do so.

Before us went the plumed hearse, a stately affair, with a bas-relief of funereal figures upon its sides. We proceeded quite across the city to the Necropolis, where the coffin was carried into a chapel, in which we found already another coffin, and another set of mourners, awaiting the clergyman. Anon he appeared, — a stern, broad-framed, large, and bald-headed man, in a black-silk gown. He mounted his desk, and read the service in quite a feeble and unimpressive way, though with no lack of solemnity. This done, our four bearers took up the coffin, and carried it out of the chapel; but, descending the steps, and, perhaps, having taken a little too much brandy, one of them stumbled, and down came the coffin, — not quite to the ground, however; for they grappled with it, and contrived, with a great struggle, to prevent the misadventure. But I really expected to see poor Captain Auld burst forth among us in his grave-clothes.

The Necropolis is quite a handsome burial-place, shut in by high walls, so overrun with shrubbery that no part of the brick or stone is visible. Part of the space within is an ornamental garden, with flowers and green turf; the rest is strewn with flat gravestones, and a few raised monuments; and straight avenues run to and fro between. Captain Auld's grave was dug nine feet deep. It is his own for twelve months; but, if his friends do not choose to give him a stone, it will become a com-

PASSAGES

FROM THE

ENGLISH NOTE-BOOKS

OF

NATHANIEL HAWTHORNE

VOL. I.

BOSTON:
FIELDS, OSGOOD, & CO.
1870.

A27.1.a: Title page. 7" × 4³/₈". Page format, 5¹/₄" (5¹/₂") × 3"

A 27 PASSAGES FROM THE ENGLISH NOTE-BOOKS

A 27.1.a
First edition, first printing [1870]

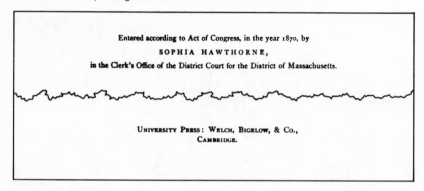

Entered according to Act of Congress, in the year 1870, by
SOPHIA HAWTHORNE,
in the Clerk's Office of the District Court for the District of Massachusetts.

UNIVERSITY PRESS: WELCH, BIGELOW, & CO.,
CAMBRIDGE.

2 vols. First and second printings both have 1870 title-page dates. Distinguishing characteristics undetermined. First printing intended for simultaneous publication with the first English edition.

I: [i–v] vi–viii [1] 2–410 [411–412]

II: [i–ii] [1] 2–393 [394]

I: π^4 1–17^{12} 18^2; also signed π^4 A–Y^8 Z^6

II: [1]^{12} 2–16^{12} 17^6 (these vol. II signature notations are on the second leaf, recto, of the gathering); also signed A–X^8 Y^6

Contents: I: p. i: title; p. ii: copyright; p. iii: dedication; p. iv: blank; pp. v–viii: preface; pp. 1—410: text, headed 'PASSAGES | FROM | HAWTHORNE'S ENGLISH NOTE-BOOKS. | [rule]'; pp. 411–412: blank.

   II: p. i: title; p. ii: copyright; pp. 1–393: text, headed 'PASSAGES | FROM | HAWTHORNE'S ENGLISH NOTE-BOOKS. | [rule] | LONDON.—MILTON-CLUB DINNER.'; p. 394: blank.

Note: A small section of *Passages from the English Note-Books* first appeared as "A Passage from Hawthorne's English Note-Books," *Atlantic Monthly,* XX (July 1867), 15–21, and was first collected in the John Camden Hotten piracy, *Passages from the Note-Books of the Late Nathaniel Hawthorne* (London, 1869), pp. 27–41. (Extract begins "Our road to Rydal lay through Ambleside . . . " and terminates " . . . while the world was in a state out of which these forms naturally grew.") See A 26.4.

Typography and paper: See illustration, A 27.1.a page format. Running heads: rectos, section titles with year; versos, 'ENGLISH NOTE-BOOKS.' with year. Parchment-tinted laid paper.

Binding: In the style of Ticknor format D (see illustration, B 1 binding), without classical male figure blindstamped on covers. Green (146. d. G) pebble-grain P cloth with blindstamped-rules panel on covers. Spine goldstamped (see illustration, A 27 bindings). Also undetermined number of the 1,000 two-volume sets of the first printing in binding uniform with *"Tinted Edition,"* with 'VOL. 17 [VOL. 18]' designation goldstamped on spine immediately below 'WORKS' (see B 1). White wove endpapers brown coated one side. Laid-paper flyleaf inserted at front and rear. All edges trimmed.

Publication: 1,000 two-volume sets printed 25 May 1870. Advertised in *American Literary Gazette,* 16 May 1870, as for 4 June. Deposited 3 June 1870. Price $4.00 per set, with Mrs. Hawthorne receiving a royalty of 40¢ per set.

Printing: Printed by Welch, Bigelow, & Co., Cambridge, Mass.

Locations: CEFC, Lilly, MH, NN, OU, PSt, ViU.

Manuscript: Manuscripts of Hawthorne's *English Note-Books* located in the Pierpont Morgan Library.

REPRINTINGS FROM THE F,O STEREOTYPE PLATES

A27.1.b
Second printing

Boston: Fields, Osgood, 1870.

500 copies of each of two volumes printed on laid paper 27 July 1870. Price $4.00 per set, royalty 40¢ per set. Also in binding uniform with *"Tinted Edition,"* some copies with 'VOL. 17 [VOL. 18]' designation goldstamped on spine immediately below 'WORKS' (see B1).

A27.1.c
Boston: James R. Osgood, 1871.

500 copies of each of two volumes printed on laid paper 9 January 1871. Price $4.00 per set, royalty 40¢ per set. Also in binding uniform with *"Tinted Edition,"* some copies with 'VOL. 17 [VOL. 18]' designation goldstamped on spine immediately below 'WORKS' (see B1).

A27.1.d
Boston: James R. Osgood, 1871.

Vols. I and II combined in two-volumes-in-one format and published as the sixth volume of the *Illustrated Library Edition.* 1,500 copies printed August 1871. Price $2.00, royalty 20¢. See B2 for reprintings of the *ILE.*

A27.1.e
Boston: James R. Osgood, 1874.

140 copies of each of two volumes printed 2 September 1874. Price $4.00 per set, royalty 40¢ per set. Also bound uniform with the *"Tinted Edition."* See B1.

A27.1.f
Boston: Houghton, Mifflin, 1880.

Vols. I and II combined with the *American Note Books* in four-volumes-in-one format and published as the sixth volume of the *Globe Edition.* 1,500 copies printed July 1880. See B3 for reprintings of the *Globe Edition.*

A27.1.g
Boston: Houghton, Mifflin, [1886].

Vols. I and II combined with the *American Note Books* in four-volumes-in-one format and published as the sixth volume of the *"New" Fireside Edition.* 1,000 copies printed May 1886. See B4.

of wash-rooms and kitchens, the bricks of which seemed half loose.

The chattels of the dead man were contained in two trunks, a chest, a sail-cloth bag, and a barrel, and consisted of clothing, suggesting a thickset, middle-sized man; papers relative to ships and business, a spy-glass, a loaded iron pistol, some books of navigation, some charts, several great pieces of tobacco, and a few cigars; some little plaster images, that he had probably bought for his children, a cotton umbrella, and other trumpery of no great value. In one of the trunks we found about twenty pounds' worth of English and American gold and silver, and some notes of hand, due in America. Of all these things the clerk made an inventory; after which we took possession of the money and affixed the consular seal to the trunks, bag, and chest.

While this was going on, we heard a great noise of men quarrelling in an adjoining court; and, altogether, it seemed a squalid and ugly place to live in, and a most undesirable one to die in. At the conclusion of our labours, the young woman asked us if we would not go into another chamber, and look at the corpse, and appeared to think that we should be rather glad than otherwise of the privilege. But, never having seen the man during his lifetime, I declined to commence his acquaintance now.

His bills for board and nursing amount to about the sum which we found in his trunk; his funeral

---

PASSAGES FROM

THE ENGLISH NOTE-BOOKS OF NATHANIEL HAWTHORNE

VOL. I.

STRAHAN & CO., PUBLISHERS
56 LUDGATE HILL, LONDON
1870

A 27.2: Title page, 7⅛″ × 5⅛″. Page format, 5⅜″ (5¹¹/₁₆″) × 3½″

OTHER EDITIONS

A 27.2
First English edition [1870]

2 vols. Published simultaneously with the first American edition.

I: [i–vii] viii–x [1] 2–472

II: [i–iv] [1] 2–453 [454–458]

I: [A]⁴ b² (-b₂) B–I⁸ K–U⁸ X–Z⁸ AA–GG⁸ HH⁴, (b₁ [pp. ix & x] a singleton pasted to the verso of [A₄] [p. viii])

II: [A]² B–I⁸ K–U⁸ X–Z⁸ AA–FF⁸ GG⁴ gg*² (-gg*₂), (gg*₁ [pp. 457–458] a singleton pasted to the verso of HH₄ [p. 456])

Contents: *I:* p. i: half title; p. ii: blank; p. iii: title; p. iv: printer's notice; p. v: dedication; p. vi: blank; pp. vii–x: preface; pp. 1–472: text, headed 'PASSAGES FROM HAWTHORNE'S | ENGLISH NOTE-BOOKS. | [rule]'.
    II: p. i: half title; p. ii: blank; p. iii: title; p. iv: printer's notice; pp. 1–453: text, headed 'PASSAGES FROM HAWTHORNE'S | ENGLISH NOTE-BOOKS. | [rule] | LONDON—MILTON-CLUB DINNER.'; pp. 454–458: ads.

Note: Contents same as in F,O edition (A 27.1.a) except for a slightly modified preface dated 'THE KNOLL, BLACKHEATH, *May,* 1870.' Preface in first American edition dated 'DRESDEN, April, 1870.'

Typography and paper: See illustration, A 27.2 page format. Running heads: rectos and versos, section titles with year. White wove paper.

Binding: Reddish brown (46. gy. r Br) P cloth with horizontal rows of black, gilt-imprinted, and blindstamped rules carrying across spine and continuing in blindstamped form only on back cover. Spine black and goldstamped in two forms: (A) with publisher's anchor device; (B) without anchor device (see illustration, A 27 bindings). White wove endpapers deep gray-blue coated one side. Edges untrimmed in most copies.

Publication: Advertised in the 26 March 1870 *Athenaeum* as "in preparation." Advertised in the 2 May 1870 *Publishers' Circular* as "in the press." Advertised in the 28 May 1870 *Athenaeum* as for June 4. Advertised in the 11 June 1870 *Athenaeum* as "new." Noted in the 15 June *Publishers' Circular* as a publication of the preceding fortnight; also advertised as "new." Listed in the 1 July 1870 *Publishers' Circular.* Reviewed in the 2 July 1870 *Athenaeum.*

Printing: Printed by Virtue and Co., City Road, London.

Locations: BM, 10348.d.10 (deposit-stamp 2 JY 70), CEFC.

A 27.3
Leipzig: Bernhard Tauchnitz, 1871.

Vols. 1139 and 1140, *Tauchnitz Collection of British Authors.* Marketed in printed wrappers and cloth. Unknown number of reprintings. Also combined in two-volumes-in-one format and bound as one volume in cloth or custom bound in leather.

A 27.4.a

[All following within red and black double-rules frame] PASSAGES | FROM | [red] The English Note-Books | [black] OF | NATHANIEL HAWTHORNE. | VOL. I. [VOL. II.] | [I: vignette of lighthouse scene] [II: vignette of castle keep scene] | [red] BOSTON: | [black] JAMES R. OSGOOD AND COMPANY, | Late Ticknor & Fields, and Fields, Osgood, & Co. | [red] 1876.

Vols. [XVII] and [XVIII], *"Little Classic Edition."* Contents same as in F,O edition (A 27.1.a). Sheets bound with James R. Osgood and, later, Houghton, Osgood spine imprints. 3,000 copies of each of two volumes printed 31 January 1876. Price $1.25 per volume, royalty 12.5 per volume. See B 5[XVII,XVIII] for reprintings of the *"Little Classic Edition."*

A 27.4.b

Boston: Houghton, Osgood, 1879.

Vols. I and II combined in two-volumes-in-one format and published as vol. VI of the *"Fireside Edition."* 500 copies printed 20 September 1879. See B 6[VI] for reprintings of the *"Fireside Edition."*

A 27.4.c

Boston: Houghton, Mifflin, [1891].

Vols. I and II combined in two-volumes-in-one format and published as vol. VII of the *Popular Edition.* 1,000 copies printed June–August 1891. See B 7 for reprintings of the *Popular Edition.*

A 27.4.d

Boston: Houghton, Mifflin, [1899].

Vols. [XVII] and [XVIII], *Concord Edition.* See B 8.

A 27.5.a1

Riverside Edition (trade), first printing, American issue [1883]

OUR OLD HOME, AND ENGLISH | NOTE-BOOKS | BY | NATHANIEL HAWTHORNE | VOL. I [Vol. II] | [I: vignette of harbor scene] [II: vignette of doorway] | BOSTON | HOUGHTON, MIFFLIN AND COMPANY | New York: 11 East Seventeenth Street | The Riverside Press, Cambridge | 1883

Vols. VII and VIII of the Riverside trade printing, with the first portion of *English Note-Books* combined with *Our Old Home* in vol. VII. Contents same as in *"Little Classic Edition"* (A 27.4.a), with "Introductory Note" by George Parsons Lathrop added. 2,000 copies of each of vols. VII and VIII printed April 1883. Price $2.00 per volume. See B 9 for reprintings of the Riverside trade printing. Also sheets of later printings with dated and undated title pages and with Riverside half title preserved issued in a two-volume set in H,M trade binding.

A 27.5.a2

Riverside Edition (trade), first printing, English issue [1883]

London: Kegan Paul, Trench, 1883.

2 vols. Sheets of vols. VII and VIII, first printing (A 27.5.a1), with cancel title, in a Kegan

Paul binding. 250 Kegan Paul title pages printed by Houghton, Mifflin, June–July 1883. Later issues noted with dated and undated Kegan Paul, Trench, Trübner title pages. See B 11.

A 27.5.b
Riverside Edition (large paper), second printing [1883]

[red] OUR OLD HOME | [black] AND | ENGLISH NOTE-BOOKS | BY | NATHANIEL HAWTHORNE | VOL. I. [VOL. II.] | [I: sepia vignette of harbor scene] [II: sepia vignette of doorway] | [red] CAMBRIDGE | [black] Printed at the Riverside Press | 1883

Vols. VII and VIII of the Riverside large-paper printing, with first portion of *English Note-Books* combined with *Our Old Home* in vol. VII. 250 copies printed May 1883. See B 10.

A 27.5.c
Boston and New York: Houghton, Mifflin, 1884.

Vols. XIV, XV, and XVI of the *Wayside Edition,* with conclusion of *Our Old Home* combined with first portion of *English Note-Books* in vol. XIV. 500 copies printed September–October 1884. See B 12.

A 27.5.d
Boston and New York: Houghton, Mifflin, [1891].

Vols. VII and VIII of the *Standard Library Edition,* with first portion of *English Note-Books* combined with *Our Old Home* in vol. VII. 500 copies printed October 1891. See B 13.

A 27.5.e
Boston and New York: Houghton, Mifflin, [1902].

Vols VII and VIII of the *"New" Wayside Edition,* with first portion of *English Note-Books* combined with *Our Old Home* in vol. VII. 500 copies printed September–October 1902. See B 14.

A 27.5.f
Boston and New York: [Houghton, Mifflin], MDCCCCIX.

Vols. VII and VIII of the *Fireside Edition,* with first portion of *English Note-Books* combined with *Our Old Home* in vol. VII. See B 15.

A 27.5.g
Boston, New York: Jefferson Press, [1913].

Vols. VII and VIII of the *"Jefferson Press Edition,"* with the first portion of *English Note-Books* combined with *Our Old Home* in vol. VII. See B 16.

PRINTINGS FROM THE AUTOGRAPH EDITION PLATES

A 27.6.a
Boston and New York: Houghton, Mifflin, MDCCCC.

Vols. XIX, XX, and XXI of the *Autograph Edition,* with conclusion of *English Note-Books* and beginning of *French and Italian Note-Books* combined in vol. XXI, all published under title 'NOTES OF TRAVEL'. Contents same as in the *Riverside Edition* (A 27.5.a₁), with some of the initials used by Mrs. Hawthorne extended to a full name and with a new introductory note provided. 500 copies. Deposited 5 March 1901. See B 20.

A 27.6.b
Boston and New York: Houghton, Mifflin, MDCCCC.

Vols. XIX, XX, and XXI of the *Large-Paper (Autograph) Edition,* with conclusion of *English Note-Books* and beginning of *French and Italian Note-Books* combined in vol. XXI. 500 copies. See B 21.

A 27.6.c
Boston and New York: Houghton, Mifflin, 1903.

Vols. XIX, XX, and XXI of the *Old Manse Edition,* with conclusion of *English Note-Books* and beginning of *French and Italian Note-Books* combined in vol. XXI. See B 22.

OTHER EDITIONS

A 27.7
The Heart of Hawthorne's Journals. Edited by Newton Arvin. Boston and New York: Houghton Mifflin, 1929.

Prints selections from the *English Note-Books* combined in one volume with selections from Hawthorne's other journals. Issued in two formats: trade printing in black-green T cloth; also 250 uncut copies in red V cloth with paper label on spine. Deposited 24 April 1929.

A 27.8
The English Notebooks. Edited by Randall Stewart. New York: Modern Language Association of America, 1941.

A reediting of Hawthorne's surviving manuscript journals in which Stewart attempted to restore as much of Hawthorne's original text as possible. Reprinted, New York: Russell & Russell, 1962.

besides much sculpture ; and especially a group above and around the high altar, representing the Magdalen, smiling down upon angels and archangels, some of whom are kneeling, and shadowing themselves with their heavy marble wings. There is no such thing as making my page glow with the most distant idea of the magnificence of this church, in its details and in its whole. It was founded a hundred or two hundred years ago ; then Bonaparte contemplated transforming it into a Temple of Victory, or building it anew as one. The restored Bourbon remade it into a church ; but it still has a heathenish look, and will never lose it.

When we entered we saw a crowd of people, all pressing forward towards the high altar, before which burned a hundred wax lights, some of which were six or seven feet high ; and, altogether, they shone like a galaxy of stars. In the middle of the nave, moreover, there was another galaxy of wax candles burning around an immense pall of black velvet, embroidered with silver, which seemed to cover, not only a coffin, but a sarcophagus, or something still more huge. The organ was rumbling forth a deep, lugubrious bass, accompanied with heavy chanting of priests, out of which sometimes rose the clear, young voices of choristers, like light flashing out of

PASSAGES FROM THE

FRENCH AND ITALIAN NOTE-BOOKS

OF NATHANIEL HAWTHORNE

VOL. I.

STRAHAN & CO., PUBLISHERS
56 LUDGATE HILL, LONDON
1871

A28.1: Title page, 7¹³/₁₆″ × 5¹/₈″. Page format, 5⁵/₁₆″ (5⁵/₈″) × 3¹/₂″

A 28 PASSAGES FROM THE FRENCH AND ITALIAN NOTE-BOOKS

A 28.1
First English edition [1871]

2 vols.

I: [i–iv] [1] 2–371 [372]

II: [i–iv] [1] 2–368

I: [A]² B–I⁸ K–U⁸ X–Z⁸ AA⁸ BB²

II: [A]² B–I⁸ K–U⁸ X–Z⁸ AA⁸

Contents: I: p. i: half title; p. ii: blank; p. iii: title; p. iv: printer's notice; pp. 1–371: text, headed 'PASSAGES FROM HAWTHORNE'S | NOTE-BOOKS IN FRANCE AND ITALY. | [rule] | FRANCE.'; p. 372: blank.

    II: p. i: half title; p. ii: blank; p. iii: title; p. iv: printer's notice; pp. 1–368: text, headed 'PASSAGES FROM HAWTHORNE'S | NOTE-BOOKS IN FRANCE AND ITALY. | [rule] | FLORENCE—*continued.*'

Note: Sections of the *French and Italian Note-Books* first appeared in eleven numbers of *Good Words,* XII (January–December 1871). See D 102.

Typography and paper: See illustration, A 28.1 page format. Running heads: rectos, section titles with year added; versos, *'FRANCE.'* and, later, *'ITALY.'* with year added. White wove paper.

Binding: Purplish blue (197. deep p B) pebble-grained P cloth in various formats, priority undetermined: (A) primary binding, with horizontal rows of black, gilt-imprinted, and blindstamped rules carrying across spine and continuing in blindstamped form only on back cover; spine black and goldstamped with publisher's device (see illustration, A 28 bindings [at A 27]) (Locations: CEFC, PSt); (B) same style as binding A, but without publisher's anchor device on spine (Locations: CEFC, LC); (C) same style as binding A, but with covers blindstamped, with publisher's anchor device on spine (Location: MB); (D) same style as binding A, but with covers blindstamped, without publisher's device on spine (Location: CtY); (E) same style as binding A, but with imprint on spine of 'Daldy, Isbister & Co.', a firm not established until 1874, probably a remainder binding (Location: MWA). White wove endpapers brown coated one side. Also white wove endpapers green coated one side. 4 pp. of Strahan & Co. ads inserted at rear of vol. I in some copies, at rear of vol. II in some copies, or omitted entirely. All edges untrimmed in most copies.

Publication: Unknown number of copies. Advertised as "nearly ready" in *Athenaeum,* 28 October 1871. Listed in *Publishers' Circular,* 1 November 1871; *Athenaeum,* 4 November 1871; *Bookseller,* (London), 4 November 1871. Advertised as "new" in *Athenaeum,* 11 November 1871.

Printing: Printed by Virtue and Co., City Road, London.

Locations: BM, 10105.bb.20 (deposit-stamp 17 NO 71) (rebound); see also binding listing.

Manuscript: The major portions of surviving *French and Italian Note-Book* manuscripts, in various hands, located in the Pierpont Morgan Library.

but the weather and walking were too unfavorable for a distant expedition; so we merely went across the street to the Louvre. . . . .

Our principal object this morning was to see the pencil drawings by eminent artists. Of these the Louvre has a very rich collection, occupying many apartments, and comprising many sketches by Annibal Caracci, Claude, Raphael, Leonardo da Vinci, Michel Angelo, Rubens, Rembrandt, and almost all the other great masters, whether French, Italian, Dutch, or whatever else; the earliest drawings of their great pictures, when they had the glory of their pristine idea directly before their minds' eye, — that idea which inevitably became overlaid with their own handling of it in the finished painting. No doubt the painters themselves had often a happiness in these rude, off-hand sketches, which they never felt again in the same work, and which resulted in disappointment, after they had done their best. To an artist, the collection must be most deeply interesting: to myself, it was merely curious, and soon grew wearisome.

In the same suite of apartments, there is a collection of miniatures, some of them very exquisite, and absolutely lifelike, on their small scale. I observed two of Franklin, both good and picturesque, one of them especially so, with its cloud-like white hair. I do not think we have produced a man so interesting to contemplate, in many points of view, as he. Most of our great men are of a character that I find it impossible to warm into life by thought, or by lavishing any amount of sympathy upon them. Not so

---

PASSAGES

FROM THE

FRENCH AND ITALIAN
NOTE-BOOKS

OF

NATHANIEL HAWTHORNE.

VOL. I.

BOSTON:
JAMES R. OSGOOD AND COMPANY,
Late Ticknor & Fields, and Fields, Osgood, & Co.
1872.

A28.2.a: Title page, 7" × 4⁷/₁₆". Page format, 5³/₁₆" (5⁷/₁₆") × 3"

A 28.2.a
First American edition, first printing [1872]

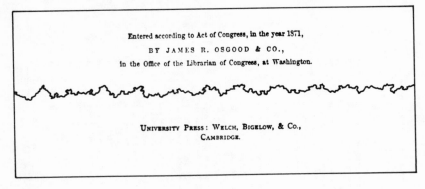

Entered according to Act of Congress, in the year 1871,

BY JAMES R. OSGOOD & CO.,

in the Office of the Librarian of Congress, at Washington.

UNIVERSITY PRESS: WELCH, BIGELOW, & Co.,
CAMBRIDGE.

2 vols.

I: [i–iv] [1] 2–307 [308]

II: [i–iv] [1] 2–306 [307–308]

I: π^2 1–12^{12} 13^{10}; also signed π^2 A–S^8 T^2

II: π^2 1–12^{12} 13^{10}; also signed π^2 A–S^8 T^2

Contents: I: pp. i–ii: blank; p. iii: title; p. iv: copyright; pp. 1–307: text, headed
'PASSAGES | FROM | HAWTHORNE'S NOTE-BOOKS IN FRANCE | AND ITALY. |
[rule] | FRANCE.'; p. 308: blank.
   II: pp. i–ii: blank; p. iii: title; p. iv: copyright; pp. 1–306: text, headed 'PASSAGES |
FROM | HAWTHORNE'S NOTE-BOOKS IN FRANCE | AND ITALY. | [rule] |
FLORENCE—*continued.*'; pp. 307–308: blank.

Typography and paper: See illustration, A 28.2.a page format. Running heads: rectos, 'FRANCE.' with year added and, later, 'ITALY.' with year added; versos, 'FRENCH
AND ITALIAN NOTE-BOOKS.' with year added. White laid paper.

Binding: Three variant bindings noted: (A) In the style of Ticknor format D (see
illustration, B 1 binding), uniform with binding of *"Tinted Edition."* Green (146. d. G)
pebble-grain P cloth with blindstamped rules and corner elements on covers. Spine
goldstamped (see illustration, A 28 bindings [at A 27]). Covers not beveled. (Locations: CEFC, MH, NN.) (B) Same as binding A with minor variations in leafy spine
ornamentation and omission of rule above 'VOL. I. [II.]'. (Locations: CEFC, NN.) (C) In
the style of Ticknor format C (see illustration, B 1 binding), uniform with binding of
"Tinted Edition." Green (146. d. G) pebble-grain P cloth with blindstamped classical
male figure, rules, and corner elements on covers. Spine goldstamped with 'VOL. 19
[20]' immediately below 'WORKS'. Both covers beveled. (Locations: MH, Turner.)
Binding C copies were intended for distribution as part of the *"Tinted Edition"* (see
B 1). White wove endpapers, brown coated one side. Flyleaves, noted in laid and
wove paper, inserted at front and rear. All edges trimmed.

Publication: 1,500 copies of each of two volumes, a number of which were bound for
marketing as part of the *"Tinted Edition"* (see binding C above). Printed 29 February
1872. Announced in the 15 February 1872 *Publishers' and Stationers' Weekly Trade
Circular* as for 24 February. Listed in *WTC,* 7 March 1872. Copy at MH presented by
publisher 27 February 1872. Price $4.00 per set, with Mrs. Hawthorne receiving a
royalty of 40¢ per set.

Printing: Electrotyped and printed by Welch, Bigelow, & Co., Cambridge, Mass.

Locations: See "Binding."

Note: The copy at MH presented by the publisher has the following errors marked for correction:

> *Volume I*
> 106.24 'ower' to be corrected to "over"
> 151.29 'Laddebach' to be corrected to "Saddlebach"
> 169.22 'crowded' to be corrected to "corroded"
> 171.22 'Vinioli' to be corrected to "Vincoli"
> 177.9 'Hillyards's' to be corrected to "Hillard's"
>
> *Volume II*
> 18.10 "Bololi" to be corrected to "Boboli"

The corrections were made in the *Riverside Edition.*

LATER PRINTINGS WITHIN THE FIRST EDITION

A 28.2.b
Boston: James R. Osgood, 1873.

Combined in two-volumes-in-one format and published as the eighth volume of the *Illustrated Library Edition.* 1,500 copies printed 17 March 1873. Price $2.00, royalty 20¢. See B 2 for reprintings of the *ILE.*

A 28.2.c
Boston: James R. Osgood, 1874.

130 copies of each of two volumes printed 4 September 1874. Price $4.00 per set, royalty 40¢ per set.

A 28.2.d
Boston: Houghton, Mifflin, 1880.

Combined with *The Marble Faun* in four-volumes-in-one format and published as the fifth volume of the *Globe Edition.* 1,500 copies printed July 1880. See B 3 for reprintings of the *Globe Edition.*

A 28.2.e
Boston: Houghton, Mifflin, [1886].

Combined with *The Marble Faun* in four-volumes-in-one format and published as the fifth volume of the *"New" Fireside Edition.* 1,000 copies printed May 1886. See B 4.

PRINTINGS FROM THE "LITTLE CLASSIC" EDITION PLATES

A 28.3.a

[All following within red and black double-rules frame] PASSAGES | FROM | [red] The French and Italian | Note-Books | [black] OF | NATHANIEL HAWTHORNE. | VOL. I. [VOL. II.] | [I: vignette of castle and roadway] [II: vignette of church among rooftops] | [red] BOSTON: | [black] JAMES R. OSGOOD AND COMPANY, | Late Ticknor & Fields, and Fields, Osgood, & Co. | [red] 1876.

Vols. [XIX] and [XX], *"Little Classic Edition."* Contents same as in JRO edition (A 28.2.a). Sheets bound with James R. Osgood and, later, Houghton, Osgood spine imprints. 2,000 copies of each of two volumes printed 29 February 1876. Price $1.25 per volume, royalty 12.5¢ per volume. See B 5[XIX,XX] for reprintings of the *"Little Classic Edition."*

A 28.3.b
Boston: Houghton, Osgood, 1879.

Vols. I and II combined in two-volumes-in-one format and published as vol. VIII of the *"Fireside Edition."* 500 copies printed 20 September 1879. See B 6[VIII] for reprintings of the *"Fireside Edition."*

A 28.3.c
Boston: Houghton, Mifflin, [1891].

Vols. I and II combined with *Sketches and Studies* in three-volumes-in-one format and published as vol. VIII of the *Popular Edition.* 1,000 copies printed June–August 1891. See B 7 for reprintings of the *Popular Edition.*

A 28.3.d
Boston: Houghton, Mifflin, [1899].

Vols. [XIX] and [XX], *Concord Edition.* See B 8.

PRINTINGS FROM THE RIVERSIDE EDITION PLATES

A 28.4.a₁
Riverside Edition (trade), first printing, American issue [1883]

PASSAGES FROM THE FRENCH AND | ITALIAN NOTE-BOOKS | OF | NATHANIEL HAWTHORNE | [vignette of church tower and dome] | BOSTON | HOUGHTON, MIFFLIN AND COMPANY | New York: 11 East Seventeenth Street | The Riverside Press, Cambridge | 1883

Vols. I and II combined in two-volumes-in-one format and published as vol. X of the Riverside trade printing. Contents same as in *"Little Classic Edition"* (A 28.3.a), with "Introductory Note" by George Parsons Lathrop added. 2,000 copies printed May 1883. Price $2.00. See B 9 for reprintings of the Riverside trade printing.

A 28.4.a₂
Riverside Edition (trade), first printing, English issue [1883]

London: Kegan Paul, Trench, 1883.

Sheets of vol. X, first printing (A 28.4.a₁), with cancel title, in a Kegan Paul binding. 250 Kegan Paul title pages printed by Houghton, Mifflin, June–July 1883. Later issues noted with dated and undated Kegan Paul, Trench, Trübner title pages. See B 11.

A 28.4.b
Riverside Edition (large paper), second printing [1883]

PASSAGES | FROM THE | [red] FRENCH AND ITALIAN NOTE-BOOKS | [black] OF | NATHANIEL HAWTHORNE | [sepia vignette of church tower and dome] | [red] CAM-BRIDGE | [black] Printed at the Riverside Press | 1883

Vols. I and II combined in two-volumes-in-one format and published as vol. X of the Riverside large-paper printing. 250 copies printed June 1883. See B 10.

A 28.4.c
Boston and New York: Houghton, Mifflin, 1884.

Vols. XIX and XX of the *Wayside Edition*. 500 copies printed September–October 1884. See B 12.

A 28.4.d
Boston and New York: Houghton, Mifflin, [1891].

Vols. I and II combined in two-volumes-in-one format and published as vol. X of the *Standard Library Edition*. 500 copies printed October 1891. See B 13.

A 28.4.e
Boston and New York: Houghton, Mifflin, [1902].

Vols. I and II combined in two-volumes-in-one format and published as vol. X of the *"New" Wayside Edition*. 500 copies printed September–October 1902. See B 14.

A 28.4.f
Boston and New York: [Houghton, Mifflin], MDCCCCIX.

Vols. I and II combined in two-volumes-in-one format and published as vol. X of the *Fireside Edition*. See B 15.

A 28.4.g
Boston, New York: Jefferson Press, [1913].

Vols. I and II combined with *Tales and Sketches* in three-volumes-in-one format and published as vol. [X] of the *"Jefferson Press Edition."* See B 16.

PRINTINGS FROM THE AUTOGRAPH EDITION PLATES

A 28.5.a
Boston and New York: Houghton, Mifflin, MDCCCC.

Vols. XXI and XXII of the *Autograph Edition*, with beginning of *French and Italian Note-Books* and conclusion of *English Note-Books* combined in vol. XXI, all published under title 'NOTES OF TRAVEL'. Contents same as in the *Riverside Edition* (A 28.4.a₁) with some of the initials used by Mrs. Hawthorne extended to a full name. 500 copies. Deposited 5 March 1901. See B 20.

A 28.5.b
Boston and New York: Houghton, Mifflin, MDCCCC.

Vols. XXI and XXII of the *Large-Paper (Autograph) Edition*, with beginning of *French and Italian Note-Books* and conclusion of *English Note-Books* combined in vol. XXI, all published under title 'NOTES OF TRAVEL'. 500 copies. See B 21.

A 28.5.c
Boston and New York: Houghton, Mifflin, 1903.

Vols. XXI and XXII of the *Old Manse Edition*, with beginning of *French and Italian Note-Books* and conclusion of *English Note-Books* combined in vol. XXI, all published under title 'NOTES OF TRAVEL'. See B 22.

OTHER EDITIONS

A 28.6
The Heart of Hawthorne's Journals. Edited by Newton Arvin. Boston and New York: Houghton, Mifflin, 1929.

Prints selections from the *French and Italian Note-Books* combined in one volume with selections from Hawthorne's other journals. Issued in two formats: trade printing in black-green T cloth; also 250 uncut copies in red V cloth with paper label on spine. Deposited 24 April 1929.

Bindings for (1) A 29.2.a; (2) A 29.1.b; (3) A 30.1.a; (4) A 31.1.a; (5) A 31.2; (6 & 7) A 34.1.a; (8 & 9) A 35.1.a; (10) A 36.1

SEPTIMIUS

A ROMANCE.

BY

NATHANIEL HAWTHORNE,

AUTHOR OF

'THE SCARLET LETTER' ETC. ETC.

LONDON:

HENRY S. KING & Co., 65 CORNHILL.

1872.

---

had stopped for some moments on the threshold, vaguely enjoying, it is probable, the light and warmth of the new spring day and the sweet air, which was somewhat unwonted to the young man, because he was accustomed to spend much of his day in thought and study within doors, and, indeed, like most studious young men, was over fond of the fireside, and of making life as artificial as he could, by fireside heat and lamplight, in order to suit it to the artificial intellectual and moral atmosphere which he derived from books, instead of living healthfully in the open air, and among his fellow-beings. Still he felt the pleasure of being warmed through by this natural heat, and though blinking a little from its superfluity, could not but confess an enjoyment and cheerfulness in this flood of morning light that came aslant the hill-side. While he thus stood, he felt a friendly hand laid upon his shoulder, and looking up, there was the minister of the village, the old friend of Septimius, to whose advice and aid it was owing that Septimius had followed his instincts by going to college, instead of spending a thwarted and dissatisfied life in the field that fronted the house. He was a man of middle age, or

A 29 SEPTIMIUS FELTON

A 29.1.a₁
First English edition, first printing, first issue [1872]

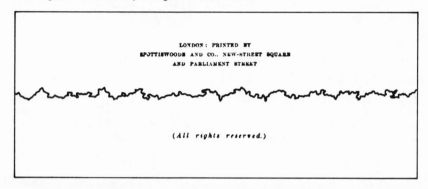

Two issues noted: (1) leaves [A]₁,₂ conjugate; preface on p. iii undated; (2) leaf [A]₂ a cancel; preface on p. iii dated 'Notting Hill, London: | *May 28, 1872'*.

[i–iv] [1] 2–298 [299–300]

[A]² B–I⁸ K–T⁸ U⁶

Contents: p. i: title; p. ii: printer's notice and rights statement; p. iii: preface; p. iv: blank; pp. 1–298: text, headed 'SEPTIMIUS. | *A ROMANCE OF IMMORTALITY.* | [rule]'; pp. 299–300: blank.

Note: Contents first appeared in serialized form in eight installments of the *Atlantic Monthly,* XXIX (January–August 1872), and in England in six installments of *St. Paul's Magazine* (London), X (January–June 1872). See D 103.

Typography and paper: See illustration, A 29.1.a page format. Running heads: rectos and versos, *'SEPTIMIUS.'* White wove paper.

Binding: Red (16. d. Red) pebble-grain P cloth. Title and author's name gilt-imprinted on front cover inside blindstamped and black-imprinted ruled panels separated horizontally by combined geometric and floral design. Same panels, without title and author's name, on back cover. Design carried across spine with title, author's name, and publisher's imprint goldstamped. White wove endpapers deep green coated one side. Verso of free front endpaper carries ad for "The Life and the Unpublished Stories of the Late Nathaniel Hawthorne," by H. A. Page. 24-page King catalogue inserted at rear. Top edges gilded; other edges untrimmed. Covers beveled.

Publication: Unknown number of copies. Noted as "in a few days" in *Publishers' Circular,* 16 May 1872. Listed as "next week" in *Athenaeum,* 18 and 25 May 1872. Listed as "this day" in *Athenaeum,* 1 June 1872.

Printing: Printed by Spottiswoode and Co., New-Street Square and Parliament Street, London.

Locations: Issues 1 and 2: MH; issue 2: BM, 12704.g.18 (deposit-stamp 5 JY 72), NN.

Manuscript: Various drafts and fragments located at Berg, CSmH, NNPM.

A 29.1.a2
First English edition, first printing, second issue [1872]

[A]² (±A2) B–I⁸ K–T⁸ U⁶, (leaf [A]2 (pp. iii & iv) a cancel)

Same as first issue (A 29.1.a1) except for canceled preface leaf, which bears two-line date at its foot (see illustration). Second-issue form of preface retained in second printing (A 29.1.b).

A 29.1.b
First English edition, second printing [1872]

London: Henry S. King, 1872.

Has new title inserted, with *'SECOND EDITION'* slug on title page and goldstamped on spine (see illustration, A 29 bindings). Preface dated 'Notting Hill, London: *May* 28, 1872'. Verso of free front endpaper carries ad for "A Memoir of Nathaniel Hawthorne, with Stories Now First Published in the Country," by H. A. Page.

PREFACE.

THE following Story is the last written by my Father. It is printed as it was found among his manuscripts.

I believe it is a striking specimen of the peculiarities and charm of his style, and that it will have an added interest for brother artists, and for those who care to study the method of his composition, from the mere fact of its not having received his final revision.

In any case, I feel sure that the retention of the passages within brackets (e.g. p. 37), which show how my Father intended to amplify some of the descriptions, and develope more fully one or two of the character studies, will not be regretted by appreciative readers.

My earnest thanks are due to Mr. ROBERT BROWNING for his kind assistance, and advice in interpreting the manuscript, otherwise so difficult to me.

UNA HAWTHORNE.

NOTTING HILL, LONDON :
May 28, 1872.

A 29.1.a2: Preface (p. iii), with dated 'Notting Hill' subscription added. A 29.1.a1 is identical except it lacks subscription.

SEPTIMIUS FELTON;

OR

THE ELIXIR OF LIFE.

BY

NATHANIEL HAWTHORNE

BOSTON:
JAMES R. OSGOOD AND COMPANY.
1872.

He tried to say to himself that he had nothing to do with this excitement; that his studious life kept him away from it; that his intended profession was that of peace; but say what he might to himself, there was a tremor, a bubbling impulse, a tingling in his ears, — the page that he opened glimmered and dazzled before him.

"Septimius! Septimius!" cried Aunt Keziah, looking into the room, "in Heaven's name, are you going to sit here to-day, and the redcoats coming to burn the house over our heads? Must I sweep you out with the broomstick? For shame, boy! for shame!"

"Are they coming, then, Aunt Keziah?" asked her nephew. "Well, I am not a fighting-man."

"Certain they are. They have sacked Lexington, and slain the people, and burnt the meeting-house. That concerns even the parsons; and you reckon yourself among them. Go out, go out, I say, and learn the news!"

Whether moved by these exhortations, or by his own stifled curiosity, Septimius did at length issue from his door, though with that reluctance which hampers and impedes men whose current of thought and interest runs apart from that of the world in general; but forth he came, feeling strangely, and yet with a strong impulse to fling himself headlong into the emotion of the moment. It was a beautiful morning, spring-like and summer-like at once. If there had been nothing else to do or think of, such a morning was enough for life only to breathe its air and be conscious of its inspiring influence.

A 29.2.a
First American edition, first printing [*1872*]

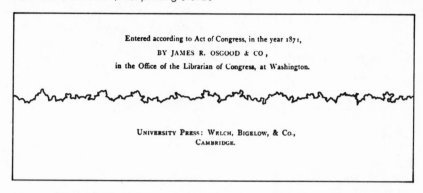

Presumably two printings with 1872 title-page dates. Presumed first printing has 't' at 42.18, which was corrected to 'lt' in presumed second printing. On the Hinman Collator, superimposition of the 1872 second printing 'lt' vs. the third printing *Illustrated Library Edition* 'lt' is exact. This suggests the plate for p. 42 with the 't' reading was corrected in both the second and third printings.

[i–vi] [1–3] 4–229 [230–234]

[1]² [2–10]¹² [11]⁸ [12]²; signed π^3 [1]¹² 2–9¹² 10⁷ [11]²; also signed π^3 [A]⁸ B–N⁸ O³ [P]²

Contents: pp. i–ii: blank; p. iii: half title; p. iv: blank; p. v: title; p. vi: copyright; p. 1: preface; p. 2: blank; pp. 3–229: text, headed 'SEPTIMIUS FELTON; | OR, | THE ELIXER OF LIFE. | [rule]'; p. 230: blank; p. 231: ads; pp. 232–234: blank.

Typography and paper: See illustration, A 29.2.a page format. Running heads: rectos and versos, 'SEPTIMIUS FELTON.' White wove paper.

Binding: Terra-cotta (43. m. r. Br) sand-grained C cloth. Green (137. d. y G) sand-grained C cloth. Blue (196. s. p B) bold-ribbed T cloth (moiréd). Also noted in green and terra-cotta smooth V cloth. Covers with blindstamped double-ruled central square with corner elements; also blindstamped horizontal decorative bands at top and bottom of covers extending around spine. Also noted with designs on front cover and spine stamped in black and title and author's name goldstamped inside central square on front cover. Spine goldstamped (see illustration, A 29 bindings). White wove endpapers brown coated one side. Flyleaves inserted at front and rear. All edges trimmed.

Note: After 1880, when Houghton, Mifflin assumed the publishing firm on the departure of James R. Osgood, unsold sheets of both the first and second printings of the Osgood edition were presumably remaindered in a Houghton, Mifflin binding. Binding noted in two forms:
A. With Houghton, Mifflin imprint on spine. Location: NN.
B. Without H,M imprint on spine. Location: CEFC, OU.

Publication: 3,000 copies printed 24 June 1872. MH copy received from the publisher 23 July 1872. Listed in *Publishers' Circular*, 25 July 1872. Price $1.50, royalty 15¢.

Printing: Electrotyped and printed at the University Press, Cambridge, Mass., by Welch, Bigelow, & Co.

Locations: Berg, CEFC, Lilly, MH, OU.

A 29.2.b
Presumed second printing

Boston: James R. Osgood, 1872.

Has corrected reading 'It' at 42.18. See A 29.2.a.

LATER PRINTINGS WITHIN THE FIRST AMERICAN EDITION

A 29.2.c
Boston: James R. Osgood, 1873.

Vol. 21 of the untitled *"Tinted Edition."* 150 copies printed August 1873. Price $2.00, royalty 20¢. See B 1[21] for reprintings of the *"Tinted Edition."*

A 29.2.d
Boston: James R. Osgood, 1873.

Combined with *Our Old Home* in two-volumes-in-one format and published as the ninth volume of the *Illustrated Library Edition*. 1,500 copies printed 7 August 1873. Price $2.00, royalty 20¢. See B 2 for reprintings of the *ILE*.

A 29.2.e
Boston: Houghton, Mifflin, 1880.

Combined with *Our Old Home, Fanshawe,* and *The Dolliver Romance* in four-volumes-in-one format and published as the third volume of the *Globe Edition*. 1,500 copies printed August 1880. See B 3 for reprintings of the *Globe Edition*.

A 29.2.f
Boston: Houghton, Mifflin, [1886].

Combined with *Our Old Home, Fanshawe,* and *The Dolliver Romance* in four-volumes-in-one format and published as the third volume of the *"New" Fireside Edition*. 1,000 copies printed May 1886. See B 4.

LATER EDITION

A 29.3
Berlin: A. Asher, 1872.

Vol. 30, *Asher's Collection of English Authors British and American. Copyright Edition.*

PRINTINGS FROM THE ''LITTLE CLASSIC EDITION'' PLATES

A 29.4.a

[All following within red and black double-rules frame] [red] Septimius Felton; | [black] OR, | THE ELIXIR OF LIFE. | BY | [red] NATHANIEL HAWTHORNE. | [black vignette of house] | [red] BOSTON: | [black] JAMES R. OSGOOD AND COMPANY, | Late Ticknor & Fields, and Fields, Osgood, & Co. | [red] 1876.

Vol. [XXI], *"Little Classic Edition."* Contents same as in first American edition (A 29.2.a). Sheets bound with James R. Osgood and, later, Houghton, Osgood spine imprints. 2,000 copies printed 18 March 1876. Price $1.25, royalty 12.5¢. See B 5[XXI] for reprintings of the *"Little Classic Edition."*

A 29.4.b
Boston: Houghton, Osgood, 1879.

Combined with *Our Old Home* in two-volumes-in-one format and published as vol. IX of the *"Fireside Edition."* 500 copies printed 20 September 1879. See B 6 for reprintings of the *"Fireside Edition."*

A 29.4.c
Boston: Houghton, Mifflin, [1891].

Combined with *The Snow-Image, Fanshawe,* and *The Dolliver Romance* in four-volumes-in-one format and published as vol. IV of the *Popular Edition.* 1,000 copies printed June–August 1891. See B 7 for reprintings of the *Popular Edition.*

A 29.4.d
Boston: Houghton, Mifflin, [1899].

Vol. [XXI], *Concord Edition.* See B 8.

PRINTINGS FROM THE RIVERSIDE EDITION PLATES

A 29.5.a₁
Riverside Edition (trade), first printing, American issue [1883]

THE DOLLIVER ROMANCE | FANSHAWE, AND SEPTIMIUS FELTON | WITH AN APPENDIX CONTAINING | THE ANCESTRAL FOOTSTEP | BY | NATHANIEL HAWTHORNE | [vignette of seated girl] | BOSTON | HOUGHTON, MIFFLIN AND COMPANY | New York: 11 East Seventeenth Street | The Riverside Press, Cambridge | 1883

Four volumes in one published as vol. XI of the Riverside trade printing. Contents same as in *"Little Classic Edition"* (A 29.4.a), with "Introductory Note" by George Parsons Lathrop added. 3,000 copies printed June 1883. Price $2.00. See B 9 for reprintings of the Riverside trade printing.

A 29.5.a₂
Riverside Edition (trade), first printing, English issue [1883]

London: Kegan Paul, Trench, 1883.

Sheets of vol. XI, first printing (A 29.5.a₁), with cancel title, in a Kegan Paul binding. 250 Kegan Paul title pages printed by Houghton, Mifflin, June–July 1883. Later issues noted with dated and undated Kegan Paul, Trench, Trübner title pages. See B 11.

A 29.5.b
Riverside Edition (large paper), second printing [1883]

[red] THE DOLLIVER ROMANCE | [black] FANSHAWE, AND SEPTIMIUS FELTON |

WITH AN APPENDIX CONTAINING | THE ANCESTRAL FOOTSTEP | BY | NATHANIEL HAWTHORNE | [vignette of seated girl] | [red] CAMBRIDGE | [black] Printed at the Riverside Press | 1883

Four volumes in one published as vol. XI of the Riverside large-paper printing. 250 copies printed May 1883. See B 10.

A 29.5.c
Boston and New York: Houghton, Mifflin, 1884.

Combined with *The Ancestral Footstep* in two-volumes-in-one format and published as vol. XXII of the *Wayside Edition*. 500 copies printed September–October 1884. See B 12.

A 29.5.d
Boston and New York: Houghton, Mifflin, [1891].

Combined with *The Dolliver Romance, Fanshawe,* and *The Ancestral Footstep* in four-volumes-in-one format and published as vol. XI of the *Standard Library Edition*. 500 copies printed October 1891. See B 13.

A 29.5.e
Boston and New York: Houghton, Mifflin, [1902].

Combined with *The Dolliver Romance, Fanshawe,* and *The Ancestral Footstep* in four-volumes-in-one format and published as vol. XI of the *"New" Wayside Edition*. 500 copies printed September–October 1902. See B 14.

A 29.5.f
Boston and New York: [Houghton, Mifflin], MDCCCCIX.

Combined with *The Dolliver Romance, Fanshawe,* and *The Ancestral Footstep* in four-volumes-in-one format and published as vol. XI of the *Fireside Edition*. See B 15.

A 29.5.g
Boston, New York: Jefferson Press, [1913].

Combined with the *American Note-Books, The Dolliver Romance,* and *Fanshawe* in four-volumes-in-one format and published as vol. [IX] of the *"Jefferson Press Edition."* See B 16.

PRINTINGS FROM THE AUTOGRAPH EDITION PLATES

A 29.6.a
Boston and New York: Houghton, Mifflin, MDCCCC.

Combined with *The Dolliver Romance* and *The Ancestral Footstep* in three-volumes-in-one format and published as vol. XIV of the *Autograph Edition*. Contents same as in *Riverside Edition* (A 29.5.a). 500 copies. Deposited 20 December 1900. See B 20.

A 29.6.b
Boston and New York: Houghton, Mifflin, MDCCCC.

Combined with *The Dolliver Romance* and *The Ancestral Footstep* in three-volumes-in-one format and published as vol. XIV of the *Large-Paper (Autograph) Edition*. 500 copies. See B 21.

A 29.6.c
Boston and New York: Houghton, Mifflin, 1903.

Combined with *The Dolliver Romance* and *The Ancestral Footstep* in three-volumes-in-one format and published as vol. XIV of the *Old Manse Edition.* See B 22.

THE

DOLLIVER ROMANCE

AND

OTHER PIECES.

BY

NATHANIEL HAWTHORNE.

BOSTON:
JAMES R. OSGOOD AND COMPANY.
1876.

had he ever been even a practitioner of the awful science with which his popular designation connected him. Our old friend, in short, even at his highest social elevation, claimed to be nothing more than an apothecary, and, in these later and far less prosperous days, scarcely so much. Since the death of his last surviving grandson, (Pansie's father, whom he had instructed in all the mysteries of his science, and who, being distinguished by an experimental and inventive tendency, was generally believed to have poisoned himself with an infallible panacea of his own distillation,) — since that final bereavement, Dr. Dolliver's once pretty flourishing business had lamentably declined. After a few months of unavailing struggle, he found it expedient to take down the Brazen Serpent from the position to which Dr. Swinnerton had originally elevated it, in front of his shop in the main street, and to retire to his private dwelling, situated in a by-lane and on the edge of a burial-ground.

This house, as well as the Brazen Serpent, some old medical books, and a drawer full of manuscripts, had come to him by the legacy of Dr. Swinnerton. The dreariness of the locality had been of small importance to our friend in his young manhood, when he first led his fair wife over the threshold, and so long as neither of them had any kinship with the human dust that rose into little hillocks, and still kept accumulating beneath their window. But, too soon afterwards, when poor Bessie herself had gone early to rest there, it is

A 30 THE DOLLIVER ROMANCE

A 30.1.a
First edition, first printing [1876]

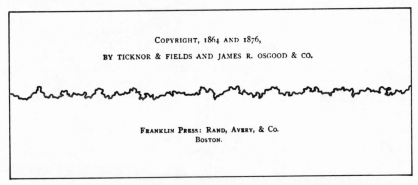

[1–8] 9–69 [70–72] 73–213 [214–216]

[1–9]¹²; signed: [1]⁶ 2⁶ [3–7⁶ 8–18⁶; also signature mark '17' on p. 191.

Contents: p. 1: blank; p. 2: ads; p. 3: title; p. 4: copyright; p. 5: contents; p. 6: blank; p. 7: 'THE DOLLIVER ROMANCE.'; p. 8: blank; pp. 9–69: text, headed 'A SCENE FROM THE DOLLIVER ROMANCE. | [rule]'; p. 70: blank; p. 71: 'TALES AND SKETCHES'; p. 72: blank; pp. 73–213: text, headed 'SKETCHES FROM MEMORY.¹ | [rule] | I. | THE INLAND PORT.'; pp. 214–216: blank.

Includes "A Scene from the Dolliver Romance,"† "Another Scene from the Dolliver Romance,"† "Another Fragment of the Dolliver Romance,"# "Sketches from Memory. I. The Inland Port,"† "II. Rochester,"† "III. A Night Scene,"† "Fragments from the Journal of a Solitary Man. I,"† "II. My Home Return,"† "My Visit to Niagara,"† "The Antique Ring,"† "Graves and Goblins,"† "Dr. Bullivant,"† " A Book of Autographs,"† "An Old Woman's Tale,"† "Time's Portraiture.—Address,"† " 'Browne's Folly'."† Daggers (†) indicate first collected appearance. The number sign (#) indicates first appearance in print. The two scenes from *The Dolliver Romance* were first printed in *Atlantic Monthly*, XIV, XV (July 1864; January 1865), 101–109, 569 (see D 95, 96).

Typography and paper: See illustration, A 30.1.a page format. Running heads: rectos, chapter titles; versos, section titles. White wove paper.

Binding: In the style of Ticknor format D (see illustration, B 1 binding), uniform with binding of *"Tinted Edition."* Green (146. d. G) pebble-grain P cloth with blindstamped rules, corner elements, and classical male figure on covers. Spine goldstamped (see illustration, A 30 bindings [at A 29]). Also probably found with 'VOL. 23' imprint immediately below 'WORKS'. Noted with covers beveled. White wove endpapers, brown coated one side. Flyleaves inserted at front and rear. All edges trimmed.

Publication: 1,000 copies printed 29 May 1876. Noted for 24 June in *Publishers' Weekly*, 17 June 1876. Noted for "this week" in *Publishers' Weekly*, 12 June 1876; also listed in same issue. Price $1.50, royalty 15¢.

Printing: Printed at the Franklin Press, Boston, by Rand, Avery, & Co.

Locations: CEFC, MH, NN, PSt.

Manuscript: Various drafts and fragments located at Berg, CSmH, MCo, NNPM and in a private collection.

LATER PRINTINGS WITHIN THE FIRST EDITION

A 30.1.b
Boston: James R. Osgood, 1876.

Combined with *Fanshawe* in two-volumes-in-one format and published as the twelfth volume of the *Illustrated Library Edition*. 1,000 copies printed 12 September 1876. Price $2.00, royalty 20¢. See B 2 for reprintings of the *Illustrated Library Edition*.

A 30.1.c
Boston: Houghton, Mifflin, 1880.

Combined with *Our Old Home, Septimius Felton,* and *Fanshawe* in four-volumes-in-one format and published as the third volume of the *Globe Edition*. 1,500 copies printed August 1880. See B 3 for reprintings of the *Globe Edition*.

A 30.1.d
Boston: Houghton, Mifflin, [1886].

Combined with *Our Old Home, Septimius Felton,* and *Fanshawe* in four-volumes-in-one format and published as the third volume of the *"New" Fireside Edition*. 1,000 copies printed May 1886. See B 4.

PRINTINGS FROM THE "LITTLE CLASSIC EDITION" PLATES

A 30.2.a

[All following within red and black double-rules frame] THE | [red] Dolliver Romance, | [black] AND OTHER PIECES. | BY | NATHANIEL HAWTHORNE. | [vignette of house] | [red] BOSTON: | [black] JAMES R. OSGOOD AND COMPANY, | Late Ticknor & Fields, and Fields, Osgood, & Co. | [red] 1876.

Vol. [XXIII], *"Little Classic Edition."* Contents same as in the first edition (A 30.1.a), with addition of appendix concerning the *"Little Classic Edition."* Sheets bound with James R. Osgood and, later, Houghton, Osgood spine imprints. 1,280 copies printed 19 September 1876. Price $1.25, royalty 12.5¢. See B 5[XXIII] for reprintings of the *"Little Classic Edition."*

A 30.2.b
Boston: Houghton, Osgood, 1879.

Combined with *Fanshawe* in two-volumes-in-one format and published as vol. XII of the *"Fireside Edition."* 500 copies printed 20 September 1879. See B 6 for reprintings of the *"Fireside Edition."*

A 30.2.c
Boston: Houghton, Mifflin, [1891].

Combined with *The Snow-Image, Septimius Felton,* and *Fanshawe* in four-volumes-in-one format and published as vol. IV of the *Popular Edition*. 1,000 copies printed June–August 1891. See B 7 for reprintings of the *Popular Edition*.

A 30.2.d
Boston: Houghton, Mifflin, [1899].

Vol. [XXIII], *Concord Edition.* See B 8.

PRINTINGS FROM THE RIVERSIDE EDITION PLATES

A 30.3.a₁
Riverside Edition (trade), first printing, American issue [1883]

THE DOLLIVER ROMANCE | FANSHAWE, AND SEPTIMIUS FELTON | WITH AN AP-
PENDIX CONTAINING | THE ANCESTRAL FOOTSTEP | BY | NATHANIEL
HAWTHORNE | [vignette of seated girl] | BOSTON | HOUSTON, MIFFLIN AND COM-
PANY | New York: 11 East Seventeenth Street | The Riverside Press, Cambridge |
1883

Four volumes in one published as vol. XI of the Riverside trade printing. Contents
includes only the three scenes from *The Dolliver Romance,* with "Introductory Note"
by George Parsons Lathrop added. 3,000 copies printed June 1883. Price $2.00. See
B 9 for reprintings of the Riverside trade printing.

A 30.3.a₂
Riverside Edition (trade), first printing, English issue [1883]

London: Kegan Paul, Trench, 1883.

Sheets of vol. XI, first printing (A 30.3.a₁), with cancel title, in a Kegan Paul binding.
250 Kegan Paul title pages printed by Houghton, Mifflin, June–July 1883. Later issues
noted with dated and undated Kegan Paul, Trench, Trübner title pages. See B 11.

A 30.3.b
Riverside Edition (large paper), second printing [1883]

[red] THE DOLLIVER ROMANCE | [black] FANSHAWE, AND SEPTIMIUS FELTON |
WITH AN APPENDIX CONTAINING | THE ANCESTRAL FOOTSTEP | BY | NATHANIEL
HAWTHORNE | [vignette of seated girl] | [red] CAMBRIDGE | [black] Printed at the
Riverside Press | 1883

Four volumes in one published as vol. XI of the Riverside large-paper printing. 250
copies printed May 1883. See B 10.

A 30.3.c
Boston and New York: Houghton, Mifflin, 1884.

Combined with *Fanshawe* in two-volumes-in-one format and published as vol. XXI of
the *Wayside Edition.* 500 copies printed September–October 1884. See B 12.

A 30.3.d
Boston and New York: Houghton, Mifflin, [1891].

Combined with *Septimius Felton, Fanshawe,* and *The Ancestral Footstep* in four-
volumes-in-one format and published as vol. XI of the *Standard Library Edition.* 500
copies printed October 1891. See B 13.

A 30.3.e
Boston and New York: Houghton, Mifflin, [1902].

Combined with *Septimius Felton, Fanshawe,* and *The Ancestral Footstep* in four-volumes-in-one format and published as vol. XI of the *"New" Wayside Edition.* 500 copies printed October 1902. See B 14.

A 30.3.f
Boston and New York: [Houghton, Mifflin], MDCCCCIX.

Combined with *Septimius Felton, Fanshawe,* and *The Ancestral Footstep* in four-volumes-in-one format and published as vol. XI of the *Fireside Edition.* See B 15.

A 30.3.g
Boston, New York: Jefferson Press, [1913].

Combined with the *American Note-Books, Fanshawe,* and *Septimius Felton* in four-volumes-in-one format and published as vol. [IX] of the *"Jefferson Press Edition."* See B 16.

PRINTINGS FROM THE AUTOGRAPH EDITION PLATES

A 30.4.a
Boston and New York: Houghton, Mifflin, MDCCCC.

Combined with *Septimius Felton* and *The Ancestral Footstep* in three-volumes-in-one format and published as vol. XIV of the *Autograph Edition.* Contents same as in *Riverside Edition* (A 30.3.a). 500 copies. Deposited 20 December 1900. See B 20.

A 30.4.b
Boston and New York: Houghton, Mifflin, MDCCCC.

Combined with *Septimius Felton* and *The Ancestral Footstep* in three-volumes-in-one format and published as vol. XIV of the *Large-Paper (Autograph) Edition.* 500 copies. See B 21.

A 30.4.c
Boston and New York: Houghton, Mifflin, 1903.

Combined with *Septimius Felton* and *The Ancestral Footstep* in three-volumes-in-one format and published as vol. XIV of the *Old Manse Edition.* See B 22.

DOCTOR GRIMSHAWE'S SECRET

A Romance

BY

NATHANIEL HAWTHORNE

EDITED, WITH PREFACE AND NOTES

BY

JULIAN HAWTHORNE

BOSTON

JAMES R. OSGOOD AND COMPANY

1883

CHAPTER V.

DOCTOR GRIM[1] had the English faith in open air and daily acquaintance with the weather, whatever it might be; and it was his habit, not only to send the two children to play, for lack of a better place, in the graveyard, but to take them himself on long rambles, of which the vicinity of the town afforded a rich variety. It may be that the Doctor's excursions had the wider scope, because both he and the children were objects of curiosity in the town, and very much the subject of its gossip: so that always, in its streets and lanes, the people turned to gaze, and came to their windows and to the doors of shops to see this grim, bearded figure, lending along the beautiful children each by a hand, with a surly aspect like a bull-dog. Their remarks were possibly and intended to reach the ears of the party, but certainly were not so cautiously whispered but they occasionally did do so. The male remarks, indeed, generally died away in the throats that uttered them; a circumstance that doubt-less saved the utterer from some very rough rejoinder at the hands of the Doctor, who had grown up in the habit of a very ready and free recourse to his fists, which had a way of doubling themselves up seem-ingly of their own accord. But the shrill feminine

A 31.1.a: Title page, 7¹/₂″ × 4¹³/₁₆″. Page format, 5¹/₈″ (5⁷/₁₆″) × 3³/₁₆″

A 31 DOCTOR GRIMSHAWE'S SECRET

A 31.1.a
First American edition (trade), first printing [1883]

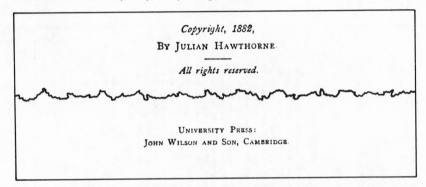

Copyright, 1882,
BY JULIAN HAWTHORNE

All rights reserved.

UNIVERSITY PRESS:
JOHN WILSON AND SON, CAMBRIDGE.

Probably published simultaneously with first English edition (A 31.2). First two print-
ings have title pages dated 1883, priority undetermined. All copies examined on the
Hinman collator have slight batter of p. 48 folio and left margin letters of first few lines.
These areas are clean in the large-paper fourth printing (A 31.1.d).

[a–b] [i–v] vi–xiii [xiv] [1] 2–368. 4-page facsimile manuscript inserted between pp.
24 and 25.

[1^8 2–16^{12} 17^4]; signed π^8 1–23^8

Contents: pp. a–b: blank; p. i: title; p. ii: copyright; p. iii: dedication to 'Mr. and Mrs.
George Parsons Lathrop'; p. iv: blank; pp. v–xiii: preface; p. xiv: blank; pp. 1–368:
text, headed 'DOCTOR GRIMSHAWE'S SECRET. | [rule] | CHAPTER I.'

Typography and paper: See illustration, A 31.1.a page format. Running heads: rectos
and versos, *'DOCTOR GRIMSHAWE'S SECRET.'* White wove paper.

Binding: Gray-green (110. gy. 0l) smooth V cloth. Title and author's name goldstamped on front cover over black imprinted scene incorporating spiders, spider
webs, books on a table, and two children. Spine goldstamped (see illustration, A 31
bindings [at A 29]). White laid endpapers. All edges trimmed. Also noted in red (16. d.
Red) remainder binding (Location: CEFC) and in light green smooth V cloth with same
design as on gray-green binding except that Osgood logo at base of spine was
replaced with Houghton, Mifflin imprint (Location: OU).

Note: Untrimmed sheets of the first printing were apparently distributed in advance
for review purposes. A notation in the Berg copy suggests that eleven such untrimmed
copies were prepared. Noted in plain, white, linen-like cloth covers, with title imprinted on otherwise plain spine (Location: Berg). Also rebound with reviewer's notations in margins (Location: CEFC). Also untrimmed sheets found in regular trade
binding (Location: Berg).

Publication: 5,000 copies (and 5,000 facsimile manuscripts), printed 13 December
1882. Noted in 16 December 1882 *Publishers' Weekly* for "this week." MBAt copy
received 20 December 1882. Price $1.50, royalty 15¢.

Printing: Printed at the University Press, Cambridge, Mass. by John Wilson and Son.

Locations: CEFC, MBAt, NN, OU, PSt, ViU.

Manuscript: Various drafts and fragments located at Berg, CSmH, MHi, NNPM.

A 31.1.b
First American edition (trade), second printing [1883]

Boston: James R. Osgood, 1883.

500 copies printed 1 March 1883. Price $1.50, royalty 15¢.

LATER PRINTINGS WITHIN THE FIRST AMERICAN EDITION

A 31.1.c
Boston: James R. Osgood, 1883.

Published in a binding uniform with the trade printing of the *Riverside Edition,* omitting Riverside half title, on white laid paper with white wove title page inserted. Top edges gilded. 500 copies printed 24 August 1883. Reprinted on laid paper, with wove 1884 Osgood title page inserted: 1,000 copies printed 31 October 1883. Officially added as vol. XIII of Riverside trade edition about 1891, with revised Riverside half title present (see B 9). Also issued in England about 1891 with cancel Kegan Paul, Trench, Trübner title with sheets of the Riverside trade printing (see B 11).

Note: Because *Grimshawe* was published by Osgood, a rival publisher, Houghton, Mifflin did not formally designate it as a volume in the *Riverside Edition* or list the work in its catalogues until about 1889 when H,M acquired rights to the property (see A 31.1.f). However, since *Grimshawe* was obviously part of Hawthorne's works, arrangements were made to insure that the Osgood title was available in bindings uniform with each of the various *Riverside Edition* formats. This arrangement was facilitated in that Osgood's publication was printed at the H,M Riverside Press. See B 9.

A 31.1.d
First edition (large paper), fourth printing [1883]

[red] DOCTOR GRIMSHAWE'S SECRET | [black] BY | NATHANIEL HAWTHORNE | [sepia vignette of graveyard scene] | [red] CAMBRIDGE | [black] Printed at the University Press | 1883

Frontispiece and vignette University Press title inserted preceding original Osgood title, which was preserved. Also 4-pp. facsimile manuscript inserted before first page of text. Binding and format uniform with large-paper printing of *Riverside Edition.* *Riverside Edition* works half title omitted and volume number not present on spine (see illustration, A 31 bindings). 270 copies printed 29 September 1883, of which 250 were numbered and bound. Price $6.00.

Location: CEFC.

A 31.1.e
Boston and New York: Houghton, Mifflin, 1889.

Remainder Osgood sheets with p. 48 batter with Houghton, Mifflin cancel title and revised copyright statement.

Location: OU.

A 31.1.f
Boston and New York: Houghton, Mifflin, 1891.

Vol. XXV of the *Wayside Edition.* See B 12.

A 31.1.g
Boston and New York: Houghton, Mifflin, [1891].

Vol. XIII of the *Standard Library Edition.* 500 copies printed October 1891. See B 13.

A 31.1.h
Boston and New York: Houghton, Mifflin, [1902].

Vol. XIII of the *"New" Wayside Edition.* 500 copies printed September–October 1902. See B 14.

A 31.1.i
Boston and New York: [Houghton, Mifflin], MDCCCCIX.

Vol. XIII of the *Fireside Edition.* See B 15.

A 31.1.j
Boston, New York: Jefferson Press, [1913].

Combined with *The Marble Faun* in three-volumes-in-one format and published as vol. [VI] of the *"Jefferson Press Edition."* See B 16.

and little Elsie did what any woman may—that is, screeched in Doctor Grim's behalf with full stretch of lungs. Meanwhile the street boys kept up a shower of mud balls, many of which hit the Doctor, while the rest were distributed upon his assailants, heightening their ferocity.

'Seize the old scoundrel! the villain! the Tory! the dastardly Englishman! Hang him in the web of his own devilish spider—'tis long enough! Tar and feather him! tar and feather him!'

It was certainly one of those cries that show a man how few real friends he has, and the tendency of mankind to stand aside, at least, and let a poor devil fight his own troubles, if not assist them in their attack. Here you might have seen a brother physician of the grim Doctor's greatly tickled at his plight; or a decorous, powdered, ruffle-shirted dignitary, one of the weighty men of the town, standing at a neighbour's corner to see what would come of it.

'He is not a respectable man, I understand, this Grimshawe—a quack, intemperate, always in these scuffles: let him get out as he may!'

And then comes a deacon of one of the churches, and several church-members, who, hearing a noise, set out gravely and decorously to see what was going forward in a Christian community.

'Ah! it is that irreligious and profane Grimshawe, who never goes to meeting. We wash our hands of him!'

And one of the select-men said—

'Surely this common brawler ought not to have the care of these nice, sweet children; something must be done about it; and when the man is sober, he must be talked to!'

DOCTOR GRIMSHAWE'S SECRET

A Romance

BY

NATHANIEL HAWTHORNE

EDITED WITH PREFACE AND NOTES

BY

JULIAN HAWTHORNE

LONDON

LONGMANS, GREEN, AND CO.

1888

A31.2: Title page, 7¹¹/₁₆″ × 5″. Page format, 5¹¹/₁₆″ (5¹⁵/₁₆″) × 3½″

A 31.2
First English edition [*1883*]

Probably published simultaneously with first printing of first American edition
(A 31.1.a).

[a–b] [i–vii] viii–xiii [xiv] [1] 2–304

[A]⁸ B–I⁸ K–U⁸

Contents: pp. a–b: blank; p. i: half title; p. ii: printer's notice; p. iii: title; p. iv: blank;
p. v: dedication to 'Keningale Cook and his Wife'; p. vi: blank; pp. vii–xiii: preface; p.
xiv: blank; pp. 1–304: text, headed 'DOCTOR GRIMSHAWE'S SECRET. | [rule] |
CHAPTER I.'

Note: Variations from the contents of the first American edition include omission of
the footnote on p. vi, omission of part of the paragraph beginning at x.24 ('There have
been included in this volume . . . ') and ending at xi.5 (' . . . Mr. Hawthorne's handwrit-
ing was singularly legible.'), a new dedication, and the addition of a new endnote at
the conclusion of the appendix distinguishing Hawthorne's Sir Edward Redclyffe from
the man of the same name who founded the hospital.

Typography and paper: See illustration, A 31.2 page format. Running heads: rectos
and versos, 'DOCTOR GRIMSHAWE'S SECRET.' White wove paper.

Binding: Gray (265. med. Gy) smooth V-like cloth. Front cover with black imprinted
title and author's name, and with black rules and decorative band carried across
spine (see illustration, A 31 bindings [at A 29]). Also on front cover blue imprinted
floral arrangement. Back cover has blindstamped central design element. White wove
endpapers imprinted with gray wall paper-type pattern one side. 12-page Longmans
catalogue inserted at rear. Top and front edges untrimmed.

Publication: Advertised in the 16 December 1882 *Athenaeum* as "now ready." Also
listed in same number.

Printing: Printed by Spottiswoode and Co., New-Street Square and Parliament Street,
London.

Locations: BM, 12705.i.4 (deposit-stamp 1 JA 83); CEFC.

PRINTINGS FROM THE AUTOGRAPH EDITION PLATES

A 31.3.a
Boston and New York: Houghton, Mifflin, MDCCCC.

Vol. XV of the *Autograph Edition*. Contents same as in first American edition (A 31.1.a).
500 copies. Deposited 5 March 1901. See B 20.

A 31.3.b
Boston and New York: Houghton, Mifflin, MDCCCC.

Vol. XV of the *Large-Paper (Autograph) Edition*. 500 copies. See B 21.

A 31.3.c
Boston and New York: Houghton, Mifflin, 1903.

Vol. XV of the *Old Manse Edition*. See B 22.

THE GHOST
OF DOCTOR HARRIS

By

Nathaniel Hawthorne

all my life as a noteworthy man; so that, when he was first . pointed out to me, I looked at him with a certain specialty of attention, and always subsequently eyed him with a degree of interest whenever I happened to see him at the Athenæum or elsewhere. He was a small, withered, infirm, but brisk old gentleman, with snow-white hair, a somewhat stooping figure, but yet a remarkable alacrity of movement. I remember it was in the street that I first noticed him. The doctor was plodding along with a staff, but turned smartly about on being addressed by the gentleman who was with me, and responded with a good deal of vivacity.

"Who is he?" I inquired, as soon as he had passed.

"The Reverend Doctor Harris, of Dorchester," replied my companion; and from that time I often saw him, and never forgot his aspect. His especial haunt was the Athenæum. There I used to see him daily, and almost always with a newspaper—the "Boston Post," which was the leading journal of the Democratic party in the northern States. As old Doctor Harris had been a noted Democrat during his more active life, it was a very natural thing that he should still like to read the "Boston Post." There his reverend figure was accustomed to sit day after day, in the self-same chair by the fireside; and, by degrees, seeing him there so constantly, I began to look towards him as I entered the reading-room, and felt that a kind of acquaintance, at least on my part, was established. Not that I had any reason (as long as this venerable person remained in the body) to suppose that he ever noticed me, but, by some subtle connection, this small, white-

A 32.1: Title page, 7¹³/₁₆″ × 5½″. Page format, 5¹¹/₁₆″ (6″) × 3³/₄″

A 32 THE GHOST OF DOCTOR HARRIS

A 32.1
First edition [*1900*]

[1–2] 3—13 [14–16]

π^8

Contents: p. 1: title; p. 2: blank; p. 3: 'Dedicated to Mrs. J. P. Heywood.'; p. 4: prefatory note signed by A. M. Wilberforce; pp. 5–13: text, headed 'THE GHOST OF DOCTOR HARRIS.*'; pp. 14–16: blank.

Note: First published in *The Nineteenth Century*, XLVII, 275 (January 1900), 88–93 (see D 109). Collected in vol. XVI of the *Autograph Edition, Large-Paper (Autograph) Edition,* and *Old Manse Edition* (see B 20, B 21, B 22).

Typography and paper: See illustration, A 32.1 page format. Running heads: rectos and versos, 'THE GHOST OF DR. HARRIS.' White wove paper.

Binding: Printed wrappers, cover title (see illustration, A 32.1 front wrapper). Floral design and title information on cover in red ink on gray-green wrapper.

Publication: No. 1 in *The Balzac Library,* published February 19, 1900.

Locations: Berg, CEFC, MH, PSt.

Manuscript: Manuscript located in the Pierpont Morgan Library.

LATER EDITION

A 32.2

THE | [red] GHOST | [black] *of* | [red] Doctor Harris | [black] *by* | NATHANIEL HAWTHORNE | [red vignette of candle] | PRINTED FOR GRATUITOUS | DISTRIBU-TION BY THE | [red] Goerck Art Press | [black] LEWIS W. GOERCK, PROP. | 925 Sixth Avenue, N.Y.

[1910]. Printed wrappers.

Location: Berg.

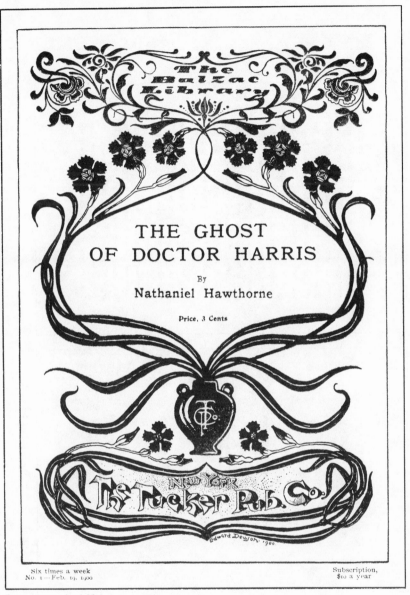

Front wrapper for A 32.1

TWENTY DAYS WITH JULIAN AND LITTLE BUNNY

A DIARY

BY

NATHANIEL HAWTHORNE

NOW FIRST PRINTED FROM THE
ORIGINAL MANUSCRIPT

NEW YORK
PRIVATELY PRINTED
1904

JULIAN AND BUNNY

if any there be. Undoubtedly, they have the least feature and characteristic prominence of any creatures that God has made. With no playfulness, as silent as a fish, inactive, Bunny's life passes between a torpid half-slumber, and the nibbling of clover tops, lettuce, plantain leaves, pig-weed, and crumbs of bread. Sometimes, indeed, he is seized with a little impulse of friskiness; but it does not appear to be sportive, but nervous. Bunny has a singular countenance—like somebody's I have seen, but whose I forget. It is rather imposing and aristocratic, at a cursory glance; but examining it more closely, it is found to be laughably vague. Julian pays him very little attention now, and leaves me to gather leaves for him, else the poor little beast would be likely to starve. I am strongly tempted of the Evil One to murder him privately, and I wish with all my heart that Mrs. Peters would drown him.

Julian had a great resource, to-day, in my jack-knife, which, being fortunately as dull as a hoe, I have given him to whittle with. So he made what he called a boat, and has declared his purpose to make a tooth-pick for his mother, himself, Una, and me. He covered the floor of the

[9]

A33.1: Title page, 9¹/₈" × 6". Page format, 5¹⁵/₁₆ (6¹/₄") × 3¹/₂"

A 33 TWENTY DAYS WITH JULIAN AND LITTLE BUNNY

A 33.1
Only edition [*1904*]

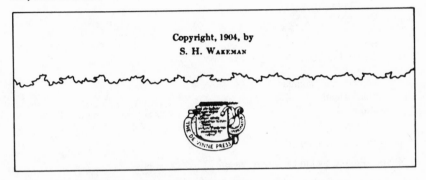

[i–viii] [1–6] 7–85 [86–88]. Frontispiece mounted on p. [2]. 4-page facsimile of Long-fellow letter inserted between pp. [4] and [5]. Also leaves excised or pasted under endpapers (see "Note one" below).

[1]⁴ [2–3]² [4–13]⁴

Note one: Leaf [1]₂ used as front pastedown endpaper and leaf [1]₁ excised or pasted under leaf [1]₂; leaf [13]⁴ excised or pasted under rear pastedown endpaper.

Contents: pp. i–vi: blank; p. vii: half title; p. viii: limitation notice; p. 1: blank; p. 2: frontispiece page with tissue guard attached; p. 3: title; p. 4: copyright; p. 5: publication notice; p. 6: blank; pp. 7–85: text, headed 'TWENTY DAYS WITH JULIAN | AND LITTLE BUNNY | BY PAPA | *July 28th,* 1851. *Monday. Lenox.*'; pp. 86–88: blank.

Note two: Extracts from *Twenty Days* were first published in Julian Hawthorne, *Nathaniel Hawthorne and His Wife* (Cambridge, Mass.: Houghton, Mifflin, 1884) (see C 47).

Typography and paper: See illustration, A 33.1 page format. Running heads: versos, 'TWENTY DAYS WITH'; rectos, 'JULIAN AND BUNNY'. White laid Van Gelder paper.

Binding: Gray laid paper-covered boards, buff V cloth shelfback. Red and black printed paper label on front cover. Leaves [1]₂,₃ used as front endpapers; true laid paper rear endpapers. Edges untrimmed. Also one copy on vellum.

Publication: Privately published by Stephen H. Wakeman. Limitation notice has 'Thirty copies only printed'. Actually, there were 29 copies on Van Gelder paper and 1 on vellum. According to a note by Wakeman in his copy (Location: Berg), copies were distributed as follows:

    2 - For copyright
    1 - Houghton, Mifflin & Co.
    1 - Wakeman (vellum)
    1 - Wakeman (paper)
    1 - John P. Woodberry
    1 - Alex W. Drake
    1 - Carter Brown Library
    1 - New York Public

    1 - Yale
    1 - Buffalo
    1 - Philadelphia
    1 - Harvard
    1 - Concord, Mass.
    1 - Columbia
    1 - Chicago
    1 - Bowdoin
    1 - Boston Athenaeum
    1 - Boston Public
    1 - Princeton
    1 - Wakeman's daughter
    1 - Frank Maier
    1 - Major Turner
    6 - Sold by Dodd, Mead & Co. at $40.

Deposited 12 December 1904.

Printing: Printed by the De Vinne Press.

Locations: Vellum: Berg; paper: Berg, CEFC, MH (see also Wakeman list above).

Manuscript: Hawthorne's manuscript located in the Pierpont Morgan Library.

and fresh into the consciousness of those whom we love. Oh what a bliss it would be, at this moment; if I could be conscious of some purer feeling, some more delicate sentiment, some lovelier fantasy, than could possibly have had its birth in my own nature, and therefore be aware that my Dove was thinking through my mind and feeling through my heart! Try—some evening when you are alone and happy, and when you are most conscious of loving me and being loved by me—and see if you do not possess this power already. But, after all, perhaps it is not wise to intermix fantastic ideas with the reality of our affection. Let us content ourselves to be earthly creatures, and hold communion of spirit in such modes as are ordained to us—by letters (dipping our pens as deep as may be into our hearts) by heartfelt words, when they can be audible; by glances—through which medium spirits do really seem to talk in their own language—and by holy kisses, which I do think have something supernatural in them.

And now good night, my beautiful Dove. I do not write any more at present, because there are three more whole days before this letter will visit you; and I desire to talk with you, each of those three days. Your letter did not come today.

9

LOVE LETTERS

OF

NATHANIEL HAWTHORNE

1839 - 1841

PRIVATELY PRINTED
THE SOCIETY OF THE DOFOBS
CHICAGO
1907

A 34.1.a: Title page, 9¹/₁₆" × 6". Page format, 5¹/₄" (5¹/₂") × 3⁵/₁₆"

A 34 LOVE LETTERS OF NATHANIEL HAWTHORNE

A 34.1.a
First edition, first printing [*1907*]

Copyright, 1907, by
WILLIAM K. BIXBY

---

2 vols.

I: [a–h] [i–iv] v–xi [xii] [1–2] 3–248 [249–256]. Frontispiece inserted facing title page. 4-page facsimile Hawthorne letter inserted between pp. 116 and 117. Also leaves excised or pasted under endpapers (see "Note one" below).

II: [a–h] [i–viii] [1–2] 3–285 [286–296]. 4-page facsimile Hawthorne letter inserted between pp. 148 and 149. Also leaves excised or pasted under endpaper (see "Note two" below).

I: [1]^8 [2]^6 [3–18]^8

Note one: Leaf [1]$_2$ used as front pastedown endpaper and leaf [1]$_1$ excised or pasted under leaf [1]$_2$; leaf [18]$_8$ used as rear pastedown endpaper.

II: [1–2]^4 [3–20]^8 [21]^4

Note two: Leaf [1]$_2$ used as front pastedown endpaper and leaf [1]$_1$ excised or pasted under leaf [1]$_2$; leaf [21]$_3$ used as rear pastedown endpaper and leaf [21]$_4$ excised or pasted under leaf [21]$_3$.

Contents: I: pp. a–h: blank; p. i: half title; p. ii: certificate of limitation; p. iii: title; p. iv: copyright; pp. v–xi: introduction; p. xii: blank; p. 1: 'LETTERS'; p. 2: blank; pp. 3–248: text, headed 'TO MISS PEABODY | [device] | Wednesday Afternoon, March 6th, 1839 | *My dearest Sophie:*'; p. 249: De Vinne device; pp. 250–256: blank.

II: pp. a–h: blank; pp. i–iv: blank; p. v: half title; p. vi: certificate of limitation; p. vii: title; p. viii: copyright; p. 1: 'LETTERS'; p. 2: blank; pp. 3–285: text, headed 'TO MISS PEABODY | [device] | *Oak Hill,* April 13th, 1841 | *Ownest love,*'; p. 286: De Vinne device; pp. 287–296: blank.

Note three: Extracts from *Love Letters* first published in "Hawthorne in the Boston Custom-House," *Atlantic Monthly,* XXI (January 1868), 106–111 (see D 100); also extracts in Julian Hawthorne, *Nathaniel Hawthorne and His Wife* (Cambridge, Mass.: Houghton, Mifflin, 1884) (see C 47); also extracts in Rose Hawthorne Lathrop, *Memories of Hawthorne* (Boston and New York: Houghton, Mifflin, 1897) (see C 55).

Typography and paper: See illustration, A 34.1.a page format. Initial chapter heads only. White laid paper.

Binding: Blue-gray cartridge paper-covered boards, vellum shelfback and corners. Spine goldstamped (see illustration, A 34 bindings [at A 29]). Leaves of first and last gatherings used as endpapers and flyleaves. Edges untrimmed.

Publication: See illustration, certificate of limitation. Deposited 5 July 1907.

THE DE VINNE PRESS CERTIFIES THAT THIS COPY OF THE
LOVE LETTERS OF NATHANIEL HAWTHORNE
IS ONE OF AN EDITION OF SIXTY-TWO COPIES,
IN TWO VOLUMES, PRINTED ON TONED
HOLLAND PAPER, FROM TYPE,
DURING THE MONTH OF
APRIL, NINETEEN
HUNDRED AND
SEVEN

A 34.1.a: Certificate of limitation

Printing: Printed by the De Vinne Press.

Locations: CEFC, MH, NN, PSt.

Manuscript: Majority of Hawthorne's letters to his wife located in the Huntington Library; one letter at Berg.

A 34.1.b
[Washington, D.C.]: A Bruccoli Clark Book, NCR Microcard Editions, 1972.

A facsimile reprint with a foreword by C. E. Frazer Clark, Jr.

was leaving me, when you go aboard. You had better come to the Rock Ferry Hotel, whence you can be transferred to the steamer. Dr. Bailey and wife are now here, intending to sail on Wednesday.

Truly yours,

Nath¹ Hawthorne.

P. S. Drive at once from the railway down to the Rock Ferry steamer, at George's Dock. It goes every half-hour through the day, and until ten o'clock p.m. Mrs. Hawthorne and the children will not excuse you, if you do not come.

Liverpool, August 24th, 1853.

Dear Ticknor,

Could not the white-faced watch be bought, with the understanding that it might be exchanged for a gold-faced one, in case the latter should be preferred? And you might select also the gold-faced one, to be sent if I return the white-face. Do you mean to bring the watch, or send it? I don't care which.

LETTERS OF

HAWTHORNE

TO WILLIAM D. TICKNOR

1851–1864

VOLUME I

NEWARK NEW JERSEY
THE CARTERET BOOK CLUB
1910

A 35.1.a: Title page, 7″ × 4½″. Page format, 4⅝″ (4¹⁵/₁₆″) × 2⅝″

A 35 LETTERS OF HAWTHORNE TO WILLIAM D. TICKNOR

A 35.1.a
First edition, first printing [1910]

Copyright, 1910, by THE CARTERET BOOK CLUB

---

2 vols.

I: [a–f] [i–vii] viii–x [xi–xiv] [1] 2–123 [124–128]. First and last leaves excised or pasted under endpapers (see "Note one" below).

II: [i–xvi] [1] 2–130 [131–136]. First and last leaves excised or pasted under endpapers (see "Note two" below).

I: [1]⁸ [2]² [3–10]⁸

Note one: Leaves [1]₁ and [10]₈ excised or pasted under endpapers.

II: [1–9]⁸ [10]⁴

Note two: Leaves [1]₁ and [10]₄ excised or pasted under endpapers.

Contents: I: pp. a–f: blank; p. i: certificate of limitation; p. ii: blank; p. iii: half title; p. iv: blank; p. v: title; p. vi: copyright; pp. vii–x: introduction; pp. xi–xiii: blank; p. xiv: facsimile Hawthorne letter; pp. 1–123: text, headed *'LETTERS OF HAWTHORNE TO* | *WILLIAM D. TICKNOR* | [rule] | Lenox, Nov. 14th, 1851. | Dear Sirs,'; pp. 124–128: blank.

II: pp. i–viii: blank; p. ix: half title; p. x: blank; p. xi: title; p. xii: copyright; pp. xiii–xv: blank; p. xvi: facsimile Hawthorne letter; pp. 1–130: text, headed *'LETTERS OF HAWTHORNE TO* | *WILLIAM D. TICKNOR* | [rule] | Liverpool, Feb. 16th, 1856. | Dear Ticknor,'; p. 131: printer's notice; pp. 132–136: blank.

Note three: Extracts from *Letters* first appeared in *Harper's Magazine,* CVIII (March 1904), 602–607 (D 110).

Typography and paper: See illustration, A 35.1.a page format. Running heads: versos, *'LETTERS OF HAWTHORNE';* rectos, *'TO WILLIAM D. TICKNOR'.* White laid paper.

Binding: Three-quarters buff (90. gy. Y) T cloth with olive-green laid paper-covered boards. Printed paper label on spine (see illustration, A 35 bindings [at A 29]). White laid endpapers of bookstock. Edges untrimmed. Bound by Stikeman & Co. In matching box, with individual protective board covers for each volume. Front cover of boy with same printed labels as on spine of books.

Publication: See illustration, certificate of limitation. Deposited 18 July 1910.

Printing: Printed at the Marion Press, Jamaica, Queensborough, New York.

Locations: CEFC, MH, NN.

The Marion Press certifies that only one hundred copies of "Letters of Hawthorne to William D. Ticknor have been printed, from type, on Holland handmade paper, and bound in two volumes. The work was begun in August, 1909, and completed in April, 1910.

This copy is number 2 4́

A 35.1.a: Certificate of limitation

Manuscript: Hawthorne's letters to Ticknor located at various libraries: Berg, CSmH, CtY, MBBC, MH, NNPM, ViU.

A 35.1.b
[Washington, D.C.]: A Bruccoli Clark Book, NCR Microcard Editions, 1972.

A facsimile reprint with a foreword by C. E. Frazer Clark, Jr.

description of rhetoric which the Irish call *blarney*, together with a few dollars advance to each, as bounty money, we gathered together about forty men and boys, and set sail, on a bright and beautiful summer's day.

Our crew was altogether as whimsical as our schooner. They reminded me, in all but numbers, of the description a downeast skipper gave of the crew of his lumber coaster, viz.: "An old man, a little boy, a 'tarnal fool, and a Frenchman." Such a hatless, shoeless, shirtless, graceless, unwashed, but not unwhipped set of ragamuffins, I believe never before indulged the gregariousness of their natures by congregating together. I had heard much of the *picked* crews of American privateers, and when I stood on the deck of the schooner, and surveyed the motley group around me, I could not but think, that we, too, had a *picked* crew, and that if the old gentleman, who has the charge of the fires in the nether regions had had the selection, he, too, would have *picked* just such another.

On board this shapeless vessel, behold me, a simple and beardless youth, installed as captain's clerk; and because the clerk's duties were likely to be, "like angels' visits, few and far between," "I was also purser to this motley crew; and because these two were not of "occupation sufficient," our worthy captain had the goodness to assign me, in the quarter bill, the post of sergeant of marines.

The
Yarn of A Yankee
Privateer

Edited By

NATHANIEL
HAWTHORNE

Introduction By
CLIFFORD
SMYTH

FUNK & WAGNALLS COMPANY
NEW YORK AND LONDON
1926

A36.1: Title page, 7³/₈″ × 5″. Page format, 5³/₁₆″ (5⁹/₁₆″) × 3¹/₂″

A 36 THE YARN OF A YANKEE PRIVATEER

A 36.1
Only edition [1926]

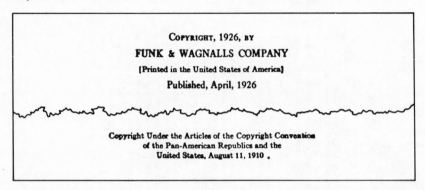

Note one: Author presumed to be Benjamin Frederick Browne. For a discussion of Hawthorne's editorial role, see *Essex Institute Historical Collections,* XIII, part II (April 1875).

[i–iv] v [vi] vii [viii] ix–xviii [1–2] 3–308 [309–310], with chapter half titles and blanks unnumbered. Frontispiece inserted facing title page. Single-page plates inserted facing pp. 14, 46, 78, 110, 154, 178, 206, 258. 2-page manuscript facsimile inserted between pp. 94–95. 2-page diagram inserted between pp. 274 and 275.

[1–20⁸ 21⁴]

Contents: p. i: half title; p. ii: blank; p. iii: title; p. iv: copyright; p. v: contents; p. vi: blank; pp. vii–viii: illustrations; pp. ix–xviii: introduction; p. 1: chapter half title; p. 2: blank; pp. 3–308: text, headed '*The Yarn of a Yankee | Privateer | CHAPTER I |* FIRST GOING DOWN TO SEA'; pp. 309–310: blank.

Note two: Large parts of *Yarn* first appeared in seven installments of *Democratic Review,* XVIII and XIX (January, February, March, May, June, August, September, 1846).

Typography and paper: See illustration, A 36.1 page format. Running heads: rectos, chapter titles; versos, '*The Yarn of a Yankee Privateer*'. White wove paper.

Binding: Green (127. gy. 0l G) crinkle-patterned cloth. Title, author's name, and silhouette of ship stamped in black on front cover and on spine (see illustration, A 36 binding [at A 29]). White wove endpapers. All edges trimmed. Published in pictorial dust jacket.

Publication: Unknown number of copies published April 1926. Price $2.00.

Locations: CEFC, CtY, Lilly, MH, NN; dust jacket, CEFC.

United States. The bust of Washington is represented on a pedestal, amid the battle-smoke and lowering clouds, but with a radiance brightening about his head, prophetic of the peaceful prosperity which his skill and valour won for us. Military emblems are displayed around him; there are the stars and stripes, which he reared so high among the banners of the nations, and there the cap which he placed on the triumphant head of Liberty; while the cannon, the musket and bayonet, the war-like drum, the pyramid of balls, and other martial insignia, are strewn at the base of the pedestal. In the back-ground, is seen the famous Passage of the Delaware. On the right, the chief figure among a group of officers, sits Washington on horseback, and downward to the bank of the river goes the ponderous artillery and all the military array. On the left, the troops are embarking, some already in the midst of the river, and others just pushing from the strand. This scene has been worthily selected to adorn the vignette of Washington; for it was one of the hero's greatest military exploits, by which, at the darkest period of the Revolution, he not only escaped a superiour enemy, but surprised and captured a large body of Hessian troops, at Trenton; and thus gave another aspect to the war.

These emblems refer exclusively to Washington's military deeds. —But it should never be forgotten, that it is not merely in the character of a hero, that his fame shines resplendent, and will remain undimmed by the gathering mist of ages. It is true, that no other man possessed the peculiar military talent, the caution mingled with boldness, the judgment, the equanimity which never sank too low nor rose too high, that were requisite to carry us triumphantly through the Revolutionary contest. Yet it may be justly said, that, even while the war was raging, his civil virtues and abilities held no inferiour place to those which marked him as a soldier. It was his moral strength of character that gave firmness to a tottering cause. Other great generals have been idolized by their armies, because victory was sure to follow where they led; their fame has been won by triumphant marches, and conquest on every field. Fortune has been the better half of all their deeds. But his defeats never snatched one laurel from the brow of Washington. In him, his

HAWTHORNE
AS EDITOR

Selections from His Writings in

THE AMERICAN MAGAZINE

OF USEFUL AND ENTERTAINING

KNOWLEDGE

by Arlin Turner

LOUISIANA STATE UNIVERSITY PRESS

University, Louisiana

1 9 4 1

A37.1: Title page, 8¹⁵⁄₁₆″ × 5¹⁵⁄₁₆″. Page format, 6½″ (6¾″) × 4″

A 37 HAWTHORNE AS EDITOR

A 37.1
Only edition [1941]

[i–iv] v–vii [viii] 1–14 [15–16] 17–52 [53–54] 55–161 [162–164] 165–212 [213–214] 215–225 [226–228] 229–259 [260–262] 263–290 [291–292], with section half titles and blanks unnumbered.

[1–17⁸ 18⁶ 19⁸]

Contents: p. i: half title; p. ii: blank; p. iii: title; p. iv: copyright; pp. v–vi: preface; p. vii: contents; p. viii: blank; pp. 1–14: introduction; p. 15: section title; p. 16: blank; pp. 17–290: text, headed '*Washington*'; pp. 291–292: blank.

Includes "Washington,"† "Major General Lincoln,"† "Commodore Dale,"† "Alexander Hamilton,"† "John C. Calhoun,"† "John Adams,"† "Jerusalem,"† "An Ontario Steam-Boat," "Old Pirates,"† "New York,"† "Captain Franklin's Expedition,"† "Mexican Custom,"† "Soldiers,"† "Death of Hindoos on the Ganges,"† "The French Soldiery,"† "Preservation of the Dead,"† "The Boston Tea Party," "St. John's Grave,"† "Unrecorded Crimes,"† "Warriours, Ancient and Modern,"† "Ancient Pilgrims,"† "Fidelity,"† "April Fools," "Martha's Vineyard,"† "Wolfe's Movement,"† "Note on the Tea Party,"† "Viscount Exmouth,"† "Coinage,"† "Tower of Babel,"† "Wolfe on the Heights of Abraham,"† "The Martyr's Path,"† "The Duston Family," "Chantrey's Washington,"† "The Royal Household Book,"† "Kissing a Queen,"† "Village of Economy,"† "Habitations of Man,"† "Wild Horsemen,"† "Historical Anecdote,"† "Cincinnati,"† "The Devil's Hill,"† "Fashions of Hats,"† "Revolutionary Sentiments,"† "Feminine Characteristics,"† "St. Clair's Conqueror,"† "Caverns,"† "Edward Drinker,"† "Laplandish Customs,"† "The Science of Noses,"† "Comparative Longevity,"† "Snakes,"† "Coffee House Slip,"† "Shot Tower,"† "Pennsylvania Hospital,"† "Nature of Sleep," "Effect of Colour on Heat,"† "Bells," "The Precious Metals, as Applied to Articles of Use and Ornament,"† "Rainbows,"† "Salt; Its Origin and Manufacturer,"† "The Dog,"† "Chinese Pyramid,"† "New York University,"† "Uses of Dead Animals,"† "Lightning Rods,"† "Influence of Music on Animals,"† "Effect of Colour on Odours,"† "Churches and Cathedrals,"† "Coal,"† [Suffolk Bank],† "Longevity of Animals,"† "Species of Men,"† "Church of Saint Sophia,"† "Weight and Substance of the Globe,"† "Incurable Disease,"† "The Puritan: A Series of Essays, Critical, Moral, and Miscellaneous,"† "Our Predecessor,"† "Fessenden's Poems,"† "John Bunyan's Works,"† "Life of Eliot,"† "Major Burnham's Orderly Book,"† "Wild Horses,"† "Editorial Notice,"# "An Obsolete Law,"† [Character],† "Bells of Moscow,"† "Fashionable Wigs,"† "Singular Accident,"† [Wars of Louis XIV],† "A Man-Mountain,"† "Enormous Still,"† "Scent of the Plague,"† "Polemical Divinity,"† "Wild Turkies and Deer,"† "Forced Abstinence,"† "Rubies,"† "A Benefactor,"† [Indian Corn],† "Dancing Horses,"† "General Picton's Helmet,"† "Combustion of a Professor,"† [A Lilliputian Book],† "Tonquinese Soldiers,"† "Saint Ursula,"† "Moorish Peculiarities, Taken at Random,"† "Public Loans,"† "American Gipsies,"† "The Looking-Glass,"† "Spider's Den,"† [Small Wit],† "A Question,"† "Rich Skeletons,"† "Theory of Tides,"† "Brazilian Ignorance,"† "Female Protection,"† "Marriage, and Long Life,"† [Wine for the Indians],† [Books],† "Americanisms,"† "A Man's Wife,"† "Be Short,"† "Botany Bay,"† "Indian Juggler,"† "Infection,"† "Doll's Eyes,"† "South American Carriers,"† "Relicts of Witchcraft,"† "A Good Rule,"† "Witch Ointment,"† "Asthma,"† "Turkish Idleness,"† "Fire Worshippers,"† "Girdle for the Earth,"† "A Musical Ear,"† "Duelling,"† "Town-Whipper,"† "Price of Victory,"† "Duels,"† "Complexion,"† "Improve,"† "Big Kettle,"† "Temperance in Iceland."† Daggers (†) indicate first collected appearance. The number sign (#) indicates first appearance in print.

Note: All contents extracted from *The American Magazine of Useful and Entertaining Knowledge,* first published in the numbers for March–September 1836 during Hawthorne's editorship. Hawthorne prepared the majority of the material, drawing on various sources. Some material was prepared by Hawthorne's sister Elizabeth.

Typography and paper: See illustration, A 37.1 page format. Running heads: rectos, section heads; versos, 'Hawthorne as Magazine Editor'. White wove paper.

Binding: Blue (204. gy. p B) fine-ribbed S-like cloth. Spine goldstamped. Stiff white wove endpapers. Published in printed dust jacket.

Publication: Published as *Louisiana State University Studies,* no. 42. Deposited 12 May 1941. Price $2.75.

Printing: Printed by the Vail-Ballou Press, Inc., Binghamton, N.Y.

Locations: CEFC, CtY, MB, MH, NN, OU, ViU.

B. Collected Works

All collected works of Hawthorne's writings through 1900 published, advertised, or sold as "Hawthorne's Works" by Ticknor and
Fields and the successor copyright holders (Fields, Osgood; James
R. Osgood; Houghton, Osgood; Houghton, Mifflin). Also selected
collected works and certain one-volume collections by other publishers through 1975, included because of their interest or for textual reasons. All works printed from the same plates are grouped
together in chronological order. Plate groups follow in the order of
the first appearance of the first work published in each group.

Note: A dagger (†) follows the first collected appearance of a work. A number sign (#) follows the first appearance in print. A section sign (§) follows a work attributed to Hawthorne.

PEDIGREE OF PRIMARY COLLECTED WORKS

Printed from the "Tinted Edition" plates

B 1   *"Tinted Edition"* (1865–1876). 23 vols.
B 2   *Illustrated Library Edition* (1871–1882). 13 vols.
B 3   *Globe Edition* (1880). 6 vols.
B 4   *"New" Fireside Edition* (1886). 6 vols.

Printed from the "Little Classic Edition" plates

B 5   *"Little Classic Edition"* (1875–1883). 25 vols.
B 6   *"Fireside Edition"* (1879–1882). 13 vols.
B 7   *Popular Edition* (1891). 8 vols.
B 8   *Concord Edition* (1899). 25 vols.

Printed from the Riverside Edition plates

B 9   *Riverside Edition (trade)* (1883–1891). 13 vols.
B 10 *Riverside Edition (large paper)* (1883). 13 vols.
B 11 *"Kegan Paul Edition"* (1883–1891). 13 vols.
B 12 *Wayside Edition* (1884–1891). 25 vols.
B 13 *Standard Library Edition* (1891). 15 vols.
B 14 *"New" Wayside Edition* (1902). 13 vols.
B 15 *Fireside Edition* (1909). 13 vols.
B 16 *"Jefferson Press Edition"* (1913). 10 vols.

Printed from the Autograph Edition plates

B 20 *Autograph Edition* (1900). 22 vols.
B 21 *Large-Paper (Autograph) Edition* (1900). 22 vols.
B 22 *Old Manse Edition* (1903). 22 vols.

Bindings for B 1: (1) Ticknor format C; (2) Ticknor format C embossed with diagonal dots; (3) Ticknor format D

B 1 "TINTED EDITION"
1865-1876

Note: First collected edition of Hawthorne's works.

"Tinted Edition," 14 vols. Boston: Ticknor and Fields, 1865. Vols. 15–18 added in 1870 under Fields, Osgood imprint. Vols. 19–20 added in 1872 under James R. Osgood imprint. Vol. 21 added in 1873 under James R. Osgood imprint. Vols. 22–23 added in 1876 under James R. Osgood imprint.

Listed in the *Cost Books* and initially advertised as the *"Tinted Edition,"* but not so identified in the works (the name apparently was derived from the parchment-tinted "tint & laid" paper supplied by Charles H. Crosby, Boston). Also referred to in the *Cost Books* as the *"Uniform Edition"* and, later, the *"Fine Edition."* Expanded works later advertised as the *"Household Edition"* in 23 vols. Printed on parchment-tinted laid paper from stereotype plates. Primary binding green (146. d. G) pebble-grain P cloth in the style of Ticknor format C. Later volumes in the style of Ticknor format D. Classical male figure centered inside rules frame, all blindstamped on front and back covers. Cover rules of Ticknor format D slightly redesigned (see illustration, B 1 bindings). Also found in the style of Ticknor format C in brown (46. gy. r Br) fine-ribbed S-like cloth embossed with pattern of bold diagonal dots. Spine goldstamped (see illustration, B 1 bindings). Ticknor & Co. imprint at base of spine replaced in reprint bindings with Fields, Osgood & Co. imprint and, later, in some copies with James R. Osgood logo. Ticknor and Fields title-page imprint replaced in reprintings with Fields, Osgood imprint and, later, in some copies with James R. Osgood & Co. imprint. Copies found with mixed title-page and spine imprints. Price of 14-volume first printing of *"Tinted Edition"* $1.50 per volume, royalty 12¢ per volume. Price of second printing raised to $2.00, royalty 20¢.

1. *Twice-Told Tales,* vol. I (1865)

"Preface," "The Gray Champion," "Sunday at Home," "The Wedding Knell," "The Minister's Black Veil," "The May-pole of Merry Mount," "The Gentle Boy," "Mr. Higginbotham's Catastrophe," "Little Annie's Ramble," "Wakefield," "A Rill from the Town Pump," "The Great Carbuncle," "The Prophetic Pictures," "David Swan," "Sights from a Steeple," "The Hollow of the Three Hills," "The Toll-gatherer's Day," "The Vision of the Fountain," "Fancy's Show Box," "Dr. Heidegger's Experiment."

500 copies printed 31 October 1864; 288 copies, September 1865; 280 copies, July 1868; 280 copies, October 1869; 150 copies, August 1873.

2. *Twice-Told Tales,* vol. II (1865)

"Legends of the Province House, I. Howe's Masquerade," "II. Edward Randolph's Portrait," "III. Lady Eleanore's Mantle," "IV. Old Esther Dudley," "The Haunted Mind," "The Village Uncle," "The Ambitious Guest," "The Sister Years," "Snowflakes," "The Seven Vagabonds," "The White Old Maid," "Peter Goldthwaite's Treasure," "Chippings with a Chisel," "The Shaker Bridal," "Night Sketches," "Endicott and the Red Cross," "The Lily's Quest," "Footprints on the Sea Shore," "Edward Fane's Rosebud," "The Threefold Destiny."

500 copies printed 31 October 1864; 288 copies, September 1865; 280 copies, July 1868; 280 copies, October 1869; 150 copies, August 1873.

3. *The Snow-Image, and Other Twice-Told Tales* (1865)

"Preface," "The Snow-Image: a Childish Miracle," "The Great Stone Face," "Main-street," "Ethan Brand," "A Bell's Biography," "Sylph Ethridge," "The Canterbury Pilgrims," "Old News, I," "II.—The Old French War," "III.—The Old Tory," "The Man of Adamant: an Apologue," "The Devil in Manuscript," "John Inglefield's Thanksgiving," "Old Ticonderoga: A Picture of the Past," "The Wives of the Dead," "Little Daffydowndilly," "Major Molineux."

500 copies printed 31 October 1864; 288 copies, September 1865; 280 copies, July 1868; 280 copies, October 1869; 150 copies, August 1873.

4. *Mosses from an Old Manse,* vol. I (1865)

"The Old Manse," "The Birthmark," "A select Party," "Young Goodman Brown," "Rappaccini's Daughter," "Mrs. Bullfrog," "Fire Worship," "Buds and Bird Voices," "Monsieur du Miroir," "The Hall of Fantasy," "The Celestial Railroad," "The Procession of Life," "Feathertop; a moralized Legend."

500 copies printed 31 October 1864; 288 copies, September 1865; 280 copies, July 1868; 280 copies, October 1869; 150 copies, August 1873.

5. *Mosses from an Old Manse,* vol. II (1865)

"The new Adam and Eve," "Egotism; or the Bosom Serpent," "The Christian Banquet," "Drowne's Wooden Image," "The Intelligence Office," "Roger Malvin's Burial," "P.'s Correspondence," "Earth's Holocaust," "Passages from a relinquished Work," "Sketches from Memory," "The Old Apple Dealer," "The Artist of the Beautiful," "A Virtuoso's Collection."

500 copies printed 31 October 1864; 288 copies, September 1865; 280 copies, July 1868; 280 copies, October 1869; 150 copies, August 1873.

6. *The Scarlet Letter, A Romance* (1865)

500 copies printed 31 October 1864; 288 copies, September 1865; 280 copies, July 1868; 280 copies, October 1869; 180 copies, August 1873.

7. *The House of the Seven Gables, A Romance* (1865)

500 copies printed 31 October 1864; 288 copies, September 1865; 280 copies, July 1868; 280 copies, October 1869; 180 copies, August 1873.

8. *The Blithedale Romance* (1865)

500 copies printed 31 October 1864; 288 copies, September 1865; 280 copies, July 1868; 280 copies, October 1869; 150 copies, August 1873.

9. *The Marble Faun; or, The Romance of Monte Beni,* vol. I (1865)

500 copies printed 31 October 1864; 288 copies, September 1865; 280 copies, July 1868; 280 copies, October 1869; 150 copies, August 1873; 140 copies, September 1876.

10. *The Marble Faun; or, The Romance of Monte Beni,* vol. II (1865)

500 copies printed 31 October 1864; 288 copies, September 1865; 280 copies, July 1868; 280 copies, October 1869; 150 copies, August 1873; 140 copies, September 1876.

11. *Our Old Home: A Series of English Sketches* (1865)

"To a Friend," "Consular Experiences," "Leamington Spa," "About Warwick," "Recol-
lections of a Gifted Woman," "Lichfield and Uttoxeter," "Pilgrimage to Old Boston,"
"Near Oxford," "Some of the Haunts of Burns," "A London Suburb," "Up the Thames,"
"Outside Glimpses of English Poverty," "Civic Banquets."

500 copies printed 31 October 1864; 288 copies, September 1865; 280 copies, July
1868; 280 copies, October 1869; 200 copies, August 1873.

12. *True Stories from History and Biography* (1865)

500 copies printed 31 October 1864; 288 copies, September 1865; 280 copies, July
1868; 280 copies, October 1869; 180 copies, August 1873.

13. *A Wonder-Book for Girls and Boys* (1865)

500 copies printed 31 October 1864; 288 copies, September 1865; 280 copies, July
1868; 280 copies, October 1869; 150 copies, August 1873.

14. *Tanglewood Tales, for Girls and Boys; Being a Second Wonder-Book* (1865)

500 copies printed 31 October 1864; 288 copies, September 1865; 280 copies, July
1868; 280 copies, October 1869; 180 copies, August 1873.

15. *Passages from the American Note-Books,* vol. I (1870)

280 copies printed 4 October 1869; 280 copies, January 1871.

16. *Passages from the American Note-Books,* vol. II (1870)

280 copies printed 4 October 1869; 280 copies, January 1871.

17. *Passages from the English Note-Books,* vol. I (1870)

Unknown number of copies of first American edition (A 27.I.a) bound with spine
stamped 'VOL. 17'.

18. *Passages from the English Note-Books,* vol. II (1870)

Unknown number of copies of first American edition (A 27.I.a) bound with spine
stamped 'VOL. 18'.

19. *Passages from the French and Italian Note-Books,* vol. I (1872)

Unknown number of copies of first American edition (A 28.2.a) bound with spine
stamped 'VOL. 19'.

20. *Passages from the French and Italian Note-Books,* vol. II (1872)

Unknown number of copies of first American edition (A 28.2.a) bound with spine
stamped 'VOL. 20'.

21. *Septimius Felton; or The Elixer of Life* (1873)

150 copies printed August 1873. Spine stamped 'VOL. 21'.

22. *Fanshawe and Other Pieces* (1876)

Fanshawe, "Mrs. Hutchinson,"† "Sir William Phips,"† "Sir William Pepperell,"† "Thomas Green Fessenden,"† "Jonathan Cilley."†

Unknown number of copies of second edition (A 1.2.a) probably bound with spine stamped 'VOL. 22'.

23. *The Dolliver Romance and Other Pieces* (1876)

"A Scene from the Dolliver Romance,"† "Another Scene from the Dolliver Romance,"† "Another Fragment of the Dolliver Romance,"† "Sketches from Memory. I. The Inland Port,"† "II. Rochester,"† "III. A Night Scene,"† "Fragments from the Journal of a Solitary Man. I."† "II. My Return Home,"† "My Visit to Niagra,"† "The Antique Ring,"† "Graves and Goblins,"† "Dr. Bullivant,"† "A Book of Autographs,"† "An Old Woman's Tale,"† "Time's Portraiture.—Address,"† " 'Browne's Folly'."†

Unknown number of copies of first American edition (A 30.I.a) probably bound with spine stamped 'VOL. 23'.

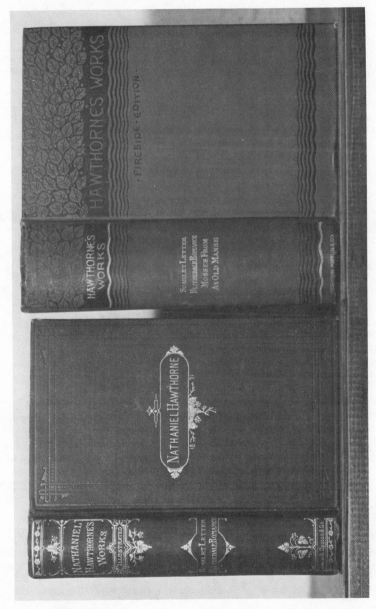

Bindings for B2 and B4

B 2 ILLUSTRATED LIBRARY EDITION
1871–1882

Illustrated Library Edition, 12 vols. Boston: James R. Osgood, 1871–1876. Vol. 13 added in 1882 under Houghton, Mifflin imprint.

Title page in each Osgood volume bears *'ILLUSTRATED LIBRARY EDITION'* designation. Primary binding green (146. d. G) pebble-grain P cloth with author's name gold-stamped on front cover and works designation goldstamped on spine (see illustration, B 2 binding). Also noted in same format bound in plum T-like cloth. James R. Osgood imprint on title page and spine replaced in reprintings by Houghton, Osgood imprint and, later, Houghton, Mifflin. Manufactured from same plates used to print the *"Tinted Edition."* Frontispiece illustration for each title added. Original price $2.00 per volume, royalty 20¢ per volume. Also sold in 6-vol. sets at $24.00 in cloth, $48.00 in half calf.

Twice-Told Tales (1871)

Vols. I and II combined in two-volumes-in-one format. 500 copies printed 16 June 1871; 500 copies, September 1871; 1,000 copies, April 1872; 500 copies, August 1873; 280 copies, March 1874; 500 copies, August 1874; 500 copies, April 1875; 500 copies, February 1876; 280 copies, September 1877; 280 copies, August 1878; 270 copies, October 1879; 270 copies, October 1880; 150 copies, March 1882; 150 copies, October 1882.

Mosses from an Old Manse (1871)

Vols. I and II combined in two-volumes-in-one format. 1,000 copies printed 3 June 1871; 500 copies, September 1871; 750 copies, May 1872; 500 copies, May 1873; 280 copies, March 1874; 280 copies, July 1874; 500 copies, February 1875; 500 copies, November 1875; 280 copies, June 1877; 280 copies, May 1878; 284 copies, March 1879; 270 copies, September 1880; 270 copies, February 1882.

The Scarlet Letter and The Blithedale Romance (1871)

Two volumes in one. 1,000 copies printed 25 June 1871; 500 copies, October 1871; 500 copies, [March] 1872; 500 copies, April 1872; 500 copies, December 1872; 500 copies, [March–August] 1873; 500 copies, September 1873; 280 copies, April 1874; 500 copies, June 1874; 280 copies, December 1874; 500 copies, March 1875; 500 copies, August 1875; 500 copies, August 1876; 280 copies, September 1877; 280 copies, May 1878; 284 copies, November 1878; 280 copies, October 1879; 280 copies, March 1880; 500 copies, September 1881; 270 copies, November 1881; 270 copies, November 1882.

The House of the Seven Gables and The Snow Image (1871)

Two volumes in one. 1,000 copies printed 15 July 1871; 500 copies, October 1871; 750 copies, [April–December] 1872; 500 copies, [March–August] 1873; 320 copies, February 1874; 500 copies, July 1874; 500 copies, November 1874; 500 copies, August 1875; 500 copies, April 1876; 280 copies, August 1877; 280 copies, August 1878; 280 copies, September 1879; 270 copies, August 1880; 150 copies, October 1882.

The Marble Faun (1871)

Vols. I and II combined in two-volumes-in-one format. 500 copies printed 27 August 1871; 500 copies, September 1871; 500 copies, March 1872; 500 copies, May 1872;

500 copies, June 1873; 500 copies, July 1873; 280 copies, March 1874; 500 copies, August 1874; 500 copies, January 1875; 500 copies, August 1875; 500 copies, April 1876; 280 copies, June 1877; 280 copies, January 1878; 280 copies, August 1878; 284 copies, April 1879; 280 copies, March 1880; 270 copies, November 1880; 500 copies, August 1881; 270 copies, September 1882.

Passages from the English Note-Books (1871)

Vols. I and II combined in two-volumes-in-one format. 1,500 copies printed August 1871; 500 copies, August 1872; 500 copies, June 1873; 280 copies, July 1874; 280 copies, November 1874; 280 copies, August 1875; 280 copies, Feburary 1876; 150 copies, Feburary 1877; 150 copies, September 1877; 174 copies, August 1878; 150 copies, October 1880; 270 copies, July 1882.

Passages from the American Note-Books (1871)

Vols. I and II combined in two-volumes-in-one format. 1,000 copies printed 26 October 1871; 500 copies, April 1872; 500 copies, [May–December] 1872; 280 copies, February 1874; 280 copies, July 1874; 280 copies, November 1874; 280 copies, August 1875; 280 copies, February 1876; 280 copies, February 1877; 174 copies, May 1878; 150 copies, August 1880; 270 copies, June 1882.

Passages from the French and Italian Note-Books (1873)

Vols. I and II combined in two-volumes-in-one format. 1,500 copies printed 17 March 1873; 280 copies, March 1874; 500 copies, September 1874; 280 copies, December 1875; 280 copies, August 1876; 174 copies, March 1878; 180 copies, March 1879; 150 copies, June 1880; 150 copies, March 1882.

Our Old Home and *Septimius Felton* (1873)

Two volumes in one. 1,500 copies printed 7 August 1873; 280 copies, July 1874; 280 copies, April 1875; 280 copies, August 1875; 280 copies, August 1876; 150 copies, 14 August 1877; 174 copies, May 1878; 150 copies, June 1879; 150 copies, August 1880; 150 copies, January 1882.

A Wonder-Book and *Grandfather's Chair* (1876)

Two volumes in one. 1,000 copies printed 23 May 1876; 188 copies, March 1879; 150 copies, March 1880; 150 copies, December 1880; 150 copies, January 1882.

Tanglewood Tales and *Biographical Stories* (1876)

Two volumes in one. 1,000 copies printed 23 May 1876; 186 copies, March 1879; 150 copies, March 1880; 270 copies, April 1881.

Fanshawe and *The Dolliver Romance* (1876)

Two volumes in one. 1,000 copies printed 12 September 1876; 175 copies, January 1880; 150 copies, August 1882.

An Analytical Index to the Works of Nathaniel Hawthorne with a Sketch of His Life, by Evangeline M. O'Connor (1882)

270 copies printed January 1882.

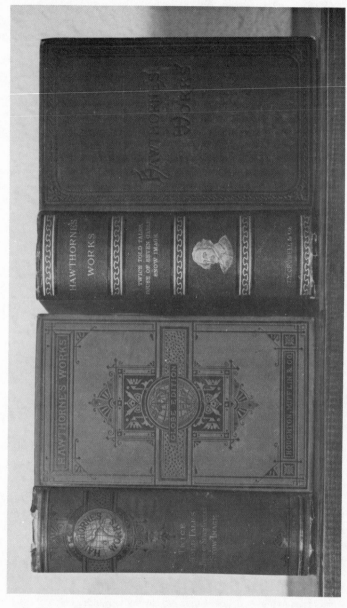

Bindings for B3: Houghton, Mifflin primary binding and T. Y. Crowell binding

B 3 GLOBE EDITION
1880

Globe Edition, 6 vols. Boston: Houghton, Mifflin, 1880.

Each omnibus-volume title page bears *'Globe Edition'* designation. Primary binding green (147. y. d G) fine-ribbed diagonal S cloth with front cover blindstamped and black imprinted, and spine goldstamped and black imprinted (see illustration, B 3 bindings). Also same format bound in reddish brown (38. d. r O) fine-ribbed diagonal T cloth. About 1884 H,M sheets issued in T. Y. Crowell binding (see illustration, B 3 bindings). Manufactured from same plates used to print the *Illustrated Library Edition.* Frontispiece illustration for each title added. Sold only in 6-vol. sets at $10.00 in cloth, $25.00 in half calf.

Twice-Told Tales, The House of the Seven Gables, and *The Snow Image* (1880)

Four volumes in one. 1,500 copies printed August 1880; 1,000 copies, September 1880; 1,000 copies, August 1881; 1,000 copies, May 1882; 270 copies, November 1883; 500 copies, February 1884; 500 copies, May 1884.

The Scarlet Letter, The Blithedale Romance, and *Mosses from an Old Manse* (1880)

Four volumes in one. 1,500 copies printed August 1880; 1,000 copies, September 1880; 1,000 copies, August 1881; 1,000 copies, May 1882; 270 copies, December 1883; 500 copies, February 1884; 500 copies, May 1884.

Our Old Home, Septimius Felton, Fanshawe, and *The Dolliver Romance, and Other Pieces* (1880)

Four volumes in one. 1,500 copies printed August 1880; 1,000 copies, September 1880; 1,000 copies, August 1881; 1,000 copies, May 1882; 270 copies, November 1883; 500 copies, February 1884; 500 copies, March 1884.

A Wonder Book, Tanglewood Tales, Grandfather's Chair, and *Biographical Stories* (1880)

Four volumes in one. 1,500 copies printed August 1880; 1,000 copies, October 1880; 1,000 copies, September 1881; 1,000 copies, May 1882; 270 copies, November 1883; 500 copies, February 1884; 500 copies, May 1884.

The Marble Faun and *French and Italian Note Books* (1880)

Four volumes in one. 1,500 copies printed July 1880; 1,000 copies, September 1880; 1,000 copies, August 1881; 1,000 copies, May 1882; 270 copies, November 1883; 500 copies, February 1884; 500 copies, May 1884.

American Note Books and *English Note Books* (1880)

Four volumes in one. 1,500 copies printed July 1880; 1,000 copies, September 1880; 1,000 copies, September 1881; [1,000 copies, May 1882]; 270 copies, November 1883; 500 copies, February 1884; 500 copies, May 1884.

B 4 "NEW" FIRESIDE EDITION
1886

"New" Fireside Edition, 6 vols. Boston: Houghton, Mifflin, [1886].

'FIRESIDE EDITION' designation on front cover only. Listed and advertised as the *"New" Fireside Edition* presumably to distinguish it from the *"Fireside Edition"* of 1879–1882 (see B 6). Primary binding brown (61. gy. Br) fine-ribbed diagonal S cloth with front cover blindstamped and black imprinted, and spine goldstamped and black imprinted (see illustration, B 4 binding [at B 2]). Manufactured from same plates used to print the *Globe Edition.* Frontispiece illustration for each title added. Same omnibus format and four-volumes-in-one title combinations as *Globe Edition.* Sold only in 6-vol. sets at $10.00 in cloth, $20.00 in half calf. 1,000 copies of each of 6 vols. printed May 1886, reprinted four times. Also 100 copies of a publisher's dummy printed April 1886.

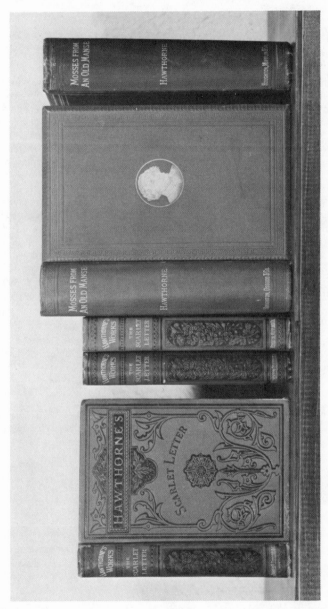

Bindings for (1) B5, *"Little Classic Edition,"* James R. Osgood; (2) B5, Houghton, Osgood; (3) B5, Houghton, Mifflin; (4) B6, *"Fireside Edition,"* Houghton, Osgood; (5) B6, Houghton, Mifflin

B 5 "LITTLE CLASSIC EDITION"
1875–1883

"Little Classic Edition," 23 vols. Boston: James R. Osgood, 1875–1876. Volume [XXIV] added in 1883 under Houghton, Mifflin imprint. Vol. [XXV] added in 1882 under Houghton, Mifflin imprint.

Listed in the *Cost Books* and advertised as the *"Little Classic Edition,"* but not so identified in the works. Edited by George Parsons Lathrop. Printed from stereotype plates made from a new setting of type. Order of arrangement of the edition and contents largely the same as the *"Tinted Edition"* (B 1) with the addition of vols. [XXIV] and [XXV]. Vignette illustrations on each title page, a frontispiece portrait of Hawthorne in vols. [XXIII] and [XXV], and a frontispiece portrait of Franklin Pierce in vol. [XXIV]. Title pages printed in black and red. Page size: $4^3/_{16}'' \times 5^3/_4''$. Primary binding green (137. d. y G) or brown (43. m. r Br) fine-ribbed diagonal S cloth with author's name and volume title blindstamped and black imprinted on front cover, and spine goldstamped and black imprinted (see illustration, B 5 bindings). All edges tinted red. James R. Osgood imprint on title page and spine replaced in reprintings by Houghton, Osgood imprint and, later, Houghton, Mifflin. Copies found with mixed title-page and spine imprints. Also later reprints published by H,M with undated title page printed in black only, in plain brown (75. deep y Br) smooth V-like cloth with spine goldstamped. Top edge gilded. Original price $1.25 per volume, royalty 12.5¢ per volume. Also sold in 23-vol. sets at $28.75 in cloth, $57.50 in half calf or morocco, $75.00 in tree calf.

[I] *Twice-Told Tales,* vol. I (1876)

3,000 copies printed 26 November 1875; 270 copies, September 1880; 270 copies, July 1881; 270 copies, March 1882; 270 copies, August 1882; 270 copies, June 1883; also reprinted after 1883.

[II] *Twice-Told Tales,* vol. II (1876)

3,000 copies printed 26 November 1875; 270 copies, September 1880; 270 copies, July 1881; 270 copies, March 1882; 270 copies, September 1882; 270 copies, June 1883; also reprinted after 1883.

[III] *The Snow-Image, and Other Twice-Told Tales* (1876)

3,000 copies printed 13 November 1875; 270 copies, June 1882; 150 copies, June 1883; also reprinted after 1883.

[IV] *Mosses from an Old Manse,* vol. I (1876)

3,000 copies printed November–December 1875; 500 copies, December 1880; 270 copies, September 1882; 270 copies, June 1883; also reprinted after 1883.

[V] *Mosses from an Old Manse,* vol. II (1876)

3,000 copies printed November–December 1875; 500 copies, December 1880; 270 copies, September 1882; 270 copies, June 1883; also reprinted after 1883.

[VI] *The Scarlet Letter (1875)*

3,000 copies printed 5 October 1875; 1,280 copies, March 1876; 500 copies, June

1877; 500 copies, November 1877; 500 copies, April 1878; 514 copies, October 1878; 512 copies, February 1879; 500 copies, July 1879; 500 copies, January 1880; 1,000 copies, May 1880; 1,000 copies, February 1882; 1,000 copies, July 1882; 1,000 copies, June 1883; 1,000 copies, February 1884; also reprinted after 1884.

[VII] *The House of the Seven Gables, A Romance* (1876)

3,000 copies printed 11 October 1875; 500 copies, January 1877; 280 copies, August 1877; 500 copies, May 1878; 510 copies, March 1879; 500 copies, December 1879; 500 copies, October 1880; 500 copies, August 1881; 500 copies, May 1882; 500 copies, December 1882; 270 copies, June 1883; 270 copies, February 1884; 270 copies, May 1884; also reprinted after 1884.

[VIII] *The Blithedale Romance* (1876)

3,000 copies printed 18 November 1875; 270 copies, December 1880; 270 copies, January 1882; 270 copies, August 1882; 270 copies, December 1883; also reprinted after 1883.

[IX] *The Marble Faun; or, The Romance of Monte Beni,* vol. I (1876)

3,000 copies printed 12 November 1875; 500 copies, August 1878; 520 copies, May 1879; 500 copies, March 1880; 500 copies, December 1880; 500 copies, January 1882; 500 copies, August 1882; 500 copies, April 1883; 500 copies, June 1884; also reprinted after 1884.

[X] *The Marble Faun; or, The Romance of Monte Beni,* vol. II (1876)

3,000 copies printed 12 November 1875; 500 copies, August 1878; 520 copies, May 1879; 500 copies, March 1880; 500 copies, December 1880; 500 copies, January 1882; 500 copies, August 1882; 500 copies, April 1883; 500 copies, June 1884; also reprinted after 1884.

[XI] *Our Old Home: A Series of English Sketches* (1876)

3,000 copies printed November–December 1875; 270 copies, December 1881; 150 copies, August 1882; 150 copies, June 1883; 150 copies, January 1884; also reprinted after 1884.

[XII] *True Stories from History and Biography* (1876)

2,000 copies printed 29 March 1876; 518 copies, January 1879; 280 copies, July 1879; 500 copies, June 1880; 500 copies, August 1882; 500 copies, April 1883; 500 copies, June 1884; also reprinted after 1884.

[XIII] *A Wonder-Book for Girls and Boys* (1876)

2,000 copies printed 28 March 1876; 500 copies, August 1878; 500 copies, February 1879; 500 copies, January 1880; 500 copies, October 1880; 500 copies, March 1881; 500 copies, February 1882; 500 copies, December 1882; 500 copies, June 1883; 500 copies, May 1884; also reprinted after 1884.

[XIV] *Tanglewood Tales, for Girls and Boys. Being a Second Wonder-Book* (1876)

2,000 copies printed 27 April 1876; 280 copies, January 1878; 510 copies, October 1878; 500 copies, July 1879; 500 copies, June 1880; 150 copies, January 1881; 500 copies, February 1881; 500 copies, January 1882; 500 copies, June 1882; 500 copies,

April 1883; 500 copies, February 1884; 500 copies, October 1884; also reprinted after 1884.

[XV] *Passages from the American Note-Books,* vol. I (1876)

2,000 copies printed 10 February 1876; 270 copies, November 1880; 270 copies, August 1882; also reprinted after 1884.

[XVI] *Passages from the American Note-Books,* vol. II (1876)

2,000 copies printed 10 February 1876; 270 copies, November 1880; 270 copies, August 1882; also reprinted after 1884.

[XVII] *Passages from the English Note-Books,* vol. I (1876)

3,000 copies printed 31 January 1876; 730 copies with cancel title, March 1882; also reprinted after 1884.

[XVIII] *Passages from the English Note-Books,* vol. II (1876)

3,000 copies printed 31 January 1876; 730 copies with cancel title, March 1882; also reprinted after 1884.

[XIX] *Passages from the French and Italian Note-Books,* vol. I (1876)

2,000 copies printed 29 February 1876; 160 copies, February 1883; 150 copies, May 1884; also reprinted after 1884.

[XX] *Passages from the French and Italian Note-Books,* vol. II (1876)

2,000 copies printed 29 February 1876; 160 copies, February 1883; 150 copies, May 1884; also reprinted after 1884.

[XXI] *Septimius Felton; or, The Elixer of Life* (1876)

2,000 copies printed 18 March 1876; 270 copies, June 1880; 150 copies, May 1882; 150 copies, July 1883; 150 copies, January 1885; also reprinted after 1885.

[XXII] *Fanshawe, and Other Pieces* (1876)

1,280 copies printed 1 September 1876; 284 copies, October 1878; 500 copies, August 1881; also reprinted after 1884. For contents see B 1[22].

[XXIII] *The Dolliver Romance, and Other Pieces* (1876)

1,280 copies printed 19 September 1876; 284 copies, October 1878; 280 copies, February 1880; 270 copies, August 1881; 270 copies, June 1883; also reprinted after 1884. For contents see B 1[23].

[XXIV] *Sketches and Studies* (1883)

Includes *Life of Franklin Pierce,* "Chiefly About War Matters," "Alice Doane's Appeal," "The Ancestral Footstep," "Appendix: Order of Arrangement of the Edition; List of Vignettes in the Edition; Index to Hawthorne's Works." 1,000 copies printed September 1883; also reprinted after 1884.

[XXV] *An Analytical Index to the Works of Nathaniel Hawthorne with a Sketch of His Life,* by Evangeline M. O'Connor (1882)

500 copies printed January 1882; also reprinted after 1884.

Note: George Parsons Lathrop, *A Study of Hawthorne* (Boston: James R. Osgood, 1876) was also published uniform with the "Little Classic Edition" and was often found with this set, although it was not listed in the order of arrangement of the edition or advertised or sold as part of the edition. 2,000 copies in *"Little Classic Edition"* format printed 17 May 1876.

B6 "FIRESIDE EDITION"
1879–1882

"Fireside Edition," 12 vols. Boston: Houghton, Osgood, 1879. Vol. XIII added in 1882 under Houghton, Mifflin imprint.

Listed in the *Cost Books* and advertised as the *"Fireside Edition,"* but not so identified in the works. Each volume has half title 'THE WORKS | OF | NATHANIEL HAW-THORNE. | *IN TWELVE VOLUMES.* | [rule] | [volume title].' Manufactured from the *"Little Classic Edition"* plates in a somewhat larger page format, and with 24 vols. combined in two-volumes-in-one format and bound in 12 vols. Title pages printed in red and black. Primary binding brown (58. m. Br) or green (46. d. G) fine-ribbed diagonal S cloth with portrait of Hawthorne goldstamped on front cover and spine goldstamped (see illustration, B6 bindings [at B5]). Covers beveled. Houghton, Osgood title-page and spine imprints replaced in reprintings by Houghton, Mifflin imprint. Later title-page imprints undated. Sold only in 13-vol. sets at $20.00 in cloth, $40.00 in half calf, $50.00 in tree calf.

I. *Twice-Told Tales* (1879)

Vols. I and II combined in two-volumes-in-one format. 500 copies printed 20 September 1879; 500 copies, May 1880; 270 copies, April 1881; 270 copies, February 1882; 270 copies, July 1882.

II. *Mosses from an Old Manse* (1879)

Vols. I and II combined in two-volumes-in-one format. 500 copies printed 20 September 1879; 500 copies, May 1880; 270 copies, April 1881; 270 copies, March 1882; 270 copies, August 1882.

III. *The Scarlet Letter* and *The Blithedale Romance* (1879)

Two volumes in one. 500 copies printed 20 September 1879; 500 copies, May 1880; 270 copies, February 1882; 490 copies, August 1882.

IV. *The House of the Seven Gables* and *The Snow-Image* (1879)

Two volumes in one. 500 copies printed 20 September 1879; 520 copies, May 1880; 270 copies, April 1881; 270 copies, March 1882; 270 copies, July 1882.

V. *The Marble Faun* (1879)

Vols. I and II combined in two-volumes-in-one format. 500 copies printed 20 September 1879; 500 copies, May 1880; 270 copies, March 1881; 270 copies, February 1882; 270 copies, July 1882.

VI. *Passages from the English Note-Books* (1879)

Vols. I and II combined in two-volumes-in-one format. 500 copies printed 20 September 1879; 500 copies, May 1880; 270 copies, May 1881; 270 copies, March 1882; 270 copies, August 1882.

VII. *Passages from the American Note-Books* (1879)

Vols. I and II combined in two-volumes-in-one format. 500 copies printed 20 September 1879; 500 copies, May 1880; 270 copies, May 1881; 270 copies, March 1882; 270 copies, July 1882.

VIII. *Passages from the French and Italian Note-Books* (1879)

Vols. I and II combined in two-volumes-in-one format. 500 copies printed 20 September 1879; 500 copies, May 1880; 270 copies, May 1881; 270 copies, March 1882; 270 copies, July 1882.

IX. *Our Old Home* and *Septimius Felton* (1879)

Two volumes in one. 500 copies printed 20 September 1879; 500 copies, May 1880; 270 copies, May 1881; 270 copies, March 1882; 270 copies, July 1882.

X. *A Wonder-Book* and *Grandfather's Chair* (1879)

Two volumes in one. 500 copies printed 20 September 1879; 500 copies, April 1880; 270 copies, May 1881; 270 copies, March 1882; 270 copies, July 1882.

XI. *Tanglewood Tales* and *Biographical Stories* (1879)

Two volumes in one. 500 copies printed 20 September 1879; 500 copies, April 1880; 270 copies, May 1881; 270 copies, February 1882; 270 copies, July 1882.

XII. *Fanshawe* and *The Dolliver Romance* (1879)

Two volumes in one. 500 copies printed 20 September 1879; 500 copies, April 1880; 270 copies, May 1881; 270 copies, February 1882; 270 copies, July 1882.

XIII. *An Analytical Index to the Works of Nathaniel Hawthorne with a Sketch of His Life* (1882)

500 copies printed February 1882; 270 copies, August 1882.

B 7 POPULAR EDITION
1891

Popular Edition, 8 vols. Boston: Houghton, Mifflin, [1891].

Identified as the *Popular Edition* on works half title present in each volume. Published in omnibus-volume format made up from the *"Little Classic Edition"* plates. Title pages printed in black only. Primary binding green (126. d. Ol G) diaper H cloth with spine goldstamped. Later printings bound in various cloths with variant spine-imprint designs. Sold only in 8-vol. sets at $8.00. 1,000 copies each of 8 vols. printed June–August 1891; 1,000 copies, May 1892; also reprinted after 1892.

I. *Twice-Told Tales* and *The House of the Seven Gables* (1891)

Three volumes in one.

II. *Mosses from an Old Manse* and *The Blithedale Romance* (1891)

Three volumes in one.

III. *The Scarlet Letter* and *The Marble Faun* (1891)

Three volumes in one.

IV. *The Snow-Image, Septimius Felton, Fanshawe*, and *The Dolliver Romance* (1891)

Four volumes in one.

V. *True Stories from History and Biography, A Wonder Book for Girls and Boys*, and *Tanglewood Tales* (1891)

Three volumes in one.

VI. *Passages from the American Note-Books* and *Our Old Home* (1891)

Three volumes in one.

VII. *Passages from the English Note-Books* (1891)

Two volumes in one.

VIII. *Passages from the French and Italian Note-Books* and *Sketches and Studies* (1891)

Three volumes in one.

B 8 CONCORD EDITION
1899

Concord Edition, 25 vols. Boston and New York: Houghton, Mifflin, 1899.

Identified as the *Concord Edition* on the title page and works half title in each volume. A remake of the original *"Little Classic Edition,"* in somewhat larger format printed on white laid paper. Title pages printed in red and black. Page size: $4^{1}/_{4}"\times 6^{9}/_{16}"$. Primary binding green T cloth with plain covers and spine goldstamped. Top edges gilded. Frontispiece illustration in each volume. Sold only in 25-vol. sets at $25.00 in cloth, $62.50 in half calf or half polished morocco.

Bindings for (1) B9, *Riverside Edition* (trade); (2) B10, *Riverside Edition* (large paper); (3) B11, *"Kegan Paul Edition"*; (4) B12, *Wayside Edition*; (5) B13, *Standard Library Edition*; (6) B14, *"New" Wayside Edition*; (7) B15, *Fireside Edition* (of 1909); (8) B16, *"Jefferson Press Edition"*, (9) B17, one of twelve separate "Paterson Edition" titles sold in cloth at 2s.; (10) B18, Walter Scott Edition; (11) B20, *Autograph Edition* (Payne binding); (12) B21, *Large-Paper (Autograph) Edition*; (13) B22, *Old Manse Edition* (dust jacket)

B 9 RIVERSIDE EDITION (TRADE)
1883–1891

Riverside Edition (trade), 12 vols. Boston: Houghton, Mifflin, 1883. Vol. XIII added about 1891.

Identified as the *Riverside Edition* on works half title in each volume. Edited with introductory notes by George Parsons Lathrop and illustrated with etchings by Blum, Church, Dielman, Gifford, Shirlaw, and Turner used as volume frontispieces and title-page vignettes. Electrotyped and printed by H. O. Houghton at The Riverside Press, Cambridge, Mass., from a new setting of type based on the *"Little Classic Edition."* Half title and title printed on a fold of white wove paper; text printed on white laid paper. Primary binding brown (58. m. Br) diaper H cloth with goldstamped label on spine (see illustration, B 9 binding). Top edges gilded. Price $2.00 per volume. Also sold in 12-vol. set at $24.00 in cloth, $48.00 in calf, $60.00 in half crushed levant.

I. *Twice-Told Tales* (1883)

"Introductory Note," "Preface," "The Gray Champion," "Sunday at Home," "The Wedding Knell," "The Minister's Black Veil," "The May-Pole of Merry Mount," "The Gentle Boy," "Mr. Higginbotham's Catastrophe," "Little Annie's Ramble," "Wakefield," "A Rill from the Town Pump," "The Great Carbuncle," "The Prophetic Pictures," "David Swan," "Sights from a Steeple," "The Hollow of the Three Hills," "The Toll-Gatherer's Day," "The Vision of the Fountain," "Fancy's Show Box," "Dr. Heidegger's Experiment," "Legends of the Province House. I. Howe's Masquerade," "II. Edward Randolph's Portrait," "III. Lady Eleanore's Mantle," "IV. Old Esther Dudley," "The Haunted Mind," "The Village Uncle," "The Ambitious Guest," "The Sister Years," "Snowflakes," "The Seven Vagabonds," "The White Old Maid," "Peter Goldthwaite's Treasure," "Chippings with a Chisel," "The Shaker Bridal," "Night Sketches," "Endicott and the Red Cross," "The Lily's Quest," "Footprints on the Sea-Shore," "Edward Fane's Rosebud," "The Threefold Destiny."

Two volumes in one. 1,500 copies printed December 1882; 500 copies, March 1883; 1,000 copies, April 1883; 500 copies, July 1883; 500 copies, October 1883; 500 copies, January 1884; 500 copies, March 1884; 500 copies, June 1884; 500 copies, October 1884; also regularly reprinted after 1884. LC (deposited 19 January 1883).

II. *Mosses from an Old Manse* (1883)

"Introductory Note," "The Old Manse," "The Birthmark," "A Select Party," "Young Goodman Brown," "Rappaccini's Daughter," "Mrs. Bullfrog," "Fire Worship," "Buds and Bird Voices," "Monsieur du Miroir," "The Hall of Fantasy," "The Celestial Railroad," "The Procession of Life," "Feathertop: a Moralized Legend," "The New Adam and Eve," "Egotism; or, The Bosom Serpent," "The Christmas Banquet," "Drowne's Wooden Image," "The Intelligence Office," "Roger Malvin's Burial," "P.'s Correspondence," "Earth's Holocaust," "Passages from a Relinquished Work," "Sketches from Memory," "The Old Apple Dealer," "The Artist of the Beautiful," "A Virtuoso's Collection."

Two volumes in one. [1,500 copies printed January 1883?]; 500 copies, March 1883; 1,000 copies, April 1883; 500 copies, July 1883; 500 copies, October 1883; 500 copies, December 1883; 500 copies, June 1884; 500 copies, December 1884; also regularly reprinted after 1884. LC (deposited 20 January 1883).

III. *The House of the Seven Gables* and *The Snow-Image and Other Twice-Told Tales* (1883)

Seven Gables: "Introductory Note," "Preface," chs. I–XXI. *Snow-Image:* "Introductory Note," "Preface," "The Snow-Image: A Childish Miracle," "The Great Stone Face," "Main Street," "Ethan Brand," "A Bell's Biography," "Sylph Ethridge," "The Canterbury Pilgrims," "Old News. I.," "II. The Old French War," "III. The Old Tory," "The Man of Adamant: An Apologue," "The Devil in Manuscript," "John Inglefield's Thanksgiving," "Old Ticonderoga: A Picture of the Past," "The Wives of the Dead," "Little Daffydowndilly," "My Kinsman, Major Molineux."

Two volumes in one. 1,500 copies printed January 1883; 500 copies, March 1883; 1,000 copies, April 1883; 500 copies, June 1883; 500 copies, October 1883; 500 copies, December 1883; 500 copies, March 1884; 500 copies, June 1884; 500 copies, October 1884; also regularly reprinted after 1884. LC (deposited 16 February 1883).

IV. *A Wonder-Book, Tanglewood Tales,* and *Grandfather's Chair* (1883)

Three volumes in one. 1,500 copies printed January 1883; 500 copies, March 1883; 1,000 copies, May 1883; 500 copies, June 1883; 500 copies, July 1883; 500 copies, November 1883; 500 copies, January 1884; 500 copies, April 1884; 500 copies, August 1884; 500 copies, January 1885; also regularly reprinted after 1884. LC (deposited 17 February 1883).

V. *The Scarlet Letter* and *The Blithedale Romance* (1883)

Two volumes in one. 1,500 copies printed March 1883; 1,000 copies, March 1883; 1,000 copies, July 1883; 1,000 copies, October 1883; 1,000 copies, January 1884; 1,000 copies, May 1884; 1,000 copies, January 1885; also regularly reprinted after 1884. LC (deposited 18 March 1883).

VI. *The Marble Faun* (1883)

Two volumes in one. 1,500 copies printed March 1883; 1,000 copies, March 1883; 1,000 copies, July 1883; 500 copies, November 1883; 500 copies, December 1883; 500 copies, March 1884; 1,000 copies, May 1884; 500 copies, October 1884; also regularly reprinted after 1884. LC (deposited 18 March 1883).

VII, VIII. *Our Old Home* and *English Note-Books* (1883)

Each volume published in two-volumes-in-one format, with *Our Old Home* and the beginning of the *English Note-Books* in vol. VII and the conclusion of the *English Note-Books* in vol. VIII. 2,000 copies of each of vols. VII and VIII printed April 1883; 1,000 copies, June 1883; 500 copies, December 1883; 500 copies, February 1884; 500 copies, May 1884; 500 copies, October 1884; also regularly reprinted after 1884. LC (deposited 16 April 1883).

IX. *Passages from the American Note-Books* (1883)

Two volumes in one. 2,000 copies printed May 1883; 1,000 copies, June 1883; 500 copies, December 1883; 500 copies, February 1884; 500 copies, July 1884; 500 copies, January 1885; also regularly reprinted after 1884. LC (deposited 19 May 1883).

X. *Passages from the French and Italian Note-Books* (1883)

Two volumes in one. 2,000 copies printed May 1883; 1,000 copies, June 1883; 500 copies, December 1883; 500 copies, February 1884; 500 copies, July 1884; 500

copies, January 1885; also regularly reprinted after 1884. LC (deposited 21 May 1883).

XI. *The Dolliver Romance, Fanshawe,* and *Septimius Felton,* With an Appendix Containing *The Ancestral Footstep* (1883)

Omnibus volume containing "Introductory Note to the Dolliver Romance," "A Scene from the Dolliver Romance," "Another Scene from the Dolliver Romance," "Another Fragment of the Dolliver Romance," "Introductory Note to Fanshawe," "Fanshawe," "Introductory Note to Septimius Felton," "Septimius Felton," "Appendix. Introductory Note to the Ancestral Footstep," "The Ancestral Footstep."†

Four volumes in one. 3,000 copies printed June 1883; 500 copies, December 1883; 500 copies, February 1884; 500 copies, July 1884; 500 copies, January 1885; also regularly reprinted after 1884. LC (deposited 18 June 1883).

XII. *Tales, Sketches, and Other Papers by Nathaniel Hawthorne,* With a Biographical Sketch by George Parsons Lathrop (1883)

Omnibus volume containing "Introductory Sketch," "Tales and Sketches. Sketches from Memory. I. The Inland Port," "II. Rochester," "III. A Night Scene," "Fragments from the Journal of a Solitary Man. I.," "II. My Home Return," "My Visit to Niagara," "The Antique Ring," "Graves and Goblins," "Dr. Bullivant," "A Book of Autographs," "An Old Woman's Tale," "Time's Portraiture.—Address," " 'Browne's Folly'," "Biographical Stories. Benjamin West," "Sir Isaac Newton," "Samuel Johnson," "Oliver Cromwell," "Benjamin Franklin," "Queen Christiana," "Biographical Sketches. Mrs. Hutchinson," "Sir William Phips," "Sir William Pepperill," "Thomas Green Fessenden," "Jonathan Cilley," "Alice Doane's Appeal,"† "Chiefly About War Matters,"† "Life of Franklin Pierce,"† "Sketch of the Life of Nathaniel Hawthorne," "Index to Hawthorne's Works."

Three volumes in one. 3,000 copies printed June 1883; 500 copies, December 1883; 500 copies, February 1884; 500 copies, June 1884; also regularly reprinted after 1884. LC (deposited 18 June 1883).

XIII. *Doctor Grimshawe's Secret A Romance . . . ,* Edited, with an introduction and Notes by Julian Hawthorne (1889?)

Published in 1883 with a James R. Osgood imprint (A 31.I.c) in a binding uniform with the *Riverside Edition,* trade printing. *Grimshawe* was not identified as vol. XIII of the *Riverside Edition* and the works were not advertised as available in 13 volumes until about 1889 following Houghton, Mifflin's acquisition of the rights to the property. (The half titles in all *Riverside Edition* volumes were revised between 1889 and 1891 to designate works in thirteen volumes.) Osgood title on wove paper, text on laid paper. Copies noted with Osgood title dated 1884. 500 copies printed 24 August 1883; 1,000 copies, 31 October 1883.

Note one: Julian Hawthorne, *Nathaniel Hawthorne and His Wife,* 2 vols. (Boston: James R. Osgood, 1885), was also published in a format and binding uniform with the *Riverside Edition* although not so identified. See C 47. The *Riverside Edition* was later advertised as available with or without the two-volume biography.

Note two: The etchings used in the *Riverside Edition* were combined with bits of the text and published as the *Hawthorne Portfolio,* with approximately 125 copies published August 1883.

B 10 RIVERSIDE EDITION (LARGE PAPER)
1883

Riverside Edition (large paper), 13 vols. Cambridge, Mass.: [Houghton, Mifflin], 1883.

Designated as 'Large Paper' works on paper label pasted on spine (see illustration, B 10 binding [at B 9]). Printed from the *Riverside Edition* plates in large-paper format. Gray-white paper-covered boards. Pages untrimmed; page size: approximately 9$^{1}/_{2}$″ × 6″. Same volume frontispieces and title-page vignettes as in *Riverside Edition* trade printing. Frontispiece and title printed on white laid plate stock, text on laid paper. Title page printed in red and black. *Riverside Edition* works half title present in vols. I–XII. Limited to 250 numbered copies; limitation notice at foot of copyright page.

Note: Houghton, Mifflin prepared 25 sets of the *Riverside Edition* (large paper) of the works of Emerson and Longfellow in 1883 with cancel English title pages presumably for distribution abroad. While no copy of the *Riverside Edition* (large paper) of Hawthorne's works has been located with a cancel English title page, it is not unreasonable to feel that H,M prepared a limited number of sets for sale by Kegan Paul in London.

I. *Twice-Told Tales* (1883)

Two volumes in one. 250 copies printed January 1883.

II. *Mosses from an Old Manse* (1883)

Two volumes in one. 250 copies printed January 1883.

III. *The House of the Seven Gables* and *The Snow-Image and Other Twice-Told Tales* (1883)

Two volumes in one. 250 copies printed March 1883.

IV. *A Wonder-Book, Tanglewood Tales,* and *Grandfather's Chair* (1883)

Three volumes in one. 250 copies printed March 1883.

V. *The Scarlet Letter* and *The Blithedale Romance* (1883)

Two volumes in one. 250 copies printed April 1883.

VI. *The Marble Faun* (1883)

Two volumes in one. 250 copies printed April 1883.

VII, VIII. *Our Old Home* and *English Note-Books* (1883)

Two volumes in one each. 250 copies each printed May 1883.

IX. *Passages from the American Note-Books* (1883)

Two volumes in one. 250 copies printed June 1883.

X. *Passages from the French and Italian Note-Books* (1883)

Two volumes in one. 250 copies printed June 1883.

XI. *The Dolliver Romance, Fanshawe,* and *Septimius Felton,* With an Appendix Containing *The Ancestral Footstep* (1883)

Four volumes in one. 250 copies printed July 1883.

XII. *Tales, Sketches, and Other Papers . . .* , With a Biographical Sketch by George Parsons Lathrop (1883)

Omnibus volume. 250 copies printed August 1883.

[XIII]. *Doctor Grimshawe's Secret A Romance . . .* , Edited, with a Preface and Notes by Julian Hawthorne (1883)

Published in 1883 in a binding and format uniform with the *Riverside Edition,* large-paper edition, and marketed as vol. [XIII] of the edition (see A 31.I.d). *Riverside Edition* works half title omitted and volume number not present on spine. See also note under A 31.I.c. 270 copies printed 29 September 1883, 250 copies numbered and bound.

Note: Julian Hawthorne, *Nathaniel Hawthorne and His Wife,* 2 vols. (Cambridge, Mass.: University Press, 1884), was also published in a binding and format uniform with the *Riverside Edition,* large-paper edition; works half title not present and volume number not present on spine. See C 47.

B 11 "KEGAN PAUL EDITION"
1883-1891

"Kegan Paul Edition," 12 vols. London: Kegan Paul, Trench and Company, 1883. Vol. XIII added about 1891 under Kegan Paul, Trench, Trübner imprint.

English issue of *Riverside Edition,* trade printing, using American sheets with cancel titles, in Kegan Paul binding. Primary binding brown (47. d. gy. r Br) fine-ribbed diagonal S cloth with spine goldstamped (see illustration, B 11 binding [at B 9]). 12-vol. *Riverside Edition* works half title present in vols. I–XII. Later printings have Kegan Paul, Trench, Trübner title-page and spine imprints and 13-vol. *Riverside Edition* works half title present in vols. I–XIII (indicating the addition of *Grimshawe*). 250 copies of twelve Kegan Paul titles printed by Houghton, Mifflin June–July 1883. Reprint Kegan Paul titles also later supplied by H,M.

B 12 WAYSIDE EDITION
1884-1891

Wayside Edition, 24 vols. Boston and New York: Houghton, Mifflin, 1884. Vol. XXV added about 1891.

Identified as the *Wayside Edition* on works half title present in each volume. Printed from the *Riverside Edition* plates revised into a 24-vol. format. Frontispiece illustrations and title-page vignettes preserved. (See illustration, B 12 binding [at B 9]). 500 copies printed September–October 1884. Also regularly reprinted after 1884. Sold in sets only at $36.00 in cloth with top edges gilded, $65.00 in half calf, $70.00 in half calf with top edges gilded, $85.00 in half levant.

I. *Twice-Told Tales*, vol. I (1884)

II. *Twice-Told Tales*, vol. II (1884)

III. *Mosses from an Old Manse*, vol. I (1884)

IV. *Mosses from an Old Manse*, vol. II (1884)

V. *The House of the Seven Gables* (1884)

VI. *The Snow-Image, and other Twice-Told Tales* (1884)

VII. *A Wonder Book for Girls and Boys* and *Tanglewood Tales* (1884)

VIII. *Tanglewood Tales* (concluded) and *The Whole History of Grandfather's Chair* (1884)

IX. *The Scarlet Letter* (1884)

X. *The Blithedale Romance* (1884)

XI. *The Marble Faun; or, The Romance of Monte Beni*, vol. I (1884)

XII. *The Marble Faun; or, The Romance of Monte Beni*, vol. II (1884)

XIII. *Our Old Home* (1884)

XIV. *Our Old Home* (concluded) and *Passages from the English Note-Books* (1884)

XV. *Passages from the English Note-Books* (continued) (1884)

XVI. *Passages from the English Note-Books* (concluded) (1884)

XVII. *Passages from the American Note-Books* (1884)

XVIII. *Passages from the American Note-Books* (concluded) (1884)

XIX. *Passages from the French and Italian Note-Books* (1884)

XX. *Passages from the French and Italian Note-Books* (concluded) (1884)

XXI. *The Dolliver Romance* and *Fanshawe* (1884)

XXII. *Septimius Felton; or, The Elixer of Life*, With an Appendix and *The Ancestral Footstep* (1884)

XXIII. *Tales and Sketches, Biographical Stories,* and *Biographical Sketches* (1884)

XXIV. *Alice Doane's Appeal, Chiefly About War Matters,* and *Life of Franklin Pierce*, With an Appendix (1884)

XXV. *Doctor Grimshaw's Secret*, With an Appendix (1891)

Grimshawe was incorporated as vol. XXV of the *Wayside Edition* about 1891, at which time the works half titles were revised to designate the edition as in 25 vols.

B 13 STANDARD LIBRARY EDITION
1891

Standard Library Edition, 15 vols. Boston and New York: Houghton, Mifflin, [1891].

Identified as the *Standard Library Edition* on works half title present in each volume. Printed from the *Riverside Edition* plates with same order of arrangement and volume titles as the 13-vol. *Riverside Edition* trade printing, with the 2-vol. biography *Nathaniel Hawthorne and His Wife* incorporated as vols. XIV and XV. Riverside frontispiece illustrations and title-page vignettes preserved. (See illustration, B 13 binding [at B 9]). 500 copies printed October 1891. Also regularly reprinted after 1891. Sold only by subscription, net $30.00 per set.

B 14 "NEW" WAYSIDE EDITION
1902

"New" Wayside Edition, 13 vols. Boston and New York: Houghton, Mifflin, [1902].

Identified as the *Wayside Edition* in thirteen volumes on works half title present in each volume, but advertised as the *"New" Wayside Edition,* presumably to distinguish it from the 1884 *Wayside Edition* (B 12). Printed from the *Riverside Edition* plates with the same order of arrangement and volume titles as the 13-vol. *Riverside Edition,* trade printing. Riverside title-page vignettes preserved. (See illustration, B 14 binding [at B 9]). Sold separately at $1.00 per volume in cloth, $13.00 per set, $32.50 per set in half calf, gilt top, or half polished morocco. 500 copies of each of 13 vols. printed September–October 1902.

B 15 FIRESIDE EDITION
1909

Fireside Edition, 13 vols. Boston and New York: [Houghton, Mifflin], MDCCCCIX.

Identified as the *Fireside Edition* on the title page and spine; no works half title present. Not to be confused with the *"Fireside Edition"* of 1879 (B 6) or the *"New" Fireside Edition"* of 1886 (B 4). Printed from the *Riverside Edition* plates with the same order of arrangement and volume titles as the original 13-vol. *Riverside Edition,* trade printing. Frontispiece illustrations in each volume. Published with printed dust jacket. (See illustration, B 15 binding [at B 9]).

B 16 "JEFFERSON PRESS EDITION"
1913

"Jefferson Press Edition," 10 vols. Boston, New York: Jefferson Press, [1913].

Known as the *"Jefferson Press Edition,"* but not so identified in the works; no works half title. Printed by arrangement with Houghton, Mifflin, using the Riverside plates in revised combinations; some material omitted. Frontispiece illustration in each volume. (See illustration, B 15 binding [at B 9]).

[I] *Twice-Told Tales*

[II] *Mosses from an Old Manse*

[III] *The House of the Seven Gables* and *The Snow-Image*

[IV] *A Wonder-Book, Tanglewood Tales,* and *Grandfather's Chair*

[V] *The Scarlet Letter* and *The Blithedale Romance*

[VI] *The Marble Faun* and *Doctor Grimshawe's Secret*

[VII] *Our Old Home* and *English Note-Books,* vol. I

[VIII] *English Note-Books,* vol. II

[IX] *American Note-Books, The Dolliver Romance, Fanshawe,* and *Septimius Felton*

[X] *French and Italian Note-Books* and *Tales and Sketches*

B 17 "PATERSON EDITION"
1885?

"Paterson Edition," 6 vols. Edinburgh: William Paterson, [1885?].

Known as the *"Paterson Edition,"* but not so identified in the works. Made from the sheets of the twelve titles separately published and distributed by Paterson, with the twelve titles bound in six two-in-one volumes; original title pages preserved. Also found with Walter Scott titles inserted, replacing Paterson titles. Paterson's practice was to package his product for different classes of trade, with each title issued in paper at 1s., in cloth at 2s., (see illustration, B 17 binding [at B 9]), and combined with another title in the six-volume *"Paterson Edition."* The "edition" was advertised in cloth, top gilded, in a paper case, at £1 1s. for the six-volume set. Same plates later used to manufacture the *Walter Scott Edition* (see B 18) in a revised format.

[I] *The House of the Seven Gables* and *The Scarlet Letter*

[II] *Mosses from an Old Manse* and *The New Adam and Eve*

[III] *Twice-Told Tales* and *Legends of the Province House*

[IV] *The Snow-Image* and *Our Old Home*

[V] *Tanglewood Tales* and *The Blithedale Romance*

[VI] *True Stories from History and Biography* and *A Wonder-Book for Girls and Boys*

B 18 "WALTER SCOTT EDITION"
1894

"Walter Scott Edition," 12 vols. London: Walter Scott, [1894].

Known as the *"Walter Scott Edition,"* but not so identified in the works. Remanufactured from the Paterson plates with a Walter Scott title page. Advertised in twelve volumes printed on antique (laid) paper, with each volume containing a frontispiece in photogravure from drawings by T. Eyre Macklin and James Torrance. Cover design for the works by Walter Crane. (See illustration, B 18 binding [at B 9]). Price 2s. 6d. per volume.

[I] *The Scarlet Letter*

[II] *The House of the Seven Gables*

[III] *The Blithedale Romance*

[IV] *A Wonder-Book for Girls and Boys*

[V] *Mosses from an Old Manse*

[VI] *Our Old Home*

[VII] *Tanglewood Tales*

[VIII] *True Stories from History and Biography*

[IX] *Twice-Told Tales*

[X] *The New Adam and Eve*

[XI] *Legends of the Province House*

[XII] *The Snow Image*

B 19 THE POPULAR TALES
1894

The Popular Tales of Nathaniel Hawthorne. Glasgow: Thomas D. Morison; London: Simpkin, Marshall, Hamilton, Kent & Co., [1894?].

One-volume collection including a biographical sketch of Hawthorne, *The House of the Seven Gables, The Scarlet Letter,* and forty-one tales. Advertised on "Mr. Morison's List of Popular Trade Books." Also published with undated New York: Wood & Clarke; Glasgow: Thomas D. Morison imprint. Continuously paged. Price 9s.

B 20 AUTOGRAPH EDITION
1900

Autograph Edition, 22 vols. Boston and New York: Houghton, Mifflin, MDCCCC.

Identified as the *Autograph Edition* on works half title present in each volume. Includes a general introduction by Rose Hawthorne Lathrop and introductory and bibliographical notes by H. E. Scudder. Limited to 500 numbered copies signed by Rose Hawthorne Lathrop and the publisher; certificate of limitation inserted in vol. I following half-title leaf. Printed title in red and black. Printed on white antique laid, decaledge, handmade paper with the 'Hawthorne | Riverside' watermark. Illustrated with 139 full-page photogravures on India paper mounted on plate stock and inserted. The works of 38 artists are represented. The frontispiece photogravure in each volume is signed in pencil by the artist. Sets were sold by subscription and offered in a variety of bindings or with other customized features to fill individual orders. A select number of sets were issued with a duplicated frontispiece in each volume hand-tinted in watercolor; a select few were issued with duplicate illustrations throughout each volume hand-tinted in watercolor. Sets were available in cloth with a printed label, in three-quarter levant, and in full levant. Also five sets only were issued in elaborate Roger Payne–style leather bindings (see illustration, B 20 binding [at B 9]) (Location: CEFC). Also a select number of sets had inserted at the front of vol. I an additional illustration of a Custom House document signed by Hawthorne; also noted with Hawthorne manuscript letters and Hawthorne family letters inserted. Also a few sets, probably less than ten, were issued with a leaf of a manuscript from an 1839 Hawthorne Note-Book purchased from Rose Hawthorne Lathrop by Houghton, Mifflin for its use (Location: CEFC). 500 extra sets of sheets were printed for use in preparing the *Large-Paper (Autograph) Edition.* See B 21.

I. *Twice-Told Tales,* vol. I (1900)

"General Introduction," "Introductory Note," "Author's Preface," "The Gray Champion," "Sunday at Home," "The Wedding Knell," "The Minister's Black Veil," "The May-Pole of Merry Mount," "The Gentle Boy," "Mr. Higginbotham's Catastrophe," "Little Annie's Ramble," "Wakefield," "A Rill from the Town Pump," "The Great Carbuncle," "The Prophetic Pictures," "David Swan," "Sights from a Steeple," "The Hollow of the Three

Hills," "The Toll-Gatherer's Day," "The Vision of the Fountain," "Fancy's Show Box," "Dr. Heidegger's Experiment." LC (deposited 20 December 1900).

II. *Twice-Told Tales,* vol.II (1900)

"Legends of the Province House I. Howe's Masquerade," "II. Edward Randolph's Portrait," "III. Lady Eleanore's Mantle," "IV. Old Esther Dudley," "The Haunted Mind," "The Village Uncle," "The Ambitious Guest," "The Sister Years," "Snowflakes," "The Seven Vagabonds," "The White Old Maid," "Peter Goldthwaite's Treasure," "Chippings with a Chisel," "The Shaker Bridal," "Night Sketches," "Endicott and the Red Cross," "The Lily's Quest," "Footprints on the Seashore," "Edward Fane's Rosebud," "The Threefold Destiny." LC (deposited 20 December 1900).

III. *The Snow-Image and Other Twice-Told Tales* (1900)

"Introductory Note," "Dedicatory Letter," "The Snow-Image: A Childish Miracle," "The Great Stone Face," "Main Street," "Ethan Brand," "A Bell's Biography," "Sylph Etherege," "The Canterbury Pilgrims," "Old News: I. Old News," "II. The Old French War," "III. The Old Tory," "The Man of Adament: An Apologue," "The Devil in Manuscript," "John Inglefield's Thanksgiving," "Old Ticonderoga: A Picture of the Past," "The Wives of the Dead," "Little Daffydowndilly," "My Kinsman, Major Molineux." LC (deposited 20 December 1900).

IV. *Mosses from an Old Manse,* vol. I (1900)

"Introductory Note," "The Old Manse," "The Birthmark," "A Select Party," "Young Goodman Brown," "Rappaccini's Daughter," "Mrs. Bullfrog," "Fire Worship," "Buds and Bird Voices," "Monsieur du Miroir," "The Hall of Fantasy," "The Celestial Railroad," "The Procession of Life," "Feathertop: A Moralized Legend." LC (deposited 20 December 1900).

V. *Mosses from an Old Manse,* vol. II (1900)

"The New Adam and Eve," "Egotism; or, The Bosom Serpent," "The Christmas Banquet," "Drowne's Wooden Image," "The Intelligence Office," "Roger Malvin's Burial," "P.'s Correspondence," "Earth's Holocaust," "Passages from a Relinquished Work At Home," "A Flight in a Fog," "A Fellow Traveller," "The Village Theatre," "Sketches from Memory The Notch of the White Mountains," "Our Evening Party Among the Mountains," "The Canal-Boat," "The Old Apple Dealer," "The Artist of the Beautiful," "A Virtuoso's Collection." LC (deposited 20 December 1900).

VI. *The Scarlet Letter* (1900)

"Introductory Note," "Preface to the Second Edition," "The Custom-House," text of *The Scarlet Letter.* LC (deposited 20 December 1900).

VII. *The House of the Seven Gables* (1900)

"Introductory Note," "Author's Preface," text of *Seven Gables.* LC (deposited 20 December 1900).

VIII. *The Blithedale Romance* (1900)

"Introductory Note," "Author's Preface," text of *Blithedale.* LC (deposited 20 December 1900).

IX. *The Marble Faun,* vol. I (1900)

"Introductory Note," "Author's Preface," text of *The Marble Faun,* I. LC (deposited 5 March 1901).

X. *The Marble Faun,* vol. II (1900)

Text of Marble Faun, II. LC (deposited 5 March 1901).

XI. *Our Old Home* (1900)

"Introductory Note," "Dedication to a Friend," "Consular Experiences," "Leamington Spa," "About Warwick," "Recollections of a Gifted Woman," "Lichfield and Uttoxeter," "Pilgrimage to Old Boston," "Near Oxford," "Some of the Haunts of Burns," "A London Suburb," "Up the Thames," "Outside Glimpses of English Poverty," "Civic Banquets." LC (deposited 5 March 1901).

XII. *The Whole History of Grandfather's Chair* and *Biographical Stories* (1900)

"Introductory Note," "Grandfather's Chair. Part I," "Part II," "Part III," "Biographical Stories. Benjamin West," "Sir Isaac Newton," "Samuel Johnson," "Oliver Cromwell," "Benjamin Franklin," "Queen Christina." LC (deposited 20 December 1900).

XIII. *A Wonder Book for Girls and Boys* and *Tanglewood Tales* (1900)

"Introductory Note," "Author's Preface," texts of *Wonder Book* and *Tanglewood.* LC (deposited 20 December 1900).

XIV. *The Dolliver Romance and Kindred Tales* (1900)

"Introductory Note," "The Dolliver Romance   A Scene from the Dolliver Romance," "Another Scene from the Dolliver Romance," "Another Fragment of the Dolliver Romance," "Septimius Felton; or, The Elixer of Life," "Appendix: The Ancestral Footstep; Outlines of an English Romance." LC (deposited 20 December 1900).

XV. *Doctor Grimshawe's Secret A Romance,* Edited, with a Preface and Notes by Julian Hawthorne (1900)

"Editor's Preface," text of *Grimshawe.* LC (deposited 5 March 1901).

XVI. *Tales and Sketches* (1900)

"Introductory Note," *Fanshawe,* "The Antique Ring," "An Old Woman's Tale," "Alice Doane's Appeal," "The Ghost of Doctor Harris,"† "Appendix. The Young Provencial"§ (G 25), "The Haunted Quack"§ (G 14), "The New England Village"§ (G 21), "My Wife's Novel"§ (G 20), "The Bald Eagle"§ (G 2). LC (deposited 5 March 1901).

XVII. *Miscellanies Biographical and Other Sketches and Letters* (1900)

"Introductory Note," "Biographical Sketches   Mrs. Hutchinson," "Sir William Phips," "Sir William Pepperell," "Thomas Green Fessenden," "Jonathan Cilley," *Life of Franklin Pierce,* "Preface to Miss Delia Bacon's Work, 'The Philosophy of the Plays of Shakespeare Unfolded',"† "Sketches and Essays   An Ontario Steamboat,"† "Nature of Sleep,"† "Bells,"† "The Duston Family,"† "Hints to Young Ambition,"§ "My Visit to Niagara," "Graves and Goblins," "Dr. Bullivant," "Sketches from Memory   I. The Inland Port," "II. Rochester," "A Night Scene," "Fragments from the Journal of a Solitary Man I.," "II. My Return Home," "A Book of Autographs," " 'Browne's Folly'," "Chiefly

About War Matters," thirteen Hawthorne letters to various people appended#. LC (deposited 5 March 1901).

XVIII. *Passages from the American Note-Books* (1900)

LC (deposited 5 March 1901).

XIX. *Notes of Travel*, vol. I (1900)

LC (deposited 5 March 1901).

XX. *Notes of Travel*, vol. II (1900)

LC (deposited 5 March 1901).

XXI. *Notes of Travel*, vol. III (1900)

LC (deposited 5 March 1901).

XXII. *Notes of Travel*, vol. IV (1900)

LC (deposited 5 March 1901).

B 21 LARGE-PAPER (AUTOGRAPH) EDITION
1900

Large-Paper (Autograph) Edition, 22 vols. Boston and New York: Houghton, Mifflin, MDCCCC.

Identified as the *Large-Paper Edition* on the works half title present in each volume and on the printed paper label on each spine (see illustration, B 21 binding [at B 9]). Limited to 500 numbered copies. Made from sheets of the *Autograph Edition*, with revised half title, limitation notice, and engraved title. Illustrations same as in *Autograph Edition*, but printed on parchment-like paper and inserted.

Note: Also "*Large-Paper Edition*" of *Nathaniel Hawthorne*, by George E. Woodberry, published and bound uniform with the *Large-Paper (Autograph) Edition* (see C 61).

B 22 OLD MANSE EDITION
1903

Old Manse Edition, 22 vols. Boston and New York: Houghton, Mifflin, 1903.

Identified as the *Old Manse Edition* on the works half title present in each volume. Printed from the plates of the *Autograph Edition*, with illustrations preserved. Published with printed dust jackets (see illustration, B 22 dust jacket [at B 9]). Sold in sets only by subscription. Originally offered in cloth, gilt top, at $1.50 per volume, later raised to $1.75; in half morocco with marbled paper sides and linings, gilt top, at $3.00 per volume, later raised to $3.50. Salesman's dummy published (Locations: CEFC, JM).

B 23 CROWELL "LENOX EDITION"
1902

Crowell "Lenox Edition," 14 vols. New York: Thomas Y. Corwell, [1902].

Advertised as the "*Lenox Edition*" but not so identified in the works. Introduction to each volume by Katharine Lee Bates. Between 1891 and 1902 Crowell published selected Hawthorne titles, with and without introductions by different authorities, in various page and binding styles but in uniform type format. In 1902 the plates of these separate editions were used to manufacture the *"Lenox Edition,"* with revised front matter and the Bates introductions, in a compact, pocket-sized format; page size: 4" × 6". Uniformly bound in limp red leatherette covers with 'HAWTHORNE'S ROMANCES' inside leafy frame goldstamped on front covers. Published same year as the *Crowell "Popular Edition"* (B 24), a new edition, priority undetermined.

[1] *Twice-Told Tales*, vol. I

[2] *Twice-Told Tales*, vol. II

[3] *Mosses from an Old Manse*, vol. I

[4] *Mosses from an Old Manse*, vol. II

[5] *The Scarlet Letter*

[6] *The House of the Seven Gables*

[7] *A Wonder-Book for Girls and Boys*

[8] *Tanglewood Tales for Girls and Boys Being a Second Wonder-Book*

[9] *The Blithedale Romance*

[10] *The Marble Faun or The Romance of Monte Beni*, vol. I

[11] *The Marble Faun or The Romance of Monte Beni*, vol. II

[12] *The Snow Image and Other Twice-Told Tales*

[13] *Fanshawe. A Tale*

[14] *The Whole History of Grandfather's Chair*

B 24 CROWELL "POPULAR EDITION"
1902

Crowell "Popular Edition," 7 vols. New York: Thomas Y. Crowell, [1902].

Advertised as the *"Popular Edition"* in 7 two-in-one volumes, but not so identified in the works. Introduction to each volume by Katharine Lee Bates. Manufactured from a new setting of type in a larger format than the *"Lenox Edition"* (B 23); page size: $5^{3}/_{16}$" × $7^{7}/_{8}$". LC set deposited 20 August 1902. LC copies have 'HAWTHORNE' inside shield-like device goldstamped on front cover. Sets also noted with Hawthorne's signature goldstamped on front cover (Location: CEFC).

[1] *Fanshawe, Grandfather's Chair, Biographical Stories*

[2] *The Marble Faun*

[3] *Mosses from an Old Manse*

[4] *The Scarlet Letter, The House of the Seven Gables*

[5] *The Snow-Image, The Blithedale Romance*

[6] *Twice-Told Tales*

[7] *A Wonder Book, Tanglewood Tales*

B 25 NEW ENGLAND ROMANCES
1904

New England Romances. London: George Newnes; New York: Scribners, [1904?].

One-volume collection including *The Scarlet Letter, The House of the Seven Gables,* and *The Blithedale Romance.* Later printing with undated London: Simpkin, Marshall, Hamilton, Kent; New York: Scribners imprint.

B 26 NATHANIEL HAWTHORNE: REPRESENTATIVE SELECTIONS
1934

Nathaniel Hawthorne: Representative Selections, With Introduction, Bibliography, and Notes by Austin Warren. New York, Cincinnati, Chicago, Boston, Atlanta: American Book Company, [1934].

American Writers Series; one-volume collection including "Introduction," "Selected Bibliography," "A Hawthorne Chronology," *American Note-Books* (selections), Hawthorne's Prefaces, and 21 tales and sketches. On copyright page of first printing: 'W.P.I.'

B 27 THE COMPLETE NOVELS
1937

The Complete Novels and Selected Tales of Nathaniel Hawthorne, Edited, with an Introduction, by Norman Holmes Pearson. New York: Modern Library, [1937].

One-volume collection including "Introduction," *Fanshawe, The Scarlet Letter, The House of the Seven Gables, The Blithedale Romance, The Marble Faun,* 19 selections from *Twice-Told Tales,* 11 selections from *Mosses from an Old Manse,* and 6 selections from *The Snow Image.*

B 28 HAWTHORNE'S SHORT STORIES
1946

Hawthorne's Short Stories, Edited and with an Introduction by Newton Arvin. New York: Knopf, 1946.

One-volume collection including "Introduction," "Chronology," and 29 tales and sketches. Published 23 May 1946; LC (deposited 26 April 1946). On copyright page of first printing: 'First Borzoi Edition'. Reprinted November 1947, March 1950, January 1954, June 1957, May 1959, May 1961.

B 29 THE PORTABLE HAWTHORNE
1948

The Portable Hawthorne, Edited, with an Introduction and Notes, by Malcolm Cowley. New York: Viking, 1948.

One-volume collection including "Introduction," *The Scarlet Letter,* and selections from *The House of the Seven Gables, The Marble Faun, The Dolliver Romance,* and

Hawthorne's *Note-Books;* also 13 tales and sketches and 11 letters; with a bibliography. On copyright page: 'Published in July 1948'. Seventeen reprintings prior to publication in 1969 of a revised and expanded "edition," which was also reprinted at least five times. Published with London: Chatto and Windus 1971 imprint.

B 30 THE BEST OF HAWTHORNE
1951

The Best of Hawthorne, Edited with Introduction and Notes by Mark Van Doren. New York: Ronald Press, [1951].

One-volume collection including "Introduction," "Biographical Table," 10 tales and sketches, *The American Note-Books* (selections), *The Scarlet Letter,* four prefaces, "Sketch of Abraham Lincoln," "Notes and Comments," "Selective Bibliography."

B 31 THE COMPLETE SHORT STORIES
1959

The Complete Short Stories of Nathaniel Hawthorne. Garden City, N.Y.: Doubleday, [1959].

One-volume collection including 72 tales and sketches from *Twice-Told Tales, Mosses from an Old Manse, The Snow-Image,* and other sources, with some attributed works. Reprints notices of Hawthorne's work by Henry James, Edgar A. Poe, Anthony Trollope, and Oliver Wendell Holmes. Also published under Doubleday's Hanover House imprint in [1959].

B 32 CENTENARY EDITION
1963–1974

The Centenary Edition of the Works of Nathaniel Hawthorne. [Columbus]: Ohio State University Press, [1963–1974].

Note: The definitive edition of the works of Nathaniel Hawthorne bearing the seal of the Center for Editions of American Authors, Modern Language Association of America.

General editors: William Charvat, Roy Harvey Pearce, Claude M. Simpson, Matthew J. Bruccoli. *Textual editor:* Fredson Bowers. *Associate textual editor:* L. Neal Smith. Eleven volumes published to date, additional volumes scheduled.

I. *The Scarlet Letter* (1963)

"Introduction" by William Charvat, "Preface to the Text" and "Textual Introduction" by Fredson Bowers. 1,942 copies published 1 February 1963; 1,040 copies, 1968; 1,070 copies, 1971.

II. *The House of the Seven Gables* (1965)

"Introduction" by William Charvat, "Textual Introduction" by Fredson Bowers. 2,000 copies published 27 December 1965; 2,000 copies, 1971.

III. *The Blithedale Romance* and *Fanshawe* (1965)

"Introduction" by Roy Harvey Pearce, "Textual Introduction" by Fredson Bowers. 1,000 copies published 27 December 1965; 1,000 copies, 1965; 2,000 copies, 1971.

IV. *The Marble Faun* (1968)

"Introduction" by Claude M. Simpson, "Textual Introduction" by Fredson Bowers. 1,969 copies published 1 July 1968; 2,000 copies, 1971.

V. *Our Old Home* (1970)

"Introduction" by Claude M. Simpson, "Textual Introduction" by Fredson Bowers. 2,458 copies published 1 September 1970.

VI. *True Stories from History and Biography* (1972)

"Historical Introduction" by Roy Harvey Pearce, "Textual Introduction" by Fredson Bowers. 2,526 copies published 1 November 1972.

VII. *A Wonder Book* and *Tanglewood Tales* (1972)

"Textual Introduction" by Fredson Bowers. 2,435 copies published 1 November 1972.

VIII. *The American Notebooks* (1973)

Edited by Claude M. Simpson. 3,000 copies published 1 May 1973; also in paperback, 1,880 copies published 1 May 1973.

IX. *Twice-Told Tales* (1974)

"Historical Commentary" by J. Donald Crowley. "Textual Commentary" by Fredson Bowers. 2,547 copies published 1 October 1974.

X. *Mosses from an Old Manse* (1974)

"Historical Commentary" by J. Donald Crowley, "Textual Commentary" by Fredson Bowers. 2,506 copies published 1 November 1974.

XI. *The Snow-Image and Uncollected Tales* (1974)

"Historical Commentary" by J. Donald Crowley, "Textual Commentary" by Fredson Bowers. 2,388 copies published 7 December 1974.

C. First-Appearance Contributions to Books and Pamphlets

First American and English publication in books and pamphlets of material by Hawthorne, arranged chronologically. Selected reprintings up through 1850 are noted to show the exposure and spread of Hawthorne's name and work prior to the publication of *The Scarlet Letter.*

Bindings for (1) C1; (2) C2; (3) C3; (4) C4; (5) C5; (6) C6; (7) C7; (8) C8; (9) C9; (10) C10; (11) C11; (12) C16; (13) C18; (14) C21; (15) D57, publisher's cloth

C 1 THE TOKEN
1831

THE TOKEN; | A | CHRISTMAS AND NEW YEAR'S PRESENT. | [rule] | EDITED BY S. G. GOODRICH. | [rule] | [four lines of verse] | [rule] | BOSTON: | PUBLISHED BY GRAY AND BOWEN. | [rule] | MDCCCXXXI.

Title page deposited with District of Massachusetts 10 August 1830. Noticed in *American Monthly* magazine October 1830.

"Sights from a Steeple," pp. [41]–51. Unsigned. See A 2.1, B 1[1], C 13.

"The Fated Family," pp. [57]–82. Unsigned, attributed. See G 10.

"The Haunted Quack. A Tale of a Canal Boat—By Joseph Nicholson," pp [117]–137. Attributed. See B 20[XVI], C 14, G 14.

"The New England Village," pp. [155]–176. Unsigned, attributed. See B 20[XVI], G 21.

C 2 THE TOKEN
1832

THE TOKEN; | A | CHRISTMAS AND NEW YEAR'S PRESENT. | EDITED BY S. G. GOODRICH | [eight lines of verse] | BOSTON. | PUBLISHED BY GRAY AND BOWEN. | MDCCCXXXII.

Reviewed in the *New-England Magazine* October 1831.

"The Wives of the Dead," pp. [74]–82. Signed 'F . . . . . .' See A 19.1, B 1[3]. Reprinted in *The Boston Pearl and Literary Gazette,* IV, 9 (8 November 1834), 70–71. In *Salem Gazette,* New Series XVII, LIII, 31 (16 April 1839), 1, 4. "By Hawthorne." In *Exeter News-Letter and Rockingham County Advertiser* (New Hampshire), IX, 8 (16 June 1839), 1. "By N. Hawthorne." In *Brother Jonathan* (New York), I, 24 (21 December 1839), 4. "By N. Hawthorne." In *United States Magazine and Democratic Review,* XIII, 61 (July 1843), 85–88. Titled "The Two Widows, By N. Hawthorne." In *Hampden Washingtonian,* II, 32, Whole No. 84 (10 August 1843), 1. "By Nathaniel Hawthorne. From the Democratic Review." In *Yarmouth Register* (Yarmouth, Mass.) (28 November 1844). In *Alexander's Messenger* (Philadelphia) (22 July 1846), p.1. Titled "The Two Widows. By Nathaniel Hawthorne." In *Salem Gazette,* LXVI, 4 (8 January 1847), 1. Titled "The Two Widows. By Nath'l Hawthorne." In *The Essex County Mercury* (Salem), New Series VIII, 2 (13 January 1847), 1. "By Nath'l Hawthorne." In *Salem Gazette,* New Vol. 120 (17 October 1851), 1. Titled "The Two Widows. [published 'at the request of a subscriber' because 'it is not to be found amongst Mr. Hawthorne's collected writings']."

"My Kinsman, Major Molineux—By the Author of 'Lights from a Steeple'," pp. [89]–116. Unsigned. 'Lights' corrected to 'Sights' in text title. See A 19.1, B 1[3].

"Roger Malvin's Burial," pp. [161]–188. Unsigned. See A 15.1, B 1[5]. Reprinted in *United States Magazine and Democratic Review,* XIII (August 1843), 186–196. "By Nathaniel Hawthorne."

"The Gentle Boy," pp. [193]–240. Unsigned. See A 2.1, A 2.2.a, B [1]. Reprinted in *Juvenile Key* (Brunswick, Maine), II, 14, 15, 16 (31 March and 14, 28 April 1832), [53]–55, [57]–58, [61]–63. "From the Token for 1832." In *Essex Register* (Salem), XXXV, 41, 42, 43, (21, 25, 28 May 1835) 1–2, 1–2, 1–2. "From the Token for 1832." In *Salem Advertiser* (May 1835).

"My Wife's Novel," pp [281]–315. Attributed. See B 20[XVI], G 20.

"David Whicher—a North American Story," pp. [349]–372. Unsigned, dated 'Bowdoin College, June 1, 1831.' Attributed. See G 5.

C 3 THE TOKEN
1833

THE TOKEN | AND | ATLANTIC SOUVENIR. | A | CHRISTMAS AND NEW YEAR'S PRESENT. | EDITED BY S. G. GOODRICH. | BOSTON. | PUBLISHED BY GRAY AND BOWEN. | MDCCCXXXIII.

Deposited with District of Massachusetts 20 October 1832. Reviewed in *New-England Magazine* November 1832.

"The Seven Vagabonds—By the Author of 'The Gentle Boy'," pp. [49]–71. See A 2.3, B 1.2.
    "The Bald Eagle," pp. [74]–89. Unsigned, incorrectly attributed. See B 20[XVI], G 2.
    "A Cure for Dyspepsia," pp. [93]–112. Unsigned, attributed. See G 4.
    "Sir William Pepperell—By the Author of 'Sights from a Steeple'," pp. [124]–134. Signed 'H********'. See A 1.2, B 1[22]. Reprinted in *Arcturus, A Journal of Books and Opinion* (New York), III, 16 (March 1842), 299–309. Attributed to Hawthorne. In *Salem Gazette*, LXVII, 10 (22 January 1848), 1. "By Nathaniel Hawthorne." In *The Essex County Mercury* (Salem), New Series IX, 4 (26 January 1848), 1–2. "By Nathaniel Hawthorne." In *The Lawrence Courier* (Lawrence, Mass.), II, 40 (24 June 1848), 1.
    "The Canterbury Pilgrims," pp. [153]–166. Unsigned. See A 19.1., B 1[3], C 13.

C 4 THE MARINER'S LIBRARY
1833

THE | MARINER'S LIBRARY | OR | VOYAGER'S COMPANION. | CONTAINING NARRATIVES | OF THE MOST POPULAR VOYAGES, | FROM | THE TIME OF COLUMBUS TO THE PRESENT DAY; WITH ACCOUNTS OF | REMARKABLE SHIPWRECKS, NAVAL ADVENTURES, THE WHALE- | FISHERY, &c,; THE WHOLE INTERSPERSED WITH NUMER- | OUS SKETCHES OF NAUTICAL LIFE, | [harbor scene] | AND ILLUSTRATED BY | FINE ENGRAVINGS. | [rule] | BOSTON: | LILLY, WAIT, COLMAN AND HOLDEN. | [rule] | 1833.

Title page deposited with District Court of Massachusetts 1 January 1833.

"The Ocean," p. 34. Unsigned. *First book appearance.* See C 9, D 1, D 2.

Two printings: (1) copyright notice pasted to verso of title page and printed on p. [iii] (also copies with pp. [iii–iv] omitted); (2) copyright notice printed on verso of title page, p. [iii] blank. Reprinted 1834. Also reprinted with New York: Leavitt & Allen, 1854 and 1855, title-page imprints. See H 19.

Locations: 1: CEFC, ViU; 2: CEFC, MH; reprints: CEFC.

C 5 THE TOKEN
1835

THE TOKEN | AND | ATLANTIC SOUVENIR. | A | CHRISTMAS AND NEW YEAR'S PRESENT. | EDITED BY S. G. GOODRICH. | BOSTON. | PUBLISHED BY CHARLES BOWEN. | MDCCCXXXV.

Reviewed in *New-England Magazine* and *Knickerbocker* magazine October 1834.

"The Haunted Mind—by the Author of Sights from a Steeple," pp. [76]–82. Unsigned. See A 2.3₁, B 1[2], C 13.

"Alice Doane's Appeal—By the Author of the Gentle Boy," pp. [84]–101. Unsigned. See B 9[XII].

"The Mermaid: A Reverie," pp. [106]–121. Unsigned. Reprinted as "The Village Uncle: An Imaginary Retrospect." See A 2.3₁.

C 6 YOUTH'S KEEPSAKE
1835

YOUTH'S KEEPSAKE. | A | CHRISTMAS AND NEW YEAR'S GIFT | FOR | YOUNG PEOPLE. | [rule] | [four lines of verse] | [rule] | [ornament] | BOSTON: | PUBLISHED BY E. R. BROADERS. | 1835.

Deposited with District Court of Massachusetts 29 November 1834.

"Little Annie's Ramble. By The Author of 'The Gentle Boy'," pp. [147]–159. See A 2.1, B 1[1]. Reprinted in *Salem Gazette*, LXV, 14 (17 February 1846), 1. "By Nathaniel Hawthorne." See C 40.

Location: CEFC, OU.

C 7 THE TOKEN
1836

THE TOKEN | AND | ATLANTIC SOUVENIR. | A | CHRISTMAS AND NEW YEAR'S PRESENT. | EDITED BY S. G. GOODRICH. | BOSTON. | PUBLISHED BY CHARLES BOWEN. | MDCCCXXXVI.

Reviewed in *Knickerbocker* magazine September 1835. Noted as "published in the middle of September" in *New-England Magazine* October 1835.

"The Wedding Knell—By The Author of 'Sights from a Steeple'," pp. [113]–124. Unsigned. See A 2.1, B 1[1], C 12. Excerpted in *Mirror of Literature*, XXVI (July–December 1835), 388–391. Part of a review of *The Token* for 1836.

"The May Pole of Merry Mount—By the Author of 'The Gentle Boy'," pp. [283]–297. Unsigned. 'May-Pole' in text title. See A 2.1, B 1[1].

"The Minister's Black Veil—By the Author of 'Sights from a Steeple'," pp. [302]–320. Unsigned. 'A Parable.*' added to text title. See A 2.1, B 1[1]. Excerpted in *Athenaeum* (London) (7 November 1835), pp. 830–831. No attribution. "From the Token, 1836." Reprinted in *The Metropolitan Magazine* (London), LVIII (May–August 1850), 97–106.

C 8 THE TOKEN
1837

THE TOKEN | AND | ATLANTIC SOUVENIR | A | CHRISTMAS AND NEW YEAR'S PRESENT | EDITED BY S. G. GOODRICH. | BOSTON. | PUBLISHED BY CHARLES BOWEN. | MDCCCXXXVII.

Reviewed in *American Monthly* magazine and *Knickerbocker* magazine October 1836.

"Monsieur du Miroir—by the Author of Sights from a Steeple," pp. [49]–64. Unsigned. See A 15.1, B 1[4].

"Mrs. Bullfrog—by the Author of Wives of the Dead," pp. [66]–75. Unsigned. See
A 15, B 1[4], C 14, C 18. Reprinted in *Salem Gazette,* LV, 80 (5 October 1841), 1. No
attribution. In *Salem Mercury,* New Series, II, 40 (6 October 1841), 3. No attribution. In
Hogg's Instructor (London), 4 (September 1846–February 1847), 154–156. "From
'Mosses from an Old Manse'."

"Sunday at Home—by the Author of the Gentle Boy," pp. [88]–96. Unsigned. See
A 2.1., B 1[1]. Reprinted in *The Salem Observer,* XV, 15 (15 April 1837), 1. "From
'Twice-Told Tales,' by Nathaniel Hawthorne."

"The Man of Adamant," pp. [119]–128. Unsigned. 'AN APOLOGUE. BY THE AU-
THOR OF THE GENTLE BOY.' added to text title. See A 19.1, B 1[3]. Reprinted in
Arcturus, A Journal of Books and Opinion (New York), III, 15 (February 1842), 191–
198. "By Hawthorne."

"David Swan," pp. [147]–155. Unsigned. 'A FANTASY.' added to text title. See A 2.1,
B 1[1]. Reprinted in *Athenaeum* (London) (5 November 1836), pp. 783–784. Part of a
review of *The Token* for 1837. No attribution. In *Salem Gazette,* XV, 67 (18 August
1837), 1. In *American Traveller* (Boston), XIII, 18 (1 September 1837), 4. "By Nathaniel
Hawthorne." In *Atkinson's Casket* (Philadelphia), 11 (November 1837), 523–525. "By
Nathaniel Hawthorne." In *Salem Mercury,* VIII, 20 (21 November 1838), 1–2. "By Na-
thaniel Hawthorne." In *American Traveller* (Boston), XV, 104 (26 June 1840), 4. "By
Nathaniel Hawthorne." In *Reynold's Miscellany of Romance* . . . , New Series 41, II (21
April 1849), 652–653. Titled "David Swan, an American Fantasy." No attribution.

"The Great Carbuncle," pp. [156]–175. Unsigned. 'A MYSTERY OF THE WHITE
MOUNTAINS. BY THE AUTHOR OF THE WEDDING KNELL.' added to text title. See
A 2.1, B 1[1].

"Fancy's Show Box," pp. [177]–184. Unsigned. 'A MORALITY.' added to text title.
See A 2.1, B 1[1]. Reprinted in *Salem Gazette,* New Series XV, LI, 21 (14 March 1837),
1–2. "By N. Hawthorne."

"The Prophetic Pictures," pp. [289]–307. Unsigned. See A 2.1, B 1[1].

C 9 AUTUMN LEAVES
1837

AUTUMN LEAVES: | A COLLECTION OF MISCELLANEOUS POEMS, | FROM | VARI-
OUS AUTHORS. | [two lines of verse] | [rule] | NEW-YORK: | PUBLISHED BY JOHN
S. TAYLOR, | Brick Church Chapel. | [rule] | 1837.

Reviewed in *Knickerbocker* magazine December 1836.

"The Ocean," pp. 95–96. *Reprint.* See C 4, D 1, D 2.

C 10 THE TOKEN
1838

THE TOKEN | AND | ATLANTIC SOUVENIR, | A | CHRISTMAS AND NEW YEAR'S
PRESENT. | EDITED BY S. G. GOODRICH. | [rule] | BOSTON: | AMERICAN STA-
TIONERS' COMPANY, | M DCCC XXXVIII.

Reviewed in *American Monthly* magazine and *Knickerbocker* magazine November
1837.

"Sylph Etherege," pp. [22]–32. Unsigned. See A 19.1, B 1[3].

"Peter Goldthwait's Treasure—by the Author of 'Twice-told Tales'," pp. [37]–65.
Unsigned. See A 2.3₁, B 1[2], C 36. Reprinted in *The Metropolitan Magazine* (London),
LVII (January–April 1850), 417–433. "By Nathaniel Hawthorne, Esq."

"Endicott and the Red Cross," pp. [69]–78. Unsigned. See A2.3₁, B1[2]. Reprinted in *Salem Gazette*, New Series XV, LI, 92 (14 November 1837), 1. "From the Token for 1838."

"Night Sketches, beneath an Umbrella," pp. [81]–89. Unsigned. See A2.3₁, B1[2]. Reprinted in *The New-Yorker* magazine, IV, 10, Whole No. 88 (25 November 1837), 563–564. "By S. G. G. From the Token for 1838" [erroneous attribution to S. G. Goodrich]. In *Salem Gazette*, New Series XVII, LIII, 7 (22 January 1839), 1. Titled "Night Sketches Under an Umbrella. By N. Hawthorne."

"The Shaker Bridal–by the Author of 'Twice-told Tales'," pp. [117]–125. See A2.3₁, B1[2]. Reprinted in *Salem Mercury*, VII, 15 (11 October 1837), 1–2. Erroneously attributed to Miss Sedgwick. In *American Traveller* (Boston), XIII, 32 (20 October 1837), 4. Erroneously attributed to Miss Sedgwick. In *Pittsfield Sun* (16 November 1837). In *The Salem Observer*, XX, 8 (19 February 1842), 1. "By Nath'l Hawthorne." In *National Aegis* (Worcester, Mass.), Series 3, V, 18 (4 May 1842), 4. "By Nathaniel Hawthorne." In *Salem Gazette*, LXV, 40 (19 May 1846), 1. "By Nathaniel Hawthorne." In *The Essex County Mercury* (Salem), VII, 20 (20 May 1846), 2. "By Nathaniel Hawthorne." In *National Anti-Slavery Standard* (New York), VII, 14, Whole No. 326 (3 September 1846), 56. In *The Metropolitan Magazine* (London), LVII (January–April 1850), 436–440.

The following reprints from the 1838 *Token* plates have been seen: *The Token, or Affection's Gift* (New-York: A. & C. B. Edwards, n.d). Spine stamped 1840 (not to be confused with *The Token and Atlantic Souvenir* [Boston: Otis, Broaders, MDCCC XL]). Also New-York: A. & C. B. Edwards undated reprintings with spines stamped 1843, 1844. Also New-York: A. Edwards, No. 3 Park Row, n.d., with spine stamped 1845. Also New-York: Ansel Edwards, n.d., with spine stamped 1846. Also Hartford: S. Andrus and Son, n.d. Also New York: Leavitt & Allen, 379 Broadway, n.d. Also New York: Leavitt & Allen, n.d.

C 11 THE PICTURESQUE POCKET COMPANION
1839

THE | PICTURESQUE | POCKET COMPANION, | AND | VISITOR'S GUIDE, | THROUGH | MOUNT AUBURN: | ILLUSTRATED WITH UPWARDS OF | SIXTY EN-GRAVINGS ON WOOD. | [rule] | [four lines of verse] | [rule] | BOSTON: | OTIS, BROADERS AND COMPANY. | [rule] | MDCCCXXXIX.

"The Lily's Quest. By Nathaniel Hawthorne," pp. [230]–239. *First book publication.* See B1[2], D42. Printed paper-covered boards, leather shelfback.

Locations: CEFC, CtY, MH, OU.

C 12 MORAL TALES, VOL. I
1840

MORAL TALES. | [rule] | VOL. I. | [rule] | Containing, | [contents list with 16 titles] | [double rules] | BOSTON: | E. LITTLEFIELD. | MDCCC XL.

"The Wedding Knell," pp. 155–165. Unsigned. *Reprint.* See A2.1, B1[1], C7.
   "David Swan. A Fantasy," pp. 165–172. Unsigned. *Reprint.* See A2.1, B1[1], C8.

Vol. 1, *Economical Library.* Printed wrappers.

Locations: CEFC, MB, MWA.

Same plates, with new front matter, later used to publish *Moral Tales* (New York: Nafis & Cornish, [c. 1840]), in clothbound format.

C 13 MORAL TALES, VOL. II
1840

MORAL TALES. | [rule] | VOL. II. | [rule] | Containing, | [contents list with 18 titles] | [double rules] | BOSTON: | E. LITTLEFIELD. | M DCCC XL.

"Night Sketches, beneath an Umbrella," pp. 39–46. Unsigned. *Reprint.* See A 2.3₁, B 1[2].
"The Canterbury Pilgrims," pp. 47–59. Unsigned. *Reprint.* See A 19.1, B 1[3], C 3.
"The Haunted Mind," pp. 89–94. Unsigned. *Reprint.* See A 2.3₁, B 1[2], C 5.
"The Man with the ____. A mystery," pp. 129–147. Unsigned, attributed. See G 12.
"Sights from a Steeple," pp. 148–155. Unsigned. *Reprint.* See A 2.1, B 1[1], C 1.

Vol. 2, *Economical Library*. Printed wrappers (see illustration).

Same plates, with new front matter, later used to publish *The Flower Basket* (New York: Nafis & Cornish, [c 1840]), in clothbound format; also noted with Boston: Shepard, Clark & Brown undated title-page imprint (Location: CEFC).

Locations: CEFC, MB, MWA.

Front wrapper for C 13 (C 12, C 14, and C 15 in same format)

C 14 TALES OF HUMOR, VOL. I
1840

TALES OF HUMOR. | [rule] | VOL. I. | [rule] | Containing, | [contents list with 17 titles] | [double rules] | BOSTON: | E. LITTLEFIELD. | M DCCC XL.

"Mrs. Bullfrog," pp. 18–27. Unsigned. *Reprint.* See A 15.1, B 1[4], C 8.
  "The Haunted Quack," pp. 56–71. Unsigned, attributed. *Reprint.* See B 20[XVI], C 1, G 14.

Vol. 3, *Economical Library.* Printed wrappers.

Same plates, with new front matter, later used to publish *Humorist Tales* (New York: Nafis & Cornish, [c. 1840]), in clothbound format; also noted with Boston: Shepard, Clark & Brown undated title-page imprint (Location: CEFC).

Locations: CEFC, ICN, MB, MWA.

C 15 TALES OF HUMOR, VOL. II
1840

TALES OF HUMOR. | [rule] | VOL. II. | [rule] | Containing, | [contents list with 23 titles] | [double rules] | BOSTON:—E. LITTLEFIELD. | M DCCC XL.

"A Rill from the Town Pump," pp. 81–88. Unsigned. *Reprint.* See A 2.1, B 1[1], C 17, D 20.
  "Mr. Higginbotham's Catastrophe," pp. 164–179. Unsigned. *Reprint.* See A 2.1, B 1[1], D 10.

Vol. 4, *Economical Library.* Printed wrappers.

Same plates, with new front matter, later used to publish *Tales for the Times* (New York: Nafis & Cornish, [c. 1840]), in clothbound format; also noted with Boston· Shepard, Clark & Brown undated title-page imprint (Location: CEFC).

Locations: CEFC, ICN, MB, MWA.

C 16 THE BOSTON BOOK
1841

THE | BOSTON BOOK. | BEING SPECIMENS OF | METROPOLITAN LITERATURE. | [rule] | BOSTON: | GEORGE W. LIGHT, 1 CORNHILL. | 1841.

Presentation copy from the publisher to J. T. Fields inscribed 23 November 1840 (Location: MH). Listed in *North American Review* Janaury 1841.

"Howe's Masquerade—by Nathaniel Hawthorne," pp. [168]–189. *First book publication.* See A 2.3, B 1[2], D 36.

C 17 THE TEMPERANCE ALMANAC
1843

Vol. I.]   T H E   [No. 5.

TEMPERANCE ALMANAC,

OF THE

MASSACHUSETTS TEMPERANCE UNION,

FOR THE YEAR OF OUR LORD

1 8 4 3:

THE SIXTY-SEVENTH YEAR OF AMERICAN INDEPENDENCE.

CALCULATIONS BY BENJAMIN GREENLEAF, Esq.

AUTHOR OF GREENLEAF'S ARITHMETIC, KEY, ETC.,

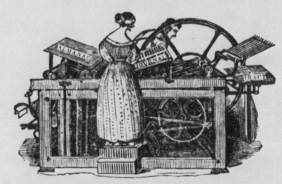

FOR THE MERIDIAN OF BOSTON,

Latitude 42 deg. 13 min. north, Longitude 71 deg. 4 min, West from Greenwich,
and 4 deg. 5 min. 3 sec. East from Washington.

BOSTON:

PRINTED BY WILLIAM S. DAMRELL, 11 CORNHILL.

Price, three dollars per hund.—*Profits devoted to the temperance cause.*

Periodical. One sheet. Postage, 100 miles, 1½ cents; over 100 miles, 2½ cents.

C 17: Cover title, 6⅞″ × 4½″

The Temperance Almanac. Boston: William S. Damrell, 1843.

"A Rill from the Town Pump. By Nathaniel Hawthorne," pp. [23–24]. An extract, with unauthorized revisions. *Reprint.* See A 2.1, B 1[1], C 15, C 19, D 20. Unpaged pamphlet, cover title.

Location: CEFC.

C 18 THE MOSS ROSE
1847

[All following within border of type ornaments] THE | MOSS ROSE: | A | CHRISTMAS | AND | NEW YEAR'S PRESENT. | EDITED BY | S. G. GOODRICH. | [rule] | NEW YORK: | PUBLISHED BY NAFIS & CORNISH, | No. 278 Pearl Street. | ST. LOUIS, MO.—NAFIS, CORNISH & CO. | [rule] | 1847.

"Mrs. Bullfrog," pp. [79]–91. Unsigned. *Reprint.* See A 15.a₁, B 1[4], C 8, C 14.

C 19 THE PROSE WRITERS OF AMERICA
1847

[All following within double-rules frame] THE | PROSE WRITERS | OF | AMERICA. | WITH | A SURVEY OF THE HISTORY, CONDITION, AND PROSPECTS OF | AMERICAN LITERATURE. | BY | RUFAS WILMOT GRISWOLD. | ILLUSTRATED WITH PORTRAITS FROM ORIGINAL PICTURES. | PHILADELPHIA: | CAREY AND HART. | 1847.

"A Rill from the Town Pump," pp. 472–474 (see C 17, D 20); "David Swan—A Fantasy," pp. 474–476 (see C 8); "The Celestial Railroad," pp. 476–482 (see D 52); "Spring" (extract from "Buds and Bird-Voices"), p. 482 (see D 53). *All reprints.*

Reprinted 1849 with "Third edition, revised slug." Also reprinted with undated Philadelphia: Henry T. Coates imprint.

C 20 ÆSTHETIC PAPERS
1849

ÆSTHETIC PAPERS. | EDITED BY | ELIZABETH P. PEABODY. | [rule] | [nine-line quotation from Spenser] | [rule] | BOSTON: | THE EDITOR, 13, WEST STREET. | NEW YORK: G. P. PUTNAM, 155, BROADWAY. | 1849.

Noted in the New York *Literary American* 5 May 1849 as "in press." Title deposited with District Court of Massachusetts 7 May 1849. Copy inscribed by James Russell Lowell 16 May 1849 (Location: PDH).

"Main-street,—N. Hawthorne, Esq.," pp. 145–174. See A 19.1. Reprinted in *The Essex County Mercury and Danvers Courier* (Salem), New Series XI, 38 (18 September 1850), 1–2. "By. N. Hawthorne. From the 1st volume of Aesthetic Papers."

Printed wrappers (see illustration, C 20 wrapper).

C 21 THE BOSTON BOOK
1850

THE | BOSTON BOOK. | BEING SPECIMENS OF | METROPOLITAN LITERATURE. | BOSTON: | TICKNOR, REED AND FIELDS. | MDCCCL.

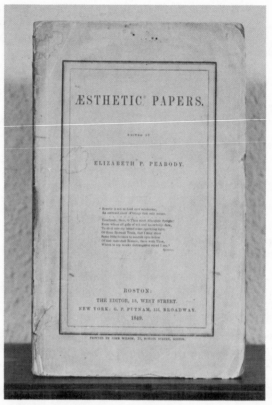

Front wrapper for C 20, 9¹/₂″ × 5⁷/₈″

1,500 copies published 1 December 1849.

"Drowne's Wooden Image. Nathaniel Hawthorne," pp. [11]–29. *Reprint*. See A 15.1.a₁, B 1[5], D 62.

C 22 THE MEMORIAL
1851

[All following within rectangular rule frame] THE | MEMORIAL: | WRITTEN BY | Friends of the Late Mrs. Osgood | AND EDITED | BY MARY E. HEWITT. | WITH ILLUSTRATIONS ENGRAVED ON STEEL BY J. CHENEY, J. HALPIN, J. I. PEASE, | AND H. BECKWITH. | NEW-YORK: | GEORGE P. PUTNAM, 155 BROADWAY. | 1851.

Title deposited with District Court of the Southern District of New York 20 December 1850. Advertised as "now ready" in *The Literary World* 28 December 1850. Deposited 13 February 1851.

"The Snow Image—A Childish Miracle: By Nathaniel Hawthorne," pp. 41–58. *First book publication* (see D 79). See A 19.1, B 1[3].

Reprinted from same plates as *Laurel Leaves* . . . (New York: Lamport, Blakeman & Law, 1854).

C 23 THE (OLD) FARMER'S ALMANACK
1851

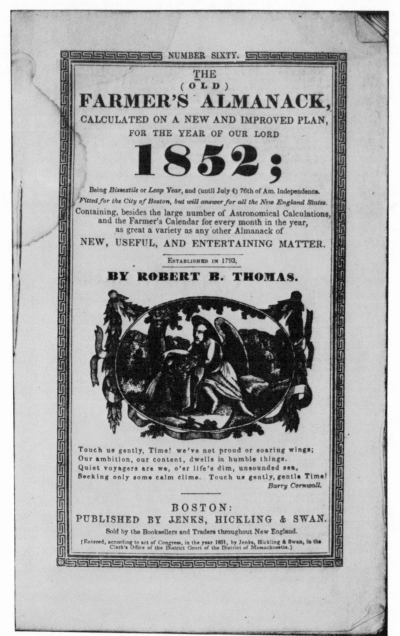

C23: Cover title, 7⁵/₈″ × 4³/₄″

The (Old) Farmer's Almanack . . . for the Year . . . 1852. Boston: Jenks, Hickling & Swan, 1851.

"The Breakfast-Table. By Hawthorne," p. 40. A slightly altered extract reprinted from *The House of the Seven Gables.* See p. 110 of A 17.1.

Pamphlet, cover title.

Also found bound in wrappers specially printed for local distribution: noted with Boston: Thomas Groom; Boston: Kidder & Cheever; Boston: John P. Jewett wrapper imprints.

Location: CEFC.

C 24 MEMORIAL OF JAMES FENIMORE COOPER
1852

Memorial | of | James Fenimore Cooper | New York G P Putnam | 1852

Advertised in the 17 April 1852 *The Literary World* for "immediate publication" and in the 8 May issue for "this week."

Letter from Hawthorne, West Newton, 20 February 1852, p. 33.

Locations: CEFC, CtY, NN.

C 25 HOMES OF AMERICAN AUTHORS
1853

HOMES | OF | AMERICAN AUTHORS: | COMPRISING | Anecdotical, Personal, and Descriptive Sketches, | BY | VARIOUS WRITERS. | ILLUSTRATED WITH VIEWS OF THEIR RESIDENCES FROM ORIGINAL DRAWINGS, | AND A FAC-SIMILE OF THE MANUSCRIPT OF EACH AUTHOR. | NEW-YORK: | G. P. PUTNAM AND CO., 10 PARK PLACE. | LONDON: SAMPSON LOW, SON & Co. | M.DCCC.LIII.

Facsimile of portion of letter from Hawthorne to George P. Putnam, Concord, 15 July 1852, inserted between pp. 312 and 313.

Reprinted with New York: D. Appleton, M.DCCC.LVII, imprint.

C 26 HOUSEHOLD SCENES
1854

HOUSEHOLD SCENES | FOR | THE HOME CIRCLE: | A Gift for a Friend. | WITH ILLUSTRATIONS BY COFFIN—ENGRAVED BY N. ORR. | AUBURN AND BUFFALO: | MILLER, ORTON & MULLIGAN. | 1854.

"Ethan Brand, or the Unpardonable Sin," pp. [75]–110. Signed. *Reprint.* See A 19.1, D 77.

C 27 THE KEEPSAKE
1857

THE | KEEPSAKE | 1857. | EDITED BY | MISS POWER. | WITH BEAUTIFULLY FINISHED ENGRAVINGS, | FROM | DRAWINGS BY THE FIRST ARTISTS, | EN-

GRAVED UNDER THE SUPERINTENDENCE OF | MR. FREDERICK A. HEATH. | [rule] | LONDON: | DAVID BOGUE, 86 FLEET STREET; | BANGS, BROTHER, AND CO., NEW YORK; | H. MANDEVILLE, 15 RUE DAUPHINE, PARIS. | [rule] | 1857.

Advertised in the 8 November 1856 *Athenaeum* for 14 November. Advertised as "now ready" in the 15 November *Athenaeum*. Also listed in the 15 November *Athenaeum*.

"Uttoxeter . . . The Author of 'The Scarlet Letter,' Etc. Etc.," pp. [108]–113. See A 24.1, B 1[11], D 82.

C 28 THE PHILOSOPHY OF THE PLAYS OF SHAKSPERE UNFOLDED
          1857

English issue

THE | PHILOSOPHY | OF | THE PLAYS OF SHAKSPERE | UNFOLDED. | BY DELIA BACON. | WITH | A PREFACE | BY | NATHANIEL HAWTHORNE, | AUTHOR OF 'THE SCARLET LETTER,' ETC. | [rule] | [three quotations] | [rule] | LONDON: | GROOMBRIDGE AND SONS, | PATERNOSTER ROW, | 1857.

Cancel title. Advertised in *Athenaeum* 11 April 1857 as ready "this day." Also listed in the 11 April 1857 *Athenaeum* and *Literary Gazette*. Also reviewed in the 11 April *Athenaeum*.

Hawthorne's "Preface," pp. [vii]–xv. See B 20[XVII].

1,000 copies were printed in London by Wertheimer and Co., Circus Place, Finsbury, at Hawthorne's expense. 500 of the copies, with a cancel title page, bound for distribution in England; 500 sets of sheets, title integral, shipped to Boston to be bound for American distribution. For details of Hawthorne's participation, see Caroline Ticknor, *Hawthorne and His Publisher* (Boston and New York: Houghton Mifflin, MDCCCCXIII), pp. 182–203.

Locations: BM, 11762.g.6 (deposit-stamp 7 MA 57); CEFC; CtY; MH; NN.

American issue

THE | PHILOSOPHY | OF | THE PLAYS OF SHAKSPERE | UNFOLDED. | BY DELIA BACON. | WITH | A PREFACE | BY | NATHANIEL HAWTHORNE, | AUTHOR OF 'THE SCARLET LETTER,' ETC. | [rule] | [three quotations] | [rule] | BOSTON: | TICKNOR AND FIELDS. | 1857.

Title integral. Listed in *Publishers' Circular* 6 June 1857.

Locations: CEFC, CtY, LC, MH, NN.

C 29 BACON AND SHAKESPEARE
          1857

BACON AND SHAKESPEARE. | [rule] | AN INQUIRY TOUCHING | PLAYERS, PLAYHOUSES, AND PLAY-WRITERS | IN THE DAYS OF ELIZABETH. | BY | WILLIAM HENRY SMITH, ESQ. | TO WHICH IS APPENDED AN ABSTRACT OF A MS. RESPECTING | TOBIE MATTHEW. | LONDON: | JOHN RUSSELL SMITH, | 36, SOHO SQUARE. | M.DCCC.LVII.

Letter from Hawthorne to William Henry Smith, Liverpool, 5 June 1857, printed on pp. 3–4 of four-page supplementary "Preface" inserted following original preface in an advertised "reissue" of this title. Text and insert on laid paper. Hawthorne sent Smith a letter of apology concerning certain statements about Smith which Hawthorne included in his "Preface" to *The Philosophy of the Plays of Shakspere Unfolded* (C 28). Smith, whose book *Bacon and Shakespeare* had just been published, arranged for publication of his letter of protest to Hawthorne and Hawthorne's reply as a four-page supplemental preface, both inserted in the reissue of *Bacon and Shakespeare*.

Copies of the insert were made available on a gratis basis to purchasers of the first issue of Smith's book, which lacked the insert. One copy noted on wove paper with insert on laid paper, inscribed by the publisher: "A copy on thick paper only 6 so printed . . . July 2/58" (Location: MB). Also noted, two proofs of the insert, one showing minor textual revisions in Hawthorne's letter (Location: MB). Also reprinted London: Skeffington & Son, M.DCCC.LXXXIV, with Hawthorne's letter included.

Location: CEFC.

C 30 THE JOSEPHINE GALLERY
1859

THE | JOSEPHINE GALLERY. | EDITED BY | ALICE AND PHŒBY CARY. | [rule] | NEW YORK: | DERBY & JACKSON, 119 NASSAU STREET | M DCCC LIX.

Announced in 15 July 1858 *Bookseller's Medium and Publisher's Advertiser* for August. Advertised in *Publishers' Circular* as "ready" 30 October 1858.

"Bertram [*sic*] the Lime-Burner. By Nathaniel Hawthorne," pp. 154–179. A reprinting of "Ethan Brand." See D 77.

Reprinted from same plates with Philadelphia: J. B. Lippincott, n.d., imprint.

C 31 FAVORITE AUTHORS
1861

[Initial letters 'F' and 'A' red, balance of two words blue] Favorite Authors, | [red] A COMPANION-BOOK | [blue] OF | PROSE AND POETRY. | [red] My Books, my best companions. | [blue] FLETCHER. | BOSTON: | [red] TICKNOR AND FIELDS. | [blue] M DCCC LXI.

"Nathaniel Hawthorne: A Virtuoso's Collection," pp. [1]–20. *Reprint.* See D 44.

Reprinted 1866.

C 32 A TREASURY OF NEW FAVORITE TALES
1861

A TREASURY | [ornament] OF [ornament] | NEW FAVORITE TALES. | FOR YOUNG PEOPLE. | [vignette of children at churn with caption 'Teaching Towzer to Churn; See page 294.'] | [rule] | EDITED AND WRITTEN. | [ornament] BY [ornament] | MARY HOWITT. | WITH ILLUSTRATIONS BY PALMER & COLEMAN. | [rule] | LONDON; JAMES HOGG & SONS.

"The Chimaera—By Nathaniel Hawthorne," pp. 194–216. Extract reprinted from *The Wonder Book.* See A 18.1.

Locations: BM, 12804.c.40 (deposit-stamped 15 JA 61); CEFC.

C 33 AUTOGRAPH LEAVES OF OUR COUNTRY'S AUTHORS
1864

AUTOGRAPH LEAVES OF OUR COUNTRY'S AUTHORS. | [vignette of female warrior] | BALTIMORE, | CUSHINGS & BAILEY | 1864.

Announced in the 12 April 1864 *The Spirit of the Fair* for 19 April. Listed in the 16 April *American Literary Gazette.*

Three-page manuscript extract, slightly altered from "Earth's Holocaust," and signed and dated 16 February 1864, pp. 30–32. At the request of the editor, John P. Kennedy, in support of the Sanitary Commission Fair, Baltimore, 1864, Hawthorne wrote out this extract for facsimile reproduction in *Autograph Leaves.*

Locations: CEFC, MH, NN.

C 34 THE HIGH TIDE
1864

THE HIGH TIDE, | BY | JEAN INGELOW, | WITH | NOTICES OF HER POEMS. | [rule] | BOSTON: | ROBERTS BROTHERS, PUBLISHERS, | 143 WASHINGTON STREET. | 1864.

One-sentence comment by Hawthorne, p. 3, in notices section.

Promotional pamphlet, printed wrappers.

Location: CEFC.

C 35 ROSES AND HOLLY
1867

[all following within red rule border] ROSES AND HOLLY: | A GIFT-BOOK FOR ALL THE YEAR. | WITH ORIGINAL ILLUSTRATIONS | BY | *GOURLAY STEELL, R.S.A. SAMUEL BOUGH, A.R.S.A.* | *R. HERDMAN, R.S.A. JOHN MACWHIRTER.* | *CLARK STANTON, A.R.S.A. JOHN LAWSON.* | *AND OTHER EMINENT ARTISTS.* | *EN-GRAVED BY R. PATERSON.* | EDINBURGH: | WILLIAM P. NIMMO. | 1867.

"A Walk Through Vanity Fair, *Hawthorne*," p. 129. Extract reprinted from "The Celestial Rail-Road." See D 52.

C 36 GOOD STORIES, PART I
1867

GOOD STORIES. | PART I. | [rule] | [contents list with six titles] | BOSTON: | TICKNOR AND FIELDS. | 1867.

"Peter Goldthwaite's Treasure. *Nathaniel Hawthorne*," pp. [61]–82. *Reprint.* See A 2.2, B 1[2], C 10.

Printed wrappers.

Location: CEFC.

C 37 GOOD STORIES, PART III
1868

GOOD STORIES. | PART III. | [rule] | *CONTENTS.* | [contents list with six titles] | BOSTON: | TICKNOR AND FIELDS. | 1868.

"The Christmas Banquet. *Nathaniel Hawthorne,*" pp. [99]–118. *Reprint.* See D 56.

Printed wrappers.

C 38 YESTERDAYS WITH AUTHORS
1872

[red] YESTERDAYS WITH AUTHORS. | [black] BY | JAMES T. FIELDS. | [red] "Was it not yesterday we spoke together?"—SHAKESPEARE. | [black] [Osgood device] | BOSTON: | JAMES R. OSGOOD AND COMPANY, | LATE TICKNOR & FIELDS, AND FIELDS, OSGOOD, & CO. | 1872.

Announced in the 15 February 1872 *Publishers' and Stationers' Weekly Trade Circular* (New York) for 17 February. Listed in the 29 February *Weekly Trade Circular.* Copy received 20 February 1872 (Location: MH).

Previously unpublished Hawthorne material from letters and manuscripts, pp. [39]–124, including first publication of Hawthorne's candid description of President Lincoln cut from Hawthorne's "Chiefly About War-Matters" as published in the *Atlantic Monthly* (see D 87).

Reprinted by Osgood and, later, Houghton, Mifflin in "Illustrated" format. Also Hawthorne chapter, with a minor revision, published separately under the Boston: James R. Osgood, 1876, imprint in the *Vest-Pocket Series.*

C 39 PERSONAL REMINISCENCES
1874

Bric-a-Brac Series | [rule] | PERSONAL REMINISCENCES | BY | CHORLEY, PLANCHE, AND YOUNG | EDITED BY | RICHARD HENRY STODDARD | [cut of books] | NEW YORK | SCRIBNER, ARMSTRONG, AND COMPANY | 1874

Letter from Mrs. Hawthorne to Henry Chorley, with postscript by Hawthorne, Leamington, 5 March 1860, pp. 61–63.

C 40 CHILD LIFE IN PROSE
1874

CHILD LIFE IN PROSE. | EDITED BY | JOHN GREENLEAF WHITTIER. | Illustrated. | [vignette of children and dog] | BOSTON: | JAMES R. OSGOOD AND COMPANY, | LATE TICKNOR & FIELDS, AND FIELDS, OSGOOD, & CO. | 1874.

Deposited 29 October 1873. Listed in *Publishers' Weekly* for 25 October 1873.

"Little Annie's Ramble," pp. [13]–21. *Reprint.* See A 2.1, B 1[1], C 6.
   Also under London: The Book Society, n.d., imprint. Listed in the 31 January 1880 *Athenaeum.*

C 41 LITTLE CLASSICS MYSTERY
1875

[all following within red and black double-rules frame] Eighth Volume. | [rule] | [red] | LITTLE CLASSICS. | [black] EDITED BY | ROSSITER JOHNSON. | [red] MYSTERY. | [black] [four lines listing contents] | [red] BOSTON: | [black] JAMES R. OSGOOD AND COMPANY, | Late Ticknor & Fields, and Fields, Osgood, & Co. | 1875.

Listed in the 20 March 1875 *Publishers' Weekly.*

"The Birthmark," pp. [207]–231. *Reprint.* See A 15.1, B 1[4], D 50.

C 42 A STUDY OF HAWTHORNE
1876

[all following within red and black double-rules frame] A | [red] Study of Hawthorne. | [black] BY | GEORGE PARSONS LATHROP. | [vignette of Hawthorne's birthplace] | [red] BOSTON: | [black] JAMES R. OSGOOD AND COMPANY, | Late Ticknor & Fields, and Fields, Osgood, & Co. | [red] 1876.

Previously unpublished material from letters and manuscript, including first publication of Hawthorne's Latin theme "De Patribus Conscriptis Romanorum," pp. 338–339. See E 2.

2,000 copies printed 17 May 1876. Price $1.25, royalty 12.5¢. Uniform with the *"Little Classic Edition"* (see B 5). Reprinted in *The Riverside Pocket Series,* Boston and New York: Houghton, Mifflin, 1886.

C 43 BRYAN WALLER PROCTER
1877

BRYAN WALLER PROCTER | (BARRY CORNWALL). | AN | AUTOBIOGRAPHICAL FRAGMENT | AND | BIOGRAPHICAL NOTES, | WITH | PERSONAL SKETCHES OF CONTEMPORARIES, UNPUB- | LISHED LYRICS, AND LETTERS OF | LITERARY FRIENDS. | BOSTON: | ROBERTS BROTHERS. | 1877.

Letter from Hawthorne to Procter, Concord, Mass., 17 June 1852, pp. 296–298.

Location: CEFC.

C 44 NATHANIEL HAWTHORNE: AN ORATION
1878

NATHANIEL HAWTHORNE. | [ornament] | AN ORATION | DELIVERED BEFORE THE | ALUMNI OF BOWDOIN COLLEGE, | BRUNSWICK, MAINE, JULY 10, 1878, | BY | JOSEPH W. SYMONDS. | [ornament] | PORTLAND: | PUBLISHED BY THE ALUMNI. | 1878.

Excerpts from unlocated Hawthorne letters probably published elsewhere.

Pamphlet, cover title.

C 45 HAWTHORNE
1879

HAWTHORNE | BY | HENRY JAMES, JUNᴿ. | London | MACMILLAN AND CO | 1879 | *The Right of Translation and Reproduction is Reserved*

Excerpts from letters previously published elsehwere.

'English Men of Letters' Series. Reprinted 1883, 1887, 1902, 1909. New York Harpers edition has 1880 title-page imprint; reprinted as no. 133, 'Harper's Handy Series,' 1887 (wrappers), 1899.

C 46 FIFTY YEARS AMONG AUTHORS
1884

FIFTY YEARS | AMONG | AUTHORS, | BOOKS AND PUBLISHERS. | [rule] | J. C. DERBY. | [rule] | [two-line quote] | [rule] | [publisher's device] | NEW YORK: | COPYRIGHT, 1884, BY | *G. W. Carleton & Co., Publishers*. | LONDON: S. LOW, SON & CO. | MDCCCLXXXIV.

Letter from Hawthorne to S. G. Goodrich, Salem, 6 May 1830, p. 113.

C 47 NATHANIEL HAWTHORNE AND HIS WIFE
1884

[red] NATHANIEL HAWTHORNE | [black] AND HIS WIFE | A Biography | BY | [red] JULIAN HAWTHORNE | VOL. I. [VOL. II.] | [sepia-tinted vignette of Custom House] | [red] CAMBRIDGE | [black] Printed at the University Press | 1884.

2 vols.

Deposited 1 November 1884.

Previously unpublished material from letters and manuscripts.

Limited to 350 numbered copies in "Large-Paper" format (see B 10, note). Also trade printing (Boston: James R. Osgood, 1885): 3,000 copies each of 2 vols. printed 22 October 1884; second printing, 1000 copies, December 1884 (see B 9 [note one]). Sheets of the large-paper printing were used to custom-bind sets on special order. (Noted in a four-volume format with a personalized supplementary title page inserted in each volume and a signed Custom House document bound in [Location: CEFC]). Also noted in a custom-bound 6-vol. set with Hawthorne-related material bound in (Location: MHarF). Also under London: Chatto and Windus, 1885, imprint. 2 vols.

C 48 LIFE OF HENRY WADSWORTH LONGFELLOW
1886

LIFE | OF | HENRY WADSWORTH LONGFELLOW | *WITH EXTRACTS FROM HIS JOURNALS AND* | *CORRESPONDENCE* | EDITED BY | SAMUEL LONGFELLOW | VOL. I [VOL. II.] | [vignette of house] [II: vignette of porch steps] | BOSTON | TICK-NOR AND COMPANY | 1886

2 vols.

Deposited 13 March 1886.

Previously unpublished material from letters.

First printing, I: 332.34 reads 'Tamerlane'; corrected to '*Tamlane*' in later printings. II: 84.25 reads 'Paige's'; corrected to 'Page's' in later printings. II: 85.4 reads 'Paige'; corrected to "Page." Also 300 numbered copies of a large-paper printing with red and black title-page imprints; publisher's imprint: Boston: Ticknor and Company, MDCCCLXXXVI, with second-printing textual variants. 4,016 copies of first trade printing printed 27 February 1886, of which 1,012 copies in sheets were shipped to London for distribution by Kegan Paul. 315 large-paper format printed 14 April 1886, bound 20–22 April 1886. Also 25 copies of large-paper format shipped to Kegan Paul 20 April 1886.

C 49 HOMES AND HAUNTS OF THE POETS
1886

HOMES AND HAUNTS OF THE POETS | Original Etchings By W. B. CLOSSON |

Portrait,	*The Wayside,*
Autograph, HAWTHORNE	*Walk on the Hill,*
Old Manse.	*The Hemlocks,*

| PUBLISHED BY L. PRANG & CO., BOSTON. [device] COPYRIGHT, 1886, BY W. B. CLOSSON.

Facsimile fragment of Hawthorne letter, undated, plate [2].

Leatherette portfolio, goldstamped 'HAWTHORNE', containing loose cover sheet and six plate pages. Noted with stamping of Hawthorne's name in two styles.

C 50 DELIA BACON
1888

DELIA BACON | A BIOGRAPHICAL SKETCH | [seven-line quotation] | [publisher's device] | BOSTON AND NEW YORK | HOUGHTON, MIFFLIN AND COMPANY | The Riverside Press, Cambridge | 1888

Previously unpublished material from letters.

C 51 LIFE OF NATHANIEL HAWTHORNE
1890

LIFE | OF | NATHANIEL HAWTHORNE | BY | MONCURE D. CONWAY | [rule] | LONDON: | WALTER SCOTT, 24 WARWICK LANE | NEW YORK: 3 EAST 14TH STREET, | AND MELBOURNE

Previously unpublished material from letters. Includes bibliographical supplement by John P. Anderson.

Small paper edition: $6^7/8'' \times 4^3/4''$.

Reprinted with title page dated 1895. Also distributed as the "*12mo Edition*" in New York by A. Lovell. Also as *Library Edition,* large-paper format, with New York: Scribner & Welford, 1890, title-page imprint.

C 52 THE DIARY OF WILLIAM PYNCHON
1890

THE DIARY | OF | WILLIAM PYNCHON | OF SALEM | *A PICTURE OF SALEM LIFE,*
SOCIAL AND POLITICAL, A CENTURY AGO | EDITED BY | FITCH EDWARD OLIVER
| MEMBER OF THE MASSACHUSETTS HISTORICAL SOCIETY | [shield device] |
BOSTON AND NEW YORK | HOUGHTON, MIFFLIN AND COMPANY | The Riverside
Press, Cambridge | 1890

Letter from Hawthorne, Lenox, 3 May 1851, pp. viii–ix.

C 53 RECOLLECTIONS
1891

RECOLLECTIONS. | BY | GEORGE W. CHILDS. | "So runs the round of life from hour
to hour." | TENNYSON. | [device] | PHILADELPHIA: | J. B. LIPPINCOTT COMPANY. |
1891.

Excerpts from an undated letter from Hawthorne to Childs, p. 23.

C 54 PERSONAL RECOLLECTIONS
1893

PERSONAL RECOLLECTIONS | OF | NATHANIEL HAWTHORNE | BY | HORATIO
BRIDGE | PAYMASTER-GENERAL U. S. NAVY (RETIRED) | [seven-line quotation] |
ILLUSTRATED | NEW YORK | HARPER & BROTHERS PUBLISHERS | 1893

Deposited 15 April 1893.

Material from letters, most previously unpublished.

Published with printed dust jacket.

Three installments first printed in *Harper's Magazine* (D 107). Also under London:
Osgood, McIlvaine, [1893], imprint.

C 55 MEMORIES OF HAWTHORNE
1897

Memories of Hawthorne | By | Rose Hawthorne Lathrop | [publisher's device] |
BOSTON AND NEW YORK | HOUGHTON, MIFFLIN AND COMPANY | The Riverside
Press, Cambridge | 1897

Deposited 18 March 1897.

Previously unpublished material from letters and manuscript.

Also London: Kegan Paul, [1897], issue.

C 56 PASSAGES FROM THE CORRESPONDENCE OF RUFUS W.
GRISWOLD
1898

PASSAGES | FROM THE CORRESPONDENCE | AND OTHER PAPERS | OF | RUFUS

W. GRISWOLD. | *Noscitur a Sociis.* | [device] | CAMBRIDGE, MASS., | W. M. GRIS-
WOLD, | 1898.

Letters from Hawthorne to R. W. Griswold, Concord, 2 July 1843, and West Newton, 15
December 1851, pp. 144, 280.

C 57 NATHANIEL HAWTHORNE
1899

NATHANIEL HAWTHORNE | BY | ANNIE FIELDS | [publisher's device] | BOSTON |
SMALL, MAYNARD & COMPANY | MDCCCXCIX

Listed in *Publishers' Weekly* 18 November 1899.

Previously unpublished material from letters.

C 58 LITERARY FRIENDS AND ACQUAINTANCE
1900

LITERARY FRIENDS | AND | ACQUAINTANCE | *A PERSONAL RETROSPECT OF* |
AMERICAN AUTHORSHIP | BY W. D. HOWELLS | ILLUSTRATED | HARPER &
BROTHERS PUBLISHERS | NEW YORK AND LONDON | 1900

Deposited 17 November 1900. Also, sheets of the trade edition used to produce an
'*Autograph Edition*' limited to 150 copies with a certificate of limitation signed by
Howells inserted at the front.

Excerpts from conversations with Hawthorne.

C 59 GAIL HAMILTON'S LIFE IN LETTERS
1901

[all following within single-rule frame divided by horizontal rules as indicated] GAIL
HAMILTON'S | LIFE IN LETTERS | [rule] | EDITED BY | H. AUGUSTA DODGE | [rule]
| *VOLUME I.* | [rule] | [shield device] | [rule] | BOSTON | LEE AND SHEPARD |
MCMI

Excerpts from conversations with Hawthorne.

C 60 STORIES OF AUTHORS' LOVES
1902

[red] Stories of | Authors' Loves | [black] [rule] | BY CLARA E. LAUGHLIN | [rule] |
WITH FORTY-FIVE PHOTOGRAVURE AND | *DUOGRAVURE REPRODUCTIONS OF* |
PORTRAITS AND VIEWS | VOL. I. [VOL. II.] | [red ornament] | [black] PHILADELPHIA
| J. B. LIPPINCOTT COMPANY | MCMII

2 vols.

Excerpts from Hawthorne letters published elsewhere.

C 61 NATHANIEL HAWTHORNE
1902

American Men of Letters | [rule] | NATHANIEL HAWTHORNE | BY | GEORGE E.

WOODBERRY | [Riverside device] | BOSTON AND NEW YORK | HOUGHTON, MIF-
FLIN AND COMPANY | The Riverside Press, Cambridge | 1902

Deposited 10 September 1902. Trade edition advertised for *"to-day"* in 20 September
1902 *Publishers' Weekly.*

Previously unpublished material from letters.

Trade printing. Also 100 special copies, with statement on copyright page: *'Of the first
edition One Hundred Copies have been* | *printed and bound entirely uncut with paper
label'* (Location: CEFC). Also *"Large-Paper Edition"* of 600 numbered copies on laid
paper, boxed and uniform with the *Large-Paper (Autograph) Edition* (see B 21) (Location: CEFC). Also London: Gay & Bird, [1902], edition.

C 62 HAWTHORNE AND HIS CIRCLE
1903

HAWTHORNE | AND HIS CIRCLE | BY | JULIAN HAWTHORNE | ILLUSTRATED |
[device] | NEW YORK AND LONDON | HARPER & BROTHERS | PUBLISHERS 1903

Published October 1903. Deposited 8 October 1903.

Julian Hawthorne quotes conversations with his father.

C 63 GEORGE PALMER PUTNAM
1903

[title-page type inside three red-ruled blocks all contained within black-ruled outer
border; inside top red-ruled block:] A Memoir of | George Palmer Putnam | Together
with a Record of the Publishing | House founded by Him | [inside middle red-ruled
block:] By | George Haven Putnam | [rule] | *Privately Printed* | Volume I | [inside
bottom red-ruled block:] G. P. PUTNAM's SONS | New York and London | 1903

2 vols.

Letter from Hawthorne to Geo. P. Morris, January 1839, I, p. 338.

New Putnam edition 1912.

C 64 THE HAWTHORNE CENTENARY AT SALEM
1904

THE | [red] PROCEEDINGS | [black] IN COMMEMORATION OF | THE ONE HUN-
DREDTH ANNIVERSARY | OF THE BIRTH OF | [red] NATHANIEL HAWTHORNE |
[black] HELD AT | SALEM, MASSACHUSETTS | JUNE 23, 1904 | [sepia vignette of
Hawthorne's birthplace] | SALEM, MASS. | [red] THE ESSEX INSTITUTE | 1904

Previously unpublished material from letters and manuscript.

C 65 HAWTHORNE AND HIS FRIENDS
1908

HAWTHORNE AND HIS FRIENDS | REMINISCENCE AND TRIBUTE | BY F. B. SAN-

BORN | [torch symbol] | THE TORCH PRESS | CEDAR RAPIDS, IOWA | NINETEEN EIGHT

Previously unpublished material from letters.

C 66 MEMOIRS AND SERVICES
1909

MEMOIRS AND SERVICES | OF | THREE GENERATIONS | [rule] GENERAL JOSEPH CILLEY | First New Hampshire Line. War of the Revolution | JONATHAN LONGFEL-LOW | Father of Sarah, wife of General Joseph Cilley | [rule] | COLONEL JOSEPH CILLEY | U.S. Senator and Officer in the War of 1812 | HONORABLE JONATHAN CILLEY | Member of Congress from Maine | [rule] COMMANDER GREENLEAF CILLEY | War with Mexico and War of 1861 | GENERAL JONATHAN P. CILLEY | First Maine Cavalry, War of the Rebellion | [rule] | REPRINT FROM THE COURIER-GA-ZETTE | [rule] | ROCKLAND, MAINE | 1909

Truncated version of Hawthorne's tribute to Cilley, pp. 9–10. *Reprint.* See A 1.2, D 39.

C 67 THE PAPERS OF FRANKLIN PIERCE
1917

LIBRARY OF CONGRESS | [rule] | CALENDAR | OF THE PAPERS OF | FRANKLIN PIERCE | PREPARED FROM THE ORIGINAL MANUSCRIPTS | IN THE LIBRARY OF CONGRESS | BY W. L. LEECH | | WASHINGTON | GOVERNMENT PRINTING OF-FICE | 1917

Paraphrased Hawthorne letters, pp. 60, 69, 70.

C 68 MEMORIES OF A HOSTESS
1922

MEMORIES OF A HOSTESS | A CHRONICLE OF | EMINENT FRIENDSHIPS | DRAWN CHIEFLY FROM THE DIARIES OF | MRS. JAMES T. FIELDS | BY | M. A. DeWOLFE HOWE | [two-line quotation] | [seal] | *WITH ILLUSTRATIONS* | THE ATLANTIC MONTHLY PRESS | BOSTON

Previously unpublished material from letters.

C 69 HAWTHORNE'S SPECTATOR
1931

HAWTHORNE'S | *SPECTATOR* | EDITED BY ELIZABETH L. CHANDLER | [Reprint from THE NEW ENGLAND QUARTERLY, Volume IV, Number 2, 1931] | COPYRIGHT 1931 BY THE SOUTHWORTH PRESS

Hawthorne's *Spectator.* See E 1.

Printed wrappers.

C 70 HAWTHORNE AND POLITICS
1932

HAWTHORNE AND POLITICS | UNPUBLISHED LETTERS | TO WILLIAM B. PIKE | EDITED BY RANDALL STEWART | [Reprint from THE NEW ENGLAND QUARTERLY, Volume V, Number 2, 1932] | COPYRIGHT 1932 BY THE SOUTHWORTH PRESS

Previously unpublished material from letters.

Printed wrappers.

C 71 HAWTHORNE GOSSIPS ABOUT SALEM
1933

HAWTHORNE GOSSIPS | ABOUT SALEM | E. B. HUNGERFORD | [Reprint from THE NEW ENGLAND QUARTERLY, Volume VI, Number 3, 1933] | COPYRIGHT 1933 BY THE SOUTHWORTH PRESS

Transcribed letters from Hawthorne to John S. Dike.

Printed wrappers.

C 72 ON HAWTHORNE'S AUTHORSHIP OF "THE BATTLE-OMEN"
1936

[Reprinted from THE NEW ENGLAND QUARTERLY, Volume IX, Number 4, 1936] | ON HAWTHORNE'S AUTHORSHIP OF "THE | BATTLE-OMEN" | DONALD CLIFFORD GALLUP | [text follows on rest of page]

Prints text of "The Battle-Omen." See G 3.

Pamphlet, title over text.

C 73 NATHANIEL HAWTHORNE AND THE MARINE MUSEUM
OF THE SALEM EAST INDIA MARINE SOCIETY
1946

Club of Odd Volumes edition

NATHANIEL HAWTHORNE | AND THE | MARINE MUSEUM | OF THE | SALEM EAST INDIA MARINE SOCIETY | OR | THE GATHERING OF A VIRTUOSO'S | COLLECTION | BY | CHARLES E. GOODSPEED | [Club of Odd Volumes seal] | *Printed for the Members of* | THE CLUB OF ODD VOLUMES | BOSTON | 1946

Facsimile reproduction of page from East India Marine Society Visitor's Book bearing Hawthorne's signature, p. 8, and facsimile pp. [193]–200 from *Boston Miscellany,* I (May 1842), where Hawthorne's "A Virtuoso's Collection" was first published. See D 44.

Limited to 99 numbered copies.

Peabody Museum edition

Nathaniel Hawthorne | AND | The Museum of the | Salem East India Marine Society | OR | *The Gathering of a Virtuoso's Collection* | BY | *CHARLES E. GOODSPEED* | PEABODY MUSEUM | SALEM, MASSACHUSETTS | 1946

A new edition manufactured in part by salvaging and rearranging large portions of the standing type used to print the Odd Volumes text. Facsimile portions preserved without change. Printed wrappers.

C 74 THE ORIGIN AND DEVELOPMENT OF LONGFELLOW'S "EVANGELINE"
1947

The Origin and Development | of | LONGFELLOW'S "EVANGELINE" | By | MANNING HAWTHORNE | & | HENRY WADSWORTH LONGFELLOW DANA | [tree ornament] | THE ANTHOENSEN PRESS | PORTLAND, MAINE | 1947

Material from previously unpublished letters.

Printed wrappers. Reprinted from the *Papers of the Bibliographical Society of America*, 41, 3 (1947).

C 75 NATHANIEL HAWTHORNE: A BIOGRAPHY
1948

Nathaniel Hawthorne | *A BIOGRAPHY* | BY | RANDALL STEWART | NEW HAVEN | YALE UNIVERSITY PRESS | LONDON • GEOFFREY CUMBERLEGE • OXFORD UNIVERSITY PRESS | 1948

Previously unpublished material from letters.

C 76 NATHANIEL HAWTHORNE: THE AMERICAN YEARS
1948

Nathaniel Hawthorne | [rule] THE AMERICAN YEARS | *by Robert Cantwell* | RINEHART & COMPANY, INC. | NEW YORK • TORONTO

LC deposited 2 September 1948.

Previously unpublished material from letters.

C 77 HAWTHORNE'S LAST PHASE
1949

Hawthorne's Last Phase | BY | EDWARD HUTCHINS DAVIDSON | NEW HAVEN | YALE UNIVERSITY PRESS | LONDON • GEOFFREY CUMBERLEGE • OXFORD UNIVERSITY PRESS | 1949

Published 9 March 1949.

Material from previously unpublished manuscript.

C 78 THE PEABODY SISTERS OF SALEM
1950

[all following within double-rules frame] The Peabody Sisters | *of Salem* | [rule] | *by* | *LOUISE HALL THARP* | [rule] | [publisher's device] | WITH ILLUSTRATIONS | [rule] | Little, Brown and Company • *Boston* | *1950*

Previously unpublished material from letters.

Also under London, Sydney, Toronto, Bombay: George G. Harrap, [1951], imprint.

C 79 THE HAWTHORNES
1951

The story of seven generations of | an American family | *THE HAWTHORNES* | [rule] | *By Vernon Loggins* | [rule] | *New York* | *COLUMBIA UNIVERSITY PRESS* | *1951*

Previously unpublished material from letters.

C 80 HAWTHORNE'S TWO "ENGAGEMENTS"
1963

THE SOPHIA SMITH COLLECTION | [title within ornamental-type panel] HAWTHORNE'S TWO "ENGAGEMENTS" | BY NORMAN HOLMES PEARSON | SMITH COLLEGE, NORTHAMPTON, MASSACHUSETTS | APRIL 1963

Excerpts from conversations with Hawthorne.

Printed wrappers.

C 81 THE PYNCHONS AND JUDGE PYNCHEON
1964

THE PYNCHONS | AND | JUDGE PYNCHEON | BY | NORMAN HOLMES PEARSON | Reprinted from | Essex Institute Historical Collections | October, 1964

Previously unpublished material from letters.

Printed wrappers.

C 82 A "GOOD THING" FOR HAWTHORNE
1964

A "GOOD THING" | FOR | HAWTHORNE | BY | NORMAN HOLMES PEARSON | Reprinted from | Essex Institute Historical Collections | October, 1964

Previously unpublished material from letters.

Printed wrappers.

C 83 NATHANIEL HAWTHORNE: POEMS
1967

Nathaniel Hawthorne | [red] POEMS | [black] Edited by Richard E. Peck

Published 1967 by The Bibliographical Society of the University of Virginia.

Various poems. See H 2, H 8–H 16, H 28–H 30, H 33–H 37.

C 84 THE NATHANIEL HAWTHORNE JOURNAL
1971

THE | NATHANIEL | HAWTHORNE | JOURNAL | 1971 | C. E. Frazer Clark, Jr., Editor | *Consulting Editor: Matthew J. Bruccoli* | University of South Carolina | NCR Microcard Editions

Published in Washington, D.C., 4 July 1971.

Includes the following previously unpublished material:
   Facsimile of Hawthorne's signature, on free front endpaper.
   Facsimile of letter from Hawthorne to Caleb Foote, Boston, 31 August 1840, pp. 2, 6.
   Arlin Turner, "Hawthorne and Longfellow: Abortive Plans for Collaboration," pp. 3–11. Material from previously unpublished letters.
   Facsimile of letter from Hawthorne to Caleb Foote, Boston, 17 January 1842, p. 8.
   Facsimile of Hawthorne inscription, p. 28.
   Francis Bennoch, "A Week's Vagabondage with Hawthorne," pp. 33–45. Quotes conversations with Hawthorne.
   C. E. Frazer Clark, Jr., " 'The Interrupted Nuptials,' A Question of Attribution," pp. 49–66. Prints text of attributed tale. Quotes from previously unpublished material.
   Letter from Hawthorne to Longfellow, Salem, 14 October 1846, p. 71.
   C. E. Frazer Clark, Jr., "Hawthorne to 'Mr. Ex-Cardinal'," pp. 72–76. Includes Geo. H. Holden's transcript of Hawthorne's letter to H. L. Conolly, Lenox, 17 June 1850.
   B. Bernard Cohen, "Hawthorne's Library: An Approach to the Man and His Mind," pp. 125–139. Quotes inscriptions and letters.
   Facsimile of "The Carriers Address" ["Time's Portraiture"], as printed in *Salem Gazette*, New Series XVI, LII (2 January 1838), p. 191. *First book appearance.*

C 85 THE NATHANIEL HAWTHORNE JOURNAL
1972

THE | NATHANIEL | HAWTHORNE | JOURNAL | 1972 | C. E. Frazer Clark, Jr., Editor | NCR Microcard Editions

Published in Washington, D.C., March 1973.

Includes the following previously unpublished material:
   Facsimile of Hawthorne's inscription to Maria L. Hawthorne, on free front endpaper.
   Facsimile of letter from Hawthorne to Samuel M. Cleveland, Concord, 8 January 1863, pp. 1–5. *First publication of complete text.*
   Undated fragment of Hawthorne letter, pp. 8–9.
   John J. McDonald, "The Old Manse Period Canon," pp. 13–39. Previously unpublished material from journals and letters.
   Facsimile of letter from Hawthorne to Samuel Colman, Concord, 20 July 1843, p. 26.

C. E. Frazer Clark, Jr., "New Light on the Editing of the 1842 Edition of *Twice-Told Tales:* Discovery of a Family Copy of the 1833 *Token* Annotated by Hawthorne," pp. 91–139. Facsimile of annotated text.

Facsimile of letter from Hawthorne to Joseph B. Boyd, Salem, 18 January 1838, p. 142.

Facsimile of Bowdoin College matriculation record, signed by Hawthorne, p. 150.

Facsimile of inscription in Hawthorne's hand on his copy of *The Vicar of Wakefield,* p. 155.

C 86 HAWTHORNE AT AUCTION
1972

HAWTHORNE | *AT* | *AUCTION* | *1984–1971* | Edited by | C. E. Frazer Clark, Jr. | With an Appendix by Matthew J. Bruccoli | [Bruccoli Clark logo] A Bruccoli [diamond symbol] Clark Book | Gale Research Company, Book Tower, Detroit

Facsimiles and transcriptions of material from previously unpublished letters, manuscripts, inscriptions.

C 87 THE NATHANIEL HAWTHORNE JOURNAL
1973

THE | NATHANIEL | HAWTHORNE | JOURNAL | 1973 | C. E. Frazer Clark, Jr., Editor | [Indian head logo] Microcard Editions Books | A Division of Information Handling Services | Denver Technological Center | 5500 South Valentia Way | Englewood, Colorado 80110

Published in Denver, Colorado, February 1974.

Includes the following previously unpublished material:

Facsimile of Hawthorne inscription to H. W. Longfellow, on free front endpaper.

Facsimile of letter from Hawthorne to William B. Pike, Lenox, 2 September 1851, pp. 1, 3.

Facsimile of signed Custom House document, p. 5.

Facsimile of Horatio Bridge's manuscript of Hawthorne's poem, "Moonlight," p. 26.

Arthur Monke and C. E. Frazer Clark, Jr., "Hawthorne's 'Moonlight'," pp. 27–34. *First book publication* of "The Battle Ground," attributed to Hawthorne. See H 20. In facsimile.

Allen Flint, *"Nathaniel Hawthorne: Poems,"* a review, pp. 255–260. *First book publication* of "The Marriage Ring." See H 24. In facsimile.

C 88 THE NATHANIEL HAWTHORNE JOURNAL
1974

THE | NATHANIEL | HAWTHORNE | JOURNAL | 1974 | C. E. Frazer Clark, Jr., Editor | [Indian head logo] Microcard Editions Books | An Indian Head Company | A Division of Information Handling Services

Published in Denver, Colorado, 4 July 1975.

Includes the following previously unpublished material:

Facsimile of Hawthorne inscription to Grace Greenwood, on free front endpaper.

John J. McDonald, ed., "A Sophia Hawthorne Journal, 1843–1844," pp. 1–30. Records conversations with her husband.

Wayne Allen Jones, "New Light on Hawthorne and the *Southern Rose*," pp. 31–46. Material from previously unpublished letters.

Facsimile of letter from Hawthorne to Mrs. Caroline Gilman, Salem, 25 September 1837, pp. 32, 34.

Raymona E. Hull, "Bennoch and Hawthorne," pp. 48–74. Material from previously unpublished letters.

Facsimile of undated fragment of Hawthorne letter, p. 61.

Facsimile of letter from Hawthorne to James T. Fields, Wayside, 18 April 1863, pp. 92, 94.

Jerome Klinkowitz, "The Hawthorne-Fields Letterbook: A Census and Description," pp. 93–103. Census includes a brief description of the contents of each Hawthorne letter.

C 89 THE NATHANIEL HAWTHORNE JOURNAL
    1975

THE | NATHANIEL | HAWTHORNE | JOURNAL | 1975 | C. E. Frazer Clark, Jr., Editor | [Indian head logo] | Microcard Editions Books | An Indian Head Company | A Division of Information Handling Services

Published in Denver, Colorado, 15 December 1975.

Includes the following previously unpublished material:

Facsimile of Hawthorne inscription to C. B. Davis, on free front endpaper.

Facsimile of letter from Hawthorne to Miss L. Jewett, 4 February 1850, p. 2.

Wayne Allen Jones, "Sometimes Things Just Don't Work Out: Hawthorne's Income from *Twice-Told Tales*," pp. 11–26. Material from previously unpublished letters.

Facsimile of manuscript leaf from Hawthorne's 1839 'Scrap-Book', pp. 27, 29.

Raymona E. Hull, " 'Scribbling' Females and Serious Males: Hawthorne's Comments from Abroad on Some American Authors," pp. 35–58. Material from previously unpublished letters.

Wayne Allen Jones, "The Hawthorne-Goodrich Relationship and a New Estimate of Hawthorne's Income from *The Token*," pp. 91–140. Material from previously unpublished letters.

D. First-Appearance Contributions to Magazines and Newspapers

First American and English publication in magazines and newspapers of material by Hawthorne, arranged chronologically. Selected reprintings up through 1850 are noted to show the exposure and spread of Hawthorne's name and work prior to the publication of *The Scarlet Letter*.

D1

"The Ocean," *Salem Gazette,* New Series III, XXXIX (26 August 1825), 1.

Verse. Signed with the initials "C. W." See C4, C9, D2, H19. Earliest located newspaper publication of Hawthorne's work.

Note: Material by Hawthorne, presumably verse, appeared in newspapers as early as 1819 according to a reference in a letter to his sister Maria Louisa dated Salem, Tuesday, 28 September 1819: "Tell Ebe [sister Elizabeth] she's not the only one of the family whose works have appeared in the papers." See *Hawthorne and His Wife,* I, 106 (C47). The work Hawthorne refers to has not been located. An article in the [*New England?*] *Palladium* on an insect attacking fruit trees published during Hawthorne's college years, possibly 1822, is credited to Hawthorne by a contemporary. See *Salem Gazette* (7 January 1887), p. 2. See also Kate Tannatt Woods, "Hawthorne's First Printed Article," *Magazine of American History,* XXIII (March 1890), 237–240.

D2

"The Ocean," *The Garland; or New General Repository of Fugitive Poetry,* I (August 1825), 44.

Verse. *Reprinted* "From the Salem Gazette." See C4, C9, D1, H19. Earliest located magazine publication of Hawthorne's work.

D3

"The Battle-Omen," *Salem Gazette,* New Series VIII, XLIV 88 (2 November 1830), 1.

Unsigned, attributed. See C72.

Reprinted in *The Daily Chronicle* (Philadelphia), III, 265, Whole No. 806 (8 November 1830), 1. In *Lowell Journal* (Lowell, Mass.), V, 37 (10 November 1830), 1.

D4

"The Hollow of the Three Hills," *Salem Gazette,* New Series VIII, XLIV, 91 (12 November 1830), 1.

Unsigned. See A2.1. See illustration.

Reprinted in *Lowell Journal* (Lowell, Mass.), V, 41 (8 December 1830), 1. No attribution. In *Ladies Cabinet of Fashion, Music, and Romance* (London), XVI (July 1839), 53–57. Titled "The Hag of the Hollow." In *The Metropolitan Magazine* (London), LIV (January–April 1849), 78–82. "By Nathaniel Hawthorne."

D5

"Sir William Phips," *Salem Gazette,* New Series VIII, XLIV, 94 (23 November 1830), 1–2.

Unsigned. See A1.2.a, B5[XXII].

411

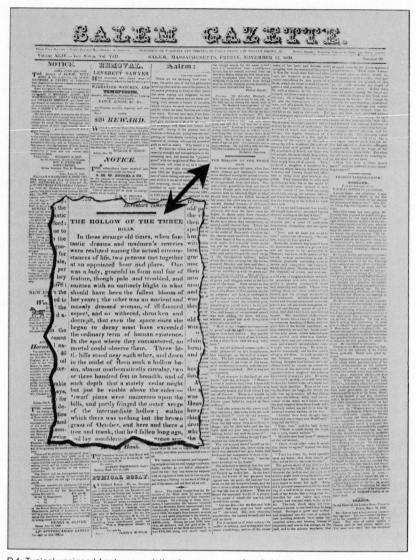

D 4: Typical unsigned front-page printing in newspaper of early Hawthorne tale

D 6

"Mrs. Hutchinson," *Salem Gazette,* New Series VIII, XLIV, 98 (7 December 1830), 4.

Unsigned. See A 1.2.a, B 5[XXII].

D 7

"An Old Woman's Tale," *Salem Gazette,* New Series VIII, XLIV, 102 (21 December 1830), 1–2.

Unsigned. See A 30.1.a.

D 8

"Dr. Bullivant," *Salem Gazette,* New Series IX, LXV, 3 (11 January 1831), 1–2.

Unsigned. See B 5[XXIII].

D 9

"The Story Teller. No. I," *New-England Magazine,* VII (November 1834), 352–358.

Unsigned. Includes interior segments titled "At Home," "A Flight in the Fog," and "A Fellow-Traveller." See A 15.3.a, where these stories are collected with selections from "The Story Teller. No. II" under the title "Passages from a Relinquished Work."

D 10

"The Story Teller. No. II," *New-England Magazine,* VII (December 1834), 449–459.

Unsigned. Includes interior segments titled "The Village Theatre," "Mr. Higginbotham's Catastrophe," and an untitled conclusion. See A 15.3.a, where all but "Mr. Higginbotham's Catastrophe" (see A 2.1), together with "The Story Teller. No. I," are collected under the title "Passages from a Relinquished Work."

"Mr. Higginbotham's Catastrophe" is collected in A 2.1 as a separate tale without the opening and concluding framework of "The Story Teller" and reprinted in *The Essex Gazette* (Haverhill, Mass.), XI, 7 (13 August 1836), 1. No attribution. In *Essex Register* (Salem), XXXVI, 66 (18 August 1836), 1. "From the New England Magazine." In *Lloyd's Penny Weekly Miscellany of Romance and General Interest* (London), V (1846), 571–573. No attribution. In *The Metropolitan Magazine* (London), LIII (September–December 1848), 374–384. "By Nathaniel Hawthorne, Esq."

D 11

"The Gray Champion," *New-England Magazine,* VIII (January 1835), 20–26.

Signed "By the Author of 'The Gentle Boy'." See A 2.1.

Reprinted in *Essex Register* (Salem), XXXV, 5 (15 January 1835), 1. "From the N. E. Magazine. By the Author of 'The Gentle Boy'." In *American Traveller* (Boston), X, 62 (30 January 1835), 4. "By the author of 'The Gentle Boy'." In *The Salem Observer,* XV, 15 (15 April 1837), 1. "From *Twice-Told Tales,* by Hawthorne." In *New-York Mirror,* XVI, 35 (23 February 1839), 1–2. "By Nathaniel Hawthorne." In *The Lowell Courier* (Lowell, Mass.), V, 645 (7 March 1839), 1–2. "By Nathaniel Hawthorne. From the New York Mirror." In *Exeter News-Letter and Rockingham County Advertiser* (New Hampshire), VIII, 50 (9 April 1839), 1. "By Nathaniel Hawthorne. From the New York Mirror."

D 12

"Old News. No. I," *New-England Magazine,* VIII (February 1835), [81]–88.

Unsigned. See A 19.1.a.

D 13

"My Visit to Niagara," *New-England Magazine,* VIII (February 1835), 91–96.

Signed "By the Author of 'The Gray Champion'." See B 20[XVII].

D 14

"Old News. No. II. The Old French War," *New-England Magazine,* VIII (March 1835), 170–178.

Unsigned. See A 19.1.a.

D 15

"Young Goodman Brown," *New-England Magazine,* VIII (April 1835), 249–260.

Signed "By the Author of 'The Gray Champion'." See A 15.1.a₁.

D 16

"Old News. No. III. The Old Tory," *New-England Magazine,* VIII (May 1835), 365–370.

Unsigned. See A 19.1.a.

D 17

"Wakefield," *New-England Magazine,* VIII (May 1835), 341–347.

Signed "By the Author of 'The Gray Champion'." See A 2.1.

D 18

"The Ambitious Guest," *New-England Magazine,* VIII, (June 1835), 425–431.

Signed "By the Author of 'The Gray Champion'." See A 2.3₁.

Reprinted in the *Essex Register* (Salem), XXXV, 45 (4 June 1835), 1–2. In *Salem Advertiser* (June 1835). In *Ladies Cabinet of Fashion, Music, and Romance* (London), IX, V (May 1836), 273–280. Unsigned.

D 19

"Graves and Goblins," *New-England Magazine,* VIII (June 1835), 438–444.

Unsigned. See B 5[XXIII].

D 20

"A Rill from the Town-Pump," *New-England Magazine,* VIII (June 1835), 473–478.

Unsigned. See A 2.1, B 1[1], C 15, C 17.

Reprinted in *Daily Evening Transcript* (Boston), VI (9 June 1835), 1. In *Worcester Palladium* (Mass.), II, 24 (17 June 1835), 1. In *Franklin Mercury* (Greenfield, Mass.), II, 43 (23 June 1835), 1. In *Old Colony Memorial* (Plymouth, Mass.), XIV, 12 (4 July 1835), 1. In *Athenaeum* (London), 413 (26 September 1835), 728. Under excerpts from the *New-England Magazine.* (See C. E. Frazer Clark, "Hawthorne's First Appearance in England," *CEAA Newsletter,* 3 [June 1970], 10–11.) In *Essex Register* (Salem), XXXVII, 22 (16 March 1837), 1. "By Nathaniel Hawthorne." In *Evening Mercury* (Salem), IX, 11 (18 September 1839), 1. As "The Town Pump." In *The Madisonian* (Washington City), IV, 123, Whole No. 674 (7 August 1841), 1. "By Nathaniel Hawthorne." In *Supplement to the Courant* (Hartford), VI, 46 (2 October 1841), 362. With a headnote from the *New London Advocate.* In *National Anti-Slavery Standard* (New York), III, 5, Whole No. 109 (7 July 1842), 20. "From the Concord *Republican.*" In *Massachusetts Cataract,* VI, 16 (6 July 1848), 1. "By Nathaniel Hawthorne. From the *New England Magazine.*"

D 21

"The Old Maid in the Winding Sheet," *New-England Magazine,* IX (July 1835), 8–16.

Signed "By the Author of 'The Gray Champion'." See A 2.3₁, where it is collected under the title "The White Old Maid."

Reprinted in *The Salem Observer,* XIII, 29 (18 July 1835), 1. "From the New England Magazine." In *The New Yorker* magazine, VII, I, Whole No. 157 (23 March 1839), 5–6. "By the Author of 'Twice-Told Tales'." *The New-Yorker* newspaper, VI, 1, Whole No. 261 (23 March 1839), 4. "By the Author of 'Twice-Told Tales'." In *Essex Register*

(Salem), XXXIX, 37 (9 May 1839), 1–2. "By N. Hawthorne." In *Arcturus, A Journal of Books and Opinon* (New York), III, 14 (January 1842), 120–130. "By Nathaniel Hawthorne."

D 22

"The Vision of the Fountain," *New-England Magazine,* IX (August 1835), 99–104.

Signed "By the Author of 'The Gray Champion'." See A 2.1.

Reprinted in *Salem Gazette,* New Series XV, LI, 23 (21 March 1837), 1. "By N. Hawthorne." In *New-York Mirror,* XV, 44 (28 April 1838), 1–2.

D 23

"Sketches from Memory. By a Pedestrian. No. I," *New-England Magazine,* IX (November 1835), 321–326.

Unsigned. Includes interior segments titled "The Notch," "Our Evening Party Among the Mountains." See A 15.3.a, where the stories are collected with "Sketches from Memory. By a Pedestrian. No. II" under omnibus title "Sketches from Memory."

D 24

"The Devil in Manuscript," *New-England Magazine,* IX (November 1835), 340–345.

Signed "By Ashley A. Royce." See A 19.1.a.

D 25

"Sketches from Memory. By a Pedestrian. No. II," *New-England Magazine,* IX (December 1835), 398–409.

Unsigned. Includes interior segments titled "The Canal-Boat," "The Inland Port," "Rochester," "An Afternoon Scene," "A Night Scene." See A 15.3.a., where the stories are collected with "Sketches from Memory. By a Pedestrian. No. I" under omnibus title "Sketches from Memory."

An extract reprinted in *The Metropolitan,* I, 45 (11 December 1835), 1.

D 26

"Old Ticonderoga. A Picture of the Past," *The American Monthly Magazine,* VII (February 1836), 138–142.

Unsigned. See A 19.1.a.

D 27

"*The Outcast,* and other Poems; by S. G. Goodrich," *Boston Daily Atlas* (23 February 1836), p. 2, col. 3.

Review signed with the initial "H."

Note: Goodrich wrote Hawthorne 17 February [1836] (Location: MeB) enclosing two copies of *The Outcast* suggesting that if Hawthorne would write a review of the book, the *Atlas* would publish it. The second copy Hawthorne was instructed to turn over to the editor of the *Salem Gazette,* where the book was also reviewed (26 Feburary 1836), but not, apparently, by Hawthorne.

D 28

"The Fountain of Youth," *Knickerbocker, or New-York Monthly Magazine,* IX, 1 (January 1837), 27–33.

Unsigned. See A 2.1, where it is collected as "Dr. Heidegger's Experiment."

Reprinted in *The Metropolitan Magazine* (London), LIV (January–April 1849), 179–187. Titled "The Fountain of Youth."

D 29
"A Bell's Biography," *Knickerbocker, or New-York Monthly Magazine*, IX, 3 (March 1837), 219–223.

Signed "By the author of *Twice-told Tales*, 'The Fountain of Youth,' etc." See A 19.1.a.

Reprinted in *The New-Yorker* magazine, II, 26, Whole No. 52 (18 March 1837), 405–406. "By the author of 'Twice-Told Tales,' &c." In *Essex Register* (Salem), XXXVII, 23 (20 March 1837), 1–2. "By the author of 'Twice-Told Tales,' 'A Rill from the Town-Pump,' Etc." In *The Boston Daily Times*, III, 344 (23 March 1837), 1, and III, 345 (24 March 1837), 1. "By the author of 'Twice-Told Tales,' 'A Rill from the Town Pump,' etc." In *Worcester Palladium* (Mass.), IV, 13 (29 March 1837), 1. "By the author of 'Twice-Told Tales,' 'A Rill from the Town Pump,' Etc."

D 30
"Edward Fane's Rosebud," *Knickerbocker, or New-York Monthly Magazine*, X, 3 (September 1837), 195–199.

Unsigned. See A 2.3₁.

Reprinted in *American Traveller* (Boston), XIII, 26 (29 September 1837), 4. No attribution. In *Salem Gazette*, New Series XVI, LII, 3 (9 January 1838), 1. In *Salem Gazette*, Tri-Weekly Series II, 72 (17 June 1848), 1–2. "By Nathaniel Hawthorne."

D 31
"The Toll-Gatherer's Day. A Sketch of Transitory Life," *United States Magazine and Democratic Review*, I, 1 (October 1837), 31–35.

Signed "By the Author of Twice-told Tales." See A 2.3₁.

Reprinted in *The Salem Observer*, XV, 44 (4 November 1837), 1–2. "A Sketch of Transitory Life. By the Author of 'Twice-Told Tales'." In *American Traveller* (Boston), XIII, 45 (5 December 1837), 4. "By the author of 'Twice-Told Tales'." In *Salem Gazette*, New Series XVII, LIII, 31 [i.e., 35] (30 April 1839), 1, 4. "A Sketch of Transitory Life. By the Author of 'Twice-Told Tales'."

D 32
"Foot-Prints on the Sea-Shore," *United States Magazine and Democratic Review*, I, 2 (January 1838), 190–197.

Signed "By the Author of 'Twice-Told-Tales'." See A 2.3₁.

Reprinted in *The New-Yorker* magazine, IV, 19, Whole No. 97 (27 January 1838), 709–710. In *The Southern Rose*, VI, 19 (12 May 1838), 298–302. "By the Author of 'Twice-Told Tales'." In *Western Messenger*, V, 4 (July 1838), 248–256. "By the Author of 'Twice-Told Tales'."

D 33
"Thomas Green Fessenden," *The American Monthly Magazine*, V (January 1838), [30]–41.

Signed "By Nathaniel Hawthorne." See A 1.2.a, B 5 [XXII].

Reprinted in *The New-Yorker* magazine, IV, 16, Whole No. 94 (6 January 1838), 660–662. "By Nathaniel Hawthorne. From the American Monthly for January." In *Essex*

Register (Salem), XXXVIII, 8 (25 January 1838), 1–2, and 9 (29 January 1838), 1. "By Nathaniel Hawthorne. From the American Monthly for January." In *Evening Gazette* (Boston), XXVI (30 January 1838), 1. "By Nathaniel Hawthorne." In *National Aegis* (Worcester, Mass.), I, 2 (31 January 1838), 1. "By Nathaniel Hawthorne. From the American Monthly for January." In *The New Havener*, III, 26 (3 February 1838), 203. "From the American Magazine. By Nathaniel Hawthorne."

D 34

"Snow-Flakes," *United States Magazine and Democratic Review*, I, 3 (February 1838), 355–359.

Signed "By the Author of 'Twice-Told Tales'." See A 2.3₁.

Reprinted in *The New-Yorker* magazine, IV, 22, Whole No. 100 (17 February 1838), 759–760. "By Nathaniel Hawthorne." In *Essex Register* (Salem), XXXVIII, 24 (22 March 1838), 1–2. "From the United States Magazine. By the Author of 'Twice-Told Tales'." *National Aegis* (Worcester, Mass.), Series 3, I, 15 (2 May 1838), 1. "From the United States Magazine."

D 35

"The Threefold Destiny. A Faëry Legend," *The American Monthly Magazine*, XI (March 1838), 228–235.

Signed "By Ashley Allen Royce." See A 2.3₁.

Reprinted in *The New-Yorker* magazine, IV, 24, Whole No. 102 (3 March 1838), 787–788. "From the American Monthly Magazine. By Ashley Allen Royce." In *American Traveller* (Boston), XIII, 75 (20 March 1838), 4. In *The Magnolia* (Cambridge, Mass.), I, 15 (28 January 1841), 1–2, and I, 16 (4 February 1841), 1–2. "By A. A. Royce." In *The New World* (New York), III, 26, Whole No. 82 (25 December 1841), 1–2. "By Nathaniel Hawthorne, Author of 'Twice-Told Tales'." In *Salem Register*, XLII, 13 (14 February 1842), 1. "By Nathaniel Hawthorne." In *Yarmouth Register* (Mass.) (28 July 1842). "By Nathaniel Hawthorne." In *Ladies Cabinet of Fashion, Music, and Romance* (London), New Series, XIII (1850), 241–245.

D 36

"Tales of the Province-House. No. I. Howe's Masquerade," *United States Magazine and Democratic Review*, II, 6 (May 1838), 129–140.

Signed "By the Author of 'Twice Told Tales'." See A 2.3₁, where it is collected as "Legends of the Province House. No. I.—Howe's Masquerade."

Reprinted in *The Hesperian, or Western Monthly Magazine* (Columbus, Ohio), I, 3 (July 1838), 234–241. Titled "Howe's Masquerade—A Tale of the Old Province House. By Nathaniel Hawthorne." In *The Boston Weekly Magazine*, I, 23 (9 February 1839), 177–178. "By N. Hawthorne." See C 16.

D 37

"Tales of the Province-House. No. II. Edward Randolph's Portrait," *United States Magazine and Democratic Review*, II, 8 (July 1838), 360–369.

Signed "By the Author of 'Twice Told Tales'." See A 2.3₁, where it is collected as "Legends of the Province House. No. II. Edward Randolph's Portrait."

Reprinted in *Salem Gazette*, New Series XVI, LII, 69 (28 August 1838), 1. "By the author of 'Twice Told Tales'." Truncated. In *The Boston Weekly Magazine*, I, 25 (23 February 1839), 193–194.

D 38

"Chippings with a Chisel," *United States Magazine and Democratic Review,* III, 9 (September 1838), 18–26.

Signed "By the Author of 'Twice Told Tales'." See A 2.3₁.

Reprinted in *Salem Gazette,* New Series XVI, LII, 80 (5 October 1838), 1. "From the U. S. Magazine. By the author of 'Twice Told Tales'."

D 39

"Biographical Sketch of Jonathan Cilley," *United States Magazine and Democratic Review,* III, 9 (September 1838), 69–76.

Signed "By Nathaniel Hawthorne Esq." See A 1.2.a, B 5[XXII] (where it is collected under title "Jonathan Cilley"), C 66.

D 40

"Tales of the Province-House. No. III. Lady Eleanore's Mantle," *United States Magazine and Democratic Review,* IV, 12 (December 1838), 321–332.

Signed "By Nathaniel Hawthorne." See A 2.3₁, where it is collected as "Legends of the Province House. No. III. Lady Eleanore's Mantle."

Reprinted in *Salem Gazette,* New Series XVI, LII, 101 (18 December 1838), 1–2. "By Nathaniel Hawthorne."

D 41

"Tales of the Province-House. No IV. Old Esther Dudley," *United States Magazine and Democratic Review,* V, 13 (January 1839), 51–59.

Signed "By Nathaniel Hawthorne." See A 2.3₁, where it is collected as "Legends of the Province House. No. IV. Old Esther Dudley."

Reprinted in *American Traveller* (Boston), XIV, 72 (8 March 1839), 4. "By Nathaniel Hawthorne."

D 42

"The Lily's Quest," *The Southern Rose,* VII (19 January 1839), 161–164.

Signed "By Nathaniel Hawthorne." See A 2.3₁, C 11.

Reprinted in *The New-Yorker* magazine, VI, 22, Whole No. 152 (16 Feburary 1839), 341–342. "By Nathaniel Hawthorne. Author of 'Twice-Told Tales'." In *Salem Gazette,* New Series XVII, LIII, 21 (12 March 1839), 1. "From the *Southern Rose.* By Nathaniel Hawthorne. Author of 'Twice-Told Tales'." In *American Traveller* (Boston), XIV, 93 (21 May 1839), 4. "By Nathaniel Hawthorne."

D 43

"John Inglefield's Thanksgiving," *United States Magazine and Democratic Review,* VII, 27 (March 1840), 209–212.

Signed "By Rev. A. A. Royce." See A 19.1.a.

Reprinted in *Boston Notion,* I, 30 (25 April 1840), 2. "By Rev. A. A. Royce. From the Democratic Review."

D 44

"A Virtuoso's Collection," *Boston Miscellany of Literature and Fashion,* I (May 1842), [193]–200.

Signed "By Nathaniel Hawthorne." See A 15.1.a₁, C 31, C 73.

D 45

"The Old Apple-Dealer," *Sargent's New Monthly Magazine of Literature, Fashion, and the Fine Arts,* II, 1 (January 1843), [21]–24.

Signed "By Nathaniel Hawthorne, Author of 'Twice-Told Tales'." See A 15.1.a₁.

Reprinted in *Salem Gazette,* LVI, 103 (27 December 1842), 1. "By Nathaniel Hawthorne. From Sargent's Magazine." In *Salem Mercury,* New Series, III, 52 (28 December 1843), 3. "From Sargent's Magazine. By Nathaniel Hawthorne."

D 46

"The Antique Ring," *Sargent's New Monthly Magazine of Literature, Fashion, and the Fine Arts,* I, 2 (February 1843), [80]–86.

Signed "By Nathaniel Hawthorne."

D 47

"The New Adam and Eve," *United States Magazine and Democratic Review,* XII, 56 (February 1843), 146–55.

Signed "By Nathaniel Hawthorne." See A 15.1.a₁.

Reprinted in *Brother Jonathan* (New York), IV, 16 (11 February 1843), 155–158. In *Salem Gazette,* LXII, 13 (14 February 1843), 1, and LXII, 14 (17 February 1843), 1. "By Nathaniel Hawthorne." In *Salem Mercury,* New Series, IV, 7 (15 February 1843), 3. "By Nathaniel Hawthorne." In *Owosso Argus* (Owosso, Mich.), II, 43 (30 March 1843), 1–2. "By Nathaniel Hawthorne. From the Democratic Review."

D 48

"The Hall of Fantasy," *Pioneer,* I, 2 (February 1843), [49]–55.

Signed "By Nathaniel Hawthorne." See A 15.1.a₁.

Reprinted in *The New World* (New York), VI, 5, Whole No. 139 (4 February 1843), 146–149. "By Nathaniel Hawthorne. From *The Pioneer.*"

D 49

"Egotism; or, The Bosom Serpent, From the Unpublished 'Allegories of the Heart'," *United States Magazine and Democratic Review,* XII, 59 (March 1843), 255–261.

Signed "By Nathaniel Hawthorne." See A 15.1.a₁.

Reprinted in *The Pathfinder* (New York), I, 5 (25 March 1843), 74–76. "Taken from *The Democratic Review.*"

D 50

"The Birth-mark," *Pioneer,* I, 3 (March 1843), 113–119.

Signed "By Nathaniel Hawthorne." See A 15.1, B 1[4], C 41.

Reprinted in *The Pathfinder* (New York), I, 4 (18 March 1843), 59–61. "Taken from *The Pioneer.*"

D 51

"The Procession of Life," *United States Magazine and Democratic Review,* XII, 58 (April 1843), 360–366.

Signed "By Nathaniel Hawthorne." See A 15.1.a₁.

Reprinted in *Salem Gazette,* LXII, 30 (14 April 1843), 1. "By Nathaniel Hawthorne. From the Democratic Review."

D 52

"The Celestial Railroad," *United States Magazine and Democratic Review,* XII, 59 (May 1843), 515–523.

Signed "By Nathaniel Hawthorne." See A 13.1, A 15.1.a₁.

Reprinted in *The Signs of the Times and Expositor of Prophecy* (Boston), V, 21, Whole No. 117 (26 July 1843), 161–164. "By Hawthorne." In *Cambridge Palladium* (Cambridgeport, Mass.), I, 31 (5 August 1843), 1. "By Nathaniel Hawthorne." In *Christian Advocate and Journal* (New York), XVII, 52, Whole No. 884 (9 August 1843), [205]–206. "By Nathaniel Hawthorne." In *Salem Gazette,* LXII, 84 (20 October 1843), 1. "By Nathaniel Hawthorne." In *Salem Mercury,* IV, 43 (25 October 1843), 1. "By Nathaniel Hawthorne." In *Gazette and Courier* (Greenfield, Mass.), LII, 2700 (14 November 1843), 1–2. "By Nathaniel Hawthorne." In *The Baptist Magazine for 1844* (London), XXXVI, Series IV, Vol. VII (January 1844), 9–12, and (February 1844), 71–76. In *The Bible Examiner* (Philadelphia) (23 February 1844). "From the Original, By Nathaniel Hawthorne. With additions and alterations." In *Voices of the True-Hearted* (Philadelphia) (November 1844–April 1846), pp. 119–125. "By Nathaniel Hawthorne." In *National Anti-Slavery Standard* (New York), VIII, 24, Whole No. 388 (11 November 1847), 96. In *The Friend, A Monthly Journal* (London), VI, 61 (January 1848), 4–8. "By Nathaniel Hawthorne. From the Non-Slaveholder." Truncated. In *Vermont Christian Messenger* (Montpelier), IV, 23, Whole No. 169 (5 June 1850), 1, 4. "By Nathaniel Hawthorne." See C 19, C 35, D 66.

D 53

"Buds and Bird-Voices," *United States Magazine and Democratic Review,* XII, 60 (June 1843), 604–608.

Signed "By Nathaniel Hawthorne." See A 15.1.a₁.

D 54

"Little Daffydowndilly," *Boys' and Girls' Magazine,* II (August 1843), 264–269 (also paged 120–125).

Signed "By Nathaniel Hawthorne." See A 19.1.a₁.

D 55

"Fire-Worship," *United States Magazine and Democratic Review,* XIII, 66 (December 1843), 627–630.

Signed "By Nathaniel Hawthorne." See A 15.1.a₁.

Reprinted in *The Bay State Democrat* (Boston), IV, 203, Whole No. 1232 (30 December 1843), 1–2.

D 56

"The Christmas Banquet. From the Unpublished Allegories of the Heart," *United States Magazine and Democratic Review,* XIV, 67 (January 1844), 78–87. See C 37.

Signed "By Nathaniel Hawthorne." See A 15.1.a₁.

D 57

"A Good Man's Miracle," *The Child's Friend* (Boston), I, 5 (February 1844), 151–156.

Signed "By Nathaniel Hawthorne."

Originally published in *The Child's Friend* by Bowles and Crosby in parts in printed wrappers. Also noted in publisher's cloth binding, probably bound at end of year from surplus parts (see illustration, D 57 binding [at C 1]).

Locations: Wrappers: PDH; publisher's binding: CEFC.

D 58
"The Intelligence Office," *United States Magazine and Democratic Review,* XIV, 69 (March 1844), 269–275.

Signed "By Nathaniel Hawthorne." See A 15.1.a₁.

Reprinted in *The Rover* (New York), III, 10 (1844), 137–141. In *The New World,* VIII, 10 (9 March 1844), 293–295. In *Salem Gazette,* LXIII, 23 (19 March 1844), 1. "By Nathaniel Hawthorne. Democratic Review." In *Salem Mercury and Weekly Gazette,* 12 (20 March 1844), 3. "By Nathaniel Hawthorne. Democratic Review." In *The Polynesian* (Honolulu), 50 (3 May 1845), 1–2, and 51 (10 May 1845), 1. "By Nathaniel Hawthorne." In *Supplement to The Courant* (Hartford), XII, 15 (31 July 1847), [113]–115. "From the Democratic Review. By Nathaniel Hawthorne."

D 59
"Earth's Holocaust," *Graham's Lady's and Gentleman's Magazine,* XXV, 5 (May 1844), [193]–200.

Signed "By Nathaniel Hawthorne." See A 15.1.a₁.

D 60
"The Artist of the Beautiful," *United States Magazine and Democratic Review,* XIV, 72 (June 1844), 605–617.

Signed "By Nathaniel Hawthorne." See A 15.1.a₁.

D 61
"A Select Party," *United States Magazine and Democratic Review,* XV, 73 (July 1844), 33–40.

Signed "By Nathaniel Hawthorne." See A 15.1.a₁.

D 62
"Drowne's Wooden Image," *Godey's Magazine and Lady's Book,* XXIX (July 1844), [13]–17.

Signed "By Nathaniel Hawthorne, Author of 'Twice Told Tales,' etc." See A 15.1.a₁.

D 63
"A Book of Autographs," *United States Magazine and Democratic Review,* XV, 77 (November 1844), 454–461.

Signed "By Nathaniel Hawthorne." See B 20[XVII].

D 64
"Writings of Aubépine," *United States Magazine and Democratic Review,* XV, 78 (December 1844), 545–560.

Signed "By Nathaniel Hawthorne." Includes interior title, "Rappaccini's Daughter." See A 15.1.a₁, where it is collected under the title "Rappaccini's Daughter."

D 65

"P.'s Correspondence," *United States Magazine and Democratic Review*, XVI, 82 (April 1845), 337–345.

Signed "By Nathaniel Hawthorne." See A 15.1.a₁.

D 66

"The Celestial Railroad," *Voices of the True-Hearted*, 8 (June 1845?), 119–125.

Reprint. Signed "By Nathaniel Hawthorne." See D 52. Originally published in eighteen (monthly?) parts, probably from 8 November 1844 through April 1846. Also noted with eighteen parts combined in one-volume format with a volume title: Philadelphia: J. Miller M'Kim, 1846.

Locations: Parts: MH, NN; bound: CEFC.

D 67

"Wiley & Putnam's Library of American Books, Nos. XIII and XIV," *Salem Advertiser* (25 March 1846).

Unsigned review of Melville's *Typee*.

Reprinted in Randall Stewart, "Hawthorne's Contributions to *The Salem Advertiser*," *American Literature*, V (1933–1934), 327–341.

D 68

"Scenes and Thoughts in Europe," *Salem Advertiser* (29 April 1846).

Unsigned review of Calvert's *Scenes and Thoughts in Europe* and Dickens's *Traveling Letters*.

Reprinted in Randall Stewart, "Hawthorne's Contributions to *The Salem Advertiser*," *American Literature*, V (1933–1934), 327–341.

D 69

"Views and Reviews in American History . . . ," *Salem Advertiser* (2 May 1846).

Unsigned review of Simm's *Views and Reviews* and Hood's *Poems*. Reprinted in Randall Stewart, "Hawthorne's Contributions to *The Salem Advertiser*," *American Literature*, V (1933–1934), 327–341.

D 70

"Orchards and Gardens," *National Anti-Slavery Standard* (New York), VII, 19, Whole No. 331 (8 October 1846), 76.

Reprint from "The Old Manse," *Mosses from an Old Manse*, 1846. See A 15.1.

D 71

"*The Supernaturalism of New England*, By J. G. Whittier. New York: Wiley & Putnam's Library of American Books," *The Literary World*, I, 11 (17 April 1847), 247–248.

Unsigned review.

D 72

Unsigned and untitled notice of a ball at Ballardvale beginning, "We had the good fortune, a week or two since, to be present at an entertainment of so peculiar a nature . . . ," *Salem Advertiser* (6 October 1847).

Reprinted in Randall Stewart, "Hawthorne's Contributions to *The Salem Advertiser*," *American Literature*, V (1933–1934), 327–341.

D 73

"Evangeline; by Henry Wadsworth Longfellow," *Salem Advertiser* (13 November 1847).

Unsigned review.

Reprinted in Randall Stewart, "Hawthorne's Contributions to *The Salem Advertiser*," *American Literature*, V (1933–1934), 327–341.

D 74

Unsigned and untitled notice beginning, "Theatrical. We dropt in at Mr. Dinneford's theatre . . . ," *Salem Advertiser* (3 May 1848).

Reprinted in Randall Stewart, "Hawthorne's Contributions to *The Salem Advertiser*," *American Literature*, V (1933–1934), 327–341.

D 75

Unsigned and untitled notice beginning, "Theatrical. Entering the theatre last Friday evening . . . ," *Salem Advertiser* (10 May 1848).

Reprinted in Randall Stewart, "Hawthorne's Contributions to *The Salem Advertiser*," *American Literature*, V (1933–1934), 327–341.

D 76

Letter to George S. Hillard, Salem, 18 June 1849, *Boston Daily Advertiser*, LXXIII, 147 (21 June 1849), 2.

Signed "Nath'l Hawthorne."

Reprinted in *Boston Semi-Weekly Advertiser*, XCI, 7122 (23 June 1849), 1. Signed "Nath'l Hawthorne." In *Salem Gazette*, Tri-Weekly Series, III, 74 (23 June 1849), 1. Signed "Nath'l Hawthorne."

D 77

"The Unpardonable Sin. From an Unpublished Work," *Boston Weekly Museum*, II, 30 (5 January 1850), 234–235.

Signed "[For the Boston Weekly Museum] By Nathaniel Hawthorne." See A 19.1 (where it is collected under the title "Ethan Brand: A Chapter from an Abortive Romance"), C 30.

Reprinted as "Ethan Brand" in *Lowell Weekly Journal and Courier*, XXVI, 20 (16 May 1851), 4. "By Nathaniel Hawthorne." In *Holden's Dollar Magazine*, VII (May 1851), 193–201. "By Nathaniel Hawthorne." In *The Lawrence Courier* (Mass.), V, 254 (28 June 1851), 1, and V, 255 (5 July 1851), 1. "By Nathaniel Hawthorne."

D 78

"The Great Stone Face," *National Era*, IV, 4, Whole No. 160 (24 January 1850), 16.

Signed "For the National Era. By Nathaniel Hawthorne." See A 19.1.a.

Reprinted in *The Essex County Mercury and Danvers Courier* (Salem), New Series XI, 6 (6 February 1850), 1–2. "By Nathaniel Hawthorne. From the National Era." In *National Aegis* (Worcester, Mass.), Series 3, XIII, 7 (13 February 1850), 1. "By Nathaniel Hawthorne. From the National Era." In *The Age* (Augusta, Maine), XX, 6 (14 February

1850), 1. "By Nathaniel Hawthorne. From the National Era." In *Lowell Weekly Journal and Courier* (Mass.), XXV, 9 (1 March 1850), 4, and XXV, 10 (8 March 1850), 4. "By Nathaniel Hawthorne."

D 79

"The Snow-Image," *International Miscellany of Literature, Art, and Science,* I (1 November 1850), 537–543.

Signed "By Nathaniel Hawthorne." See A 19.1.a, C 22.

Note: Hawthorne furnished "The Snow-Image" to Rufus Griswold for inclusion in a volume memorializing Fanny Osgood (see *The Memorial,* C 22). Griswold, a member of the Osgood memorial committee, apparently feeling that it would help promote the sale of *The Memorial,* secured permission to publish Hawthorne's story in advance in the *International Miscellany,* a magazine of which Griswold was also editor. *The Memorial,* which was printed first but not released until early in 1851, served as printer's copy for the magazine.

Reprinted in *Lowell Weekly Journal and Courier* (Mass.), XXV, 46 (15 November 1850), 4. "By Nathaniel Hawthorne. From the Memorial." In *Salem Gazette,* Tri-Weekly Series 4, 135 (15 November 1850), 1, and 4, 136 (16 November 1850), 1. "By Nath'l Hawthorne." In *The Essex County Mercury and Danvers Courier* (Salem), New Series XI, 47 (20 November 1850), 1–2. "By Nath'l Hawthorne. From the Memorial . . . ." In *Boston [Weekly] Museum,* III, 27 (14 December 1850), 211. "From the Memorial . . . ."

D 80

"Feathertop: A Moralized Legend," *International Monthly Magazine of Literature, Art, and Science,* V, 2 (1 February 1852), 182–186, and V, 3 (1 March 1852), 333–337.

Signed "Written for the International Monthly Magazine. By Nathaniel Hawthorne." See A 15.3.a.

D 81

"Antaeus and the Pygmies," *The Evening Post* (New York), LII (24 August 1853), 1.

Signed "By Nathaniel Hawthorne. From the Tanglewood Papers, in the press of Ticknor, Reed and Fields of Boston." See A 22.2.a.

Reprinted in *Lowell Weekly Journal and Courier* (Mass.), XXVIII, 39 (16 September 1853), 4. "By Nathaniel Hawthorne. From the Tanglewood Papers; given in advance of publication in The Evening Post."

D 82

"Lichfield and Uttoxeter," *Harper's New Monthly Magazine,* XIV (April 1857), 639–641.

Signed "By Nathaniel Hawthorne."

"Uttoxeter" segment *reprinted* from *The Keepsake,* 1857. See C 27.

D 83

"Letter from Hawthorne," *The Weal-Reaf. A Record of the Essex Institute Fair, Held at Salem, Sept. 4, 5, 6, 7, 8, with Two Supplementary Numbers, Sept. 10, 11,.* no. 2 (5 September 1860), p. 14, and no. 3 (6 September 1860), p. 24.

Signed "Nathaniel Hawthorne." See B 5[XXIII], where it is collected under the title "Browne's Folly."

A newspaper published for the Essex Institute Fair in 8 parts: no. 1 (4 September), no.

2 (5 September), no. 3 (6 September), no. 4 (7 September), no. 5 (8 September); two supplementary numbers: no. 6 (10 September), no. 7 (11 September); and an extra as no. [8].

Note: Later remaindered by the Essex Institute, prospectus published.

D 84
"Some of the Haunts of Burns by a Tourist Without Imagination or Enthusiasm," *Atlantic Monthly,* VI, 36 (October 1860), 385–395.

Unsigned.

See A 24.1.a.

THE

𝕼𝕮𝖊𝖆𝖑-𝕽𝖊𝖆𝖋.

A RECORD OF THE

ESSEX INSTITUTE FAIR,

HELD AT SALEM,

SEPT. 4, 5, 6, 7, 8,

WITH TWO SUPPLEMENTARY NUMBERS,

SEPT. 10, 11,

1860.

D 83: Cover leaf of *The Weal-Reaf,* no. 1

D 85

"Near Oxford," *Atlantic Monthly,* VIII, 48 (October 1861), 385–397.

Unsigned.

See A 24.1.a.

D 86

"Pilgrimage to Old Boston," *Atlantic Monthly,* IX, 51 (January 1862), 88–101.

Unsigned.

See A 24.1.a.

D 87

"Chiefly About War-Matters," *Atlantic Monthly,* X, 57 (July 1862), 43–61.

Signed "By A Peaceable Man." See B 9[XII].

Note: Hawthorne had included a candid description of President Lincoln in the manuscript of "Chiefly About War-Matters" which James T. Fields felt was in poor taste. Fields advised Hawthorne against publication and the Lincoln profile was omitted when the piece was printed in *Atlantic Monthly.* Nine years later, after Hawthorne's death, Fields published the Lincoln profile and discussed the circumstances surrounding the editorial cut in *Yesterdays with Authors* (C 38), pp. 98–101.

The manuscript of "Chiefly About War-Matters" is in the C. Waller Barrett Collection at The University of Virginia.

D 88

"Leamington Spa," *Atlantic Monthly,* X, 60 (October 1862), 451–462.

Signed "A Peaceable Man."

See A 24.1.a.

D 89

"About Warwick," *Atlantic Monthly,* X, 62 (December 1862), 708–720.

Unsigned.

See A 24.1.a.

D 90

"Recollections of a Gifted Woman," *Atlantic Monthly,* XI, 63 (January 1863), 43–58.

Unsigned.

See A 24.1.a.

D 91

"A London Suburb," *Atlantic Monthly,* XI, 65 (March 1863), 306–321.

Unsigned.

See A 24.1.a.

D 92

"Up the Thames," *Atlantic Monthly,* XI, 67 (May 1863), 598–614.

Unsigned.

See A 24.1.a.

D 93
"Outside Glimpses of English Poverty," *Atlantic Monthly*, XII, 69 (July 1863), 36–51.

Unsigned.

See A 24.1.a.

D 94
"Civic Banquets," *Atlantic Monthly*, XII, 70 (August 1863), 195–212.

Unsigned.

See A 24.1.a.

D 95
"A Scene from *The Dolliver Romance*," *Atlantic Monthly*, XIV, 81 (July 1864), 101–109.

Unsigned.

See A 30.1.a.

Five excerpts beginning, " 'Pansie, darling,' said Dr. Dolliver cheerily . . ." reprinted in *Examiner* (London) (5 September 1864), p. 569.

D 96
"Another Scene from *The Dolliver Romance*," *Atlantic Monthly*, XV, 87 (Janaury 1865), 1–7.

Unsigned.

See A 30.1.a.

D 97
Letter to Buchanan Read, Concord, 30 April 1863, *Boston Evening Transcript*, XXXVII, 10933 (12 December 1865), 1.

Signed "Nath'l Hawthorne."

D 98
"Passages from Hawthorne's Note-Books," *Atlantic Monthly*, XVII, nos. 99–104 (January–June 1866), 1–10, 170–178, 257–266, 422–432, 565–571, 725–734, and XVIII, nos. 105–110 (July–December 1866), 40–47, 189–196, 288–295, 450–460, 536–544, 682–697.

Serialized in twelve installments. See A 26.1.a.

D 99
"A Passage from Hawthorne's English Note-Books," *Atlantic Monthly*, XX, 117 (July 1867), 15–21.

See A 27.1.a.

Excerpts from "Passages from the *English Note-Books* of Nathaniel Hawthorne" reprinted in *Pall Mall Gazette* (17 August 1870), p. 12, and in *Pall Mall Budget*, IV, 99 (20 August 1870), 27–28.

D 100
"Hawthorne in the Boston Custom-House. [Extracts from his Private Letters.]," *Atlantic Monthly*, XXI, 123 (January 1868), 106–111.

Prints extracts from Hawthorne's letters to his wife. See A 34.1.a.

D 101

"Nathaniel Hawthorne. Letter to 'My Dear B_____,'" *Once a Week, an Illustrated Miscellany of Literature, Art, Science, and Popular Information,* New Series, I (June 1868), 562–563.

Undated letter from Concord.

D 102

"First Impressions of France and Italy," *Good Words* (London), XII (January–December 1871), 25–31, 129–136, 205–212, 357–364, 432–440, 501–512, 578–584, 642–647, 699–703, 794–799, 830–838.

Serialized in eleven installments, beginning with the entry for January 6, 1858, and ending with the description of Powers in Florence, published in advance of the *French and Italian Note-Books.* See A 28.1.

D 103

"*Septimius Felton,*" *Atlantic Monthly,* XXIX, nos. 171–176 (January–June 1872), 5--14, 129–138, 257–266, 475–484, 566–576, 645–655, and XXX, nos. 177–178 (July–August 1872), 1–16, 129–144.

Serialized in eight installments. See A 29.1.a.

Also serialized in six installments as "Septimius. A Romance of Immortality," *St. Paul's Magazine* (London: Strahan; Philadelphia: Lippincott), X, nos. 52–57 (January–June 1872), 1–20, 113–129, 225–241, 345–367, 457–475, 569–595; also published in clothbound format with spine imprint "Readings from Hawthorne, Disraeli, etc."

Also Julian Hawthorne transcribed in four installments unpublished passages from a second draft of the "Septimius" manuscript in "Nathaniel Hawthorne's 'Elixer of Life' / How Hawthorne Worked," *Lippincott's Monthly Magazine,* XLV (January–April 1890), 66–76, 226–235, 412–425, 548–561.

D 104

"The Ancestral Footstep," *Atlantic Monthly,* L, 302 (December 1882), 823–839, and LI, nos. 303–304 (January–February 1883), 47–63, 180–195.

Signed "By Nathaniel Hawthorne." See B 9[XI].

D 105

"A Look Into Hawthorne's Workshop. Being Notes for a Posthumous Romance," *Century Magazine,* XXV, 3 (January 1883), [433]–448.

Julian Hawthorne supplied *Century Magazine* with his father's manuscript notes for *Doctor Grimshawe's Secret* that had not been published in the book (A 31.1.a.).

D 106

"Unpublished Letters of Nathaniel Hawthorne," *Athenaeum,* MDCCCLXXXIX, 3224 (10 August 1889), 191–192, and MDCCCLXXXIX, 3225 (17 August 1889), 225.

Reprinted in *Critic,* XII (31 August 1889), 104–105, and XII (7 September 1889), 115–116.

D 107

Horatio Bridge, "Personal Recollections of Nathaniel Hawthorne," *Harper's Magazine,* LXXXIV (January–March 1892), 257–265, 359–373, 510–521.

Serialized in three installments, later expanded in book form. Material from letters. See C 54.

D 108
"One of Hawthorne's Unprinted Note-Books [While at the Boston Custom House, 1839]," *Atlantic Monthly*, LXXVII, no. CCCLIX (January 1896), 1–5.

Untitled 1839 scrapbook covering the period 7–19 February 1839. See pp. 253–265 of B 20 [XVIII].

Reprinted in Rose Hawthorne Lathrop, *Memories of Hawthorne*, 1897, pp. 35–45 (C 55). See also C 89.

D 109
"The Ghost of Dr. Harris," *The Nineteenth Century, A Monthly Review*, XLVII, 275 (January 1900), 88–93.

Signed "Nathaniel Hawthorne." See A 32.1.

Reprinted in *The Living Age*, CCXXIV, 2901 (10 February 1900), 345–349. In *Critic*, XXXVI (April 1900), 368–372.

D 110
Julian Hawthorne, "A Group of Hawthorne Letters," *Harper's Magazine*, CVIII (March 1904), 602–607.

D 111
Rose Hawthorne Lathrop, "The Hawthornes in Lenox, Told in Letters by Nathaniel and Mrs. Hawthorne," *Century Magazine*, XXVII (November 1904), 86–98.

E. Special Material and Selected Ephemera

Arranged chronologically.

E 1 THE SPECTATOR
1820

Manuscript newspaper edited by Hawthorne. See illustration.

Hawthorne produced seven numbers by hand for distribution among his family: vol. I, no. 1, undated, 2 pp.; no. 1, 21 August 1820, 4 pp.; no. 2, 28 August 1820, 4 pp.; no. 3, 4 September 1820, 4 pp.; no. 4, 11 September 1820, 4 pp.; no. 5, 18 September 1820, 4 pp.; no. 6, 25 September 1820, 4 pp. See C 69.

Location: MSaE.

E 2 DE PATRIBUS CONSCRIPTIS ROMANORUM
1824

Hawthorne's manuscript Latin composition assigned as part of 1824 October Exhibition at Bowdoin College. 2 pp. First published in *A Study of Hawthorne* (C 42). See also p. 256 of *Hawthorne at Auction* (C 86).

Location: MBe.

E 3 THE OCEAN
1836

Sheet music. Words of Hawthorne's poem "The Ocean" (D 1) set to music by Edward L. White. See illustration. Deposited 1836 with District Court for the Eastern District of Pennsylvania.

Locations: CEFC, MH.

E 4 AN ADDRESS
1843

AN | ADDRESS | TO THE | PEOPLE OF THE UNITED STATES | IN BEHALF OF THE | AMERICAN COPYRIGHT CLUB, | Adopted at New-York, October 18th, 1843. | [rule] | NEW-YORK: | PUBLISHED BY THE CLUB | [rule] | MDCCCXLIII.

Printed address. Pamphlet, cover title, 20 pp. Hawthorne was listed as an associate member.

Location: CEFC.

Note: Hawthorne was also a signer of a printed letter published in New York on 25 April 1862 urging defeat of "A Bill to amend the Act respecting Copyrights" then before the House of Representatives.

433

THE SPECTATOR.

No. 1.   EDITED BY N. HATHORNE & Co.   Vol. 1.

CONDITIONS.
Published on Wednesdays.
Price 12 cts. per annum.
Payment to be made at
the end of the year.

PROSPECTUS.
To commence a periodical
publication at a time in
which the Press is alread-
y overflowing with them,
may appear to many too
be unnecessary, and to
raise it to eminence a-
mong the crowd of its ri-
vals, is certainly a work
requiring both industry &
talent. The personal in...
...to such an at-
tempt must be considera-
ble; for wealth does not lie
in the path of literature;
and the wreath of Genius
is not bestowed upon ef-
forts so humble as these.
Although we would not in-
sinuate that in commencing
this Publication, we are gui-
ded solely by disinteres-
ted motives, yet the con-
sideration that we may
reform the morals, and
instruct and amuse the
minds of our Readers,
that we may advance
the cause of Religion,
and give to truth and
Justice a wider sway,
has been of the great-
est weight with us.
It shall be our object in
the Spectator, to accom-
modate ourselves, as
far as possible, to all men,
and to endeavour to please
all except the vicious. That
our paper...
...ly...
...ne...
...le s...
qua... ...every
appearance of impiety
and immorality.
To conclude, keeping in mind
our duty to a higher pow-
er, we shall use our best
endeavours to benefit mankind.

MISCELLANY.
For the Spectator.
THE END OF THE YEAR.
Upon finding ourselves advanced one stage farther in the
journey of existence, we naturally look back upon the
space we have passed, and
recall to mind the various
events which have befallen
us. In a retrospection of
this kind there is much to
sadden the heart, and to
damp the expectations of
future happiness. The gleams
of joy which enlightened the
path, have vanished like
the fading beams of sun-
shine, but the wounds of
sorrow still rankle deep in
the bosom. Yet it is the nature of man still to look
forward with undying hope,
and in every situation, and under every calamity, still to prove
that "Man never is, but always
to be blest."
Perhaps, during the past year,
the grave has closed over
friends, whom we beheld at
its commencement with as
fair a prospect as ourselves.
of long happiness and extensive
usefulness. With a voice from
their tombs louder than that
of the living, they warn us
also to be ready, and remind
us that, when a few more years
have rolled away, we must
sleep with them.
Though time, when past, can
never be recalled, and the faults
and frailties which marked
its course cannot now be rem-
edied, yet we may place them
as beacons for our future lives,
and learn from the errors of
others, and of ourselves, to steer
in safety down the tide of existence.

For the Spectator.
ON SOLITUDE
Man is naturally a sociable being,
not formed for himself alone, but
destined to bear a part in the
great scheme of nature. All
his pleasures are heightened,
and all h... ...ed
by partic...pation... ...ly in
Society that the full energy of
his mind is aroused, and all its
powers drawn forth.
Apart from the World, there are
no incitements to the pursuit of
excellence; there are no rivals to
contend with; and therefore there
is no improvement.
Perhaps life may pass more tran-
quilly, estranged from the pur-
suits and the vexations of the
multitude, but all the hurry
and whirl of passion is prefer-
able to the cold calmness of
indifference.
The heart may be more pure
and uncorrupted in solitude,
than when exposed to the influence of the depravity of
the world; but the benefit of
virtuous examples is equal to
the detriment of vicious ones, &
both are equally lost.

E 1: Manuscript newspaper, vol. 1, no. 1

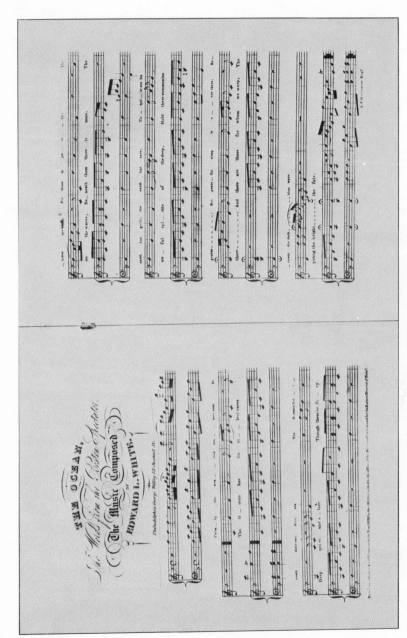

E3: Sheet music. Single sheet, 19⁷/₈″ × 13³/₁₆″, folded to 9⁷/₈″ × 13³/₁₆″; verso blank

F. Selected Bibliographic Material

Arranged chronologically.

F 1
Anderson, John P. "Bibliography." In *Life of Nathaniel Hawthorne.* By Moncure D. Conway. London: Walter Scott, [1890], pp. [i]–xiii.

See C 51.

Includes works, contributions to magazines, biography and criticism, and chronological list of works.

F 2
Stone, Herbert Stuart, comp. *First Editions of American Authors. A Manual for Book-Lovers.* With an Introduction by Eugene Field. Cambridge, Mass.: Stone & Kimball, MDCCCXCIII.

Includes section on Hawthorne, pp. 91–94.

Trade printing. Also 50 numbered copies in large-paper printing.

F 3
Foley, P. K. *American Authors 1795–1895. A Bibliography of First and Notable Editions.* With an Introduction by Walter Leon Sawyer. Boston: [P. K. Foley], 1897.

Includes section on Hawthorne, pp. 117–121.

Trade printing. Also 500 numbered copies.

F 4
"Bibliography of the Writings of Hawthorne." *Book Buyer,* XV (October–November 1897), 218–220, 326–327.

F 5
Exercises in Commemoration of the Centennial of the Birth of Nathaniel Hawthorne by the Essex Institute Salem Massachusetts Thursday Afternoon 23 June 1904. [Salem: Essex Institute, 1904].

Prints list of Hawthorne's writings.

Printed wrappers.

F 6
Paltsits, Victor Hugo. "List of Books, Etc., By and Relating to Nathaniel Hawthorne, Prepared as an Exhibition to Commemorate the Centenary of His Birth." *Bulletin of the New York Public Library,* VII (July 1904), 311–322.

Quotes and paraphrases letters.

Booklet, cover title.

F 7

Browne, Nina E., comp. *Bibliography of Nathaniel Hawthorne.* Boston and New York: Houghton, Mifflin, MDCCCCV.

550 numbered copies printed.

F 8

Cathcart, Wallace Hugh. *Bibliography of the Works of Nathaniel Hawthorne.* Cleveland: The Rowfant Club, MCMV.

91 copies printed.

F 9

First Editions of the Works of Nathaniel Hawthorne Together with Some Manuscripts, Letters and Portraits Exhibited at The Grolier Club from December 8 to December 24, 1904. New York: The Grolier Club, 1924.

Quotes letters.

Printed wrappers. Also a large-paper edition "of forty copies on Van Gelder handmade paper, with frontispiece portraits, additions to text, and index." Paper-covered boards, numbered, boxed.

F 10

Original Manuscripts, Drawings, and Printed Books Exhibited in the Cole Reading Room of Herring Library at St. Lawrence University 6 June to 31 August 1925. [Canton, N.Y.: St. Lawrence University, 1925].

Quotes letters.

Booklet.

F 11

A Catalogue of an Exhibition of First Editions, Association Books, Autograph Letters, and Manuscripts of Nathaniel Hawthorne. April 21 to May 22, 1937. Buffalo, N.Y.: Lockwood Memorial Library, University of Buffalo, 1937.

Quotes inscriptions and letters.

Printed wrappers.

F 12

Wilson, Jean C. S., and Randall, David A., eds. *Carroll A. Wilson: Thirteen Author Collections of the Nineteenth Century.* New York: Scribners, 1950.

Includes description of Wilson Hawthorne collection, pp. [119]–154. Quotes letters and inscriptions.

F 13

Gordan, John D. *Nathaniel Hawthorne: The Years of Fulfillment, 1804–1853, An Exhibition from the Berg Collection First Editions, Manuscripts, Autograph Letters.* New York: The New York Public Library, 1954.

Quotes from letters and manuscripts.

Printed wrappers.

F 14
Labaree, Benjamin W., and Cohen, B. Bernard. "Hawthorne at the Essex Institute." *Essex Institute Historical Collections,* XCIV, 3 (July 1958), 297–308.

Describes Hawthorne letters and manuscripts at the Essex Institute.

F 15
Blanck, Jacob, comp. *Bibliography of American Literature.* Vol. 4, *Nathaniel Hawthorne to Joseph Holt Ingraham.* New Haven and London: Yale University Press, 1963.

Omits periodical and newspaper appearances.

F 16
The Centenary Edition of the Works of Nathaniel Hawthorne. [Columbus]: Ohio State University Press, [1963–1974].

11 vols. See B 32.

Each volume includes bibliographical and textual apparatus.

F 17
Bruccoli, Matthew J. *An Exhibition of Books, Manuscripts, and Letters 4 July 1804 Nathaniel Hawthorne 19 May 1864 at the Main Library, Ohio State University, marking Hawthorne Day 15 May 1964.* [Columbus: Ohio State University, 1964].

Quotes from letters and manuscripts.

Pamphlet, cover title.

F 18
Austin, Gabriel C. *A Descriptive Guide to the Exhibition Commemorating the Death of Nathaniel Hawthorne 1804–1864.* New York: The Grolier Club, 1964.

Quotes from letters with a full transcript of Hawthorne's letter to J. L. O'Sullivan, Boston, 19 May 1839.

Printed wrappers.

Note: The Grolier exhibit ran from October 20, 1964, through December 5: A more detailed listing of the material in the exhibit was published as Andrew B. Myers, "Nathaniel Hawthorne, A Checklist," *Gazette of The Grolier Club,* New Series, V (October 1967), 2–20.

F 19
Harwell, Richard. *Hawthorne and Longfellow: A Guide to an Exhibit.* Brunswick, Maine: Bowdoin College, 1966.

Quotes letters and inscriptions with a facsimile of a section of a letter from Hawthorne to Horatio Bridge, 13 October 1853.

Printed wrappers. Also a few copies specially bound for presentation.

F 20
Clark, C. E. Frazer, Jr., comp. *The Merrill Checklist of Nathaniel Hawthorne.* Columbus, Ohio: Charles E. Merrill, [1970].

Includes books, separate publications, contributions, editions, letters, bibliographies and checklists, biographies and memoirs, scholarship and criticism.

Printed wrappers.

F 21

Nathaniel Hawthorne . . . An Exhibition July 15–20, 1971 from the Collections of C. E. Frazer Clark, Jr. and the Liverpool City Libraries. Liverpool, England, 1971. Bloomfield Hills, Mich.: C. E. Frazer Clark, Jr., 1971.

Prints facsimiles of letters and quotes letters.

Pamphlet.

Colophon: '500 Copies Printed for the LIVERPOOL SHOW 1971 *The Nathaniel Hawthorne Journal* _____'.

Also 300 copies of an invitation published with a facsimile of a Fourth of July invitation sent to Hawthorne by the American residents in Liverpool.

F 22

Clark, C. E. Frazer, Jr. "Hawthorne and the Pirates." In *Proof: The Yearbook of American Bibliographical and Textual Studies.* Edited by Joseph Katz. Vol. I. Columbia, S.C.: University of South Carolina Press, 1971, pp. 90–121.

Prints a facsimile of a letter from Hawthorne, Liverpool, 15 August 1857, and facsimiles of title pages of selected English printings of Hawthorne's writings. Includes a checklist of English printings.

F 23

Hawthorne's Hand. An Exhibition from the Collection of C. E. Frazer Clark, Jr. 31 October through 8 December at The Grolier Club, New York, 1973. Bloomfield Hills, Mich.: C. E. Frazer Clark, Jr., 1973.

Prints facsimiles of letters and manuscripts and quotes letters.

Pamphlet.

Colophon: '200 Copies Printed for The Grolier Exhibit 1973'.

F 24

Nathaniel Hawthorne The College Experience. An Exhibition from the Collection of C. E. Frazer Clark, Jr. 16 May through 21 June at the Kent State University Libraries . . . Kent, Ohio, 1974. Bloomfield Hills, Mich.: C. E. Frazer Clark, Jr., 1974.

Prints facsimiles of letters and manuscripts and quote letters.

Printed wrappers.

Colophon: '500 Copies Printed for The Kent State University Libraries'.

F 25

Nathaniel Hawthorne. The American Experience. An Exhibition from the Collection of C. E. Frazer Clark, Jr., 25 November 1974–17 January 1975. William L. Clements Library, The University of Michigan, Ann Arbor, Michigan. [Bloomfield Hills, Mich.: Clark, 1974].

Quotes from letters.

Folder.

G. Prose Material Attributed to Hawthorne

Arranged alphabetically.

G 1

"The Adventures of a Rain Drop," in *The Token* (Boston: S. G. Goodrich, MDCCCXXVIII), pp. 78–83.

Attributed to Hawthorne by F. B. Sanborn, "A new 'Twice-Told Tale' by Nathaniel Hawthorne," *New-England Magazine,* New Series XVIII (August 1898), 688–696. Since identified as by Lydia Maria Child. See Ralph Thompson, *American Literary Annuals and Gift Books* (New York: H. M. Wilson, 1936), p. 70.

G 2

"The Bald Eagle," in *The Token* (Boston: Gray and Bowen, MDCCCXXXIII), pp. [74]–89.

See C 3.

Attributed to Hawthorne by F. B. Sanborn, "A new 'Twice-Told Tale' by Nathaniel Hawthorne," *New-England Magazine,* New Series XVIII (August 1898), 688–696. Written by Longfellow. See Luther Samuel Livingston, *A Bibliography of . . . the Writings of Henry Wadsworth Longfellow* (New York: privately printed, 1938), pp. 134, 375, 387.

G 3

"The Battle-Omen," *Salem Gazette,* New Series VIII, XLIV, 88 (2 November 1830), 1.

First attributed to Hawthorne by J. E. Babson ("Tom Folio"), a Boston bibliophile, who researched Hawthorne's uncollected writings for J. R. Osgood and was probably responsible for some of the "pieces" being first published by Osgood in *Fanshawe and Other Pieces* (A 1.2). "The Battle-Omen" appears on Babson's manuscript "finding list" located in the Clark collection. The story was known to P. K. Foley, Boston antiquarian dealer and author of *American Authors 1975–1895* (Boston, 1897), which was published for subscribers. Foley provided transcripts of the story for select customers, like Daniel Edwards Kennedy (Foley's transcripts of various material attributed to Hawthorne by him are located in the Clark collection). Foley also informed Stephen H. Wakeman (see p. 184 of *Hawthorne at Auction* [C 86]) about Hawthorne's probable authorship. See Donald C. Gallup, "On Hawthorne's Authorship of 'The Battle Omen'," *New England Quarterly,* IX (December 1936), 690–699 (C 72). Included in *The Snow Image, and Uncollected Tales,* vol. XI of the *Centenary Edition* (B 32). See C 72.

G 4

"A Cure for Dyspepsia," in *The Token* (Boston: Gray and Bowen, MDCCCXXXIII), pp. [93]–112.

See C 3.

Attributed to Hawthorne by Moncure D. Conway in "Hawthorne, His Uncollected Tales in 'The Token,' Beginning with 1831," *New York Times Saturday Review of Books and*

Art, 8 June 1901, pp. 397–398. Rejected by Nelson F. Adkins, "The Hawthorne Canon" (Unpublished typescript, Ohio State University Center for Textual Studies), p. 19.

G 5
"David Whicher—a North American Story," in *The Token* (Boston: Gray and Bowen, MDCCCXXXII), pp. [349]–372.

See C 2.

Attributed to Hawthorne by Irving Richards, "A Note on the Authorship of 'David Whicher'," *Jahrbuch für Amerikastudien* (Heidelberg), VII (1962), 294. Attributed to John Neal by Hans-Joachim Lang, "The Authorship of 'David Whicher'," *Jahrbuch für Amerikastudien,* VII (1962), 288–293. Attributed to Longfellow by Alfred Weber, "Der auto von 'David Whicher' und das geheimnis der grünen brille," *Jahrbuch,* X (1965), 106–125. Rejected by *Centenary Edition,* vol. XI, p. 408.

G 6
"The Downer's Banner," *The American Monthly Magazine,* I, 6 (September 1829), 387–400.

Attributed to Hawthorne by George E. Woodberry, *Nathaniel Hawthorne* (Boston and New York: Houghton, Mifflin, 1902), pp. 34–35. Rejected by *Centenary Edition,* vol. XI, pp. 405–406.

Note: Story reprinted in four parts in *Yeoman's Gazette* (Concord, Mass.) (7, 14, 21, 28 November 1829). Unsigned.

G 7
"Eastern Lands," *The Essex Banner and Haverhill Advertiser* (17 November 1838), p. 1.

Proposed as a possibility in *The Centenary Hawthorne News-Sheet,* 4 (1968), 3. Listed by C. E. Frazer Clark, Jr., in *The Merrill Checklist of Nathaniel Hawthorne* (Columbus, Ohio: Charles E. Merrill, 1970), p. 6. Rejected by *Centenary Edition,* vol. XI, p. 402. Unsupported and doubtful.

G 8
"Ethan Allen, and the Lost Children," in *Twice-Told Tales* (Dublin: James M'Glashan, MDCCCL), pp. 262–286.

Included without comment in this collection but nowhere else attributed to Hawthorne. See A 2.5.

G 9
"The Fairy Fountain," in *Twice-Told Tales* (Dublin: James M'Glashan, MDCCCL), pp. 296–301.

Included without comment in this collection but nowhere else attributed to Hawthorne. See A 2.5.

G 10
"The Fated Family," in *The Token* (Boston: Gray and Bowen), MDCCCXXXI, pp. [57]–82.

See C 1.

Attributed to Hawthorne by Moncure D. Conway in "Hawthorne, His Uncollected Tales in 'The Token,' Beginning with 1831," *New York Times Saturday Review of Books and*

Art, 8 June 1901, pp. 397–398. Rejected by Nelson F. Adkins, "The Hawthorne Canon" (Unpublished typescript, Ohio State University Center for Textual Studies), p. 21.

G 11
"The First and Last Dinner," in *A Practical System of Rhetoric,* by Samuel Phillips Newman, 2nd ed. (Portland: Shirley & Hyde; Andover: Mark Newman, 1929), pp. 218–221.

Attributed to Hawthorne by Louise Hastings, "An Origin for 'Dr. Heidegger's Experiment'," *American Literature,* IX (January, 1938), 403–410. Written by William Mudford. See Nolan E. Smith, "Another Story Falsely Attributed to Hawthorne: 'The First and Last Dinner'," *Papers of the Bibliographical Society of America,* LXV (1971), 172–173.

G 12
The Flower Basket (New York: Nafis & Cornish, n.d. [ca. 1840]).

Reprinted almost entirely from the plates used to print vol. II of *Moral Tales* (C 13), a collection S. G. Goodrich had assembled that included four Hawthorne tales first printed in *The Token.* Presumably unaware of the circumstances, a Samuel T. Sukel attributed the entire contents of *The Flower Basket* to Hawthorne in "14 'Unknown' Tales Held Hawthorne's," *New York Times* (13 September 1948), p. 16. Of the 14 tales in the Goodrich collection, 4 are by Hawthorne and all but one of the remaining tales have been assigned to other authors by Nelson F. Adkins, "Notes on the Hawthorne Canon," *Papers of the Bibliographical Society of America,* LX (1966), 365–367. One sketch in the collection, "The Man with the _____," has not been assigned, but it is unlikely that Hawthorne wrote it.

G 13
"Graves and Goblins," *New-England Magazine,* VIII (June 1835), 438–444.

Included in *The Dolliver Romance and Other Pieces* (A 30.1.a). Probably attributed to Hawthorne by J. E. Babson; title included in Babson's manuscript "finding list" (see G 3). Included in *The Snow Image, and Uncollected Tales,* vol. XI of the *Centenary Edition* (B 32).

G 14
"The Haunted Quack. A Tale of a Canal Boat—By Joseph Nicholson," in *The Token* (Boston: Gray and Bowen, MDCCCXXXI), pp. [117]–137.

See C 1.

Included in *Tales and Sketches,* vol. XVI of the *Autograph Edition* (B 20[XVI]). Attributed to Hawthorne by F. B. Sanborn, "A new 'Twice-Told Tale' by Nathaniel Hawthorne," *New-England Magazine,* New Series XVIII (August 1898), 688–696. Included in *The Snow Image, and Uncollected Tales,* vol. XI of the *Centenary Edition* (B 32); see p. 399 of that volume for supporting evidence.

G 15
Hawthorne's First Diary. With an Account of its Discovery and Loss, by Samuel T. Pickard (Boston and New York: Houghton, Mifflin, 1897).

Book based on a series of articles that appeared in the *Portland Transcript* purportedly written by a "W. Sims" (William Symmes?). The articles appeared 25 June, 9 July, 6 August, 23 November, 31 December 1870 and 11, 18, 25 February, 4, 18 March, 8, 22 April, 6 May 1871. Also a note appeared 21 June 1873 and 13 July 1892. George Parsons Lathrop questioned the authenticity of the articles in *A Study of*

Hawthorne (Boston: James R. Osgood, 1876), pp. 83–100, [333]–337. Nina Browne quotes Julian Hawthorne as calling the *Diary* "a clumsy and leaky fabrication," in *A Bibliography of Hawthorne* (Boston and New York: Houghton, Mifflin, MDCCCCV), p. 103. Pickard himself later became doubtful about the genuineness of the book and often presented his doubts in inscriptions he wrote on the endpapers of various copies (Location: CEFC). He published his doubts in *The Dial* (Chicago) (16 April 1902), p. 155. Pickard also caused a single-sheet disclaimer entitled "Note to page 61" to be printed and tipped to the free front endpaper of remaining copies. The disclaimer reads in part: "When I published this book, in 1897, I had no doubt as to the genuineness of the alleged Diary, notwithstanding the mystery with which Symmes surrounded himself. . . . But I soon after found that one item—this on page 61—could not have been written by Hawthorne when he was a boy, because Jackson was drowned, as here related, in September, 1828, when Hawthorne was 24 years old. I also found . . . . As soon as I learned these facts, I ordered the publishers to destroy the plates, and to send me all the copies that remained unsold of this first and only edition. Of the edition of 1100 copies, only about 50 are still unsold." Dated May 1907. How many remaindered copies Pickard had may be a question as he continued to advertise and promote the sale of the title himself (see Pickard correspondence in Clark collection).

Published in brown, blue, and green bold-ribbed T cloth, top edges gilded, with printed dust jacket. Also untrimmed copies in red V-like cloth with paper label on spine; reportedly 100 such copies produced (Location: CEFC). Listed in *Publishers' Weekly* 16 October 1897. Also American sheets with cancel London: Kegan Paul, Trench, Trübner & Co., 1897, title. Listed in *Athenaeum* 16 October 1897.

G 16
"Hints to Young Ambition," *New-England Magazine* (June 1832) 513–514.

Included by Horace Scudder in vol. XVII of the *Autograph Edition* (B 20). Rejected by George E. Woodberry in *Nathaniel Hawthorne* (Boston and New York: Houghton, Mifflin, 1902), p. 46.

G 17
"An Indian's Revenge," in *Twice-Told Tales* (Dublin: James M'Glashan, MDCCCL), pp. 287–295.

Included without comment in this collection but nowhere else attributed to Hawthorne. See A 2.5.

G 18
"The Interrupted Nuptials," *Salem Gazette,* XLI, New Series V (12 October 1927), 1.

First attributed to Hawthorne by P. K. Foley who prepared transcripts (Location: CEFC) of the story and presented them to D. E. Kennedy. Foley also presented a copy of the *Salem Gazette* containing the story to Parkman D. Howe stating that in his opinion the tale was written by Hawthorne. This opinion was supported by Professor Norman Holmes Pearson. See C. E. Frazer Clark, Jr., " 'The Interrupted Nuptials,' A Question of Attribution," in *Nathaniel Hawthorne Journal 1971* (Washington, D.C.: NCR Microcard Edition, 1971), pp. 49–66. Rejected by *Centenary Edition,* vol. XI, pp. 407–408.

G 19
"The Modern Job; or, The Philosophic Stone," in *The Token* (Boston: Charles Bowen, MDCCCXXXIV), pp. [269]–319.

Attributed to Hawthorne by F. B. Sanborn, "A new 'Twice-Told Tale' by Nathaniel Hawthorne," *New-England Magazine*, New Series XVIII (August 1898), 688–696. Attributed to Edward Everett by George E. Woodberry in *Nation*, LXXV (9 October 1902), 283.

G 20

"My Wife's Novel," in *The Token* (Boston: Gray and Bowen, MDCCCXXXII), pp. [281]–315.

See C 2.

Attributed to Hawthorne by F. B. Sanborn, "A new 'Twice-Told Tale' by Nathaniel Hawthorne," *New-England Magazine*, New Series XVIII (August 1898), 688–696. Attributed to Edward Everett by George E. Woodberry in *Nation*, LXXV (9 October 1902), 283. Also attributed to Everett by Wallace Hugh Cathcart, *Bibliography* . . . (Cleveland: The Rowfant Club, MCMV), pp. 5–6.

G 21

"The New England Village," in *The Token* (Boston: Gray and Bowen, MDCCCXXXI), pp. [155]–176.

See C 1.

Included by Horace Scudder in vol. XVI of the *Autograph Edition* (B 20). Supported by Gerald R. Griffin, "Hawthorne and 'The New England Village': Internal Evidence and a New Genesis of *The Scarlet Letter*," *Essex Institute Historical Collections*, CVII (1971), 268–279. Rejected by *Centenary Edition*, vol. XI, pp. 406–407.

G 22

"An Old Woman's Tale," *Salem Gazette*, New Series VIII, XLIV (21 December 1830), 1–2.

Included in *The Dolliver Romance and Other Pieces* (A 30.1.a). Probably attributed to Hawthorne by J. E. Babson; title included in Babson's manuscript "finding list" (see G 3). Included in *The Snow Image, and Uncollected Tales*, vol. XI of the *Centenary Edition* (B 32).

G 23

"Sir Henry Vane," *New-York Mirror*, III, 33 (11 March 1826), 260–261.

Attributed to Hawthorne by L. Neal Smith, Associate Textual Editor, *Centenary Edition*, in correspondence with CEFC.

G 24

"A Visit to the Clerk of the Weather," *The American Monthly Magazine* (May 1836) pp. 483–487.

Attributed to Hawthorne by George E. Woodberry, *Nathaniel Hawthorne* (Boston and New York: Houghton, Mifflin, 1902), p. 61. See C 61. Included in *The Snow Image, and Uncollected Tales*, vol. XI of the *Centenary Edition* (B 32).

G 25

"The Young Provincial," in *The Token* (Boston: Carter and Hendee, MDCCCXXX), pp. [127]–145.

Attributed to Hawthorne by F. B. Sanborn, "A new 'Twice-Told Tale' by Nathaniel Hawthorne," *New-England Magazine*, New Series XVIII (August 1898), 688–696, and accepted by Moncure D. Conway in "Hawthorne, His Uncollected Tales in 'The Token,' Beginning with 1831," *New York Times Saturday Review of Books and Art* (8 June 1901), pp. 397–398. The story was attributed to W. B. O. Peabody by *Springfield Republican* (25 November 1829), p. 1, and *Essex Register* (3 December 1829), pp. 1–2. Rejected by *Centenary Edition*.

H. Verse by Hawthorne and Verse Attributed to Him

Arranged chronologically.

H 1

"The charms of sweet Music . . . ." Undated manuscript (Location: ViU). Signed "Nathaniel Hathorne [*sic*]."

[ca. 1815]. Four lines of untitled verse in a copy book. Reproduced in facsimile in the Manning sale catalogue; see *Hawthorne at Auction,* p. 232 (C 86).

H 2

"Moderate Views." Letter, 13 February 1817 (Location: MSaE).

Eight lines of untitled verse beginning, "With passions unruffled . . . ." Published in *Nathaniel Hawthorne: Poems,* p. 2 (C 83).

H 3

"Lady fair, will you not listen . . . ." Quoted in a letter from Elizabeth M. Hawthorne to Julian Hawthorne, 20 December 1865 (Location: CU).

[ca. 1817]. Four lines of untitled verse attributed to Hawthorne by his sister. Noted by Maurice Bassan, "Julian Hawthorne Edits Aunt Ebe," *Essex Institute Historical Collections,* C, 4 (October 1964), 278.

H 4

"Then, oh Thomas, rest in glory!" Quoted in a letter from Elizabeth M. Hawthorne to Julian Hawthorne, 20 December 1865 (Location: CU).

[ca. 1817]. Untitled four-line epitaph attributed to Hawthorne by his sister. Noted by Maurice Bassan, "Julian Hawthorne Edits Aunt Ebe," *Essex Institute Historical Collections,* C, 4 (October 1964), 277.

H 5

"Oh, earthly pomp is but a dream . . . ." Included by Hawthorne in a letter to his sister Elizabeth, 28 September 1819 (Location: NNMor).

Eight lines of untitled verse. Published in *Hawthorne and His Wife,* I, p. 105 (C 47).

H 6

"I saw where in his lowly grave . . . ." Included by Hawthorne in a letter to his sister Elizabeth, 28 September 1819 (Location: NNMor).

Four lines of untitled verse. Published in *Hawthorne and His Wife,* I, p. 106 (C 47).

H 7

"Oh, do not bid me part from thee . . . ." Included by Hawthorne in a letter to his sister Elizabeth, 28 September 1819 (Location: NNPM).

Eight lines of untitled verse. Published in *Hawthorne and His Wife,* I, p. 106 (C 47).

453

H 8
"I left my low and humble home . . . ." *The Spectator* MS, 21 August 1820 (Location: MSaE). See E 1.

Published in *Nathaniel Hawthorne: Poems*, p. 8 (C 83).

H 9
"Go to the grave where friends are laid . . . ." *The Spectator* MS, 28 August 1820 (Location: MSaE). See E 1.

Published in *Nathaniel Hawthorne: Poems*, p. 9 (C 83).

H 10
"I have seen the oak . . . ." *The Spectator* MS, 28 August 1820 (Location: MSaE). See E 1.

Published in *Nathaniel Hawthorne: Poems*, p. 10 (C 83).

H 11
"Oh could I raise the darken'd veil . . . ." *The Spectator* MS, 4 September 1820 (Location: MSaE). See E 1.

Published in *Nathaniel Hawthorne: Poems*, p. 11 (C 83).

H 12
"Oh I have roam'd in rapture wild . . . ." *The Spectator* MS, 4 September 1820 (Location: MSaE). See E 1.

Published in *Nathaniel Hawthorne: Poems*, p. 12 (C 83).

H 13
"Days of my youth, ye fleet away . . . ." *The Spectator* MS, 11 September 1820 (Location: MSaE). See E 1.

Published in *Nathaniel Hawthorne: Poems*, p. 13 (C 83).

H 14
"Ye forms of Heroes slumb'ring here . . . ." *The Spectator* MS, 11 September 1820 (Location: MSaE). See E 1.

Published in *Nathaniel Hawthorne: Poems*, p. 14 (C 83).

H 15
"How sweet the silver Moon's pale ray . . . ." *The Spectator* MS, 18 September 1820 (Location: MSaE). See E 1.

Published in *Nathaniel Hawthorne: Poems*, p. 15 (C 83).

H 16
"The billowy Ocean rolls its wave . . . ." *The Spectator* MS, 18 September 1820 (Location: MSaE). See E 1.

Published in *Nathaniel Hawthorne: Poems*, p. 16 (C 83).

H 17
"On Walter Scott's Poem of Waterloo, By Lord Erskine." Undated manuscript.

[ca. 1820]. Four lines of verse in a copybook beginning, "On Waterloo's ensanguined plain . . . ." Listed in the Manning sale catalogue. See *Hawthorne at Auction*, p. 233 (C 86).

H 18
"The moon is bright in that chamber fair . . . ." Unsigned manuscript (Location: CtY).

[ca. 1820]. Twenty-four lines of verse. Reproduced in facsimile in the Julian Hawthorne sale catalogue. See *Hawthorne at Auction*, pp. 275–276 (C 86). See also *Hawthorne and His Wife*, I, pp. 102–103 (C 47).

H 19
"The Ocean," *Salem Gazette*, New Series III, XXXIX (26 August 1825), 1. Signed with the initials "C.W."

Sixteen lines of verse beginning, "The Ocean has its silent caves . . . ." Identified by Horatio Bridge. Attributed to Hawthorne by James T. Fields, *Yesterdays with Authors*, p. 68 (C 38). Confirmed by Horatio Bridge, *Personal Recollections of Nathaniel Hawthorne*, pp. 36–37 (C 54). See also C 4, D 1, D 2.

H 20
"The Battle Ground," *Salem Gazette*, New Series III, XXXIX (30 August 1825), 1. Signed with the initials "S.T."

First attributed to Hawthorne by P. K. Foley who provided D. E. Kennedy with a transcript (Location: CEFC). See Arthur Monke and C. E. Frazer Clark, Jr., "Hawthorne's 'Moonlight'," *The Nathaniel Hawthorne Journal 1973*, pp. 27–34 (C 87). See also Allen Flint's review of *Nathaniel Hawthorne: Poems* in *NHJ 1973*, pp. 255–260 (C 87).

H 21
"Moonlight," *Salem Gazette*, New Series III, XXXIX (2 September 1825), 1. Signed with the initials "P.S."

Twenty-one lines of verse beginning, "We are beneath the dark blue sky . . . ." Identified by Horatio Bridge. Attributed to Hawthorne by George Parsons Lathrop, *A Study of Hawthorne*, pp. 122–123 (C 42). Confirmed by Horatio Bridge, *Personal Recollections of Nathaniel Hawthorne*, pp. 35–36 (C 54). See also Arthur Monke and C. E. Frazer Clark, Jr., "Hawthorne's 'Moonlight'," *The Nathaniel Hawthorne Journal 1973*, pp. 27–34 (C 87).

H 22
"Dreams," *Salem Gazette*, New Series III, XXXIX (11 November 1825), 1. Unsigned.

Presumably feeling that it was remotely possible that Hawthorne had written this verse, P. K. Foley supplied a transcript to D. E. Kennedy (Location: CEFC).

H 23
"Lines to M.B.D," *Salem Gazette*, New Series IV, XL (24 February 1826), 1. Signed with the initial "G."

Presumably feeling that it was remotely possible that Hawthorne had written this verse, P. K. Foley supplied a transcript to D. E. Kennedy (Location: CEFC).

H 24
"The Marriage Ring," *Salem Gazette*, New Series IV, XL (20 June 1826), 1. Signed with the initial "G."

Attributed to Hawthorne by Allen Flint in a review of *Nathaniel Hawthorne: Poems* in *The Nathaniel Hawthorne Journal 1973,* pp. 255–260 (C 87).

H25
"Fairies," *Salem Gazette,* New Series IV, XL (29 August 1826), 1. Signed with the initials "P.T."

Presumably feeling that it was remotely possible that Hawthorne had written this verse, P. K. Foley supplied a transcript to D. E. Kennedy (Location: CEFC).

H26
"To a Cloud," *Salem Gazette,* New Series IV, XL (2 September 1826), 1. Signed with the initials "T.P."

Presumably feeling that it was remotely possible that Hawthorne had written this verse, P. K. Foley supplied a transcript to D. E. Kennedy (Location: CEFC).

H27
"The Consumptive," *Salem Gazette,* New Series IV, XL (8 December 1826), 1. Signed with the initials "C.W."

Presumably feeling that it was remotely possible that Hawthorne had written this verse, P. K. Foley supplied a transcript to D. E. Kennedy (Location: CEFC). Foley noted that the poem was signed with the same initials as those on "The Ocean." See D1.

H28
"The wine is bright, the wine is bright . . . ." *Fanshawe* (1828), ch. V, p. 60 (A1).

Sixteen lines of verse. Also published in *Nathaniel Hawthorne: Poems,* p. 20 (C 83).

H29
"I've been a jolly drinker . . . ." *Fanshawe* (1828), ch. V, p. 62 (A1).

Four lines of verse. Also pubished in *Nathaniel Hawthorne: Poems,* p. 20 (C 83).

H30
"Oh, Man can seek the downward glance . . . ." "The Threefold Destiny. A Faëry Legend," *The American Monthly Magazine,* XI (March 1838), 234 (D 35).

Eight lines of verse. Also published in *Nathaniel Hawthorne: Poems,* p. 22 (C 83).

H31
"Walking on the Sea," *Scenes in the Life of the Savior,* ed. R. W. Griswold (Philadelphia: Lindsay and Blakiston, 1846), pp. [95]–96. Signed "Hawthorne."

Five five-line stanzas beginning, "When the storm of the mountain . . . ." Attributed to Hawthorne by George Parsons Lathrop, "Some Forgotten Hawthorne Verses," *New York Times Saturday Review* (12 March 1898), pp. 161–162. Rejected by Ralph Thompson, *American Literary Annuals and Gift Books 1825–1865* (New York: H. W. Wilson, 1936), p. 154. Rejected by Joy Bayless, who proposed a Walter Hawthorne, a contributor to *Graham's* magazine during Griswold's editorship, as the author, in her *Rufus Wilmot Griswold Poe's Literary Executer* (Nashville, Tenn.: Vanderbilt University Press, 1943), p. 83.

Note: Scenes published October 1845. Reprinted without date on title page. Also reprinted as *The Bible Gallery* (Philadelphia: Lindsay and Blakiston, 1858). "Walking on the Sea" reprinted in *Christ and the Twelve,* ed. J. G. Holland (Springfield, Mass.: Gurdon Bill; Chicago: Charles Bill; Cincinnati: H. C. Johnson, 1867), pp. 108–109. "Walking on the Sea" listed in the table of contents as by "Nath'l Hawthorne."

H 32
"The Star of Calvary," *Scenes in the Life of the Savior,* ed. R. W. Griswold (Philadelphia: Lindsay and Blakiston, 1846), pp. [164]–167. Signed "Hawthorne."

Eleven six-line stanzas beginning, "It is the same infrequent star . . . ." Attributed to Hawthorne by George Parsons Lathrop, rejected by Thompson and Bayless (see H 31). Also see H 31 for reprintings.

H 33
"There dwelt a Sage at Apple-Slump . . . ." Undated manuscript (Location: CSmH).

Eight lines of "Nonsense Verse." Published in *Hawthorne and His Wife* (1884), II, p. 322 (C 47). Also published in *Nathaniel Hawthorne: Poems,* p. 28 (C 83).

H 34
"There was an old Boy . . . ." Undated manuscript (Location: NNMor).

Seven lines of "Nonsense Verse." Published in *Hawthorne and His Wife* (1884), II, p. 322 (C 47). Also published in *Nathaniel Hawthorne: Poems,* p. 29 (C 83).

H 35
"There was an Old Lady of Guessme . . . ."

Five lines of "Nonesense Verse." Published in *Hawthorne and His Wife* (1884), II, p. 322 (C 47). Also published in *Nathaniel Hawthorne: Poems,* p. 30 (C 83).

H 36
"There was a young man went to college . . . ." Undated manuscript (Location: CSmH).

Five lines of "Nonsense Verse." Published in *Nathaniel Hawthorne: Poems* (1967), p. 31 (C 83).

H 37
"Oh snow that comes . . . ." Undated manuscript (Location: CSmH).

Sixteen lines of "Nonsense Verse" composed jointly by Hawthorne and his daughter Una. Published in *Nathaniel Hawthorne: Poems* (1967), p. 32 (C 83).

Attributed to Hawthorne by Allen Flint in a review of *Nathaniel Hawthorne: Poems* in *The Nathaniel Hawthorne Journal 1973*, pp. 255–260 (C 87).

H 25

"Fairies," *Salem Gazette*, New Series IV, XL (29 August 1826), 1. Signed with the initials "P.T."

Presumably feeling that it was remotely possible that Hawthorne had written this verse, P. K. Foley supplied a transcript to D. E. Kennedy (Location: CEFC).

H 26

"To a Cloud," *Salem Gazette*, New Series IV, XL (2 September 1826), 1. Signed with the initials "T.P."

Presumably feeling that it was remotely possible that Hawthorne had written this verse, P. K. Foley supplied a transcript to D. E. Kennedy (Location: CEFC).

H 27

"The Consumptive," *Salem Gazette*, New Series IV, XL (8 December 1826), 1. Signed with the initials "C.W."

Presumably feeling that it was remotely possible that Hawthorne had written this verse, P. K. Foley supplied a transcript to D. E. Kennedy (Location: CEFC). Foley noted that the poem was signed with the same initials as those on "The Ocean." See D 1.

H 28

"The wine is bright, the wine is bright . . . ." *Fanshawe* (1828), ch. V, p. 60 (A 1).

Sixteen lines of verse. Also published in *Nathaniel Hawthorne: Poems*, p. 20 (C 83).

H 29

"I've been a jolly drinker . . . ." *Fanshawe* (1828), ch. V, p. 62 (A 1).

Four lines of verse. Also pubished in *Nathaniel Hawthorne: Poems*, p. 20 (C 83).

H 30

"Oh, Man can seek the downward glance . . . ." "The Threefold Destiny. A Faëry Legend," *The American Monthly Magazine*, XI (March 1838), 234 (D 35).

Eight lines of verse. Also published in *Nathaniel Hawthorne: Poems*, p. 22 (C 83).

H 31

"Walking on the Sea," *Scenes in the Life of the Savior*, ed. R. W. Griswold (Philadelphia: Lindsay and Blakiston, 1846), pp. [95]–96. Signed "Hawthorne."

Five five-line stanzas beginning, "When the storm of the mountain . . . ." Attributed to Hawthorne by George Parsons Lathrop, "Some Forgotten Hawthorne Verses," *New York Times Saturday Review* (12 March 1898), pp. 161–162. Rejected by Ralph Thompson, *American Literary Annuals and Gift Books 1825–1865* (New York: H. W. Wilson, 1936), p. 154. Rejected by Joy Bayless, who proposed a Walter Hawthorne, a contributor to *Graham's* magazine during Griswold's editorship, as the author, in her *Rufus Wilmot Griswold Poe's Literary Executer* (Nashville, Tenn.: Vanderbilt University Press, 1943), p. 83.

Note: Scenes published October 1845. Reprinted without date on title page. Also reprinted as *The Bible Gallery* (Philadelphia: Lindsay and Blakiston, 1858). "Walking

Index

Index